ADVANCED CHAKRA HEALING

ADVANCED CHAKRA HEALING

Energy Mapping on the Four Pathways

CYNDI DALE

THE CROSSING PRESS
Berkeley | Toronto

The Crossing Press
A Division of Ten Speed Press
P.O. Box 7123
Berkeley, California 94707
www.tenspeed.com

Distributed in Australia by Simon & Schuster Australia, in Canada by
Ten Speed Press Canada, in New Zealand by Southern Publishers Group,
in South Africa by Real Books, and in the United Kingdom and Europe
by Airlift Book Company.

Cover and text design by Lisa Buckley

Disclaimer: The author fully recognizes and accepts the value of the traditional medical profession. The
ideas, suggestions, and healing techniques in this book are not intended as a substitute for proper medical
attention. Any application of these ideas, suggestions, and techniques is at the reader's sole discretion.

Library of Congress Cataloging-in-Publication Data is on file with the publisher.

ISBN-10: 1-58091-161-7
ISBN-13: 978-1-58091-161-0

Printed in the United States of America
First printing, 2005

1 2 3 4 5 6 7 8 9 10 —08 07 06 05

Contents

Acknowledgments

Advanced Chakra Healing is truly the product of minds already illuminated by truth. Infinite thanks go to Dr. Michael Isaacson for his
invaluable insights and knowledge, and to Amy Rost, who edited the
working copy of this book. Her precision wrapped each concept in the
right words.

I hold everlasting gratefulness for Jo Ann Deck of Celestial Arts/
Crossing Press, who believed in this work and all other works that
attempt to show a new way to change old problems. She is a light unto
the world. Annie Nelson was the brilliant editor who shaped the book
over and over, helping me through the stages in which it was strewn in
several sections around my kitchen.

To Nathan Uri, for his amazing technical and creative talent in
designing my website.

To Ellen Sue Stern, my phenomenal agent, friend, and companion
in soul sojourns, only and always my best.

And finally, a big thanks to the young people in my life and home,
Michael, Gabriel, and Katie, who learned to not disturb me when I was
writing (except to suggest take-out food, as I was too busy to cook—to
their delight).

Introduction

Since the publication of my book *New Chakra Healing* in 1996, I've been asked dozens—if not hundreds—of times to write a sequel. When I pointed out, in *New Chakra*, the existence of chakras that few had previously seen, I broke new ground in the energy-healing world by expanding on the then-current model of the human energy system. I obviously ignited a flame, for to my surprise, since its American-based inception *New Chakra* has gone on to be published in several languages around the world. Then again, I shouldn't have been so shocked. People around the world share an ancient bond: our common ancestors used chakra-based healing thousands of years ago.

Your energy system is the invisible you, the one that links your physical and your spiritual self. The chakras are energies of light that, when activated and used properly, allow miraculous change. Science is finally catching up to ancestral wisdom, substantiating the existence of these swirling vortexes of light by using special photographic, computer-based, and electromagnetic devices. The holistic healing field has responded in kind, embracing ideas such as chakra-based healing, chakra clearing, and chakra diagnostics. I predict that in a few years chakra therapies will be mainstream. Already, I can go to certain spas and get a chakra assessment, receive a chakra massage, and buy chakra lotions to pamper my way to chakra heaven!

When I began thinking about how to approach a *New Chakra Healing* sequel, my initial idea was to simply expand on the original points introduced in my first book. With encouragement from several publishers, I began to do so. In fact, I wrote three hundred pages. I covered the nuts and bolts of working with the chakras to increase physical well-being. My subject areas included using the chakras to deal with beliefs and emotions, the soul and the spirit.

However, the entire time I was writing, my client work was changing focus. I was still a chakra-based consultant, working with more than a hundred clients a month, some in person and some over the phone, using intuitive means to help them problem-solve. I continued teaching about chakras in my classes and workshops. I was also completing a chakra-based book on intuitive development. But my use of the chakras had evolved since writing *New Chakra Healing*. I continued to strongly believe in the information in *New Chakra*, but my application of it—my healing philosophy—had changed.

Instruction in a New Reality

I had been forming and practicing a model of healing different from that typically considered holistic. *New Chakra Healing* was based on years of cross-cultural study in the United States and abroad, meditation and revelation, discussion with learned experts, and client experience. Many of my new learning venues were similar, but the most intense and, frankly, practical teachings were being revealed to me during Dreamtime—that time period during sleep in which our consciousness is open to instruction.

For several years, I had been receiving teaching from a physically present source of wisdom, to which I responded with a valiant attempt to learn. Christ had been entering my dreams and offering guidance and instruction about the true nature of healing. About a year ago, these visitations increased and began to occur when I was wide awake. One visit actually left me floating above my own bed! And these waking-state drop-in visits were never arranged by appointment. They would happen whenever and wherever I was, and regardless of what I was doing.

(I understand the boldness of my assertion that it was Christ who was mentoring me. I can only respond that if you had been there you would have believed it, too. I wasn't being instructed in religious dogma— Christ didn't attempt to save my soul or assert Christianity as the one true path of true healing. There was no religion involved in the process.)

As the teaching times unfolded, I began to grasp an idea of reality different from the one I had previously held. I saw that a person isn't divided into parts—physical, emotional, mental, and spiritual—as the holistic model might describe it. These are only categorical perceptions. Rather, there is a Greater Reality unifying everything and everyone within it. But it isn't entirely uniform. Not everything that we see "here" is present in the Greater Reality. In the Greater Reality, there is no sickness or greed or fear, because there is no perceived need for these ways of being.

This Greater Reality can be described as a little like heaven on earth. The physical is spiritual and the spiritual is physical. There is no difference between the two. There are, in fact, no separations at all within the self; there are only different spaces or places from which to see the self and the rest of the world. From one viewpoint, the physical may look physical; from another, emotional. But we're supposed to make our decisions based not on ideas that separate, but on truths that unify.

You see, there are no different truths, only different ways of perceiving the truth. In our human condition, however, we think that these various perceptions *are* truth instead of ideas *about* truth. Because we've forgotten our implicit wholeness and interconnectedness, we manifest our lives from a belief in brokenness and disconnection. To change our lives, we must change our perceptions. We must heal by emphasizing wholeness and by eliminating that which isn't true. We must take the bold steps necessary to believe in goodness again.

This is a big leap. To make it, we're encouraged to walk on one or all of four distinct pathways or realities. Each is a valid way to embrace this Greater Reality. Each is its own plane, place, or space, and each provides a different perspective on the self and the world. But all offer opportunities to achieve the awakened state that brings true healing. As we learn to see with greater insight, healing follows.

It has taken me a long time to identify the structure of the Four Pathways. I worked diligently to practice the concepts and techniques that I was being taught. And I know that what I was taught works—for all people, not just a chosen few.

The Key to Wholeness

I saw amazing results with my clients, but I knew that I didn't have the final key. Finally, in light of my new learning, I ripped up my first draft of *Advanced Chakra Healing* and started over.

That same day I met a new client I'll call Antoinette. (I haven't used anyone's real name in this book.) Antoinette was in constant pain from a rare form of osteoarthritis. She feared that soon she would be wheelchair-bound and dependent on her children. She didn't want to be a burden, but neither traditional nor alternative medical care had made the slightest bit of difference in her condition, and she was steadily worsening.

As Antoinette listed her prior attempts at healing, I could see that she really had tried it all, from botox shots to crystal healing. I needed to provide help beyond the usual intuitive assessment or hands-on healing. I decided to draw on my newest learning and work with the Four Pathways system, with which I had been experimenting for only a few years. But I didn't know where to start; I had no sense of what to do to help this woman. So I asked for spiritual guidance.

Usually, I perceive images with my inner eye. This time, I was overwhelmed with a vision that was as vivid as the moving pictures on a movie screen. I saw an Antoinette who was already well in the physical sense of the word. She was vibrant, happy, pain-free, and able to play with her grandchildren. Internally, I asked how she had shifted from her current state to this imagined state, and on my internal screen I saw a picture of the four pathways of reality. They were stacked atop each other, yet each was able to touch all the others. Stark white, swirling funnels of light ran through each of the four realities, interconnecting all four pathways. These funnels looked like stairways to heaven, DNA strands of pure white.

I knew what I was seeing. I had been doubting the applicability and universality of the chakras, and now I was perceiving one of the highest functions of these units of light. Chakras serve as tunnels into the various aspects of reality, each independent chakra a doorway connecting one reality to another.

I immediately knew what to do for Antoinette. I could see the pathway and the chakra that she would most likely respond to. With Antoinette's permission, I intuitively shifted energy.

And she fell over.

When she rose, she said that she felt "unusual." Sitting before me, she reported a tingling in her legs. After a few moments, she said that she believed that the arthritis in her legs was gone. A few minutes later, I worked with a different chakra on a different pathway, and her arms cleared up.

Antoinette called a few weeks later and said that she didn't need to come back. She was well. I never saw her again.

Antoinette definitely allowed a miracle that day. Not every client is cured nor are all of my life problems solved. Sometimes working with a pathway provides a truth or a plan of action. Other times, a pathway requires a release of the need for a healing. I can say, however, that I've seen lives—including my own—changed for the better.

Advanced Chakra Healing may have started as a sequel to *New Chakra Healing*, but it has evolved into a book with its own healing paradigm. My hope is that you can take all or part of the information in *Advanced Chakra Healing* and use the Four Pathways to awaken to your own state of wholeness. In doing so, you will be using your chakra system for its true purpose: to allow your true self to unfold in every area of your life.

part one

A New Way of Healing

chapter *one* » A New Way of Healing

*What is the meaning of
thy struggle?*

*The man who did
not know how to answer
this question would
resign himself, while
another, one who sought
a meaning to existence,
feeling that God had been
unjust, would challenge
his own destiny. It was
at this moment that
fire of a different type
descended from the
heavens—not the fire that
kills but the kind that
tears down ancient walls
and imparts to each
human being his true
possibilities. Cowards
never allow their hearts to
blaze with this fire; all
they desire is for the
changed situation to
quickly return to what it
was before, so they can
go on living their lives
and thinking in their
customary way.* [1]

—Paulo Coehlo,
The Fifth Mountain

A Broken Paradigm

The phrase "to heal" actually means "to make whole." Most of us expend a lot of energy trying to create wholeness where there is brokenness. As a society, we're spending billions upon billions of dollars every year on traditional and complementary medical care, all to fix our broken parts. We feel sick; we list our symptoms and see our general practitioner, who tells us what is "wrong" with us. If we don't get better, we wait until we feel worse and then see a medical specialist. Traditional healing is a process of uncovering the origin of the symptoms. If we can locate a particular cause, we have a disease. If we can't figure out the foundation of the presenting problems, we have a syndrome. Basically, the traditional medical model is a search for the broken physical part.

Until a few decades ago, our path stopped there. Then came holistic health care—also called alternative medicine, complementary health care, and integrative medicine—which was supposed to fix the deficiencies of this model. The basic idea of holistic healing is that the human self is made up of several components: the physical, mental, emotional, and spiritual. Healing is now just a matter of finding which category of the "whole self" contains the broken piece, not just which part of the physical self needs repair. This reductionistic approach, often not reimbursed by insurance, is reducing our available pocket monies, but is it increasing our health? Though there are benefits to working mentally, emotionally, or spiritually to address physical complaints, there are also deficiencies in this model.

Understanding the Limitations
of Traditional Healing Approaches

The Mind-Body Approach Consider the mind-body philosophy. There is no doubt that the mind can be stronger than the body. For example, when spinal tapping was new, medical providers were told that headaches were an expected side effect. These informed doctors relayed this expectation to their patients and in fact, seven out of fifteen patients given the warning did get headaches. Then in 1981, on the island of Kiribati, doctors failed to warn their patients of this side effect. Only one in thirteen patients got a headache. [2]

I also remember a story relayed by a client of mine, who had just returned from medical-missionary work in Kenya. The nuns in the African clinic distributed medicine but had run out. So they mixed food coloring with water and passed out this "new medicine" to treat ailments from colds to HIV. My client, a nurse, was astonished at the results. Patient after patient reported being cured. The rainbow water and the nuns' reassurance combined to create the belief in the water's healing property. What we think and how we think can fix what's broken.

But the mind-body connection can also backfire. There are hundreds of reported cases of something called the nocebo effect— becoming sick because you believe that you're supposed to get sick. In his book *Timeless Healing*, Dr. Herbert Benson points out several such cases occurring on the mass or epidemic level, including a situation in which seven hundred people in New Zealand became ill from fumes said to be toxic. In fact, the fumes were nonlethal. [3] People became ill because they believed they would become ill.

If you're expected to die of cancer, might not your expectation create the reality? If your parents think that you're a failure, might their belief explain your financial problems? If your spouse is afraid you'll stray, could you be overeating to remain unattractive? Whether or not the belief provoking a problem originates in you, if you take it to heart, it becomes your belief. *Your* mind—not someone else's—is what affects your body. And yet, how often do we know what beliefs are affecting us, much less their sources and why we've assumed them? There are simply too many beliefs and too many sources of beliefs to ever manage them all. Can you ever dig deep enough to ferret out the mental trigger for a physical illness? What if the problem isn't in the mind, but lies somewhere else? Those who shudder at the complexities of the mind-body approach often turn to other holistic venues for healing. That's where feelings come in.

The Healing by Feeling Approach The emotionally minded believe that every illness is a result of a repressed or mistaken feeling. When working with my clients, I constantly find correlations between disease and feelings. When people fail to feel and express their feelings, their physical bodies become tense and rigid. From a mechanical point of view alone, an inflexible body won't operate smoothly. If your muscles are tight, for instance, your lymph system won't flow correctly. The lymph releases toxins, and if these waste products are not passed out of the body, they'll be stored where you least want them. For women, this might be in the breast tissue, thereby creating the conditions for breast cancer. For men, the repositories could include the stomach, hence the heavy gut that increases the chance of heart disease.

There's no question that an inability to deal with feelings creates a less joyful life, as well as physical maladies. You don't want to feel sad? Backed-up tears create a cold person. Who wants to be in a relationship with someone who is distant or unavailable? This is a setup for a lonely life. You don't think it's okay to get angry? Without anger, we allow others to take advantage of us. Pretty soon we're so stressed, we get sick.

However, healing by feelings, as I call it, has had as limited success as has mind-body healing. *Process* is the word coined to describe the expression of a feeling. The term fits, since emotional healing can be a very long process indeed. You can spend forever feeling your feelings about the past, and there's no guarantee that you are processing the feeling that links to a presenting disease. It's not so easy to separate the "good" feelings from the "bad" feelings. You can get so busy processing yesterday's emotions that it's easy to forget that you have a life to live in the here and now.

In holistic thinking, specific feelings are often linked to specific diseases. For instance, feeling-healing experts usually say that repressed grief can cause lung disease and stored anger can result in liver problems. When teaching healing, I cautiously share this information with my students. (In fact, I will be presenting a list of these associations in this book, pages 176–77.) However, I would never say that a feeling is actually causing a disease. It could be, but so could a germ. Having a feeling within a disease context merely means that there is a relationship—sometimes—between certain diseases and certain feelings. When feelings are involved, I have typically found a complex relationship between feelings, beliefs, memories, chemicals, spiritual forces, and more. The intricacies of working with feelings are often oversimplified in typical feeling-healing work.

My personal view is that people are much more complicated and individual than the feeling-body theory allows. For instance, feeling-based healers often connect hopelessness with cancer. I worked with one client with breast cancer who was the most hopeful and upbeat woman I've ever met. She did recover from her cancer, but only after she began using symbolic healing tools rather than emotionally or mentally based ones. During our work, she never processed a repressed feeling.

It's also difficult to figure out which feelings might be causing a physical problem and which ones might result from that problem. I had a client with rheumatoid arthritis who displayed a lot of anger. Several holistic-minded providers insisted that the anger was the root of her disease; if she dealt with the anger, she would get well. I had a sense that my client's anger wasn't causing her arthritis; rather, she was angry because she had arthritis! By assuming that my client already held the condition of wholeness inside, I developed a healing process that resulted in the elimination of the arthritis within three sessions. The only feeling my client ever expressed was relief.

Accepting and expressing your feelings is an important task in getting well. Then again, it's also a necessity for living a full, vital, and juicy life. We need to keep the emphasis on feelings in perspective and recognize that emotion-based healing has its limitations.

The Soul-Spirit Healing Approach The belief in spiritual healing is as old as the hills. It's actually the oldest type of healing. Part the mists of time and you'll see shamans drumming, medicine healers mumuring, and mystics chanting for purposes of soul healing. Soul healing is one aspect of spiritual healing—the calling forth of wisdom and curatives from the invisible to produce effects in the physical. The basis for soul healing is essentially the same, culture to culture: to correct karma, life's collateral damage held by the soul. The challenge with soul healing is that it is an inexhaustible endeavor. We all have a past. How will we ever erase all the yesterdays to catch up with today? Healing the past, be it in this lifetime or others, is a valuable step on the healing path, as long as we don't get stuck there.

The more modern or religious supporters of spiritual healing skip the soul altogether and insist upon a more direct involvement with the Divine. Several studies indicate that people with religious associations are often healthier, recover faster from disease, and live longer than those without these associations. For instance, a study of nearly two thousand older adults in North Carolina found that individuals attending church regularly had healthier immune systems than those who didn't.[4]

Perhaps believing in something greater than the self, or even having loving relationships such as those formed in a religious context, can affect our actions. If we feel loved, we're going to be more loving toward ourselves. We'll adopt healthier habits, such as eating well and exercising, and we'll abstain from obviously unhealthy behaviors, such as smoking and drinking.

However, many studies question the effectiveness of spiritual healing in general. Louis Rose, a British psychiatrist, spent twenty years investigating faith-healing cures, using questionnaires and information from doctors. He couldn't find evidence of a single miracle cure.[5] Another investigator, William Nolen, M.D., followed twenty-five people who reported being miraculously healed during the 1970s by the famous Christian evangelist Katherine Kuhlman. Nolen reported that none of the twenty-five individuals exhibited a long-term cure of any organic disease.[6] A more recent study, conducted in 2003 by Duke University Medical Center cardiologists, produced similar results. Reported in the *Telegraph of London*, the three-year study, involving 750 heart patients in nine hospitals and twelve prayer groups of different faiths around the world, yielded no scientific evidence that the prayer had any effect.[7] Working the world of spirit without taking any other action is a questionable avenue to health.

» Healing the Whole Self

ASPECTS OF MENTAL, emotional, and spiritual healing do work on physical illness, and we can hope that strides will continue to be made in these applications. But just like traditional physical healing methods, these approaches have their limitations.

In treatment of disease, there has been a considerable upsurge in the use of alternative therapies to battle stress, major diseases, and emotional challenges. According to statistics provided by the National Center of Complementary and Alternative Medicine, a 2002 edition of a survey by the National Health Center for Health Statistics revealed that 36 percent of all Americans use some form of complementary or alternative health care. If including figures for megavitamin therapy and prayer, this figure rises to 62 percent. In 1997, the U.S. public spent between $36 and $47 billion on these therapies, representing more than was paid out-of-pocket for all hospitalizations and half of what was paid for out-of-pocket physician services. Much of these monies are spent on warring against stress and disease.[8]

In spite of these enormous amounts of monies spent, there has been no significant reduction in reported cases of stress, deaths from major illnesses, or emotional problems. Consider that upward toward nine of ten visits to the doctor are stress-related, according to statistics from the American Psychological Association.

Look also at the ceaseless increase in heart disease, cancer, and diabetes, three of the top seven national killers. The age-adjusted annual rate of cancer death has increased rather than decreased in the recent decades, a rise of 8.7 percent despite the increased use of alternative modalities. As suggested in an article called "Progress Against Cancer?" by Harvard researchers John C. Bailar III and Elaine M. Smith, "Some thirty-five years of intense effort focused largely on improving treatment must be judged a qualified failure." As stated by the astute evaluator Michael Lerner in his book *Choices in Healing,* there has been "no decisive and scientifically documented cure for cancer among the complementary cancer therapies." Rather, there are therapies which seem "possibly to extend survival with specific cancers." Holistic medicine might assist, but it's not doing the full job, at least in the arena of cancer.

Meanwhile on other fronts, heart disease continues to be the nationwide, number one cause of death. Approximately 60 million Americans currently have coronary heart disease, with women's rates increasing each year. And diabetes

The Four Pathways:
An Invitation to the Miraculous

This book introduces the Four Pathways, an entirely fresh design for holistic healing. It moves away from fixing parts to ensuring wholeness; from working hard at healing to making simple changes that deliver healing.

The goal of this model is to increase your personal effectiveness at healing. Adopting the Four Pathways idea can help you create those true leapfrogging, quantum-jumping, heart-popping wonders that we call miracles.

The term *miracle* is usually applied to a phenomenon that can't be explained. There are small and large miracles. A small miracle is having your car start in the middle of winter when a minute ago the engine only rolled over. A large miracle is when the cancer tumor disappears after doctors have given up hope. The truth is that the illogical, supernatural part of a miracle is a matter of perspective. The supernatural

currently affects at least 6.3 percent of the American population. Think that figure isn't astounding? Consider that diabetes cases rose 61 percent between 1991 and 2001.

We're losing the health battle, in spite of the best efforts of holistic weaponry—and maybe the struggle for happiness, too. Consider the increased numbers of individuals employing anti-depressant and anti-anxiety medications, failing to notice significant differences when using over-the-counter alternative treatments like herbal remedies. It's not that alternative therapies aren't helpful. Statistically, however, the overwhelming availability of holistic remedies and the amounts of monies spent on them should at least touch our health measurements, all of which have worsened not strengthened over time, despite the considerable increase in use of the alternative treatments.

The problem with the current idea of holistic healing is that it is not actually holistic. Healing isn't a matter of sorting every broken bit into its appropriate category. Separating ourselves into the categories of physical, mental, emotional, and spiritual only emphasizes the belief that we are not whole. There aren't four or six or even ten parts to the human self. You are a circle, not a pie chart.

A story that well illustrates my point takes me back ten years. My father had given a Mighty Morphin' Power Ranger gun to my son, Michael. This particular species of toy may or may not be recognizable to you, but take my word for it, it was a big deal. This gun was cool. It could dial alien-busting tones and high-alert frequencies, while generating enough power to save the world. It was a five-year-old boy's dream gun. Soon, it accompanied Michael to bed, bath, and beyond. Until it broke.

Not one for mechanics, I did my best to fix the switch that was stuck. I tried every unjamming technique known to mothers since time began, including the use of eyebrow tweezers and nail cutters. I even superglued another piece of plastic to the broken switch. Nothing helped. Finally, I admitted defeat. I sadly informed my five-year-old that the gun was dead and might as well be thrown out. He looked at me like I was akin to the aliens on the Mighty Morphin' Power Rangers' television show. "But, Mom," he noted sagely, "it's still the same gun that it was, even if one part doesn't work."

No matter how many broken pieces you have, you are only one, complete self. *You are not a being subdivided into four or even a thousand categories. Trying to heal by subdividing yourself isn't as effective as healing the whole self all at once.* It's time for a healing model that addresses the whole self all at once.

is merely a layer of reality existing alongside and within the one we typically call "real." If you could see the energetics underpinning a miracle—the scene behind the scenery, the visible behind the invisible—you could explain and create the miraculous.

There are four realities, but only one real you. You are fully "here" in the material universe. You have access to and are made of all the powers and forces of the natural and supernatural worlds. You are a magical being and can perform enchantments. And you are fashioned from pure consciousness and can shift all of reality through conscious awareness.

In the Four Pathways model, there are four layers, planes, or realities of human existence. These different realities add up to a Greater Reality, while independently offering equally valid ways to make and create change. Each pathway has its own set of rules, principles, and systems; all of them can create the so-called miraculous.

The beauty of the Four Pathways is that they all interact. If you make a modification on one pathway, you'll see exponential change in that and all other pathways, simultaneously. For instance, you might work one of the Four Pathways to forgive your parents for cruelties they did to you when you were young. As soon as you alter your energy on this pathway, the other three pathways shift and modulate. Suddenly, other areas of your life miraculously change! Your arthritis clears up. Your boss gives you a raise. You start sleeping better at night. You hear from a long-lost friend. Your spiritual gifts open up; you begin to receive visions at night that inform you of things to come the next day.

The current holistic model would divide you into subcategories to solve the problem. You haven't forgiven your parents for mistreating you? That's an emotional issue. Sure, emotions impact the physical body, but you need to work on this issue solely as an emotional one or it won't go away. You have a broken feeling and it needs to be fixed.

In the Four Pathways approach, you're considered whole already. There's a solid, viable reason that you're holding onto an unwillingness to forgive. The emotions involved are expressed throughout all four pathways of the Greater Reality and add up to your current reality. Shift your experience of your parents on any of the Four Pathways and your entire reality will shift. Now you're making exponential change. You're creating miracles.

Chakras: The Doors of Light

As I became aware of the Four Pathways, I became concerned. Partitioning the personality in four directions was complicated enough. Now four realities? My fear was alleviated as I noticed that all four pathways are accessible through doorways available to us all: the chakras. Chakras are the key focal points of the human energy system, a complex set of energy bodies that regulate all components of the self. Energy bodies are of particular interest to contemporary scientists and healers alike because of their seemingly magical properties. Through the chakras, we can diagnose disease, predict outcomes, clear problems, and attract what we need.

Chakras are paired with another set of energy organs, the auric fields. The auric fields are perhaps better known as the auric system. Ever seen a halo in a medieval painting? That's a representation of part of the auric fields. In general, the chakras run the inside of you and the auric fields regulate the energy outside of you. Together, the chakras and auric fields connect you to the Four Pathways, so you can access any or all of the pathways at any given moment.

» Four Levels of Reality

ENVISION THESE FOUR healing pathways as a three-dimensional checkers game. There are four boards stacked on top of each other:

The Elemental Pathway
The Power Pathway
The Imagination Pathway
The Divine Pathway

A pocketbook description of each:

The elemental pathway	Material reality
The power pathway	Powers and forces
The imagination pathway	Magic
The divine pathway	Consciousness

Because you exist on all four levels of reality at the same time, any shift of position on any of the pathways creates change in the nature of the energy in and around you. You open to new energies that could provide healing. You allow release and attraction—releasing what hurts and attracting what helps. When you reach critical mass, all the boards shift at once.

All four pathways are in the here and now. These are not different dimensions, though each pathway incorporates certain of the various dimensions and planes of existence. Each pathway involves the physical, emotional, mental, and spiritual aspects of being human, but these distinctions are blurred together within and between the pathways. You can take an herb and alter your consciousness, because of the link between the elemental pathway and the divine pathway. You can command the wind to blow and heal a tumor, because of the connection between the power pathway and the elemental pathway. You can picture a circle and create abundance—a result of the relationship between the imagination pathway and the power pathway. You don't have to worry about the differences between physical, emotional, mental, or spiritual energies. No matter which pathway you are using, you are working with your entire self.

Chakras are situated inside and outside of the human body. Because of this local placement, they are considered material bodies. They can actually process sensory energy, which is energy that can move slower than the speed of light. All energy contains information. This means that chakras can energetically converse with all aspects of the human self and its environment, exchanging data and influencing activity. Chakras can sort psychic energy—that is, information-energy that can move faster than the speed of light. They can also exchange slow energy for fast and vice versa; this conversion skill is what gives chakras their appearance as swirling units of light.

I've worked with chakras for most of my life and can testify to the advantage of living life and doing healing through the chakra system. If you can fold a tumor, which is a sensory mass, into a psychic fold of energy, you can potentially shift it out of the body. If you can capture your speeding thoughts, you can change the messages you give to the world and attract more abundance. I've come to realize, however, that working with the chakras in the current holistic model is limiting. Using them, instead, as doorways to the higher realities is the key to the miraculous. Seen through the model of the Four Pathways, the chakras are truly doorways of light. Through them, you can project yourself onto any of the pathways, which is equivalent to walking through walls!

» Shifting Energy

MY FRIEND JACK, a physical laborer, was considering quitting his much-loved profession because of the severity of his back pain. He didn't place much stock in chakras, auric fields, and the like, and he insisted that if you can't see something, you can't really be sure of its existence. I joked that he couldn't see his back pain, either, but it was still there. Jack finally reached the end of his rope and arrived at my doorstep, asking for an "invisible healing," although he did specify that he wanted visible results.

Within one minute, Jack's back pain had disappeared. It has now been gone for months. I didn't even bother to diagnose the origin of the pain. I couldn't tell you today whether I was working on his lumbar or his sacral vertebrae. Nor did I do any laying on of hands or prayer as we would recognize prayer. I simply entered Jack's chakra system with my consciousness and traced the doorway of light to the pathway that was open for healing. I easily perceived that Jack was open at the divine pathway and that the "Jack there" was already healed. By shifting the divine healing energy into the rest of Jack through the chakras, all the rest of Jack's chakras opened. Psychic energy converted into material energy. Through my inner eye, I watched Jack's vertebrae, nervous system, and muscular structure break down and rebuild. I didn't heal Jack—Jack healed himself. In my work with Jack, I used a technique that I've come to call **energy mapping**.

Energy Mapping for Chakra Healing

To make use of the Four Pathways, you have to find them. Energy mapping is a technique that allows you to intuitively access all four pathways. Through energy mapping, you can do the following:

- Activate the chakras as doorways
- Select the correct chakras to use for a particular problem
- Picture your life issues so as to construct helpful solutions

- Mobilize resources for healing
- Shift your problems out of reality
- Open to the miracles you desire

With a traditional map, you can determine where you are in relation to streets, buildings, and other landmarks. Once you know where you are, you can figure out how to travel to wherever you want to go. In the same way, an energy map shows your current position on a given pathway in relation to the energies around you. From there you can intuitively follow the chakric doorways, energy lines, principles, and walkways toward the origin of your problems—the wholeness lying latent, waiting to be activated. Then you can determine which energetic changes or shifts in perspective you need to make in order to encourage wholeness at all levels. By seeing what to release and what to attract, you can chart your own course for healing.

You can energy map any life issue. In Part Five, the energy-mapping section of this book, I present several energy maps of common life complaints. Some of these are the garden-variety illnesses that annoy us all, like colds and flu. Others are the tragic ones that befall too many, including cancer and heart disease. After examining and working with these energy maps, you will know how to construct your own.

In order to energy map the pathways, you must first understand the Four Pathways system. Parts Two and Three of this book are devoted to explaining how energy works and the basics of each of the pathways. Much about this system is still unknown; I will provide the concepts and data that I've tested and used in my work and teachings. Once you understand the Four Pathways and the basic process of energy mapping, it will be easier for you to come up with your own ideas.

Using Your Innate Intuition

To access the pathways and create energy maps, you need to use your own inner ability for reading energies. You are psychic. This isn't an eerie, occult, or even paranormal concept; it's a fact. Being psychic is nothing more or less than reading the information contained in energy that moves faster than the speed of light. Anytime you sense another's pain, feel a storm coming days before it strikes, or guess who is on the phone before you answer, you are reading fast information-energy. You are being psychic.

Your psychic abilities shift on each pathway, because energy moves at different speeds and in different packages on each pathway. With a little practice, you can adapt these skills to working each of the pathways. In chapter 10, I've provided ways to help you better define your personal psychic gifts. Knowing which of the many psychic gifts are easiest for you to use will also help you decide which pathway you will be able to work most easily and effectively.

Onward to Healing

Before studying the Four Pathways approach, I want you to take a minute and consider the concept of honesty. As is said in the *I Ching*, an ancient Chinese mystical tract:

Whenever a feeling is voiced with truth and frankness…a mysterious and far-reaching influence is exerted. At first it acts on those who are inwardly receptive. But the circle grows larger and larger…the effect is but the reflection of something that emanates from one's own heart. [9]

I realize that when you're sick, you don't feel whole. You may feel bad or sad or mad, dangerous or cranky or obtuse, but you probably don't feel whole. Relationship breakups, financial disasters, parenting problems, poor bathroom plumbing—the stuff of life seems determined to break us down rather than build us up.

In working the pathways, you automatically stretch your consciousness beyond its fixation on your problems. But to assume wholeness doesn't mean to lie about your problems or how you feel about them. Working the pathways requires frank and full disclosure of what you're really going through. Feelings, reactions, and needs are messages leading toward, not away from, wholeness. By following our anger, we find the self that requires boundaries. By experiencing our sadness, we are led to the love of that which seems lost. By complaining about our boss, we're challenged to find our own authority. We only get into trouble when we stop being honest, when we refuse to follow the thread of our own perceptions to their truest conclusions.

As you learn about the pathways and the doorways of light open to you, remember to always be honest with yourself. That's the secret to opening the doorways into the greatest light of all—the Divine.

The Four Pathways
of Healing

two chapter

*I know, Master Niketas,
that the center of the
universe is your city here,
but the world is vaster
than your empire, and
there's even Ultima
Thule and the land of
the Hiberians.* [1]

—Umberto Eco,
Baudolino

Each of the Four Pathways is like a different universe—self-contained yet linked to the others. Each is a place yet also a process. Each place is a *where* that has its own language, rules, principles, and energies. Each *where* promises different types of miracles—if you know what you're doing!

The Elemental Pathway:
The Brooding Universe

"And in the beginning, the spirit hovered over the waters...."

So begins one of the most famous creation stories, found in Genesis, the first book of the Jewish Torah and the Christian Old Testament. This image illustrates the elemental pathway: darkness consumed by emptiness, and then the presence of something unfathomable, unattainable, and invisible, yet so powerful that from it emerges water, mud, and the breath of life.

The elemental pathway is usually the most comfortable because most of us close the doorways to the other three pathways at our first explosion into the world. As a child waiting in the womb to be born, you were bathed in the blood and waters of the elemental, but also in the light and remembrances of other dimensions, the planes you had just left. When you were born, you opened your eyes to the elemental pathway. You then learned to identify mainly with the physical rather than the spiritual, forgetting even that the physical itself is holy and that the elemental is itself a doorway to the mystical and the miraculous.

The elemental should not, however, be confused with the physical level of reality. Even though the elemental operates on physical laws and material energies, it is more than chemicals and biology. It is a blend of matter and spirit—just as you are. It is just that the energy involved on the elemental is more tangible to the everyday seeker than the energy accessed through the other three pathways.

Your elemental energy system is made of the **managing energy bodies.** The chief energy bodies are the chakras, which link the physical with higher abilities and planes. The chakras become more effective as you yearn to understand what lies beyond that which can be seen, heard, smelled, touched, or shared. Prisms of elemental reality, the chakras also respond to the awakening of superhuman abilities and mystical knowledge.

Miracles occur on the elemental pathway when you redefine your physical self as the elemental self. The elemental self includes not only your brain but also your mind; certain aspects of your soul and spirit; and vehicles for accessing the past, present, future, and potential realities.

For instance, you can work physically by visiting an allopathic or traditional doctor and taking a prescribed medication. You allow the miraculous, however, when you join certain energies or information with the medications so as to transform elemental-based issues at their center. And sometimes, you don't even need the medications.

My patient Claire provides an elemental miracle example. For twenty years, she had tried almost anything, from integrative and inspirational to medical and therapeutic, to help her chronic fatigue. Without intervention, the energetics causing a problem continued to have a malignant effect on her system. I psychically looked at Claire's energies to see what was either malformed or not conforming to the optimum health available to her. I perceived many misinformed beliefs creating the conditions for the chronic fatigue, all centered in a certain chakra or energy body. What would unpin everything at once?

I simply asked Claire to consider that *she didn't need to still be the person who originally allowed this sickness into her body.*

At this suggestion, Claire turned hues of red and purple and shook violently. Within a couple of minutes, she calmed and stretched her arms.

"My aches, they're gone!" she said.

She was well and continued to be well. Claire had allowed herself to shift to a higher reality in the elemental pathway; to stop identifying with the past so she could use the energy available in her "right-now" body to get well. She had unconsciously held the reason for her illness in her body, and I was able to perceive this reasoning in one of her chakras. Freed of the rationale for being sick, her unconscious could clear up the energetics of the disease. Her body took care of the viral component while her consciousness or "informed self" took care of the rest.

Here is how it works. You negotiate healing on the elemental path through *energetic marksmanship*. You use your psychic strengths to look for malformation and the causes of presenting problems. Then you direct the energy of the elemental to clear causal issues and change the structure of a problem. The more intense you are, the more effective you are. The more potent, decided, intentional, and action-based your healing endeavors, the more likely it is they will work.

These are skills anyone can learn because we already exercise them. Have you any idea how much energy it takes to hold a tumor in the body? What if you could direct the same energy toward getting rid of the tumor? Maybe even a tad more energy, so it really leaves? The key is to recognize what you've been doing and why and then to gain control of your psychic abilities. The best way to do this is to better understand aspects of the human energy system called the managing energy bodies, which include the chakras and the auric fields. We'll be covering this information in chapter 7.

If you need more muscle to make broader and more sweeping changes, consider the next pathway of healing: the power path.

The Power Pathway: The Radiant Reality

Have you ever looked at the sun and then looked around you? The world looks different; each figure is lit. Your companion glows, the leaves are tinted, and you're aware of the play between shadow and light. This is what it's like to peer into and play within the power reality. While you live full-time in the elemental pathway, you also live full-time in the power pathway. Most of us don't know it because our inner eyesight isn't attuned to this radiant reality.

The power pathway, like the elemental, is most readily available through the human energy system. You enter the power pathway through the chakras, the main control switches of the elemental. From there, you work the *seals*, the *power doors*, and others of the *power energy bodies* described in chapter 6.

By working the power pathway, you access points of truth that allow you to use supercharged energy. Through the power pathway, you can command the forces, powers, and energies that create substantial and authoritative change.

We all work the power reality, whether consciously or not. A person stuck in a poverty cycle, for instance, may be directing elemental and power energies. On the elemental level, our seeker of wealth may be stuck in negative and self-defeating beliefs, repressed emotions, and probably past-life patterns. The elemental pathway illustrates and plays out every issue causing his life problems. Consequently, our would-be financial wizard could use elemental processes to break through his entrenched patterns and obtain wealth. He could gain control of his managing energy bodies, alter his beliefs, express his repressed feelings, and open to a higher spiritual calling. But he also has another choice.

As his guide on the power pathway, I would coach him to put on his luminized glasses and see what I see. He is not accessing the force of Abundance. And the virtue of Honesty is not plugged into his spine. Little wonder; he isn't allowing energy sources—the Powers, the Forms, or the Masters—to help him. Instead, he's connected to the force of Poverty and a nonvirtue of niceness. He believes that nice men aren't rich—an elemental-based block big enough to keep him from using his power potential. If he can learn to shift power energies through his power energy bodies, however, our debt-ridden friend can shift his life into high-speed earning.

I worked with someone with the same issue as our hypothetical friend. Max had been unemployed for six months and was just about out of money. After learning how to access his Abundance force, Max received a phone call within twenty-four hours. He was offered a job—one that he wanted, even!

I remember the first time I became aware of my own power-level powers. I was four. I was mad at my sister. My dad was praising her Cinderella-looking outfit while I was being ignored. I focused my jealousy and pictured my sister's outfit ripping. Within seconds, it did, falling in pieces at her feet.

Later, in seventh grade, I endured a lecture on the occult. The visiting pastor levitated trumpets to give us an example of what demons in Native American sweat lodges can do. I went home and tried the same in my corner room downstairs, except with books. It worked! After nearly getting knocked out by a dictionary, I decided this might not be a smart activity. I knew this type of thing must be evil, because the preacher said so. Yet secretly, I still practiced commandeering energies. I knew intuitively that power could be used for good or bad, but that you could never do good without power.

We all have the innate capabilities and rights to command energies. The first step toward working the power pathway is to own your powers. Own your right to radiate.

But if you're going to do so, learn about the next pathway, the imagination. You don't want to mix up the differences between good and bad, negative versus positive intentions. The energies available on the elemental or the power pathways can be used for good or bad, or for a mix of both.

The Imagination Pathway: The Disappearing Cosmos

The mystical healers of Hawaii follow a healing path called *kahuna*. When studying in Kauai with Serge King, a kahuna master, I learned that the kahunas believe that all of life is a dream. You live in a dream and are the dreamer of your life, as I am in my life. Coming to this awareness enables us to live a fruitful and true existence.

This perspective allows me to detach from what "is" and connect with what "really is." Both the elemental and the power levels deal with what "is," even if the power forces are mainly invisible. What "is" includes the money in your pocketbook, the type of car you drive, and the nature of your relationship with a mate. Working the elemental and the power pathways calls for *attachment*, or involvement in the process of taking action to make change. The imagination pathway introduces the idea of *detachment*—the idea of accomplishment by doing nothing.

There is no energy on the imagination pathway, only a rearrangement of projections created from *antiparticles*. Antiparticles operate the antiuniverse. The antiuniverse, also called the antiworld, is a reality that matches our own. If there's a particle-based chair on your deck, its opposite—a space where no chair exists—exists in the parallel world of the antiuniverse.

Understanding the imagination level takes thinking logically. Science now insists that certain particles only exist in the third dimension when we look at them. Mystical physicists explain the appearance of ghosts—they might only be there when we desire to see them. This leaves the question: where are the particles—the ghosts of reality—when not being observed? That somewhere is the antiworld.

Imagination doesn't exist, but your imagination can lead you toward what you desire to bring into existence. This is the process of *illusion*—an impression of truth that isn't actually that truth.

You have probably heard of Thomas Edison, the inventor of the light bulb. He had to believe in the possibility of a light bulb in order to create it. It took him over 300 tries before he finally struck light and shifted the light bulb from his imagination into the real world. By believing in his dream, which started as an illusion, Edison eventually manifested a product now used around the world.

In this world, you might have only the whisper of a dream. Your wish is an illusion. It's not real in the third dimension, but it does exist in the antiworld. Upon proper application of your imagination, you can link to the antiworld and transfer antiparticles into this world. What was once a thought, a wish, or a hope is now a solid reality. Every invention, including the wheel, cars, and packaged foods, once started as an illusion.

Illusions of the imagination can be used to visualize a new and desired reality. Your imagination itself is the most important tool on the imagination level. By gaining conscious control of your illusion efforts, you use the child's game of pretend to help your imagination call "true reality" into the elemental reality.

However, on the imagination pathway, you also need to separate illusion from *delusion*—an impression based on a lie. An illusion is true because it leads to something real, and a delusion is false because it leads to a lie. A delusionary imagination is like the mirage, a deceptive image of an oasis that leads nowhere but over the sands and toward death. Using imagination to create delusion makes you vulnerable to the victimization of *fantasy*, or the adherence to lies.

Delusions can include and cause mistaken beliefs. Is money really evil? Is it bad to want sex? Are you really ugly? Are you really undeserving of happiness? Is that tumor really real? Is it leading toward a greater truth or a lie? If you have body image issues, fears about money, doubts about whether you're deserving, anger at being powerless, you are in delusion. And the separation of mind, body, soul, and spirit is a major delusion!

Delusions are usually caused by our own elemental minds or by the shifting seas of the power level. They may be phantom programs from family systems, religious institutions (especially fear-based or fanatical groups), or cultures. They may even be coercion from invading, otherworldly spirits. They can be created consciously or unconsciously.

But delusions actually hold no power, for they themselves have no consciousness. A convincing delusion will attract elemental or power energies and seem to become real. Healing on the imagination path involves becoming conscious of delusions and dispelling them.

This brings us back to detachment. The Buddhists, like the kahuna, understand that nothing exists, so nothing is all that is real. This concept can be critical in reaching for and accepting healing. If nothing exists, nothing is all that is real. If nothing is real, then your tumor isn't real. If money isn't real, then you aren't lacking money. This is detachment at work.

Working the imagination can be very powerful. In the energy mapping section, I'll teach a simple technique in which you examine the center of the chakra involved in an issue. If you alter the information determining what's in this world versus the antiworld, you can shift the balance between the two and alter elemental reality.

My patient Ben was having a difficult time letting go of his former wife. He insisted that he was still in love with her, even though she treated him disrespectfully and cruelly. We worked through his heart chakra, the obvious source of relationship challenges. I had Ben define the image in the center of this chakra. He saw a broken circle. Circles, as I'll describe more fully in a later section, relate to completion. The real issue wasn't really Ben's relationship with his former wife, but Ben's relationship with relationships! All of his relationships exhibited some form of incompletion.

On the elemental pathway, we might have tracked this effect back to its cause. On the power pathway, we might have summoned powers or forces to correct the situation. On the imagination pathway, we simply altered the symbol by completing the circle. We then energized this process using other techniques. The so-called worlds on either side of Ben's heart shifted. By the next morning, he reported feeling "done" with his former wife and life and ready to move on.

The Divine Pathway: A Daily Celebration

To illuminate means to make something or someone shine or become lit. "Illumination" is a celebratory word, and celebration is what the divine path brings.

We all exist on the level of divine reality. We aren't aware of it, because we aren't willing to allow ourselves the unconditional love and access to power provided through the divine. The divine is a space and an awareness that is hard to explain or describe, as are its effects. It is a lighted path, leading to a place of formlessness, timelessness, and perfection. This is the reality of the so-called instant miracle, although these miracles can be unexpected.

The divine is nothing more or less than *awakened perception*. The door to this pathway cannot be entered with deeds, intention, knowledge, or words, nor influenced with any of these. But there is a walkway to it. Just as the chakras open to the power seals, they are also channels of light to the divine. The energy bodies on the divine pathway include the *body of the eternal*, the *body of the infinite*, the *seven bowls of existence,* and the *seven lamps,* all of which are described in chapter 7. You can become illuminated through the energetic system, but only if you know the overriding truth of the divine: *You must be as you really are, right here.*

As do the other paths, the divine has particular energy portals, powers, structure, records, passwords, language, and purpose. Unlike the other pathways, however, the divine doesn't require that you "work" for a healing.

When you are illuminated, you are lit with understanding. This is the nirvana that Buddhists strive to achieve, the heaven that Christians desire to reach. The Chinese idea of the *hsien,* or illuminated master, describes the practicing illuminary.

There is an ancient Chinese story of a young female *hsien.* After she was murdered, her body did not grow cold, but instead emanated a fragrant, flowery smell. Later, the coffin was found to contain nothing more than a slipper. Like Cinderella, she forgot her slipper when she left the ball. The young *hsien* was an illuminated being and, upon death, became what she had always been: pure consciousness.

Some illuminated or wakeful beings just plain skip the dying process. Yet another known *hsien,* Yu Tzu, was said to never die. Instead, he took off heavenward and was never seen again. Christians believe that three days after Jesus died, he rose in his transfigured body and that in this form he still was able to perform human functions, such as eating. Consider also the stories of Simeon Toko, from Angola [2]. A missionary from a Baptist Missionary Society in Angola had a dream that a Great King was now alive in infant form. He was led to Simeon, who at that time was a weak and sick baby. The pastor turned around in dismay, doubting the voice that had led him there.

When older, Simeon joined a Baptist church, and manifested such abilities and powers that white missionaries thought him guilty of black magic. He and others left that church.

Following a surge of spiritual powers, Simeon and his followers were persecuted. Finally, two agricultural foremen decided to reap the reward offered for Simeon's life, and they attempted to murder him.

Sending Simeon to work on a tractor, the driver started it up, activating the seed sower. Simeon's body was severed into several pieces. The driver shifted into reverse, while the other murderer flashed a "thumbs up" signal. And then—the body of Simeon recomposed itself.

Simeon continued to perform miracle after miracle while walking the earth in physical form, including commanding a plane to stop and restart in mid-air. When he finally died in 1984, many people asserted that he continued to visit in an apparitional body and in dream states. Another story is told, however, that makes us question the finality of this death. It is said that doctors decided to experiment upon Simeon's corpse. After cutting out Simeon's heart, he supposedly sat up, stared around the operating room, and asked why he was being persecuted this way.

And then there are natural substances seemingly imbued with supernatural healing powers. The dirt at a certain Catholic church in New Mexico is said to have healed hundreds of parishioners' complaints. How can dirt accomplish such a miracle? Is it in fact accomplished by the faith connected to the dirt, as some might suggest?

These are examples of illuminated events, but they don't describe the process of illumination healing. Basically, you create an illuminated healing through expanded consciousness or awareness. By refusing to fight what exists, you can see beyond it and own a different choice. Everything and anyone conscious will assist.

Entering the state of divine feels like expanding oneself into a neutral state. In neutrality, I hold no judgment about anything or anyone; I assume that everything that "is" is some reflection of love. I also assume that all abilities and powers are available to me, as long as I'm willing to allow myself to be changed into a more divine state when providing a healing for someone else.

I gave my first divine healing to my friend Jane. She was extraordinarily stressed, so she was constantly tired, gaining weight, and abnormally cranky. On the divine pathway, it doesn't matter where you begin a healing, just that you do so. I arbitrarily placed my hands on her adrenals, assumed the divine state, and began to link with her first chakra.

Jane immediately began to feel hot. Over the next few minutes, she was able to relay everything that was occurring within her body, as well as the truths unfolding to her. She reported that the energy was clearing a future case of breast cancer; that her hypothalamus—a gland in the brain—was permanently correcting a heart arrhythmia; and that her lungs were ridding themselves of secondary smoke she had inhaled as a child. She also revealed several understandings that were coming to her, such as the need to accept love from others and a hidden desire to play more.

After the healing, Jane was completely wiped out and hardly moved for hours. Over the course of just a few months following the healing, she lost twenty pounds, quit one job and started one that she likes, and began writing a book that she had always wanted to write. She now reports greater peace in her marriage and more joy in her parenting. Quite simply, she feels more alive!

A Cross Comparison

Here is a comparison of miracle workers on the Four Pathways.

An elemental miracle worker could be a doctor who uses skill and compassion to guide a cancer patient through surgery and chemotherapy. Yet another elemental wunderkind might use psychic gifts to reveal the issues underlying the cancer, thereby assisting the patient with clearing the causal issues. This technique could be called medical intuition; I often use it and then send the client to qualified professionals—other elemental workers—for traditional treatment.

A power miracle worker might intuitively sense the energetic forces at play in a disease process. After diagnosing the forces, she can shift energetic bodies, lines, forces, or powers to provide an influx of new energy and reestablish physical balance. Many energy medicine workers excel at this level. I once used power techniques to summon a regeneration force to combat a client's uterine cancer. This seemed a critical step in the cancer's eventual disappearance.

An imagination wonder worker could use imagination to fool a client into health; the placebo effect does the rest. One common imagination tool is the use of mirrors, shamanic instruments, and symbols to produce effects. Imagination work doesn't have to look mystical or magical, however. I once used an imagination technique to help a married couple of thirty years face the delusion of their marriage. All they talked about was how much they loved each other, and yet neither wanted sex with the other partner. I simply took information from the other world—the truths that were denied and therefore lingering in the antiworld—and shared this data with my clients. Whatever they cheerfully said, I stated the opposite. Finally, both began to cry and complain about the other person. After two hours of "clearing the air," they began to relate more honestly with each other. Since this session they've reported back that they now have an active and satisfying sex life.

A divine miracle maker knows that in the healing there is no miracle; there is only a shift in perspective that allows love to become incarnated.

Another comparison of the Four Pathways was given to me in the dream state. I actually fell asleep, dreamed, and then awakened four times that night. Each dream was part of the larger dream; each dreampart taught me about one of the Four Pathways.

While dreaming, I found myself in my kitchen, accompanied by Christ. In part one, Christ pointed at my refrigerator. The fridge was under lock and key. Christ assigned me the task of making dinner, and obviously my first job was to get into the refrigerator. At this juncture, I used elemental techniques to find the key and open the refrigerator.

I searched the entire kitchen, on ladders and on my hands and knees, until after a long time I finally found the hidden key. Feeling successful, I woke from my dream.

When I fell asleep again, I was back in my kitchen staring at the same locked refrigerator. This time, I asked Christ how to use power forces to accomplish the task. At his bidding, I unplugged the fridge from the electrical socket and used some sort of magnetic device to decode the lock. Even while sleeping, I understood the analogy. On the power level, you can ask for higher help and engineer efforts with various forces and powers.

When I awoke again, I felt pretty proud of myself, until I slipped back into slumber and found myself again in front of the locked Amana. What was next? I went for the imagination. I simply sat down and pretended that I had already made dinner. That worked, for a while. I could see that it might be an easier task for a real master, the guru who can truly live on air. I decided that this wasn't my preferred means of operating.

When I woke again, I was not surprised to immediately doze back off. There was the refrigerator, locked again. This time, I noticed a small bowl on the top of the refrigerator. Christ said to me, "If you change your perception of the problem, the problem will change." Without knowing exactly what I was doing, I pictured myself setting the problem in the bowl. I asked for a solution. And then I walked away.

I didn't have far to walk. When I looked at the refrigerator again, the lock was gone. I heard these words: "When there is no resistance to the problem, it then shifts out of existence." I knew that I was now on the divine pathway, the place of knowing what needs to be known. I also knew that I didn't have to solve my own problems. Unconditional Divine Love is present for us all, as are the powers necessary to make changes. Owning any version of this truth causes a shift in awareness, and this shift alters reality as we know it.

Where the Pathways Lead

Walking the Four Pathways can be done in any order. Some people prefer to first learn the elemental, then the power, and so on. My own journey has involved learning and using all at once. You'll find your own way.

If you look at the Four Pathways in a progressive order, which our linear minds are apt to do, you will find that they mirror the stages of human development often outlined by some of the brightest and keenest minds; for example, the stages proposed by mythologist Joseph

Campbell, who compares everyone's life to a hero's journey. As a hero in our own life, we must all undergo a multiphase process of searching for meaning—first in the immediate environment, then in the world, then inside of the self, and finally in the self through which the universe flows. These stages are parallel to the Four Pathways, as well as the four mind states experienced by searchers for meaning.

The stages leading to enlightenment were observed by researchers R. Masters and J. Houston, who used mind-altering drugs to analyze subjects for authentic religious experiences. Dr. James Austin describes the study in his book *Zen and the Brain*. [3] He reports that Masters and Houston were looking for transformative experiences that included a true encounter with a supreme being and led to permanent change. By analyzing over two hundred subjects, Masters and Houston came up with four stages leading toward authentic religious experience:

1. *The sensory level.* A highly visual stage that seemed interesting, but most of the pictures had little meaning for the subject experiencing them.

2. *The recollective-analytical level.* Here, visual images were personal and seemed to carry a message or purpose. The subjects reported more intense emotions; they also said that the boundary between the conscious and the unconscious seemed to disappear. There appeared to be emotional healing on this level.

3. *The symbolic level.* Themes at this level were mythological and ritualistic. Some subjects reported undergoing rites of initiation. Others reported a sense of a beneficial "climate" or energy behind the scenes.

4. *The deep integral level.* This was the only level involving true religious experiences—an emotionally charged, personalized encounter with "the ultimate level of reality." This level seems to give way to a spiritual consciousness, carrying the "flavor of eternity." Masters and Houston noted that only about 5 percent of all subjects got to this level, and that these individuals were particularly mature and well-developed people.

In Austin's analysis of these findings, he emphasizes that while half of the subjects in the study had ecstatic experiences, most of them did not transform. Only a few reached the deep integral level by having a "personal encounter with what was perceived as 'Ultimate Being.'" Only those who reached this level were permanently changed by the experience. And of these, only six individuals—6 percent of those who had ecstatic experiences—qualified for a special category within the fourth stage, called "Unitary Consciousness" by Masters and Houston. In this subgroup, subjects achieved a state devoid of all sensual or empirical data, and they returned from the experiment truly transformed.

What made these six people different? They shared the following characteristics: They were over forty and had more mature brains. All were intelligent, creative, and responsible. They had also spent years seeking out mystical experiences through various spiritual disciplines. During the experiment, all of them experienced their personalities dissolving into a "boundless being" within an extreme light. They became one with that which is, and afterward they became even more interested in their everyday lives—permanently. As Austin points out, this is the "essential aspect of Zen transformation"—the living of life more fully.[4]

This advanced spiritual stage was characterized by the Zen master Pai-Chang hundreds of years ago as one of freedom. "When you are unhindered by bondage or freedom, this then is called liberation of mind and body in all places."[5] The Soto Zen master Dogen uses a different phrase: "Everyday life is enlightenment."[6] In other words, when you are unhindered by bondage or freedom, you are expressing your original self in total freedom. Living is the ultimate mystical experience.

We can all reach the ultimate level of consciousness, what I call the illuminated reality of *Wakefulness*. True miracles and happiness are possible when we're able to be our original selves—magical, mystical, and powerful in daily reality. By learning about the world around us, we accept the elemental self and own the importance of the everyday. By accessing our power gifts, we dissolve the false boundaries between "in here" and "out there" and know ourselves as citizens of the universe. By facing the imagination, we realize that we are the creation of our own creative powers. We learn how to walk as "real" and "not real," in form and formlessness. By surrendering to the wakeful state of the divine, we become connected. We become what Eastern religions describe as the enlightened master serving tea to his servants.

It takes long and hard work, as shown in the study by Masters and Houston. You don't have to be over forty, as their study suggested, but you do need to walk a disciplined path and understand the rules. Otherwise, you may spin out, into either the depression of reaching the pinnacle and then falling, the hallucinations of fantasy, the pride of having all those powers, or the hopelessness of never trying. Learning the rules of any one or all of the pathways provides you with the discipline and the structural support you need to be real and original in your stretch for wholeness.

Energy Basics

The Nature of Energy

Working Energies

Because healing on the Four Pathways is done energetically, to comprehend how the Four Pathways function you need to understand working with energy.

Working energetically means that you create change by changing the energy of a problem. To accomplish this goal, you can either bring in energy that establishes your desires, alter the energy holding a problem in place, or actually change the nature of a particular energy. All of these strategies compose what I call *shift healing*. They allow the possibility for life-enhancing and sometimes miraculous change.

By working energetically, you bypass the difficulties of jumping back and forth among physical, emotional, mental, or spiritual considerations. You don't have to figure out where an issue lies. You need only work with the energies causing a presenting problem—or the energies that will allow wholeness to become more three-dimensional. By shifting energy on a certain pathway, you automatically change the physical, emotional, mental, and spiritual components of that issue. And by creating such a change on one pathway, you immediately transfer energy to all other pathways, which can then conform to a more healed state.

Some of us blank out when forced to learn about energy. The subject can sound a bit abstract or overly theoretical. Personally, discussing energy is one of my passions. Everything in the world—and, I might add, not yet in it—is fashioned from energy. Grasp the importance and the basic concepts of energy and you hold the key to the universe in your hands. Reconfigure the energy of yesterday and you can fashion a new today. Figure out the energy forming today and you can create a new tomorrow. And don't we all want tomorrow to be a little better than today?

The Energies Creating Today

Your world is as it is for one reason: the energies creating today are locking your current reality into place.

Everything in your world is made of energy, as are you. And there are energies holding what currently exists in place. If you want to change what's around or inside of you, you have two main options: change what's in place, or change what's holding reality in place.

We perform both of these energy tasks constantly. Let's say I'm wearing a purple sweater and I don't like it. By taking off the purple sweater, I'm changing energies. I'm getting rid of an energy that's been in place. When I put on a new sweater—say, my favorite blue one—I'm continuing to change what's in place, this time through an exchange of energy.

Problems are similar to purple sweaters. If they're relatively easy to deal with, we simply move energy until we've gotten the problem "off our back." Sometimes, though, it's not that simple. Issues can be like too-tight sweaters. Ever tried on an old high-school shirt and then wished that you hadn't? It's not so easy to wiggle out of some problems. When we can't simply change what's in place, we need to change the energy holding the undesirable energy in place. It's easy if the challenge is to simply unbutton a sweater. If the barnacle is cancer or a paranoia or impending financial doom, however, it's far more difficult to figure out which energy is handcuffing us to disaster.

Working the pathways is dependent on being able to identify and change the energies that keep you stuck and bring in energies that enhance wholeness and health. To accomplish any of these goals, you have to analyze the energy involved in a situation according to two criteria: the information in the energy and the qualities of the energy, such as motion, speed, and intensity.

If you can learn how to break an issue down into its energetic parts, you can assert the energy necessary to free yourself from a problem. Likewise, by eliminating the frozen, limiting, or imprisoning energies that are causing you difficulties, you allow breathing room for healing. You create the pauses necessary to make forward jumps.

Ideas about Energy

I'll be listing and describing the particulars of energy in the next chapter. Here, I want to present an overall picture to provide context.

For quite some time, physicists have known that energy—such as electricity, magnetism, and light—existed in the form of waves. If all energy moves in waves, it's easy to predict what energy is going to do. But at the turn of the twentieth century, physicist Max Planck performed an experiment that erased this assumption about energy. By measuring the relationship between light shining on a metal plate and the actual electricity produced, he deduced that energy doesn't always flow in continuous waves. Rather, it is made of individual units, which he called quanta. Quantum physics was born.

A few years later, Albert Einstein started writing equations on his tablecloths in between naps. His work established the fact that energy can't be destroyed—it merely changes form. He also showed that light was composed of particles called photons. When light was shone on a metal plate, the light would splinter off electrons, creating electricity. But Einstein wasn't sold on quantum theory. As he saw it, matter can't move faster than the speed of light. This meant that quantum theory couldn't explain the pesky, unexplainable behavior of the so-called quanta.

And these quanta were certainly causing problems. They just wouldn't—or couldn't—stay in place. Ever watched toddlers on a day-to-day basis? One day they can't sit still, another day they keep disappearing, the next day they're glued to the television set. Quanta exhibit the same inconsistent behavior. Sometimes they act like waves and sometimes like particles. Sometimes two particles might relate though separated by millions of miles. Sometimes two particles might date for a while and then—poof!—one of them will disappear, and no amount of searching can ferret out the hiding spot.

Einstein didn't appreciate the inconsistency and kept trying to come up with an explanation that would tie Newtonian physics with quantum physics. He even selected a name for this theory: the Unified Field Theory. He never found an equation deserving of the name.

But then, Einstein was missing information that we now have. We now know that certain energies can move faster than the speed of light. This fact is crucial to working the pathways and performing shift healing. What if you could eliminate a problem before it even exists? This is possible on some of the pathways.

There was yet another idea being touted during Einstein's time that he refused to corroborate. Einstein didn't believe in what a layperson might call the theory of other worlds. The idea keeps gathering strength, however, probably because it explains the strange behavior of quanta.

The other world theory suggests that you and I exist in "this world." In any given moment, there are infinite possibilities. As soon as you move forward, you cancel out most of these possibilities because you've made a choice.

As an intuitive-based consultant, I constantly hear complaints about the need to make life-changing choices. Every day, individuals insist that I must tell them their future so they'll have a guaranteed outcome. *Then* they'll make their choices! The truth is, *you cannot see your future until you step into it.* Only then does it totally create around you. However, the paths not chosen are not lost forever. According to the other world theory, the unchosen is spun into one of the other worlds in the multiverse. The journeys not taken may even create their own world.

In all probability, there are hundreds—if not infinite numbers—of other worlds, many of them now being labeled the antiworld. We know that there are antiworlds that mirror our own—their occupants often exact duplicates, yet in reverse. For instance, a weighted particle in this world is weightless in the antiworld. A positively charged, this-world quanta will be a negatively charged antiparticle over there.

The other world theory explains certain forms of psychic phenomena. That sudden psychic revelation you get could be a faster-than-light quanta dropping in from the antiworld, where it's been hiding for, say, a few centuries. Not that psychic energy only reflects the past; it may have been inspired to visit you from the future!

The antiworld also explains the whereabouts of disappearing quanta. If something is here one moment and gone the next, it must go somewhere—or to some time, at the least! Einstein established that energy can't be destroyed, but merely changes form. And antiworlds aren't really such a bizarre concept if you think of them as a series of rooms just partitioned off in your house. In the quanta world, we're constantly adding onto our house, but most of us are still learning how to open the doors to these new rooms. The imagination pathway in particular encompasses working in both this world and the antiworlds. While the effects are magical, the techniques for negotiating this type of change are actually quite simple.

Lack of Predictability

It would be convenient to assume that everything here is mirrored in everything in the antiworld; that there is symmetry to life. That's the idea behind holistic thinking, after all. As above, so below. What is in me is mirrored in the Greater All. This theory has been substantiated, in part, by the work of Juan Maldacena of the Institute for Advanced

Study in Princeton, New Jersey. He found that what was going on in reality was mirrored by the physics taking place on a bounding surface. But the details were different. In one arena, there were perhaps four interacting dimensions; in the other, there would be five.[2]

The outcome of Maldacena's experiment points out the lack of predictability in reality. It's not true that all actions produce an equal and similar reaction, as we were taught in ninth-grade science. A certain mental belief may or may not be reflected as a certain disease in the body; a particular herb may or may not effect the desired change. Working energetically is a lot more complicated than following all the rules. Current thinking has identified thirty-two different types of quanta. If scientists are like cereal manufacturers, within a few years there will be an additional thirty-two "new and improved" versions. Quanta are complicated, that much we know.

We energy workers aren't left in the lurch, however. The fact that energy can move in waves, the existence of particle formation—these are critical factors in our favor. If you can work or change waves, you can move mountains. If you can control or alter a particle, you can pinpoint an issue and change it. The power lies in knowing what to do when and where.

Working the Four Pathways helps you do more than "shoot in the dark" when performing healing. Each pathway has its own set of energies, energy rules, and potential outcomes. Before you start moving and shifting energies on any of these realities, you need to be able to figure out what to do and why. This is called *reading energy*. If you can read the information that's telling energy what to do, you've moved beyond trying; you can track all those speeding bullets and moving forces or predict the possible outcome. You take charge of matters.

Influential Energy

You can push and push on a boulder, but if it's anything like the boulders I try to move, it isn't going to budge. It's easy to say that you can change reality by moving energy, but some energies are simply too stubborn or big to move—and some are too small and slippery to even find!

The good news is that you don't have to do all the work with brute force—or positive thinking, soul understanding, or spiritual prayer. Instead of creating change by applying power, you need only to convince energy to move itself!

Am I really saying that you can rid a farm field of stones by talking to the stones? Technically, I am. Science is substantiating an important idea that can be truly life changing, if not life saving. Energy equals information. This fact is vital to any and all healing processes, for it proposes that *one way to create change is to work not only the energy itself, but also with the information within and affecting energy.*

This revolutionary thought means that you have more healing options than traditional or even alternative medicine might propose. You can certainly continue to work directly on a tumor. You can biopsy, cut, and probe. You can image white light and a new life. You can hold positive thoughts and down vitamin-enriched antidotes. But you can also work to change the information telling the tumor it needs to be a tumor. And if the tumor, like a too-tight purple sweater, still doesn't want to exit, you can work with the information that's maintaining the tumor. Unpin the tumor and the body can't hold onto it.

The concept of energy equaling information was the basis of experimentation conducted by Drs. Gary Schwartz and Linda Russek. Schwartz, a professor of psychology, neurology, and psychiatry and director of the Human Energy Systems Laboratory at the University of Arizona, joined with Russek, a research psychologist at Harvard University Student Health Center and Human Energy Systems Laboratory, to create the Dynamic Systems Memory Field. Their research demonstrates that all physical systems exchange influential energy. Because this energy is influential, it must contain information that creates an effect. [3]

These joint works are noted in several papers but are summarized best by Dr. Paul Pearsall in his book *The Heart's Code: Tapping the Wisdom and Power of Our Heart Energy.* He says that because information is seeded within all energy, everything that exists has energy that is "full of information." [4]

This means that everything you do, think, eat, believe, or say is information packaged and carried by energy. Change information and you change energy and its effects. Change the information you're putting out into the world and the world changes what it's sending you.

Intelligent Pathway Healing

Pathway healing involves being both conscious of the information that you're working with and aware of the forces that can change or direct that energy. For example, let's say you want to get rid of cancer cells. Shift healing could involve moving energy by changing the information in (1) the malignant cells, (2) the healthy cells around them, or (3) the forces maintaining either the illness or the healing process. Instead of dividing your actions into physical, emotional, mental, or spiritual, you only have to consider the information involved in creating or maintaining a problem, or the information that will reassert wholeness and healthiness. Which method you use depends on which pathway you work.

However, before you can affect energy via a certain pathway, you have to learn the language and principle of each one. When you're in Germany, it's less effective to speak French than to speak German. Let's look at examples of what each pathway offers for healing a malignant growth in the body.

On the elemental pathway, one of the principles is that might is right. A typical mind-body enthusiast might suggest that you think pretty thoughts to get rid of a tumor. A holistic healthcare professional might give you herbs, while a soul healer might conduct a soul healing. These are incomplete tools unless the energy that might assert wholeness and healing is stronger than the energies creating and maintaining the tumor. To boost the potency of the energy for healing, you must direct the information accordingly.

There are several ways of working information on the elemental pathway. You could read the information establishing the tumor as a physical reality and exchange it for different information. You could analyze and alter the information causing the body's weakness in relation to the growth and thus bolster the body's defense mechanisms. You might support the healing properties of an herb by adding additional information that boosts its effectiveness. You might decrease the tenacity of a tumor by rewriting its energetic patterns. You could work with waves, which change consciousness patterns, or particles, which can subdivide a tumor so natural forces can conquer it. You could even expand a particle that's already healthy and thus grow a new reality that could eventually overtake the current one! On the elemental level, you have a lot of options. But all are going to require the ability to increase the potency of the positive forces and decrease the intensity of the negative energies. To do that, you must work the information creating the current static state.

Do you really want to blast a tumor out of existence? Then you're talking about leaping to the next pathway: the power. On the power pathway, a tumor isn't a tumor; it's a blank space, an area lacking the necessary support of certain vital forces. If you direct the correct positive forces at this site, the blank space is replaced with healthy energy, which encourages the growth of healthy cells. If you eliminate the forces creating the blank space first, your job is even easier. The power pathway is about forces. It can provide the key to making the physical changes you desire on the elemental pathway, upon which "might is right."

On the imagination pathway, a tumor is simply an idea that you've accepted as true. Change your mind, the tumor disappears.

And on the divine pathway, the tumor is a malady afflicting not only you, but all of humankind. Through Divine Love and other spiritual principles, you can achieve the consciousness necessary to allow the tumor to disappear. It never needed to become.

Change information, change reality.

The Chakras as Information Doorways

One of the reasons I recommend working through the chakra system is that changing information can be a long, slow process. The chakras are able to convert slow energy to fast and fast energy to slow. They can shift waves to particles and particles to waves. You must consciously direct these efforts to produce the desired effects, but anyone can learn to do this! Energy mapping will introduce you to several simple techniques that will activate your innate skill at shifting reality.

Working the chakras on the pathways allows you to make change more easily, more quickly, and with less mess. Again, we're talking about the nature of energy. All energy contains information, and you can change, alter, eliminate, and add information. You can also use information to direct the energy waves or particles themselves. This is possible because of various qualities of energy, such as speed, intensity, and motion.

Light-Speed Healing

Besides information, speed is the other important factor when seeking miracles or performing shift healing. If you want a miracle, you have to either make a healing go faster than normal or completely stop the problem. According to new physics, both are possible.

Studies are showing that light can move faster than the established speed of light. This means that you potentially can direct or redirect information-energy and create an instant effect.

Speeding Up Energy A breakthrough experiment at the NEC Research Institute in Princeton, New Jersey, proved that light can move at speeds beyond the established speed of light. Scientists broke this cosmic limit when they caused a pulse of light—a collection of waves—to travel many times faster than the speed of light. In fact, the light accelerated so fast, it escaped the test chamber before it could even enter it![5]

This means the information contained in that energetic pulse of light was also transferred faster than the speed of light. It also shows that when consciously working with information, you can use the chakras to create a desired effect, maybe even at a speed faster than a speeding bullet!

The applications of fast energy are innumerable. If mass—and, therefore, information—can move faster than the speed of light, then cause can follow effect. You could actually make a tumor disappear before it appears.

Picture a chamber filled with freezing liquid. The chamber is open at both ends. Now imagine a beam of light shot through one of the openings. There are millions of photons carried on this light, but we're only interested in "Fred the Photon."

If Fred were to move slower than the speed of light, he would enter the chamber and then exit the other side after a negotiated amount of time. But Fred is quicker than your average photon. Fred moves so fast, he's out the chamber door before he's even entered the chamber! Fred isn't magic. Fred didn't break any laws of nature. Fred just moves really fast.

Pretend that Fred is a tumor. If a tumor can move faster than the speed of light, or the information telling your cells to create a tomorrow can do the same, this suggests the following:

- You can get rid of a tumor before you get it. If you can focus on the "future" tumor, you can shift it out of existence before it's established in your body.
- You can shift to the future and "look back" at a tumor that you haven't yet gotten, and plausibly keep it from occurring. By looking at an earlier version of your tumor, you can change the conditions that "provoked" it.
- You can perceive your tumor in two places at the same time. At some crossover point, the tumor lingers at either end of the chamber—the chamber being comparable to your physical body. If you can "freeze" the tumor at the ends, why, it will never lock into physical form!

Shift healing doesn't bend the rules of time and space. It merely puts you in charge of them.

Stopping Energy What about stopping energy in its tracks? What if you could halt cancer and buy time to bolster the immune system? What if you could freeze-frame an oncoming car long enough to get out of its way? You're talking about something that mystics have experienced since time began. It's called reaching the *zero point*—the human ability to reduce time to a standstill.

Science substantiates this ability. Researchers knew that many substances, including water, could slow light. But it wasn't until Dr. Lene Vestergaard Hau and other researchers began using sodium and other substances that they actually stopped light from moving. In 2001, Hau and fellow researchers absorbed a pulse of light into a cloud of sodium, which halted the light and its imprint at zero velocity for one-thousandth of a second. This process, termed *freezing light*, involves turning a laser beam on an opaque material, then manipulating the light with a second laser beam. At the zero point, the light vanishes, but the imprint does not! A second or coupling beam regenerates the pulse. [6]

Even more recently, in 2003, Harvard researchers topped this achievement when they actually completely stopped the light before sending it on its way. [7] Repeating and expanding on this experiment can potentially lead to information storage and processing capabilities, with the human body serving as a power quantum computer.

I believe that the human ability to freeze light explains many mystical phenomena, such as the shamanic acts of slowing time, walking in two geographic places at once, and stopping the dying process. To understand this aptitude, you need only think of the human being as a formation of light. As asserted by Dr. Richard Gerber, a pioneer in energy medicine, "the physical universe is composed of orderly patterns of frozen light." [8] Chakras are seen as conduits for and transformers of light, able to alter the frequencies of the various energies necessary for human existence. Really, the total human being is nothing more or less than a giant light converter!

What if certain people, such as the shaman trained in the mystical practices of altering reality, have beaten science to the punch? What if these and other amazing individuals are simply aware of means for stopping and starting the movement of light—or even the means to split certain waves of light or motivate certain particles of light at will? If so, it would be possible for the knowledgeable to consciously freeze the light present at a certain moment in time-space, step forward into the Greater Reality, perform a desired task, slip back into the bubble of frozen time when ready, and unfreeze what's been stopped. There will be an imprint or memory of both events, which, from a certain perspective, occurred at the same time.

Intensity

One of the other important considerations in pathway healing is intensity. Intensity refers to the amount of applied force you need to move energy. There are times you need to increase or decrease the force on information-energy to alleviate a situation.

Remember the analogy of the energy as a boulder? Actually moving an energy boulder might take a little elbow grease. Some are so heavy that to lighten the load you have to work first with information inside of the energy. You might have to change the coded program of energy—say, tell cancer particles to transform into air particles. It's easier to move air than rock.

Motion

One of the other critical healing factors is the motion of energy. Motion is much more complicated to manage and control than you might think, but it's very important to gain skill in this area if you want powerful healing results.

Everything in the physical reality is in motion. Even a solid desk is composed of moving particles, each bouncing into the others yet held together by gravitational properties. Conceivably, you could use the idea of motion to produce astounding healing effects.

Want to get rid of a tumor? How about simply moving it out of the body? I recently performed just such a technique through the power pathway. The growth, a benign tumor on a friend's hand, disappeared over a few days and didn't return. It still exists, but not on him! I simply "motioned" the tumor away.

There's another way to create motion for change. It's called working with spin.

Spin is usually seen as the revolution or rotation of an object around an axis or center point. The easiest way to begin healing an issue on the Four Pathways is to figure out the spin of a disease. A problem is causing either a depression, which is a depression or inversion of energy, or anxiety, which is a speeding or expenditure of energy. Sometimes, all you need to do with a problem is correct the energetic spin, or change your axis or center point. By considering the direction or directions of energy, by setting motions at will, you can conceivably move your problems out of your life and attract more desirable situations.

Scientists used to believe that objects or particles had coordinated spins, that there was a logic to the motion of waves or particles. In the microworld, it's a bit more complicated than that. Quanta don't just slip back and forth. You can't just figure out a quanta's spin or track its movements by figuring out which points on a plane they pass through.

Numbers don't mean much in the quanta world. You can't measure everything in a linear fashion. Some quanta form certain geometric figures when they spin. Others create strange and bizarre patterns. Certain spins produce exponential effects, meaning the "off-diagonal" movements get bigger and bigger over time.

These days, scientists are starting to measure these motions using a matrix. Matrix patterning is the basis for healing techniques prevalent around the world. Reiki is a Japanese healing system teaching the application of universal energy through symbology. A symbol is a matrix. All diseases are patterned on individual matrices. Breast cancer cells, for instance, will spin in a certain way. Prostate cancer cells will generate their own matrices. Working spin involves changing the structure or spin of these cells, the spin of the information in the cells or the energies emanating from these cells. If you alter the spins of enough malignant cells, you change the conditions allowing cancer.

» The Speeds of Energy

FOR HEALING PURPOSES, we need to know about four main speeds of energy. Certain speeds are available on certain pathways and others are not. Knowing this will help you consciously direct informed energy to meet your goals.

Slower Than the Speed of Light Quarks are particles that move slower than the speed of light. Sensory information, noted through your five senses, is composed of quarks. You can measure and manage slow energy with natural physical laws.

Faster Than the Speed of Light Tachyons are particles that can move faster than the speed of light. Tachyons are actually antiparticles. In the antiworld, they carry weight; in the physical universe, they hold negative weight. Tachyons help explain psychic phenomena and many miraculous happenings. In this world, they carry information faster than the speed of light, which explains how psychic data gets transferred so quickly. They also describe certain miraculous events. A collection or wave of tachyons existing in the antiworld, if suddenly appearing in the physical, can cause the instant appearance of an object, the solution to a long-term problem, or even a new problem!

Think back to the suggestions made earlier about Fred the Photon. Moving energy quickly can essentially help you prevent problems before they occur, shift them into a different existence, and present choices that enable health.

Zero Point At the zero point, light is frozen into a fixed imprint. This imprint will remain in place, even though the light can be freed to move forward. This offers the knowledgeable several capabilities. As shamans have done for centuries, you could freeze yourself or an aspect of yourself in a certain place and time while projecting yourself forward to accomplish a set task. This is the process used in remote viewing, a psychic technique involving the projection of consciousness to obtain information or gather energy. If you need information for healing purposes, you could project an aspect of your consciousness, find the data, and bring it back. When working certain pathways, you can establish the zero point to also gather healing energy.

Stillness When you reach a certain speed that is faster than the speed of light, you arrive at stillness. Stillness isn't lack of movement; rather, it is movement so fast that you are simultaneously moving and at rest. Stillness connotes "all time" with no dualities. It is usually described in spiritual circles as an acceptance of what is. This state of tranquility or peace is an especially prized commodity in Eastern spiritualities.

It's important to understand the physics of stillness as containing immeasurable movement. This implies that if you can unconditionally accept what is, you can change it as well. You can potentially walk around with a tumor indefinitely, awaiting the shift in perception necessary to spin it out of physical existence.

To work spin effectively, you must figure out the spin of the problematic energy and possibly also envision the desired spin. Significant breakthroughs in medical technology allow some of these measurements and, therefore, spin healings. You can also use your own mind and intuition to effect spin healing. As in times long ago, simply imaging accurate symbols, colors, geometries, numbers, or tones can alter spin and therefore affect outcome. Imagine, for example, that breast cancer cells spin on a certain matrix. In working with a breast cancer caused by issues from the past, we'll most likely perceive a counterclockwise spin. There are dozens of symbolic variations, but most depressed spins will have squared-off corners. Imagine, then, the cancer cells are spinning counterclockwise in a rectangular type of shape. One way to eliminate these errant cells is to permanently change their spin! Moving them into a clockwise rotation and a different shape, for instance a spiral, can unpin the hold of the cancer and potentially allow the body's immune fighters to now attack these cells with force.

Speed, Intensity, and Motion on the Pathways

You have to work energy differently on each of the Four Pathways to produce change. Here is a pathway-by-pathway comparison in regard to speed, intensity, and motion.

The Elemental On this pathway you can work speeds faster and slower than the speed of light. You must increase or decrease the intensity mechanically to produce effects. Motion is measurable, and you must apply pressure or intensity to create real change. Your consciousness must be supported by physical behavior or energies to create changes; therefore you'll obtain the best results when holding your body, mind, emotions, soul, and all other aspects of yourself in total alignment with a single focus.

The Power On this pathway you can work speeds faster and slower than the speed of light, but advanced power workers can achieve the zero point. You access various powers and forces to change intensities and usually work with waves to change motion.

Forces can move faster or slower than the speed of light. A force is similar to a wave but is also subdivided into subwaves and formational particles. Through conscious manipulation, you can apply forces, rather than the limiting mechanics of the elemental pathway, to create change. You can also change the composition of a force, as well as the direction, intensity, and speed of any single force or of any of the particles or subwaves within a force.

The Imagination Fast and slow energies can have an impact, but the zero point is the natural state. In a way, you could say that there is no energy on the imagination pathway. Anything created on this pathway is from the antiuniverse. Illusions or delusions, however, can attract elemental energy or power forces of any sort. Any freed or escaped light is not real on the imagination pathway; it is simply a projection from another pathway.

Shift healing is actually quite easy on the imagination pathway, once you understand that on this pathway nothing is real. What is not real can be changed. It can be eliminated or magnified. You need only stand in the middle of an imagination pathway—available through the center point of every chakra—to act as your own imagination maestro.

An easy way to picture the imagination pathway is to see it as a mirror with two sides, centered in an energy body of any sort. The most graphically accurate way to portray the imagination pathway is to envision a Möbius Strip. Here's how to construct such an image in your mind.

Conjure a ribbon that is circular, much like a latched necklace. One of the ribbon's flat sides is white and the other is black. The white represents the antiworld and the black, the world as we know it.

Now twist the ribbon so it forms a crossed-over figure eight. Envision a multilayered form that seems to crisscross with white and black. Unlike this physical ribbon illustration, in a true Möbius Strip the black and white are actually separate and yet they lie on the same plane. "Healing" occurs when energy shifts from black to white, which transfers energy from 3-D reality to the antiworld. Energy can never be destroyed, but it can change form—and sides of reality! The elimination of a visible problem is simply an energetic shift of energy from black to white, or here to there. "Manifestation" happens when energy moves from white to black. Now, what hasn't been suddenly appears.

The Divine This pathway uses all four energy speeds, with most changes occurring in stillness. All intensities are available and matrices exist in their purest form. That which you need is present.

Importance of the Divine Science

Understanding the science of the divine helps you see the potential of pathway healing. Working the divine is like being in graduate school. Everything that you learned in elementary school, high school, and undergraduate school suddenly comes together in a whole. Data acquired in the lower grades was accurate and relevant, but it is usable in a more coordinated fashion when integrated "at the top."

To best visualize the science of the divine, picture a point in which vibrates all the known energy of the universe, so fast that it appears perfectly still. The intensity is so great that the point holds no weight. This point generates a half-life, a harmonic set of waves that emanate as do ripples on water when you toss in a rock. If you could mathematically analyze the flow of the wave, you would find that every wave relates to every other wave in a proportional sequence, that of phi.

Phi has also been called the Golden Ratio, the Golden Number, the Golden Section, and the Divine Proportion. We don't really know who first calculated this number, but we do know that in 300 B.C.E., Euclid of Alexandria explained phi by drawing a straight line. When you cut it in a certain place, it produces an "extreme and mean ratio." In other words, all lines, no matter their length, can be cut in the same place and produce two lines of a similar ratio.

A   **C**   **B**

The ratio of AC to CB is the same as AB is to AC. This is an indication that you have placed "C" or cut the line on its Golden Ratio.

The actual numerical value of phi is an endless, nonrepeating number: 1.6180339887..., and so on. This number describes the symmetry of the rose, in that it measures the positions of the petals; as well, it reflects the curve of the conch and, some believe, the movement of stocks in the stock market. When seen in an apple, the Golden Ratio forms a five-pointed star; through the life of a mollusk, the spiral of its shell. If you were to continue connecting lines related with the Golden Ratio, you would create a spiral, the measurements of which could be converted to a five-pointed star.

The spiral is key in many mystical communities. Some people believe that the soul enters the body on a clockwise spiral and exits counterclockwise. I use the spiral for imagination healing; a clockwise spiral centered in the chakra will summon energy toward the direction in which it is guided. A counterclockwise spiral will release energy. If you use a spiral in a chakra, you will automatically create an inverse reaction.

Another set of numbers related to the Golden Ratio is critical in understanding the divine pathway in terms of physics. These are called the Fibonacci numbers, and, interestingly, they explain why the world is imperfect rather than perfect—a key fact to accept if you are to shift heal on the divine pathway.

Johannes Kepler, an astute astronomer, mathematician, and metaphysician of centuries past, wrote an essay in 1606 discussing the shape of the six-pointed snowflake. He stated that this and other regular solids, including the pentagram, are formed with divine proportions that can be measured by numbers that, when added, create the next number. These numbers, called the Fibonacci numbers, converge to the Golden Ratio.

This is how the Fibonacci numbers work: If you start with one and add it to itself, you get two. Two plus two equals four, four plus four equals eight, eight plus eight makes sixteen, and so on. There is a symmetry in creation and we are onto its code.

This symmetry is often call *self-symmetry* because at first we don't see a pattern or a purpose. Symmetry only emerges on something called a *size scale*. A standard emerges over time. Much has been made of the size scale symmetry of seemingly different and unrelated objects or appearances in a body of work called fractal geometry.

The term *fractal* means broken or fragmented. Fractals are the main phenomenon analyzed by chaos theory—a branch of thinking devoted to determining whether or not there are patterns in chaos or in seemingly disordered and even unrelated objects or energies. Science is formulating that fractals are indeed mathematically related and can be reduced to measurements that are just one over the Golden Ratio. This formula is called the Golden Tree. According to this theory, way back at the beginning of time, but after the so-called Big Bang, our universe was trapped in a vacuum state for a time period. The rate of expansion is faster than that which occurs during a state of decay. (Incidentally, the current trend, in that we are moving away from the center, is one of decay.) When held in a vacuum or void, energy can expand faster. Infinite numbers of pocket universes were born within this vacuum and the Golden Tree measurement superseded the Golden Ratio.

Similarities have also been deduced with the numbers one and ten, which can be generated to produce what is called the Golden Sequence. For a long time, mathematics has been formed around the base of 10; you will find that most of the healing in this book indicates an advantage to exponentially increasing energies used by units of ten, positive or negative. As the ancient mystics knew, the zero is the void, the emptiness from which we all emerged. The One? The I Am That I Am. And you are an "I Am," a generating and moving, singular being, as well.

And in the center of all shapes designed with the Golden Ratio? A fish shape. This shape is esoterically considered the entry or portal into the divine—the mirror in the middle of the imagination, that connection between heaven and earth that we long to establish ourselves within on the divine pathway. It is also the shape formed by our vertebrae in our spinal column and in the centers of certain organs and cells. There is great uniformity among all that exists "in heaven as on earth." Science points this out, but it also affirms an equal and complete opposite concept. Stay with me, and I'll explain.

Let's return to the stillness, that central still point I described when discussing the speeds of energy. This is the middle of the divine, the place of all potential, similar to the idea of the single atom that illuminated into the Big Bang that created the universe.

For just a minute, let's not join our thinking with that of the experts. Let's not assume a Big Bang. Let's say that there was no explosion, no single volcanic eruption. There is, as there always has been, a slow creative generation of energy in wavelike form from the center point.

In that there is endless energy contained within this core, which could be called the central "I Am," there are infinite energies reflecting from it. Certainly, these forces might be generating in harmonic and perfect sequences—and some of them must be, in that we can determine the ratio of the Golden Mean behind almost everything. The closer you are to the source, the more intense the energy and the more symmetrical and perfect the laws governing the behavior of this energy. The power pathway is based on these laws of perfection. If you use the laws of perfection, you can access the forces emanating from the source.

We have, however, determined that there are measurements different from those of the Golden Mean. What exists besides the Golden Tree? Maybe Pear or Apple Tree worlds, as well? It scarcely matters, for, having established a different set of perfect measurements, we have the basis for both the elemental and the imagination pathways. The elemental pathway obviously has chaos and order, fractals and wholes, the Golden Ratio and the Golden Tree. The predominance of chaos explains why we have to work so hard to repair our elemental-related problems. Unless you put increased energy behind a moving object or an oscillating atom, it gradually grinds to a halt.

The concept of pocket universes offers at least a partial explanation for the imagination pathway. The antiworld is very much a pocket universe that has remained in its vacuum state. There are laws and rules governing energy in a vacuum and they are related to—yet slightly different from—those in "reality." By figuring out these rules and ordering the relationship between the pockets and this reality, we can shift energy between these places and states to create change in the here and now.

And so I'm back to the divine, which, again, we could conceive of as the state of perfection. But it's not! Think of the Fibonacci numbers. What of the "non-Fibonacci" numbers? If forces and energies are constantly emanating from a source in line with the spiral dynamic, then there are also forces and energies that operate in opposition. For every energy that is rippling in perfection, there are energies with different measurements that aren't perfect—which merely means that they are different and perhaps not uniform.

We all wonder what is making Mona Lisa smile in Leonardo da Vinci's most famous painting. Perhaps a greater mystery is the rationale for the obvious asymmetry present in the background and some suggest, in the coloration and shading of the main figure herself. If you study the painting, you'll notice that the landscape behind our regal beauty fails to coordinate or match up horizontally. Look also at the winding and serpentine gorge near Mona Lisa's right shoulder, which isn't accounted for at her left shoulder. Students of math and the esoteric have both postulated that da Vinci, a brilliant scientist and mathematician, was revealing the nature of the Fibonacci numbers. I would also suggest that his work incorporates the existence of the Golden Tree in addition to the Golden Ratio; the idea of imperfection married with perfection. Logic says that a perfect universe would be static. Perfect order would not break down. Although perfection doesn't necessitate correction, neither does it require creativity. For new orders to be created, there must be an element of disorder. The mere idea of evolution assumes that there must be a higher order to reach.

Almost every religion mandates the One God as the Creator. If God were perfect and the universe already complete, why create? Certainly, the central still point of The Great I Am could be considered perfect, but it's not. You need imperfection for creativity.

Divine Love would mean nothing without imperfection. If God or the Divine is the norm, then God is also the aberration, the One capable of loving the imperfect or "not set" into increased capabilities and power.

You must grasp the blessedness of allowing imperfection to achieve the divine. The only healing power that works is Divine Love, and the human being cannot accept Divine Love unless in acceptance of imperfection.

Wakefulness, as I defined it earlier, is a certain type of consciousness. Supreme awareness requires the acceptance of the imperfect with the perfect, the dynamic with the static, the incomplete with the complete. Awareness is a developmental process, one that describes the goal of all of our journeys. The awareness required to perform shift healing is basically a call to consciousness.

Consciousness on the Pathways

Science buzzes with an attempt to figure out the meaning of consciousness. Here is a brief description of the different types of consciousness according to pathways. I have included two examples showing the connection between consciousness and healing in each description. One is a basic example; the other is taken from the Bible, which I consider to be one of the best instructional sources for universal healing. I also use a religious tract to stress the point that all pathways are holy or of wholeness, each in their own way.

Elemental Consciousness

This is the awareness of the self and one's own strengths. Healing is accomplished through direct manipulation to that which does not have consciousness, such as objects, and persuasion to others that have consciousness, such as animals or other humans.

An example of a higher use of elemental consciousness is herbal medicine, in which a healer uses his or her own intuitive faculties to determine which plant might help the ill. In the Bible, we find that Leviticus and other Old Testament books are full of elemental-based recommendations, such as regulations about mildew, infectious skin diseases, and dietary controls. These laws are provided for the prevention of and recovery from disease. **The key to elemental healing is acting with intention.**

Power Consciousness

This is the awareness of powers outside of the self. Healing occurs through becoming conscious of one's own ability to command what is not conscious, such as forces, and that which is conscious, such as spiritual guides.

An example of an excellent use of power consciousness is spirit medicine, in which a healer commands the spirit of a plant to help heal a sick person.

In the Bible we find many cases of power healing. Peter, walking in the ways of Christ, heals a crippled man by commanding him to walk. As recorded in Acts 3:6–7, Peter proclaimed, "Silver and gold I do not have, but what I have I give you. In the name of Jesus Christ of Nazareth, walk…" Instantly the man's feet and ankles become strong. A great Old Testament example is that of Moses, following God's orders, commanding water from rock and dividing the waters of the Red Sea. **The key to power healing is commanding.**

Imagination Consciousness

This is the awareness of nothing or the void. The existence of nothing allows the self to use invisible powers to change that which doesn't have consciousness into different forms.

Shamans constantly perform imagination healing. I met two shamans from Siberia who used symbology right in front of me to heal a man's broken arm. The circle creates connection, and the energy infused from one plane to another during the healing connected bone cell to bone cell, until the tissues reflected the wholeness that lay underneath.

The Bible opens with one of the greatest imagination stories ever told. In the beginning, God creates the heavens and the earth, while the earth was "formless and empty, darkness was over the surface of the deep, and the Spirit of God was hovering over the waters." (Genesis 1:1–2) That which is without form and empty is a vacuum, representing the great void. From nothing, the Spirit creates something—not based on a model or a template, but from the dual sparks of imagination and desire. The key to imagination pathway healing is imagining.

Recently, I worked the imagination pathway for a client with cancer. She had refused surgery, an elemental-based technique for dealing with breast cancer. Nor did she believe that she had the power to effect change, a prerequisite to accessing power forces. We couldn't jump to the divine because she didn't believe that God wanted her healed. She felt that she deserved the cancer because of her "earlier sins." I had no choice but to use imagination.

My client underwent two biopsies, three weeks apart. The first biopsy tested malignant; the second did not. The only difference was the work that we had done in between, which took about one minute. I simply had my client envision a door in the center of the lump and asked her to permit the malignant cells to shift to the other side of reality. In its place, she shifted in the breast tissue that she'd had when younger. The lump remained; actually, she had lived with this particular lump for over twenty years. But the cancer was gone.

We sealed the work with symbols, so that she couldn't immediately tempt the cancer back into her body. You'll use symbol healing in chapters 11, 12, 13, and 14. While techniques similar to this one may or may not work for you, the key is in knowing that you aren't conducting healing. My client's cancer still exists, as will any "problem" that you address and supposedly eliminate through the imagination but in the antiworld, not in this world. Wholeness on the imagination pathway isn't the same as curing on the elemental pathway. A "whole self" has cancer on one side of the Möbius Strip and no cancer on the other side. You simply choose which side of the strip will face "in" rather than "out."

Divine Consciousness

This is the awareness of the All, which is in constant motion toward becoming more of Itself. The acceptance of Divine Love ultimately allows one to bring consciousness into that which is not conscious and to invite that which is conscious to become more conscious.

Most miracle healing is divine in basis. I recently talked with a client from San Francisco who had been diagnosed with terminal cancer six years earlier. At that time, Jan was given three months to live. She simply decided that since her body was a temple of God, it didn't need to be destroyed by a malignancy. She prayed for a healing from Above, so that her body would reflect her beliefs. Jan has tested cancer-free now for six years.

There are countless indications of divine healing in the Bible. One initiated by the Divine is described in I Samuel, 10:10–11, in which Saul is visited by the Spirit of God, which "came upon him in power," so that Saul joined the prophets in prophesying. Saul is a conscious being, now made more conscious by a higher consciousness.

Christ's rising from the dead best illustrates the ability to infuse the nonconscious with consciousness. Prior to rising, he compares himself with living water. In John 4:13, he declares that whoever drinks of the living water shall never thirst again. Living water is conscious water. It holds physical substance and yet is animate and aware of the effects it has on others. Christ is asserting that his consciousness will one day actually be able to animate even that which has no life—including the flesh of his own earthly body, which, after he rises, continues as if living. **The key to divine healing is petitioning**.

Learning Pathway Healing

The remainder of Part Two is devoted to helping you apply energetic concepts to each of the pathways. I encourage you to follow your own learning style. For example, I'm a kinesthetic learner. This means that I learn only by doing. I'll often push ahead and try something, then back up to figure out exactly what I'm doing. Some people have to read the rules before anything makes sense; others develop a picture in their head. You know your style. When learning the pathways, it's not important to learn all the details up front; simply hold the right intention and have a good heart.

At the same time, I have found it important to know the details of each pathway. A close friend of mine once said that if you want to lighten a dark room, you have only to turn on a flashlight. But if you want to find something in particular in the room, you have to know where to direct the flashlight. This analogy applies to the Four Pathways. Want to know how to work each one? Then you must know what to look for. Toward this end, the next chapter is a compilation of specific energy terms.

Of Positive, Negative, and Everything in Between: Life Energies and Kundalini

*But we who would
be born again
indeed, must wake
our souls unnumbered
times a day.*[1]

—George MacDonald,
Diary of an Old Soul

In this chapter, we will make our first exploration into the energetic concepts needed to make full use of the Four Pathways. You've been introduced to the basic physics ideas in relation to the pathways, and now we're going to venture into even more specific energy and metaphysical particulars. Here are the basics regarding energetic charges; subsequent chapters will discuss energy and the differences among the pathways.

Energy Particles and Charges

When conducting healing, it's important to know whether you're working with positive, negative, or neutral energy. If you can read the charges of a diseased state, you can figure out what's needed to create balance. Too much positive, you want negative, and vice versa.

Protons are particles with a **positive charge**, which makes them magnetic in nature. Magnetic energy draws what we need to us and therefore performs the attraction aspect of healing. Seen psychically, magnetic energy appears as a yellow color. When illuminated, its colorations can become gold.

Positive charges could be called light energies. Everything exists on a spectrum that includes light and dark charges. Light charges are closer to infrared and are usually easier for the human eye to see. Different charges hold different meanings, or types of information. On the power level, for instance, light charges hold spiritual or love-based data.

Electrons are particles with **negative charges** and are electric in nature. Electrical energy repels, using conflict to create movement and to shape reality. Therefore, electrons perform the release function of healing. Electrical energy appears blue when seen psychically. When illuminated, these energies can appear white or more typically, deep black.

As dark charges, electrons are closer to ultraviolet and difficult to perceive with the naked eye. Dark charges hold energies different from those of the light charges. On the power level, dark charges hold energies relating to power and might.

Neutrons have **neutral charges**, which means they can carry positive or negative charges in their field. They can be programmed to attract or repel, and will do so based on the information loaded into them or in their fields. The programmable energy created by neutrons is psychically seen as pink, red, or clear.

Although the neutral particles more or less remain still, they carry information that tells other charges what to do; therefore, they compose the basis matter that impacts reality.

The three energy particles are composed of subatomic particles. There are hundreds of kinds of such particles. As noted in chapter 3, the most important particles for healing purposes are quarks, which move slower than the speed of light, and tachyons, which move faster than the speed of light. There are also subatomic particles theorized to have tiny whips on their ends; these are able to transfer through time and exist solely within space.

Energy particles form molecules and atoms. Most of life is organized around three basic types of molecules and atomic structures. These molecules are (1) carbon, which assists in the material aspect of life, as in the body; (2) hydrogen, which relates to the water element of life and the mind; and (3) oxygen, which relates to the fire element of life and the blood, soul, and spirit.

Energy Entities and the Four Pathways

Here's how these different types of energy work according to pathway:

Elemental Pathway. Protons fabricate light matter and reveal physical reality. Electrons are the particles most typically perceived as "real" and tangible; they underlie dark matter and compose the substance and structure of reality. Neutrons can attract dark and light matter for manifesting.

Power Pathway. Protons hold spiritual forces and ideas, electrons command forces and ideas of power, and neutrons formulate the impartial spaces from which to command.

Imagination Pathway. Protons create illusions, electrons create delusions, and neutrons make up the place of nothingness.

Divine Pathway. Protons represent the energy of love, electrons add movement to the stillness of love to create grace, and neutrons function as the center point of Divine Love.

Life Energies

Every culture suggests the presence of an indefinable vital force or energizing material, sometimes called the *fifth force* or *ether*. The key to healing is actualizing this indescribable vital force. It is carried in the spirit, but available on every plane and pathway of existence. It holds the properties of stillness but can also translate into all other speeds, carrying eternal truth within it. Each of the four main pathways can access this vital force, which I call the *vital source energy*.

There are several forms of vital source energy. All reflect the parenting energy of the Divine, yet they work differently on the various pathways without compromise.

Basic life energy is the fundamental, elemental version of vital source energy. Different cultures call it chi, life force, *prana*, orgone, mana, and other terms. Western science explains basic life with chemical reactions and has yet to explain how these chemicals can create life. Eastern medicine takes a more broad-minded approach, allowing for a powerful version of energy that motivates spirit into being. I would suggest that both Western and Eastern thoughts are correct and yet incomplete. Even on the elemental pathway there is an energy capable of emitting consciousness and life force, if awakened fully. This energy is the basic life energy animated into the material version of vital source energy. Magical elemental healing involves this complete magnification of basic life energy.

The power pathway functions on *life spirit energy*, a version of vital source energy capable of carrying all frequencies of matter and spirit, plus the spiritual energetic forces. This spirit-based energy joins with the basic life energy of the elemental and allows you to access and move the spiritual energetic forces necessary to free the vital source energy trapped within the body. A highly evolved power worker can create reality-based changes by directing life spirit energy, rather than specific forces.

The imagination pathway carries no vital source energy. As theorized by some physicists, there are universal arenas that were and are similar to vacuum pockets. No energy exists within these spheres—and yet, potential is everything. Consider the research of Nikola Tesla, who was fascinated by the vacuum state. Constructing a perfect vacuum, he was surprised to find that a substance—hydrogen—had somehow leaked into or formed itself within the void. Nothing either attracts something or, from some deep place within itself, creates something. Vital source energy does not require the substantiation of physical, energetic, or spiritual matter to exist.

Life forms on all pathways can follow the flow of vital source energy to develop supernatural healing ability. Many societies have tracked this evolution, although chiefly through the elemental. The best-known term for energetic transformation is the *kundalini process*.

Rising through the Ashes: The Kundalini Process

Kundalini is an ancient Hindu term for the spiritualization of an energy system. Each pathway has its own kundalini process, and the process sometimes differs for men and women. When undergoing a kundalini process on a certain pathway, all energies and dualities are merged into unity. Personal evolution and healing fundamentally involves following the graduating process of kundalini.

Kundalini on the Elemental Pathway: Of Physical Power There are many facts about kundalini unknown to contemporary humans. I believe that these are important to healers, as they are fundamental to the seeking of healing.

On the elemental pathway, kundalini originates with basic chemical reactions that begin before we're even born. Know what's behind conception, the fire that blends egg and sperm? Kundalini.

At its baseline, kundalini involves both fusion and fission. You had your first kundalini process at conception, when the genes from your mother's egg merged or fused with the genes from your father's sperm. Two basic life energies and—boom!—there was fission, the atomic explosion that gave you life though cellular multiplication. Your primary kundalini experience was a complex set of biochemical chain reactions and included the movement of genes, the splitting of cells, and the dance of development.

As you became older, these chemical equations became more complex. Have you ever stopped to consider how many exchanges of molecules, liquids, lipids, hormones, proteins, enzymes, vitamins, minerals, and other physical properties probably occur at any given moment within your body? This complicated exchange of matter is a fundamental kundalini process, one not usually noted by spiritual masters.

The primary kundalini is the level of modern medicine. Can you keep track of the trillions of cells keeping your body habitable for your spirit? If you can't do this for yourself, how could a physician do this for you? We're not going to beat disease by trying to comprehend the infinite number of formulaic processes that impact health.

The ancients and the mystics share an understanding that kundalini can evolve, even as the human being must over time. Esoteric masters know how to progress their elemental-based basic life energy, increasing the speed, force, and spin of the energy of matter. The body basic now leaps from physical or sensory to include spiritual or psychic. The chakras ignite, and health now becomes the concern of the human energy system.

The ancient practice of kundalini is simply a methodical means of stimulating basic life energy into a more fully activated state. By consciously controlling and increasing your energy, you can galvanize your system into optimum performance. While basic life energy stimulates and runs your biochemistry—and therefore your organic functions—it also feeds your *managing energy bodies,* the energetic structures of the elemental body. Your chakras and auric fields are the primary managing energy bodies. Basic life energy can carry quarks and tachyons, and when it is fully activated within the physical body it will trigger and connect all managing energy bodies.

Because the originators of this process encouraged starting the kundalini progression in the red-colored first chakra and then moving it upward, kundalini is often envisioned in the form of an uncoiling snake, which is why I call it the *red* or *serpent kundalini process.*

In men, serpent kundalini usually begins in the first chakra, as the ancients would have it. This ever-increasing basic life energy moves upward and seeds the entire system with the energy needed to awaken the pineal gland, located in the brain, which serves as the center of the seventh chakra. The pineal is coded with spiritual destiny. In turn, the pineal activates the seed of destiny—one of the elemental-based managing energy bodies—and the spiritual genetics, a set of light-bearing codes that instruct the physical genes to operate as the Divine Spirit designed. (We will be considering these and other managing energy bodies in the next few chapters.)

Once ignited, the body is better prepared to evolve spirit into body, as the body frequencies are now more apt to resonate with the higher-order spiritual frequencies. Good health is a by-product; as the spirit vibrates at an incredibly high frequency, the prepared body has most likely shed much of its negative and disease-ridden processes to mirror the spirit. Perfect health is not necessary for spiritual fulfillment, but there is a purification process that increases well-being and happiness.

Over time, the serpent energy rises upward until it pops through the ninth chakra. From there, it fully accesses the spiritual points, a set of twenty chakralike energies that work in the same way as the chakras, except with higher energies, such as faith, wisdom, and love. (You can learn more about these points in my first energy manual, *New Chakra Healing.*) After looping through and capturing the essence of these spiritual energies, the now extremely potent kundalini reenters the system through the tenth chakra. There it rests, assisting the man in being grounded and practical in reference to his spiritual goals.

The success of the male kundalini process depends on the ability to deal with the interpersonal problems and issues latent in each chakra. Sometimes the most difficult issues to confront lie within the first chakra, the originating point of the male kundalini. The initial inflammation of this chakra often triggers latent sexual issues, violence, repressed desires, emotions, and addictions. Resolution of these issues isn't complete with the circling of the serpent kundalini. The *golden kundalini process*, which enlivens all the power bodies, provides the spiritual understandings required to allow full acceptance of one's male energies, as well as generic human and divine qualities.

In women, the serpent kundalini starts in the second chakra, usually setting off emotional and sensuality issues, which are ideally resolved through creative inspiration. Why this chakra difference? History. In recent times, women have typically held little status or wealth in society. This was not the case thousands of years ago, when their community importance was measured by degrees of their fertile and supernatural powers. The first chakra was biologically of less consequence than the second chakra for women. Men were the hunters of animals and defenders of the clan. Both jobs required taking life. Issues and energies about life and death are integral to the first chakra. Thus early men developed potent first chakra abilities to provide for clan and families. Women, on the other hand, were the child-bearers and food gatherers. Gestation is a second chakra function, whether involving the growth of a child or the nurturing of crops.

The second chakra centers in the womb, from which spin life, emotions, and spiritual creativity. Women's elemental-based programming is therefore central to the second rather than the first chakra.

As with men, in women the kundalini energy undulates through the ninth chakra and the spiritual points, then emerges through the tenth chakra before coming to rest in the first chakra, thus enabling women to achieve lifelong monetary, sexual, and success goals that contribute to their spiritual destiny.

The end point of the serpent kundalini for both men and women is the beginning of the golden kundalini process involving the power process. The golden kundalini provides a more intense sense of spiritual purpose.

The red and golden kundalini processes can occur simultaneously. I have shown people how to blend energies together, and I've seen instant healing of specific problems occur through the intentional merging of these powerful energies. One woman's self-esteem issues disintegrated; another woman remembered childhood abuse and was able to forgive herself for ways she had acted as a result. A man allowed a clearing of twenty years of low back pain.

Joining kundalini energies doesn't "finish" either the red or golden kundalini processes instantly, however. Even with the assistance of the golden kundalini energy, the red serpent energies will take time to completely rise and circle. Even when merged with red serpent energies, the golden kundalini energy will intensify and increase over time. Working the two processes together simply makes both kundalini processes more enjoyable, safer, and quicker. In relation to the red kundalini process, the golden kundalini offsets possible physical reactions, soothes and smoothes emotional feedback, and provides motivation to go through necessary life changes. In relation to the golden kundalini process, the red kundalini bolsters spiritual learning, encourages the use of power forces, and strengthens the spiritual seals. Seals are a chakra-related set of energy bodies through which you receive the full implosion and access to spiritual energetic forces.

Kundalini on the Power Pathway: Of Spiritual Energy The power pathway functions on *life spirit energy*, which is able to carry all frequencies of matter and spirit plus the spiritual energetic forces. This spirit-based energy is really another version of the elemental-originating basic life energy. The main difference is that power kundalini originates in spirit-matter, whereas elemental kundalini initiates in the physical. Over time, power kundalini allows you to access and move the spiritual energetic forces necessary to free the vital source energy trapped within the body.

When you reach a certain intensity and spin of life spirit energy, you activate the golden kundalini process. Intensification of the golden kundalini process can result from many factors. The golden kundalini process is often activated when the red kundalini process reaches a certain level of intensity, usually following years of physical discipline and devotion to a spiritual way. With intention, you can also trigger the golden kundalini process concurrently with the red kundalini process. Conscious setting of the power seals will advance a golden kundalini process. Deliberate work with the spiritual points will evolve a golden kundalini process. As well, critical life experiences—such as Near Death Experiences, visitations of spiritual beings, or direct revelation from the Divine—also set a golden kundalini process in motion.

The golden kundalini process usually begins in the highest spiritual point, moves through the ninth and eighth chakras that align over the head, and then enters the body through the seventh chakra at the top of the head. It completes only after the setting of your seals, which involves shifting the placement of your seals through a process described in chapter 13.

Both women and men have golden kundalini experiences. Women usually have to shift focus from their pituitary to their pineal gland to achieve the optimum benefits. Men, on the other hand, need to incorporate their pituitary with their pineal to achieve the right male-female balance and to access the left and right hemispheres of the brain equally.

Kundalini on the Imagination Pathway There is no energy on the imagination pathway, therefore there is no form of life energy. However, our imaginations do effect change through belief, desire, sorcery, and intention in any of the pathways, and this can convince you into a kundalini process. Often, you will find that certain people store their red or golden kundalini on one side of the imagination or the other. Those who repress their serpent kundalini in the antiworld often experience great difficulties with everyday life concerns, including their health. Those who suppress their golden kundalini in the antiworld may have access to at least certain aspects of the red kundalini and thereby achieve at least some modicum of worldly success, but they typically lack spiritual integrity and balance. You must bring both kundalini processes forward into the "real world" of the body to actualize your material and spiritual selves.

Kundalini on the Divine Pathway Divine initiation speeds up the red and gold kundalini processes. In fact, these cannot be completed until you are on the divine pathway. Only on the divine pathway are you able to face the deepest human issues, metaphorically contained in the seven bowls representing the seven deadliest human pains, which we will cover in chapter 7. By drawing upon divine truths, you access the strength and wisdom needed to support the final kundalini process of transmuting pain into love. This ultimate conversion can take from a few months to years, as it is stressful on the body. The divine self doesn't deal in harsh and complicated healings.

I use a specific term to describe divine kundalini: *radiating kundalini*. The kundalini process on the divine pathway isn't really a process, especially in comparison to the red kundalini process of the elemental pathway and the golden of the power pathway. Think of what it means to radiate light. You simply turn the light on, and it spreads 360 degrees. There are only two decisions to make: Are you going to turn on the light or not? Are you going to intensify the glow or not? Radiating kundalini divines the true self from within your deepest core and allows your spirit full access to every cell of your body, every thought in your mind, and every sense of your soul. This unified spiritual connection can bring instantaneous healing and immediate awareness, or meet any other deep-seated need.

Energy Communication

Working the Four Pathways involves using various means of communicating—ways of receiving, interpreting, sending, or projecting information-energy. This chapter covers various forms and types of energy and the energy laws that affect and influence such communication, from energy languages to time and space dimensions.

Energy Communication Methods

There are five basic ways to communicate energetically: sensory, psychic, intuitive, phantasmal, and spiritual. Each is a different method for transferring information and energy.

Sensory communication occurs through the body-based senses and physical organs with quarks—information-energy moving slower than the speed of light.

Psychic communication occurs through the energy system and the body, using quarks and tachyons. These are converted through the energy system from slower to faster than the speed of light and back again.

Intuitive communication occurs through the energy system and the mind. These two interface to translate fast tachyons to slow quarks and back again.

Phantasmal communication refers to energies that aren't real but merely perceived as real. Phantasmal messages are made of depictions of information-energy, not the energy itself.

Spiritual communication uses zero point and lightning-fast energies of all nature to communicate through transmission or instant transfer. There are several forms of spiritual communication, including *charismatic communication,* in which the recipient serves as a vessel for

Divine messages and healing, and *numinous communication*, in which your communication reflects the Divine within.

Part Three offers two complete chapters on the subject of energy communication and includes a personalized test, so you can figure out the communication style that will best help you energy map.

Energy Languages

Language refers to our ability to accept the information-energy or consciousness that makes sense to us or that helps us make sense to someone or something else.

Our communication can be sensory, psychic, intuitive, phantasmal, or spiritual, and each type can use one of the main energetic languages accessible to human beings:

Language of matter. This language involves communicating with sensory information. You must be able to hear, see, touch, or smell information to converse in matter.

Language of feeling. Emotions and feelings can be shared through frequency, vibration, harmonics, transmission, and other states. Through the language of emotion, you can sense or feel your own and others' feelings. You can also direct physical and spiritual forces and energetics with strong emotions.

Language of heart. There are three levels to the heart: the Lower Heart, the Middle Heart, and the High Heart. With this language, you can transfer information to and from any of these chambers to create loving and bonding connections or to break destructive links.

Language of light. Light, both its dark and light vibrations, is encoded with information. On certain pathways, you can transfer data, concepts, messages, and consciousness in and on light.

Language of shadow. I call this language the *shadow language* because it involves sharing ideas and energies without actually sending or receiving data.

Language of unity. The language of unity communicates only truth and creates oneness with all. Consequently, you can actually receive all other languages and types of communication through this language. Sharing through this medium requires achieving a certain state of consciousness rather than vocabulary.

You can use all of these languages on some of the pathways, and only some of the languages on others. On the elemental pathway, you can use any type of language once you fully connect with the other pathways. The power pathway allows for language of the heart and light. The imagination pathway involves the language of the shadow, and the divine pathway, the language of unity.

Separating Fact from Fiction, Belief from Feeling

It's important to separate feeling from belief for pathway results. Sometimes people confuse the two. It's easy to think that a thought is logical and well defined, yet a thought can be joined with a feeling that controls it. My client Max provides an example. Max had experienced three heart attacks because he believed he needed to work himself to success. The voice of logic said that he had to overwork to succeed, but the motivating factor was an intense fear from childhood. Max was scared that he would be a failure, like his alcoholic father.

We can also confuse our ideas the other way, considering a belief to be a feeling. My client Clarissa thought herself an overly emotional person. "I have too many feelings," she would cry. Consequently, she couldn't hold a primary relationship longer than a month or two; the men would give up in agony. We were able to trace her feelings to a single belief: that she didn't deserve love. From this pinpoint, Clarissa's psyche had produced feeling responses that substantiated her belief.

Two main types of feeling- or belief-oriented problems are frequently present in pathway blocks. These are mental and emotional strongholds, and they appear on all the pathways. Clearing these can often make a distinct impression in your life.

Strongmen and Strongholds

Strongholds are energetic bonds that hold you imprisoned. They

» Energy Packages

THE INFORMATION IN energy can be packaged in many ways. Here are the main ideas you'll need to remember to conduct pathway healing:

Thoughts are individual units of energy that hold a single idea, concept, or fact. You can also call a thought a consciousness particle.

Beliefs are a subset of thoughts that direct consciousness and can also be directed by consciousness. There are six primary types of beliefs:

Primary Belief	Negative Aspect	Positive Aspect
Worthiness	I am unworthy.	I am worthy.
Deserving	I don't deserve.	I do deserve.
Power	I am powerless.	I am powerful.
Value	I have no value.	I am valuable.
Love	I am not lovable.	I am lovable.
Goodness	I am bad (or evil).	I am good.

Feelings are frequencies that carry strong charges and communicate information that motivates. Feelings are highly personal. What makes me sad might make you happy. As shared by author Brian Hines in *God's Whisper, Creation's Thunder,* "Feeling is what we do when we are in the private and subjective domain of our consciousness."[2]

Every type of feeling can be identified by one of the five basic feeling constellations, or headings:

- Fear
- Anger
- Sadness
- Disgust
- Happiness

Emotions are *beliefs* paired with *feelings;* emotions can direct consciousness or can be directed by consciousness. Feelings are incredibly important to someone seeking healing. A weak feeling looks like a single frequency and has a weak affect on reality. A strong feeling, however, forms a wave that can alter reality on any of the pathways. It can pound away a tumor, force a need, or summon spiritual help. Likewise, a potent feeling can negatively impact reality, causing disease, anguish, and life problems.

are like strongmen, or muscle men, that won't let go until you figure out why the two energies are bonded together. Strongholds are the key issue underneath *patterns*—established responses that hold you fixated in a problematic state. To break a pattern, which is the structure holding all disease or issues in place, you need to address strongholds.

A *mental stronghold* is two or more beliefs paired together in a permanent relationship. Mental strongholds always inhibit our success by adversely directing behavior. For instance, you might believe that "girls are weak" and that "weak people don't deserve success." If you're a girl, you'll consider yourself weak and therefore not deserving of success. You'll sabotage every opportunity that comes your way.

Most mental strongholds are made of an observation, which can consist of a thought, or a thought form, and the negative aspect of one of the six main beliefs. A thought form is a single thought of immense power and intensity, able to overpower independent thinking. But you can also create a mental stronghold with a positive aspect of one of the beliefs. For instance, you might believe both that "I am a woman" and that "only women are worthwhile." Therefore, you believe "I am more worthwhile than a man." Either way, you are limiting your full functioning.

An *emotional stronghold* is an emotion that is locked into place and directs behavior adversely. It is made of at least one feeling paired with at least one belief. Emotional strongholds are even more potent than mental strongholds; they are strong inhibitors to growth and healing. The feeling serves as the motivator, while the belief directs the feeling energy.

Sometimes you can cancel out the belief aspect of an emotional stronghold. For instance, the negative belief "I am unworthy" might be paired with the feeling of self-shame. You can break the emotional stronghold by eliminating the *thought* "I am unworthy." The shame might remain intact, however, and continue to cause problems.

Feelings that have been freed from a belief yet are still affecting your life are called *emotional charges.* To deal with an emotional charge, I usually recommend that the client work the pathways to figure out the *original message* of the feeling. What prompted the feeling in the first place? You'll be learning the meaning of the various feelings throughout this book, which will assist you in answering this question. I also suggest that clients remember the power of feeling.

You can change reality with a directed feeling. Feelings are frequencies and can be used for good! By attaching a helpful instead of harmful belief, message, or voice to a feeling, you can direct a feeling toward achieving a higher goal. For instance, I might tell a client with shame to eliminate the beliefs holding the shame in a stronghold.

Now left with an emotional charge, I direct the client to establish a marching order for the shame, such as "I will be embarrassed if I do *not* achieve my goals" or "I will show myself that I am worthy of love." This technique is best oriented on the elemental, power, or imagination pathways, as dualities do not exist on the divine pathway.

Elemental Elements

Since humanity began practicing the healing arts, it has worked with the fundamentals of nature. Almost every civilization has performed healing with the elements, the most basic of which include fire, air, water, and earth. Some cultures add more elements to this list. The Four Pathways system expands it further to include ten elements:

fire	water	metal	stone	star
air	earth	wood	ether	light

Elements exist on each of the pathways; they may appear or interact in various ways. On the elemental pathway, the ten elements are baseline, very physical. Look around! The world does seem to be composed of fire, air, water, and the other elements. So is the body, as well as the other aspects of self, matter, and spirit on the elemental level.

I almost always include elements in my elemental pathway healing. This is because many conditions can be corrected with a shift of elements. Too much fire, for instance, will cause inflammation of tissue where the fire is located. If you want to subdue inflammation and perhaps the pain associated with it, you can add elements that will eliminate or control the fire energy. Water will quench fire, but sometimes you don't want to drown a fire. Stone can create boundaries for a fire; earth can suppress it. Metal can deflect fire energy, and if you add ether, you end up igniting a star! Elements can be added psychically or through the use of nutrition, supplements, herbalism, color or light therapy, crystal stone therapy, or several other means. Be careful, however, and think through the use of elements so you don't cause further problems. Once I worked with a client who forced the element of water into a broken bone. He had learned about the elements when studying the Chinese medicine system. I'm not sure what made him think that water was the accurate resource, and it wasn't. The bone was unhealed three months into the recovery process, remaining mushy and weak. During our session, we substituted stone for water, and the bone healed within a week.

On the power pathway, elements are extremely important for increasing the effectiveness of the spiritual energetic forces. Elements are the basis of the powers, energies that add substance and potency to the spiritual forces. Powers are actually formed of a spiritual version of the various elements. Let's say that you have an intestinal yeast infection on the elemental level. Elementally, you have too much water in your abdomen, which encourages an overgrowth of yeast and fungus. On the elemental pathway, you can add star energy to the abdomen, using spiritual truths as fodder for burning off the excess water element. By attaching a power force to this process, you increase the effectiveness of the healing. If you summon a power made of fire and attach it to the spiritual force, the water will burn away or steam off even more quickly.

On the imagination pathway, elements don't exist, and yet they can serve as effective healing tools through applied imagination. All change on the imagination pathway occurs through a transfer of possibilities

» Key Applications of the ten basic elements on the elemental pathway

Fire. Eliminates, purges, and burns away. Adds life energy, excitement, new life. Is the basis of all kundalini processes and is therefore an important healing tool; for instance, fire can be used to purify the blood or lymph system of toxins.

Air. Transmits ideas and ideals. Allows the spread of energies from place to place or person to person. Active when moving and directed; inactive yet ripe with potential when still. Can be a potent force for destruction or redirection when used with strength, as in a tornado or gale. Can set or change the spins of energies; for instance, it can wipe your mind free of imposing or inaccurate beliefs.

Water. Transmits psychic and feeling energies, soothes and heals, washes and cleanses. Can be strong force, as in a hurricane, to effect change. Used for psychic divination or obtaining information, such as when imagined in a bowl and used to spy for information. Can be imaged as a waterfall to cleanse your body of psychic buildup or leftover feelings.

Earth. Builds, solidifies, and protects. Is the basis for holding malleable structures, such as cell walls and thought forms. Grounds, centers, and forces practical and tangible applications when used; for instance, it can be used after surgery to rebuild cut tissue.

Metal. Protects, defends, and deflects. Is the basis for armaments, such as safety mechanisms in the body and certain types of cellular or energy body walls. Is also like a mirror in that it reflects or deflects other energies; for instance, it can be used in an auric field to avert others' energies.

Wood. Adds buoyancy, adaptability, and a positive nature. A porous structure that decays over time; ideal as a temporary measure to bring good cheer to a depressed state, or help someone adapt to a new life change; for instance, you could surround a transplanted heart with wood to enable the body to integrate the new tissue.

Stone. Strengthens, holds, and toughens. A foundational energy. Can be used to wall off and hold other elements in place, such as building a "lake" for water needed to soothe inflamed tissue, or to hold fire energy in the first chakra and between the antiworld and this world. You can empower this transfer by imagining the energy of fire, for instance, to speed the exchange of an idea. You could provide protection when endangered by envisioning yourself surrounded by armor.

The divine pathway is composed of all elements, and then some! The elements swirl in expectation on the divine pathway, all in the basin of stillness. Through the divine pathway, you can access spiritual qualities and elements that don't even exist in our universe. In fact, you can create new forces, forms, and energies at will, if these will further the cause of the Divine. You don't need to figure out which elements to summon on the divine pathway, but I find it interesting to see which ones effect change when you petition for a cause.

There is strong correlation between the elements and several other medically viable healing concepts, including pH and nutrition. Elements

so increase metabolism and life energy. Can also be streamlined into a system; for example, you could streamline it directly into bone tissue and thus help heal osteoporosis or bone cancer.

Ether. Holds spiritual truths and can be used to infuse any system, energy body, mind, or soul with such spiritual truths. Ether is liquid gas. It is actually the "fifth element"—the spiritual energy that scientists and metaphysicians have attempted to define for centuries—and the vital source energy of the divine pathway made manifest on the elemental pathway.

Light. Can be directed, spun, fashioned, summoned, or eliminated to produce almost any desired effect. Light is electromagnetic radiation of various wavelengths. *Dark light* is composed mainly of electrons that carry intelligence about power; *light light* is fashioned chiefly from protons that hold intelligence about love. If you're depressed, you could add light and gain a higher perspective on a seemingly hopeless situation. If you're too anxious, you could work with dark light and move yourself into action.

Star. Accomplishes purification of physical matter through spiritual truth, and also uses spiritual truths to form physical matter. A star is made of fire and ether; fire burns the ether and gives off gas, which in turn ignites fire. You could use star energy to eternally burn spiritual truth in any of your chakras, thus enabling them to replenish physically and psychically without fail.

How can these elemental concoctions assist in healing? Consider again the inflammatory process. Heart disease is linked to inflammation in the blood vessel, impacted by plaque buildup. Fire is a result of the blockage. The body thinks it's doing you a favor by increasing the fire element; after all, ideally fire can burn out the increasing fat buildup. Unfortunately, the swelling is causing further restriction in the vessel. You might visualize the energy of stone surrounding the fire and confining it to the fatty buildup, thus burning out the fat while protecting the surrounding tissue. Washing the inflamed area with water can soothe the damaged tissue, then rebuilding it with earth can restore it to health. After eliminating the lipid blockage, you might repair it with metal, which can deflect further waste storage.

are actually the basis of a healthy pH balance. The pH level measures the balance between acidity and alkalinity in your body. You can often shift pH by transferring, adding, or eliminating elements, which we will consider in the chapters devoted to elemental and power healing.

Nutritional health is based on the correct balance, use, and elimination of basic fats, proteins, sugars, and liquids. Every nutrient or substance is composed of certain key elements, the balance of which differs according to the substance. Fats, for instance, have considerably more water than do proteins. A fat will ideally contain a healthy mix of water and ether. Water serves as a conduit for the spiritual truth of the ether. Unfortunately, our unconscious or programming has usually substituted misperceptions for truths. I commonly find that people's fats are loaded with the types of untruth that attract shame. This is important, because many diseases or lifestyle problems are shame-based. Multiple sclerosis (MS), for instance, involves a breakdown in the fatty sheaths surrounding the nerves. You could say that MS is an attack on shame. Obesity is technically a condition of storing too much fat—or of holding your power in your tissue because you are ashamed of it. You can not only work to change the beliefs stored in the body, but you can also change the elemental balances in the energy and physical bodies affected by these problems. Adding earth to the myelin sheath, for instance, might stave off further neuron deterioration until the person stricken with MS could work on the causal issues. Igniting the first chakra with star energy can increase the power, life energy, and will power of someone trying to lose weight, thus burning off some of the shame and therefore the fat. We will consider further elemental applications in later chapters.

The Bottom Line: Working Intelligence and Consciousness

All pathway healing is really a matter of working with information. A feeling like shame can overwhelm the strongest personality and reduce the best of us to the mental state of a frightened rabbit. The belief "I am bad" creates the type of patterns that put people in jail, as they attempt to live this belief as truth. Strongholds are simply units of information that attract energetic forces. When information and energetic constructs are joined together, you get effect. You produce the patterns that underlie problems. Break a problem into its energetic components and you break it apart. Now that's called working intelligently. Here are some additional concepts to understand how to effectively work energetically.

Intelligence is just another word for information. This word describes the programming or information within particles and sub-atomic particles, as well as that in various charges and all other energies.

Consciousness is where awareness, action, and the ability to adjust come together. An individual can operate on various levels of consciousness, some levels of a higher spiritual order than others. There are forms of consciousness alive and not. I use the term *animate consciousnesses* for beings or energies that are completely self-directed and can direct things outside of themselves with choice.

Consciousness forms, also called *thought forms*, are clumps or organized categories of individualized thoughts. A thought form represents a unified idea. Thought forms are especially dominant in running certain parts of the mind, most typically the Lower and Middle Minds. A thought form often keeps the Lower Mind vulnerable to harmful and self-defeating reactions, and the Middle Mind initiating behaviors injurious to one's well-being.

Consciousness waves carry thoughts or consciousness particles to all parts of the universe.

A **consciousness paradigm** is a unified ideal made up of similar consciousness particles that are carried on consciousness waves. There are three basic types of consciousness paradigms: those about power, love, or grace.

Consciousness forces are natural, energetic, or spiritual fields or forces that move energy when consciously directed.

Ultimately, as you gain control of yourself on the pathways you gain the ability to consciously select which information or intelligence you want to base your life upon.

Patterns, Boundaries, and Habits

As I've said, all presenting illnesses, problems, and addictions stem from patterns. *Essentially, healing is about releasing or changing patterns.* However, it is important to differentiate patterns from boundaries and habits. Here is a brief key to distinguishing the three entities, followed by detailed descriptions.

- **Patterns.** These are repetitive events, thoughts, or feelings that inhibit an expression of your whole self, or limit the ways you can express yourself lovingly.

- **Boundaries.** "Bad" boundaries make you too flexible or too rigid and therefore also qualify as patterns. "Good" boundaries retain your sense of self yet allow an exchange of love.
- **Habits.** A "bad" habit is a pattern and will create problems; a "good" habit will keep you healthy.

A **pattern** is a fixated, energetic lock that causes us to re-create the same situations and responses over and over. A stronghold is a pattern. An addiction is a patterned response; for instance, you might smoke whenever you're lonely. Take away the pattern and you're left with the problem. You can have a pattern on any of the pathways. Because of this, you can free yourself from any one particular pattern through any pathway, if you have the skill.

A **boundary** is an energetic partition that provides containment. It keeps what is within us inside of us, and keeps things that are not of us on the outside. Patterns are fixed, but boundaries will shift and move. On one day, we might smoke when we're stressed; the next day, we'll confront the source of the stress. Boundaries are necessary to function in health in the world. They determine the "self" versus the "not self." Knowing this, you can decide what to increase and what to reduce in your life.

The best boundaries are *parameters*, which define facts or circumstances that restrict how something can be done while allowing for positive results. In the world of energy, a parameter is a decision that limits which energies can enter or engage with you, while enforcing your overall well-being. Some people confuse boundaries with walls, erecting a fortress that is impenetrable—and induces loneliness. What would happen if everyone who experienced heartache decided to "never love again," and built an energy barrier that let no one of the desired sex anywhere near? This decision doesn't qualify as a parameter, which would encourage engagement with healthy individuals, while discouraging relationships with harmful individuals.

If you think in terms of four related pathways, you ideally want to set a boundary or limitation on one pathway that automatically alters so as to work on another pathway. For instance, I often encourage truly psychic people to establish psychic boundaries. When I'm teaching, one of my favorite phrases is "Just because someone is dead doesn't mean that he or she knows anything more than someone who is alive." Psychic people are often vulnerable to the influences of interfering or intruding entities. On the elemental pathway, you would set a parameter to allow linkage to only Divine-approved entities. This parameter will restrict supernatural contact on the elemental pathway to helpful sources; it can also transform into appropriate parameters on the other pathways, keeping you safe from unsavory spiritual forces on the power pathway and dangerous antiparticles on the imagination pathway. On the divine pathway, only the Divine is recognized as valid, so this parameter serves as a perfect means to figure out which truths apply to you in a given moment and which do not.

A **habit** is an adaptive response that creates boundaries. You can develop the habit of brushing your teeth at night: this is a behavioral boundary helping to create good health. However, you may also develop a pattern whereby you *have* to brush your teeth or you cannot fall asleep—not a good situation-response combination if there's no toothbrush nearby!

Forms of Energy

In working the pathways, you will be called to understand the various forms of information-energy. Consider these scientifically based definitions of energy:

Waves are a fundamental theory of quantum physics. This theory explains how energy can sometimes act like a particle and sometimes behave like a wave. Think of particles as tiny dots punctuating a space, and a wave as either many dots moving together or a single dot becoming its own streaming sunbeam.

Knowing about waves is important because information is carried on waves. Certain forces are also carried on waves. This can explain anything from how a disease can energetically spread from one person to another, even without physical contact, to how a thought can be shared across the globe. A wave that moves faster than the speed of light can share the information upon it the same way that a computer can perform "instant messaging," the no-lag-time delivery of an email over the Internet.

A **frequency** can be the wave on which a signal is broadcast. Many waves carry one or more particles of information-energy. Frequency indicates the number of times a wave oscillates or cycles within a given time period. When you're conducting healing work, you must often look for the frequency patterns of a disease or a problem. Each disease has its own frequency or "spin cycle," as does each healing energy. You can analyze frequencies in order to decide which one to bring in to heal, but you can also figure out a reverse frequency—one that might cancel the problem right out!

To **vibrate** something involves moving it back and forth or in different directions. Every time something or someone moves or oscillates, you produce an effect in the moved object and what's around it. You can measure a vibration by figuring out what's called a *fixed reference point* at which to start measuring the cycling. When and if you make a complete turn or loop, you have a full vibration or rotation.

In terms of healing, all problems generate their own vibrations or cycling of energy, as do all solutions. That's why so many healers are turning to what's called *vibrational medicine* to figure out how to treat people with energetic means. The key to vibrational healing is to figure out the correct fixed reference point or point of view. Do you want to "look at" cancer through the lens of the cancer? Through the eyeglasses of illness? Through the assumption of health and wholeness? You will perceive very different information depending on where you start.

A **harmonic** is a single oscillation of a special type of frequency. This special frequency is an *integral multiple* or necessary ingredient of a more fundamental frequency. Several harmonics can produce a single frequency or tone. For instance, take a frequency that is 220 hertz (Hz) and one that is 330 Hz. Both harmonize into a frequency that is 110 Hz.

A harmonic is also an overtone given off tonally, almost like an afterglow, when you play a certain vibrating note. In this way, a harmonic can continue to make a certain vibration play long after you're done vibrating it.

Knowing about harmonics is very important in healing. Let's say that a certain disease is caused by an A frequency, and that A has Q and Z inside of it. Perhaps Q is healthy and helpful, but Z is in error or isn't supposed to be present. If you get rid of Z, you may correct the problem.

Certain pathways present the opportunity to conduct harmonic healing, either by reading inside of a problematic frequency or by energetically studying the afterglow.

Harmonic Healing

Pathway healing allows shifts in all aspects of the affected self and on all levels of reality. This is possible, in part, because all four aspects of your personhood, including your spirit, share positive harmonics—the unique band of frequencies, vibrations, and resolutions that emanates from your spirit or essential self. You can perform healing by attempting to fix the energetics that are "out of tune," and also by magnifying the harmonics that mirror your spirit.

Everyone of us is attuned to his or her own set of harmonics, which, if heard, would sound like a musical composition. Seen psychically, it presents an astounding display of oscillating and dancing fireworks. Harmonics include almost every higher quality, such as joy, justice, or faith. By strengthening your ideal and spirit-based harmonics, you allow the body, mind, or soul to adapt to wholeness and thus heal.

This idea of harmonic healing is not new. The ancients suggested that all of life is a harmony of the spheres. Playing your own harmonic is necessary for the greater composition.

The basic spiritual harmonies often underlie your spiritual purpose, the divine truth seeded in your spirit. Your spiritual destiny is to express this purpose in every way.

In chapter 13 you'll find a list of harmonics associated with the power pathway, which presents the easiest way to work with harmonics.

Plowing the Field: Of Fields and Forces

We've been discussing the ways that energy moves in sequence and waves. These waves don't come out of nowhere. Energy can move in waves and particles, and certain energies move from one state to another. Understanding this will give you control when shift healing. Think of what you could do if you could reduce a wave to particle state and blow away a tumor, or expand a particle of healing into a healing wave and renew your immune system! To do this, you must comprehend the relationships among particles, fields, and forces.

All particles cast a field around them, as do people and objects. Certain of these fields produce forces. Electricity running through a wire, for instance, generates a magnetic force. Certain express or "bullet" trains in Japan are now running on top of the magnetic force and seem to be actually flying through space. Current studies are showing that the body is surrounded by a magnetic field. "Every event in the body, either normal or pathological, produces electrical changes...and alterations of the magnetic fields in the spaces around the body," says James Oschman in his book *Energy Medicine*.[3] This means that disease can start with the smallest of particles. Through vibration, a particle emanates on a frequency that generates a field. This field can become a force that, if strong enough, can overpower the body. The parasite causing malaria, for instance, is extraordinarily potent. Certainly the intracellular destruction caused by the spreading parasites is one of the causes of the incredible damage, but so is the energetic construct holding the malaria frequency in place.

Even doctors wonder why certain germs, viruses, or bacteria are carried by all people, but only some become sick. Staph, for instance, is present in almost everyone, but only strikes certain people and then only at certain times. What profile typically falls prey to a staph infection? Someone who has had surgery. Studies show that up to 50 percent of surgical patients experience some sort of post-surgical staph infection, which can kill. A cut in the body disturbs the energetic fields. A damaged particle emits a warped field, one lacking immunity to the field generated by staph particles.

Changes in particles and fields can spawn disease. Altering the fields and forces affecting a living organism can also carry out healing.

Here is a list of the fields I find most important in healing work. I introduced auric fields in chapter 1, and I will have more to say about them in later chapters relating to the various pathways; the other three fields will be discussed in this chapter.

- **The auric fields.** Graduating layers of light that manage the energy outside of your body.
- **The morphogenetic fields.** Fields of energy that surround every animated being, body, organ, or cell.
- **The physical energetic fields.** Physical energies often form different systems that conduct information. There are several types of physical energetic fields, all of which lie on what is called the *Secondary Grid.*
- **The spiritual energetic fields.** Energies capable of shifting between speeds faster and slower than the speed of light are sometimes organized as spiritual truths. These spiritual energetic forces are available on what is called the *Primary* or *Star-Point Grid.*

The Morphogenetic Fields

Morphogenetic fields link similar beings together and provide a means for sharing information and learning. They exist in and around these groups in particular:

- Imagination, power, and elemental-based energy bodies or boundaries
- The multiverse
- The universe
- The planet earth
- Specific continents
- Time zones
- Specific species or population groups, including human cultures based on ethnicity, religion, gender, age, education, passions and interests, soul groups, or common issues and problems

- Family groups, either from this or other lives
- The individual aspects and subaspects of any one individual.
  An aspect of a person is a core component of the self, such as your body, mind, or spirit. A subaspect is a subdivision of one of these aspects. For instance, the body reduces into parts like the ego and inner children.

Morphogenesis, a scientific term for the formation and differentiation of tissues and organs, comes from the Latin for creation or birth of form. Back in the 1930s, physicist Paul Weiss suggested that all living creatures generate morphogenetic fields—learning-sensitive fields that can be altered through vibration to create change. In *A New Science of Life*, English biologist Rupert Sheldrake proposes that morphogenetic fields are actually organizing fields that "act across both space and time."[4] When we're sharing data along the morphogenetic fields, we're conducting what Sheldrake calls *morphic resonance*. He explains that morphic resonance occurs when "a system is acted upon by an alternating force which coincides with its natural frequency of vibration."[5]

Morphogenetic fields can account for inherited information. Sheldrake claims that memories themselves are not "confined to individual brains." They can pass from person to person in a sort of "pooled" memory that "could be inherited from countless individuals in the past."[6]

Morphogenetic fields can explain how certain types of information can transfer on the elemental pathway. When a unit of information becomes intense or powerful enough, it ignites along shared fields. On the power pathway, forces can translate this same way. Space and time are formal constructs on the elemental and power pathways, but absent on the imagination pathway. Morphogenetic fields don't really exist on the imagination pathway; rather, the information from the elemental or the power pathway convinces you to shift energy from one side of the imagination pathway to the other, which then causes changes in reality. On the divine pathway, time and space are condensed to an eternal Here and Now. However, decisions on the divine pathway transfer instantaneously into the morphogenetic realities on the other pathways.

The Physical Energetic Fields

The physical energy fields fashion an energy form, the Secondary Grid, that is especially important to understand in shift healing. This construct connects all of physical reality on an interlocking set of energetic lines. Once you learn how to perceive and work this form, you can pinpoint problems and shift them phenomenally fast.

The Secondary Grid looks like a giant net connecting millions of smaller nets. The lines conduct information-energy and double as units of time—meaning that on the Secondary Grid, information is transferred inside of linear time. The lines are like strings that make sure information-energy is sent from the past to the present and then into the future.

The pockets between the lines are space—a neutral area that can still be programmed by intense concentration. In relation to energy types, neutrons occupy space; they can attract protons to achieve form and electrons to spread fields. On some of the pathways, you can perform healing by inserting new thoughts into the spaces and transferring these energies into time.

The Keys of Enoch by J. J. Hurtak, a source of esoteric knowledge that can be compared to much of the references in the New Testament book of Revelations, explains this grid as the "central geometric form for all biophysical and consciousness evolution."[7] In *The Keys*, Hurtak states that the grid is organized in units of eighteen energies connected with a five-pointed pyramidal structure that is hydrogen-based. Recall our earlier discussion about the relationship between a five-pointed star and the Fibonacci numbers, and add to this knowledge the results of the experiment by Nikola Tesla, who as mentioned in chapter 4, created a vacuum that leaked hydrogen.

The Secondary Grid is built on universal principles that incorporate the basic structures of natural law, as well as how change occurs in the fractal-like, imagination-based vacuum state. Hurtak says that the grid collects knowledge about biomes, ecosystems, astronomic forces, evolution, geology, and energy working. It then passes this information through an inner planetary network. The Secondary Grid has so far been activated and organized by human beings only for purposes of furthering physical reality. When fully activated, the Secondary Grid will transform into its correct shape, what I call the Primary Grid.

The Secondary Grid is composed of the following types of energy lines:

· Earth, dimensional, spatial, and heavenly body-based *ley lines*
· Morphogenetic fields and lines
· The Vivaxis
· Emotional and mental strongholds that transform into power levels
· Power levels
· Power fields
· Natural energy forces and properties

Ley lines are energy-based nets that maintain electromagnetic or other natural forces. Because your body is electromagnetic, it is highly affected by the energy of ley lines. There are ley lines in the earth, coming from planets and stars, and emanating from other planes and dimensions. These can all form geometric shapes that hold or alter physical reality.

Vivaxis is a word coined by Judy Jacka, N.D., in her book *The Vivaxis Connection*. It refers to the "sphere of energy created during the last weeks before birth that connects our etheric and electromagnetic energy fields with that of the earth."[8] I believe that the Vivaxis is a form of the morphogenetic fields linked into the greater Secondary Grid System. It is an aspect of the Secondary Grid that serves as a personal ley line between an individual and the planet.

The Vivaxis theory suggests the presence of receptors that connect us to the earth's energetic lines. The energy in the receptors can move clockwise or counterclockwise. Researcher Fran Nixon discovered that during an earthquake or planetary disturbance the normal spin of the electromagnetic field, which is vertical, is disturbed.[9] Changes in spin can account for environmental sensitivities, astrological influences, the "off" feeling we have around certain people (their spin disturbs our own), and even the seeming rigidity of a disease or life problem. If we're locked into an adverse spin, we're not going to be balanced. We won't be able to shift unless we shift our spin.

Power levels are consciousness waves that hold two dualistic notions together. Many Secondary Grid lines are actually made of a single strand of one power level. This line is like a continuum of a single idea. For example, on one side of a power level line is the idea of being a victim; on the other side is the energy it takes to be a victimizer.

Power levels can captivate your thoughts and energies and keep you strangled in your mental and emotional strongholds. For instance, you might be operating in a mental stronghold that says, "I am bad" and "Bad people deserve to be punished," so you adhere to a power level relating to victim-victor: you are bad, so you deserve to be victimized.

The major power levels include

Victim-victor	Fear-love
Ignorance-knowledge	Innocence-guilt
Holding-sending	Bad-good

Power fields are a progressive order of energetic fields that stair-step you through the human development process into owning your divinity. Using the fields enables practical decision-making, problem solving, diagnostics, healing, and spiritual awareness. (I learned of the power fields from David Hawkins, author of *Power versus Force: The*

Hidden Determinants of Human Behavior. [10] Based on his insights, I have been working with these fields for quite a while, and though my assessments have come to be somewhat different from his, I very much recommend his book.)

In my understanding, a power field is a vibrational level in the Secondary Grid. Each power field represents a certain type of life necessity or achievement. Most exponential growth occurs to the power of 10. To accomplish your life directives, you must achieve a 100 mark at each of the main power fields. Once you reach the 100 mark at each and every power field, you suddenly leap to 1,000 plus one. This isn't a stopping point, but symbolizes that now you're able to access your divine as well as your human abilities.

Theoretically, you could reach the 100 mark in every area except, let's say, the first power field. Here, you might still be stuck on a survival issue—for instance, on good versus bad. If you never get unstuck from thinking of yourself as either "good" or "bad," you could conceivably never reach the 100 mark. Although you can realize the achievement of every other power field, you won't be fully secure and therefore fully "here."

All sorts of situations can cause us to be stuck on a power field, including mental and emotional strongholds, power levels, programming, and delusions.

There are currently four recognized *natural energy forces* or extended fields:

- The *electromagnetic fields*, which are generated from charged particles or waves
- The *gravitational field*, which pulls objects of weight toward it
- The *strong nuclear field*, which pulls together the nucleus in atoms
- The *weak nuclear field*, which can break a nucleus apart
- In addition to these well-known energy forces, there are many undecipherable forces that are still being determined by science.

The Spiritual Energetic Fields

The spiritual energetic fields are energies that flow between heaven and earth, between spiritual and material dimensions. They emanate from and compose the Primary or Star-Point Grid. Our spirits are connected with this and only this system.

Although the power levels on the Secondary Grid act in concert with natural law and serve as a conduit for sensory and psychic information-energy, the points on the Primary Grid work only with the highest and very lowest frequencies of light. I often refer to it as the Star-Point Grid because information and even beings in this field look like points or streams of various colors of light.

The nickname of the Star-Point system also comes from Hurtak's esoteric writings in *The Keys of Enoch*. Remember Hurtak's assertion that the original grid is organized in five-point formations and linked to hydrogen? He insists that if you look at a platinum crystal under a field ion microscope, you will see the bubble formations that form the pyramid shapes of the grid. This five-pointed system is the base

Following is my outline of the basic power fields. I have included samples of the types of power levels that can keep us stuck on a power field.

Power Level/ Power Field	Power Level	Power Field	Physical Energetic Property	Basic Purpose
1/100	Good-bad Life-death	Survival	Informed charges	Existence
2/200	Doing-being Holding-sending	Functional	Frequencies	Productivity
3/300	Success-failure Knowledge- ignorance	Ego	Vibrations	Accomplishments
4/400	Together-apart Innocence-guilt	Relational	Waves	Joined efforts for exponential gain
5/500	Worth- worthlessness Self-others	Recognition	Harmonics	Knowledge of Higher Power and powers
6/600	Deserving- not deserving Acting-not acting	Transformation	Composition	Cocreation with Higher Power/powers
7/700	Victim-victor Inside-outside	Applied power	Disharmony	Ability to direct forces on own
8/800	Attachment- detachment Something-nothing	Transmutation	Emptiness	Conversion of one force to another
9/900	Virtuous-not virtuous Good-bad	Truth	Generating	Manifestation from universal truths
10/100	One-all	Unity	Formlessness	Dark completed in light; become source of all energy
1,000 + 1	None	In-spirited; in the spirit	None; use spiritual energetic forces	Spiritual infusion

structure that requires activation for the higher levels of consciousness and the divine pathway. Until you activate yourself on the Star-Point System, you must consciously direct the Primary Grid energies and forces for your well-being; before full activation, however, these energies can be detrimental as well as supportive.

The Spiritual Energetic Forces *Forces*, in general, are fields that continue expanding; matter produces fields that, in turn, create forces. We've already considered some of the Secondary Grid natural forces, such as electromagnetism and gravity. In relation to the Primary Grid, forces are spiritually oriented principles, ideals, ideas, and conscious and unconscious energies that generate change. The main ones to consider are

- Spiritual forces
- Powers
- Virtues
- Rays

From this point on, when I use the term *forces* alone, I am speaking about natural forces, natural and spiritual forces, and forces in general. When I use the term *spiritual energetic forces*, I am speaking of all the *energies*—including spiritual forces, virtues, powers, and rays—that are specifically available through the Primary Grid. (In chapter 6 I will be introducing the concept of the Forces, which are conscious entities that employ all forces for higher purposes.)

The **spiritual forces** are beams of energy set in motion by the Divine with which we are to create our destinies. These emanate from the Star-Point Grid, but can be made available on the Secondary Grid.

On the elemental pathway, both natural and spiritual forces feed the managing energy bodies, which include the chakras and the auric fields, as well as the spine itself. Only spiritual forces supply energy to the spiritual points. Spiritual energetic forces can also be called *power forces*, because the easiest way to access and manage them is on the power pathway.

The basic spiritual forces are outlined in chapter 13. For now, it's sufficient to note that there are two main types of spiritual forces: the generative and the degenerative. The power pathway, like the imagination and the elemental pathways, is dualistic; every positive or creative spiritual force is balanced by a negative or destructive spiritual force. Consider the need for both. As a tree grows through creative properties, so does it die and decay through destructive elements, thereby providing food for its offspring and other forest life. Cancer on the power pathway actually involves an imbalance between degenerative and generative spiritual forces. Cancer cells grow unchecked, fed by generative spiritual forces. Destructive spiritual forces would destroy the chaotic cells.

Powers are wave patterns of energy that motivate change in the other forces. While they can operate on natural forces, they are usually most effective as augmentations of spiritual forces. This is because they are composed of spiritual truths unified for particular reasons but applied as elements. For instance, the *power* of fire can exponentially increase the strength of the *spiritual force* of truth. Those who know about the powers can summon them at will. If used, powers increase the intensity of any energy in tenfold increments.

Powers are easiest to perceive as reflections of the elements: earth, air, metal, wood, fire, water, stone, ether, light, and star. If you could see powers in "outer space"—that is, beyond the perceptions of the physical self—they would appear as shifting, spinning bands of long energies, a little like Christmas ribbon candy or moving barbershop poles, made of pure spiritual "matter." When they shift from the Star-Point Grid to the Secondary Grid, these swirls of energy resonate as elements. A power that soothes and comforts will transmit as a water power once it "hits" the physical planes. A power that protects and defines will reverberate as a metal power upon arrival in the here and now.

Although the idea of powers as elemental in formation may imply they have a high physical construction, this is misleading. Powers are spiritual forces and are so powerful that they can't safely connect to physical structures, such as organs or cells—or even the chakras, usually, unless the chakras have completely converted into the channels of light that they become through divine adapting. Powers can literally overwhelm physical structures and obliterate them—as happens in rare but documented cases of spontaneous combustion, in which someone literally explodes into a ball of fire. This type of situation is caused by the inadvertent attachment of a power to a person. Why can't chakras usually tolerate an infusion from a power? Chakras and other energy bodies are composed of psychic and physical substances and the physical substances are easily imbalanced, unless fixated in pure divine truths.

Powers can perform multiple functions, so there are powers that are seemingly composed of several elements. Usually, however, only one major element becomes "activated," and that is in accordance with the spiritual force attached to it. Spiritual forces are so focused that they actually "select" or seemingly "speed dial" the element embodied in the power that is most needed for a particular situation.

Later in this chapter, I'll discuss another type of power—powers that are conscious. Called the Powers, these are forms or beings that represent a specific type of power.

The easiest way to access the powers—or the Powers—is on the power pathway. When working with powers, you can either summon a desired power or allow the spiritual forces used on the power to attract the most helpful power. If you are commanding your own power, I suggest referring to the list of elements covered earlier in this chapter and summoning the power that mirrors the element most needed on the elemental pathway. For instance, if you need air for clear thinking on the elemental pathway, call for an air power.

Virtues are consciousness waves that support divine, or enlightened, decision-making and behavior. On the elemental and power pathways, the virtues often feed the back of the chakras and are often selected based on accessibility to the spiritual points.

Many healers think that they are working virtuously or even working with the virtues when in fact they are not. The virtues are energies that represent universal truths. People easily form energetic constructs from emotional or mental strongholds or power levels and then ascribe a virtuous interpretation to them. For instance, a lot of people confuse kindness, which is a virtue, with niceness, which is a false, artificially produced construct. You can be kind while not being nice. Sometimes, a kind act will involve being rude or even crude, as in shouting at someone to stop hitting a child. A "nice" person won't even raise his or her voice.

Energetically, a virtue and a nonvirtue may look alike. The only way to really tell the difference through psychic viewing is to consider whether the posing energy emanates from the divine pathway or not. As you get comfortable with the divine, this becomes easier and easier to do. And it's important to do. Often, people won't release their negative issues or energies because they think it's wrong or that it's virtuous to hold onto them. For instance, I often find people holding onto their parent's energy, thinking that it is virtuous to help out a parent. Energy from elsewhere always causes problems in our own bodies and often underlies stress-related and degenerative diseases. And it's all in the name of "niceness."

Following is a list of key virtues and the qualities that masquerade as those virtues:

Virtue	Nonvirtue
Kindness	Niceness
Cleanliness	Sanitization
Courage	Bravado
Selfness	Selfishness
Discernment	Judgment
Integrity	Morality
Self-esteem	Arrogance
Inscrutability	Deviousness
Perkiness	Hyperness
Vulnerability	Neediness
Carefulness	Pickiness
Innocence	Ignorance
Tolerance	Foolishness
Transparency	Exposure
Modesty	Self-deprecation
Wisdom	Knowledge

Rays are horizontally accessed energies that feed our energy system, linking us with both the Primary and the Secondary Grid. They are energy bands that emit from the Primary Grid, yet attach to each of the chakras and move through the body. Rays provide a means for "moving in place," for opening to energies on all places within a power level. If we're stuck in being a victim, for instance, one of the six major rays can access another place on the victim-victor power level continuum. Maybe a little victor will balance us? In short, rays establish our horizontal power base.

The rays enter through the front side of our chakras, whereas the virtues enter through the back side. Because of this, the rays primarily affect our conscious decision-making and therefore our everyday, visible lives.

Each of the six major rays weaves into and through two particular chakras, connecting them so that we can obtain a second perspective on each and every issue.

- First Ray: Will power
- Second Ray: Love and kindness
- Third Ray: Intelligence
- Fourth Ray: Unity
- Fifth Ray: Knowledge
- Sixth Ray: Idealism

Times and Places

There are hundreds of time-space "places," including various planes of existence, energy planes, worm holes, vibrational zones, spheres, and more. In this section, we'll be looking at those that are most helpful for shift healing. To apply this information, you need to understand not only the linear and uniform natures of time and space, but also the nonlinear and nonuniform ones.

We're most comfortable dealing with time as linear or methodical, such as the time told in increments on your watch. This is the basis of elemental pathway time measurement. Space, too, is usually considered in measurable terms and has traditionally been thought of as uniform. Though Einstein considered the universe as curved, he proposed that gravity responded to this curvature in measurable ways.

Recent thought, however, is raising questions as to the equilibrium of time and space, or *spacetime* as it is often called. A theory called loop quantum space suggests that in the quantum world, space creates nodes and lines called spin networks. When spin networks move and shift, the nodes meet in something called *spin foam.* This shifting would mean that not only do particles and fields move and change, but so does the geometry of space. It would also suggest that this geometry evolves through a series of abrupt and not always uniform moves, not continuously. Time can thus be seen as a series of clock ticks; in positing this, the theory is similar to the concept of linear time. However, one tick might find a single quantum area present in the third dimension, but at the next tick, the area is gone. The disappearance of the quantum area is said to now define the tick, not the other way around. Actually, however, time does not exist in between the ticks. In fact, there is no in-between "in the same way that there is no water in between two adjacent molecules of water." [11]

I'll be describing the types of time and space ideas needed for shift healing. It's important to remember the new discoveries about time and space, however, because they will unlock you from your standard thinking. If time shifts, so can that which is created in the third dimension over time. If space is discontinuous, then you can move objects from "space to space."

I once applied this idea twice in a single day, the first time to "change timing" for a young man in the middle of a cold-sore attack. He was going on a date the next day and really wanted the cold sore to disappear. Because I understood that there are "spaces between time," I worked from the divine pathway to shift the viral component of the cold sore out of existence and into the space between "time clicks." The cold sore was gone within an hour and didn't return.

I used the same thinking to work with a woman on her sister, who was four hundred miles away. Testing had detected a huge mass in Jackie's right breast, and the doctors were sure that it was malignant. My friend and I concentrated on Jackie, while I slipped the mass into the "space between ticks." The next day, Jackie returned for an ultrasound. Not only was there no malignancy, there was no mass.

Yet again, I applied the quantum loop theory when working with a woman with severe phobias. I was able to help Vicki change her perspective of risk and thereby to increase her success in everyday life endeavors. Using a divine-based idea, I first told her that she was living her life in linear time and uniform space. She was like a moving object, rushing through the universe so fast that she felt out of control. Risk meant moving faster, which was scary. Vicki agreed that this was a valid description of her life and an explanation for her being frightened of doing so much as travel in an airplane. I then helped her shift her perspective and imagine herself as centered in the middle of the loop in between time and space. Vicki pictured herself occupying the space between space, in a land in which time held no meaning. In this place, she was still. People, ideas, events—all these were lines and points that seemed to come toward her in slow motion, giving her time to select which to interact with. Vicki was suddenly able to see herself as the center of her own life, capable of deciding what to respond to and how. Her instrumental phobias disappeared overnight, and Vicki is now able to take risks previously impossible for her to even consider, such as grocery shopping after dinner instead of in broad daylight.

What if you understood that every time you took a risk, you were safer? Think of the difference this idea might make in your life! *Seeing reality in a different way actually changes reality.*

You don't need to be a super scientist to allow physics to work for you. Shift healing is dependent upon perspective. Simply breaking free of your previously limiting viewpoints frees you to explore new healing possibilities. On all the pathways, you'll be using various ideas about time and space to make changes. These ideas will include knowledge about the dimensions and the planes of light, as well as various applications of energy laws.

Dimensions

I will now introduce the thirteen dimensions, as I know them. Descriptions of dimensions one through eight are based on mathematical and scientific ideas. The remaining descriptions relate to esoteric concepts from texts including those of ancient Egypt, which I have adapted for the Four Pathway system. These dimensions occupy various places in the spacetime continuum. You will be accessing these dimensions through energy symbology, tones, colors, and shapes, which are covered in a later section of this chapter, "Energy Laws."

First dimension. A point; the zero place of the beginning; space. For anything or anyone to manifest, it must have a place of departure that has only one factor.

Second dimension. Lines, namely vertical and horizontal lines, combined to form shapes with length and width. This dimension introduces measurement, because you have points relative to each other, and therefore a possible beginning, end, and middle. With vertical and horizontal lines, you can create a rectangle and length and width. The lines represent actual reality and the middle area, unmanifested reality—the zero or the imagination. Without height, however, you are still in flat line space.

Third dimension. A cube; structure. We add height and volume. Objects now exist and you exist within the structure of the cube—in which you have six manifested lines, or planes, and also twelve lines—as well as the space in the middle, which represents the void or unmanifested potential. If you cut the corners of the cube, you produce triangle shapes and a tetrahedron, the sign of balance and equilibrium. The tetrahedron is the sign of Divinity.

The cube is the most well known of all elemental dimensions, but when shaped into pyramid or cross structures, it becomes the basis of the power and the imagination pathways as well. The cube represents the basic shape of the elemental pathway in the physical, its spiritual properties represented by pyramid structures; the chakralike seals of the power pathway are set with a cross; and the imagination pathway is composed of the undisclosed middle space of third-dimensional forms. The divine pathway itself has shadings in the third dimension, in that it is best represented by the reflection of two tetrahedrons in perfect complement within a divine tetrahedron.

Fourth dimension. A point outside the cube. You are still in the cube but can access time outside of the box to shape the cube. You can perceive the power from the elemental.

Fifth dimension. A cube with lines outside of it. You now exist within or outside of the cube, but not in both places at once. Within time, you can link the power with the elemental and consciously direct the relationship between them.

Sixth dimension. The cube lines dissolve and leave only disconnected points. Each point becomes an opening for creation. You are in the power pathway, but also the imagination pathway. Here, the elemental pathway is created from the imagination pathway.

Seventh dimension. No points and no lines. You are pure consciousness. If you have a body, you can choose to operate on any of the pathways through this dimension and, if you desire, to combine pathways and work on two or more at once.

Eighth dimension. Nothing and everything; pure imagination. Living on the divine pathway within the eighth dimension provides pure power to create or alter anything in "reality" or unreality.

Ninth dimension. Pure expression of love.

Tenth dimension. Grace.

Eleventh dimension. Purity with all.

Twelfth dimension. Unity with the Creator.

Thirteenth dimension. Cocreation.

Planes of Light

When the body dies, there are thirteen planes the soul follows to merge back into spirit. When most people die, their souls select one of several energetic tunnels as exit points. The lower tunnel leads to lower vibrational spacetime dimensions, all refractions of the first two dimensions, the bottom of which we call Hell. It is simply the plane of one's own subconscious.

The middle tunnel has several tracks. One tunnel leads directly into the etheric realm of the third dimension, upon which souls live as ghosts—souls that refuse to leave the third dimension. Through this tunnel, souls escape facing the consequences of their lives and the benefits of healing through death, and they remain locked into linear spacetime until they free themselves or are freed.

Other middle-space tunnels exit into the first three of the thirteen Planes of Light. Some souls enter the Plane of Rest, which is another aspect of the third dimension, except that there time is not linear. The Plane of Evaluation is akin to the fourth dimension, and the Plane of Healing is available to several different dimensions and, therefore, spacetime zones.

The higher tunnel proceeds directly out of spacetime as we know it to the upward dimensions and the higher Planes of Light, where dwell masters, avatars, and other ascended beings. The very highest tunnel leads directly to the thirteenth dimension or above and is an invitation directly into the Light or heart of the Divine.

The goal of this development process is reunification of one's own soul (or various soul bodies) with one's own spirit, and thus to recognition of perfect unity with The All. At any point, a being can reenter the world of physical matter and live another lifetime. Of course, you don't have to die to make this progression. The point of the pathways is to welcome this unification here and now. You can conduct pathway healing through any of these Planes of Light; by doing so, you gain a perspective that releases you from your everyday thinking and speeds up your healing process.

- **Plane of Rest.** Place of peace and restoration.
- **Plane of Evaluation.** Place of conducting a life review following death.
- **Plane of Healing.** Place for healing from life damage or making amends for difficulties caused to others.
- **Plane of Knowledge.** Plane of interconnecting lines and forms that gather data into organized "storage libraries."
- **Plane of Wisdom.** Place for the integration of knowledge and life experiences.
- **Plane of Truth.** Place for learning the ancient laws, universal truths that run all of reality.
- **Plane of Peace.** Place to gather peace within the self.
- **Plane of Momentum.** Place for assignment of acts of goodwill to share peace with others. These others might number among the living or the dead. Many once-humans return to the earth to serve as guides for the living.
- **Plane of Love.** Plane of illumination, upon which one's own spiritual truth becomes reflected and developed.
- **Plane of Power.** Place for receiving advanced instruction and testing in application of powers and forces.
- **Plane of Charity.** Place to practice the art of selflessness. The call to love through action requires elimination of the self.
- **Plane of Mastery.** The place of the "Christing decision," the opportunity to become your own Enlightened Consciousness.
- **Plane of Consciousness.** The place of being the Creative within the Creator.

Zones of Life and Death

There are several zones that assist the soul in its alchemical processes between life, death, and the space in between lives. Many ancient texts, including those of the Egyptians, early Mesopotamians, and Mayans, have described states of existences predating and following incarnation. Several science studies suggest a place of decision-making before birth, the concept behind the White Zone. These ideas, along with my professional experience, has led me to the awareness of these four zones.

- **The White Zone.** The space without time in which the soul determines upcoming life goals, lessons, and events.
- **The Gray Zone.** The place where space and time meet while the soul is exiting the White Zone and beginning its entry orbit into an awaiting body.
- **The Red Zone.** The place where space and time meet while the soul is still lingering in the body, but just about to exit into the Black Zone. It's called the Red Zone because the soul is still linked to the elemental pathway's basic life energy.
- **The Black Zone.** The space without time just after death in which the soul pauses before deciding which way to go through the tunnels or Planes of Light.

Spin and Energy

Healing is affected by how you direct, shape, and form energy. Light doesn't just go in a straight line. Energy, energy particles, energy waves, and spacetime can move in crooked or straight lines, from dot to dot, or in jumpstarts and stops. Energies can form into circles or squares. They can move around corners and double back on themselves.

Spacetime often organizes in geometric patterns, as do your energy bodies. Even more important, the fields around energies often oscillate in measurable geometric patterns. When we're "at ease" or healthy, our cells, subatomic particles, organs, tissues, and energy bodies are spinning correctly and thus holding correct shapes. Disease can be seen as a matter of incorrect spin. When you injure a tissue, such as through a paper cut, the tissue is damaged, but so is the spin of the cells and the field emanating from the tissue. Spin affects spins. When enough cells, physical or etheric, are spinning uncontrollably, they begin to shape themselves into new geometric patterns, ones that will now hold a disease in place, until reversed or changed again.

I often diagnose a disease based on shape and, therefore, spin. It's easy to see if someone is emotionally depressed: the person always has some form of life energy stuck in a boxlike shape inside his or her body; the box often spins backwards, in a repressed or depressed fashion. Depression is compressed energy that moves counterclockwise.

Depressed spin can create more than just an emotional problem. Fibromyalgia and chronic fatigue also result from depressed spins. The energy becomes so stuck, the spin so slow, and the resulting geometric shape so rigid, the various forms of life energy can't move through the body.

Anxiety psychically appears like a clockwise spin that lacks form. Many forms of cancer are a product of high-anxiety spins. The energy around the cells spins so fast, it can't hold form and loses shape, hence the appearance of the misshapen cancer cells. When enough cells are communicating in this new, formless pattern, other cells join in the song, and soon the cancer spreads.

Spins are hard to see—the spins of individual cells or subatomic particles are so fast that even scientists have a difficult time measuring them. The easiest way to set and evaluate spin is by checking for the symbols in the center of the chakras. On all pathways, each chakra determines and reflects the spin that manages its own territory. Symbols can be appraised by looking at spin itself, geometric patterns, numerical values, energy colors, and tones. Whichever technique you use, you are essentially working with symbology.

Even using everyday words to command wholeness involves working with the symbolism of words and encompasses spin, shape, tone, color, and numerical representations. You need only remember this: If you change shape, you change spin. If you change the spin of a disease into the spin of being at ease, you heal.

When I started studying the chakras more than twenty years ago, one of the first lessons I was taught related to spin. Your chakras, both front and back, are supposed to spin clockwise. A fully functioning chakra will do that; this is a sign of good health.

Counterclockwise movements can indicate clearing but also imbalance.

Shifting the spin of a chakra, receptor, or other energy is possible on or through any of the Four Pathways. It requires working vibrationally, which allows you to convert one sort of particle to another or to bring in a certain type of particle or force to overcome one that you don't want. The way to manage this process is to figure out which energy laws operate on which pathway, and to use these laws for gain rather than injury.

Energy Laws

All energy moves according to well-established laws that tell it what to do. Want to change spin? Change direction? Establish new shapes, symbols, and speeds? These are the energy laws that govern such changes. Some will work on one pathway but not on another. In Part Three, I will differentiate the laws according to the pathways. Here are brief descriptions of the three main types of energy laws:

Natural Laws. Rules that allow movement and change on a pathway.

Conversion Laws. Energy laws that govern the exchange of information-energy to produce an effect.

Spiritual Laws. Laws that govern movement and reality of the spirit. The different realities have different spiritual laws, which is why miracles aren't seen as miraculous on one level, but are on another.

Breaking the Energy Laws

You might wonder at the use of symbols and spin to break energy laws and create damage. We all break energy laws and cause damage to ourselves and others, usually inadvertently. An emotional stronghold wounds our bodies and energy systems and can be psychically detected as a harmful symbol in the chakras and other energy bodies, as well as in the cells of the physical body. As problematic as these accidental conditions and their effects are, intentional manipulation is even worse.

Sometimes, harmful symbols—and, therefore, changes in spin—are established through intention; this is called *sorcery*. Sorcerers can be alive or dead. They seek power over others by creating or manipulating forces. In other words, sorcerers are experts at bending spins so as to bend others' wills to their own will.

There are many types of "black magic" forces. All involve the creation of energetic *bindings* that overpower the energies of other people. A binding is any energy force that puts its creator in charge of a certain type of energy. For instance, one lover can bind another to eternal love. Now the two will reappear together, lifetime after lifetime, whether or not the "bindee" desires the relationship.

I recently worked with a woman from Africa who had experienced social problems and back pain her entire adult life. She had been bound by an entity in a prior life, which promised to be her friend forever. This entity attached to her neck. Every time Elaine made a new friend or received a client's compliment as a hairdresser, the entity would perceive the other person as a threat and psychically stab her in the neck.

I still reread Elaine's letter to me. As soon as we released the entity to its correct dimensional home, her life changed. Her back problems disappeared, she began to retain her previously disappearing client base, and she established solid friendships.

A *curse* is a binding established over a group of people. Curses are often passed down in families and establish family *miasms*, or negative patterns, which result in common diseases, financial issues, relationship problems, and the like. Multiple sclerosis can perhaps be considered an "accursed condition," caused by a negative energy that settled on the Irish during the potato famine. Research this statement; you'll find it interesting that there is a high prevalence of multiple sclerosis among people with Irish ancestry during the famine time. The curselike energy creates a miasm that causes a high susceptibility to fungus and mold, the afflictions that damaged the potatoes in that era. Curses almost always involve the tenth chakra and are held in the morphogenetic field.

Sometimes the original perpetrator of a curse or its first victim becomes a ghost and continues to plague the cursed group for generations to come. Entities that won't release into death are called *hauntings*, and their effects on the living are called *interference. Ancestral hauntings* are entities from the living's actual lineage. There are many other beings that can cause interference, including demons, phantoms, and other ghosts. (See chapter 6 for this list.)

A *spell* is a binding held over an individual. An individual often casts a spell over another to maintain control, inhibit the other's success, or ensnare them in love. Spells can also cause disease. Any inhibition of energy changes spin and, therefore, the patterns and symbols in the body.

People can accidentally create bindings. These bindings are typically weak and often unconsciously refused or broken by the victim. When set intentionally, however, bindings can last nearly forever. Strong sorcerers set bindings by actually reshaping natural or spiritual forces into unnatural shapes. They might change a circle into a square, cast binding forces into someone's body, invert a number, surround the victim with an "off tone," or infuse a symbol with inappropriate energy. Many occultists choose to make these changes to rob the victim of his or her vital life energy and use it personally. What can be done for good can also be done for evil.

For example, by establishing the geometric symbol of the cross over an activated chakra-seal, the primary energy body of the power pathway, you ensure energetic protection and cancel out imagination delusions. A crooked cross, such as the Nazi swastika, placed on a seal will access the power forces to establish group consciousness, the basis for fanaticism, fundamentalism, and brainwashing.

All energetic bindings are a result of energetic contracts that inhibit the function of the chakras and therefore, a person.

Energetic Contracts

All chakras are susceptible to *energetic contracts*—restrictions on accessing spiritual gifts, powers, and destiny. These can affect every area of life, from physical to relationship health. In general, *bindings* appear as elastic bands or symbols that connect at least two beings or energies. They are often present in the first, fourth, fifth, ninth, and tenth chakras. Following are descriptions of some specific types of bindings.

Energetic cords appear like garden hoses. The older and more limiting the contract, the thicker the tubing. Energy flows through the middle of these cords. If you read this energy, you can interpret the nature of the contract. You know you have an energy cord if you can't detach from a certain person or people system no matter how hard you try. Yellow energy, for instance, means exchange of beliefs; orange might indicate that feelings are being swapped.

Life energy cords look a lot like energetic cords, but are psychically red or orange in color because the energy flowing through them is basic life energy. These cords can exist between parts of the self, such as from current-life to a past-life self, or between a person and any other individual or group. They work like wires running off a mainframe that deliver electricity to the different end users, thus splitting your basic life energy into several outlets. Energy depletion, chronic or severe illnesses, chronic fatigue, and adrenal problems usually involve life energy cords.

Curses look like tubules of thick, dark filaments bound together. They, too, can run between a person and any other individual or group. Curses are not empty at the center; the energy is bound in the tubes themselves. Curses hold in place many diseases, as well as sexual and monetary disorders.

An *energy marker* looks like a clump of counterclockwise, swirling charges forming a symbol. This symbol will instruct others how to treat the marked person. An energy marker in the tenth chakra is usually mirrored in at least one other chakra and also patterned in the corresponding, affected auric fields. If you're always treated disrespectfully, for instance, no matter what your behavior, you might have an energy marker.

An *enigma* is an attachment that ends at the physical body. It looks like an energetic accessory in one of the auric fields or elemental energy bodies.

If someone's life is stuck, I look for *holds*—energy restrictions placed by one on another. Many parents put holds on their children, usually to keep them safe, but sometimes to ensure a steady diet of basic life energy. Very immature and overly mature (bored) individuals are often the product of holds.

Energy contracts disappear only after you figure out your *payoff*, or the reason you are holding onto your end of the contract. Traditional therapy can be extremely helpful, as can using the techniques covered in Part Four and Part Five. Energy contract healing techniques can also be found in chapter 11.

Unified Energy Healing

How does energy from all four pathways come together for shift healing? Pierre, a client from France, provides an example.

Pierre was experiencing severe atrial tachycardia, a fast heartbeat originating in the upper chambers or atriums of the heart. To me, the elemental causes of the arrhythmia seemed related to a low-grade and long-term strep infection, which made further sense when he relayed that he had been plagued by a sore throat and a slight body rash for years. I suggested he undergo blood evaluations, but I continued to explore other reasons for his tachycardia.

Strep causes inflammation, but it wouldn't be considered the true cause of a condition energetically, but rather the disease attracted to a causal situation. What was going on inside of Pierre that would magnetize a strep infection? Pierre's main issue involved feeling unbelievably sad about the state of the world. He was fanatically involved in acting as a change agent, serving on several committees and in dozens of organizations working toward world peace. Every time he heard about world problems, his tachycardia kicked in.

On the elemental pathway, we understand a fast heartbeat as indicating an issue in the fourth chakra. The quick spin of this chakra as perceived psychically reflects an anxiety-related situation based on a misinformed spiritual belief. This "magnetic" condition was attracting the strep bacteria, which in turn depleted many of the nutrients in his system. The shortage of core nutrients, such as magnesium, furthered the fast pulse. Elementally, Pierre's feeling of powerlessness in affecting change had created air holes in his auric field and set up a strange syncopation in regard to the fire in his adrenals. When he became incensed, the first chakra stoked the fire of his adrenals as if to propel him to fight for human rights. This fire forced adrenaline into the bloodstream, which compelled the heart into a fast beat. Upon seeing the ineffectiveness of his drive, Pierre would become sad, and water would flood his system, creating the condition for further strep (and other bacterial) overgrowth.

This complicated patterning was easier to see on the power pathway. There Pierre was "overly virtuous" in his heart, using virtues to promote world change instead of personal development. His natural harmonics were Peace and Harmony. Like all harmonics, these are threaded with secondary spiritual qualities, including Happiness. Pierre was refusing to accept the "strand of Happiness" corded throughout these harmonic energies. How could he be happy when the world wasn't happy? Hence we arrive at his core misperception: *I can't be happy unless everyone else is happy first.*

The placement of the various power forces imitated this misperception, as did the energies on the imagination pathway. There, Pierre was rejecting happiness, refusing to allow it to enter from the anti-world. Instead, he was clutching unhappiness. The divine pathway illustrates his basic need—to know that the Divine wanted him happy!

Always, the divine pathway reveals the truth that can replace all elemental-based misperceptions. A divine truth is like a living consciousness. The acceptance of it automatically transforms all other energies from all other pathways. Consequently, as soon as Pierre understood that he could create more peace and harmony for the world by being personally happy and making choices that would increase his personal happiness, all the pathways began to shift. He called a few weeks later and reported that all strep-related symptoms had disappeared within a few days of our session and that he hadn't had a tachycardia attack since the day that we had met.

Energy Sources and Connections: Who's Out There?

[Merlin speaks]
"I am unique, I assure you." He smiled gleefully at the legate's wide-eyed distress. "It is no great difficulty for me to be in two places at once, for I am not corporeal in the manner of people… Oh, in the Great Tree, I am solid enough. But here in Middle Earth I find it easy to work in multiples." [1]

—A. A. Attanasio,
The Serpent and
the Grail

You are constantly interacting with the world of energy, and you can decrease the negative side effects of this relationship by becoming more conscious of what's out there and what to do about it.

A *source* is the origin of information or energy. For our purposes, consider *sourcing* to involve tracking a cause of a problem or information back to an animate and conscious being, consciousness, or energy. Diagnosing, on the other hand, involves tracing a situation back to any of its root causes. An animate source such as an entity or ghost might be only the formative cause of a presenting issue.

Conscious and unconscious sources constantly move between the spiritual and the material dimensions. It's easy to become the object of an energetic attraction without knowing it, or to think a message is for you when it's not! But sources are also helpful for healing and can be called upon for information and energy. Here are a few terms to understand in reference to sourcing.

Animate sources are potentially conscious of self; *inanimate sources* cannot be. A belief or a feeling can be an inanimate source of a problem, but the source of the belief or feeling is probably animate.

Some animate sources are physically alive and some are not. In general, animate sources meet the following three criteria:

- They run life energy
- They can and do generate original consciousness or intelligence
- They can change consciousness or intelligence at will

Helpful sources encourage the internalizing of your personal spirit in your body; harmful sources discourage this internalization. Determining whether a particular source is helpful or harmful requires a subjective analysis. The answer is based on your spiritual destiny; the same source could be helpful to someone with a particular destiny, yet harmful to someone on another path.

Graceful or grace-filled sources further the Divine (love in action), while interfering sources interfere with the Divine plan, for personal or selfish ends.

Deciding whether a source is good, bad, or evil is another subjective decision. Typically, good supports divine will and increases love, while bad involves going against divine will and decreases love, consciously or unconsciously. Evil is an anticonsciousness; it seeks to destroy the consciousness or life of others. The short-term goal of an evil source is to gain energy and power, which it refuses to generate for itself through natural means. The long-term goal of evil is to cancel itself and everything else out of existence.

Sources on the Level of the Natural

Natural forces include the wind, storms, rain, sunshine, earthquakes, and any great natural movements of climate and the elements. Many cultures believe that spirits control the natural forces. Some imbalances can be corrected by assuming the energy available through natural forces. By breathing in a missing force, you can greatly enhance recovery from colds and flu.

Natural spirits are usually associated with environmental issuance, such as volcanoes, streams, glens, or mountains. In most countries, special sites are assigned culturally specific names and local natural spirits are called upon for beneficent purposes.

Nature spirits are different from local natural spirits in that they aren't restricted to a particular environmental factor or location. These basically break down into the following categories:

Beings of the underworld or netherlands. These include beings on the astral plane, such as dragons and dwellers upon each of the post-death planes of light.

Beings of the faery realm. These include fairies and unicorns, centaurs and phoenixes. The underworld and the faery realm differ mainly in their location in the spacetime dimensions and in their vibration. The Celts of old believed there were three worlds: the underworld, the middle world, and the higher world. Energetically, the underworld is made of lower vibrations and is inhabited by beings that reflect dark energies and powers. The middle world is that of mankind and nature as we understand it; the higher realms are light-based in frequency and replete with beings that run at a high vibration, such as the fairies and devas. In actuality, all of these worlds exist within and inside of each other, though the terms usually evoke the image of one under the ground, another on earth, and yet another in the sky.

The elemental beings. Asian medicine has highlighted five basic elements or properties from which all is made: fire, water, metal, air, and wood. I add earth, stone, star, light, and ether. All of these elements can be reduced to the major three life components—carbon, hydrogen, and oxygen—that govern the physical world. There are various types of animate beings that live off of and also generate these core elements.

- *Fire beings* live in the center of the earth, keep the earth balanced, and send energy for purifying and transmuting. When transplanted into the body, they can become viruses and feed off the oxygen in the blood, eventually causing circulation and heart issues.

- *Water beings* are amoeba-shaped forms that dwell in wetness. In their element, they can be called upon for cleansing and renewing. When stuck in your body, they create bacteria and throw off your hydrogen molecules. Bacteria can cause numerous problems, including immune and autoimmune issues and some types of cancers.

- *Earth beings* are solid and solidifying. They can rebuild, strengthen, and maintain. Out of their element, they affect the carbon balance of your body and often underlie yeast, mold, and fungus, which cause digestive disturbances, confusion, some cancers, and autoimmune diseases like MS. When *crystal dwellers,* a type of earth being, become lost in bone instead of stone, they cause bone disorders.

- *Metal beings* are protective and solid. They don't absorb energies or information but they do deflect both. They are ideal for protective uses, but when absorbed into the body because of fear they will attract physical heavy metals that cause toxicity.

- *Air beings* transmit ideas and ideals. They will bring data on an as-needed basis, but can also underscore inaccurate concepts and thus promote negative thinking or "eat holes" in energy body walls and thus encourage leakage of energy or the induction of negative energies.

- *Wood beings* bring balance and calm. If present where they shouldn't be, they can cause stubbornness and a refusal to budge. As they decompose, they emanate various toxins and rot.

- *Stone beings* are exactly what they sound like. They are typically the historians of nature, storing data, energy, and information that psychic individuals can then access for healing or other purposes. A stone being laden with information disharmonious to your being could turn bone into slush, for instance, but when placed accurately it can help connected energies hold form, shape, and integrity.

• *Star beings* generate universal truths that burn with eternal light. Truth is truth, but not all truths are applicable to every situation. Certain spiritual misperceptions can be fed by a star being that emphasizes a truth that doesn't fit for you. This is often the case in chakra-based misperceptions.

• *Light beings* carry love or power intelligence. As with star beings, holding the wrong ideas in the wrong places underscores illness and life problems.

• *Ether beings* generate spiritual truths and qualities, and can be supportive of your own personal wisdom. As with star and light beings, they can also underpin ideas that are wrong for you.

Beings of the stars. Examples are extraterrestrials (ETs), which include the Blue People and the Grays. The Blue People are considered inhabitants of the Blue Planet of water and emanate divine truth to this planet; I was introduced to them by a Peruvian shaman whose grandmother consulted them for healing work. The Grays are thought to be an intrusive group of ETs who harvest eggs from living women to seed with their own sperm.

Beings of Earth. These are plants and animals and their souls or spirits, which often serve the human race. Helpers assist either for a particular task or throughout someone's life. Different animals represent different types of messages. A *totem* is a guiding figure that assists a particular family or clan. A *power animal* or being is a helper spirit. *Familiars* are mammals, reptiles, or birds that have been enchanted, entrapped, or manipulated so that their powers are available to a person. Plants, too, can provide divine or harmful guidance; many plants and trees have their own spirits and provide instruction. *Spirit plant medicine* is the invocation of the mystical to connect with the actual personality or knowledge of the plant world.

Shamans often direct the powers or energies latent in many *natural objects* for healing ends. You can also program objects for your own use or access the information-energy already in the implement.

Indigenous healers can access the spirit of a plant through special preparation and *natural ceremony*. The resulting drugs are used for healing and divination.

Sources on the Level of Spirits

There are two spirit categories of great interest. These are usually termed the angels and the demons, though technically both are the same. We'll look at various types of these and then list the other common spirit sources. In this section, I use the term *God* instead of *Divine*, as much of the information about angels comes from religions that use that label.

Angels

Jews, Christians, and Muslims believe that in creating heaven, God brought forth the heavenly hosts of angels, which makes angels older than humans. In the Old Testament, angels are attendants at the heavenly court, and their job is first to worship God, then to convey God's will to earth. The word *angelos* itself means *messenger*, but the Israelites also assigned these beings the roles of servants, ministers, hosts, holy ones set apart, and watchers. It's important to remember that there are harmful as well as helpful angels, though only helpful ones are available on the divine pathway.

Angels have spirits but don't have souls, unless they are or have been incarnate in a physical body, at which point most develop souls. Because of their spiritual nature, angels remain linked to the Primary or Star-Point Grid at all times; those with souls can get trapped on the Secondary Grid system. If we're open spiritually, as in through the divine pathway and sometimes the power pathway, angels can contact us directly through the Primary Grid. They can then deliver help or assistance immediately. If an angel is forced to go through the Secondary Grid, it might materialize through the Primary into the Secondary. From that point, angels can deliver words, visions, senses, a touch, or insight, directly or through others. Basically, they closet themselves in one of the connection spaces in the Secondary Grid and project holographically through time and space. This is why they can appear in many places at the same time or take on different forms.

There are several types of angels. These include the *cherubim*, who, according to the Israelites, support God's chariot and also act as guardian spirits. The term *seraphim* comes from a word meaning *to burn*; these angels surround God's throne and sing. It is suggested that the Jewish seraph is akin to the chimera of the ancient Near East as well as the Egyptian god Serapis, who inhabited the burning circle, or lower realm.

Archangels are the chief angels. Like the well-known archangel Gabriel, they deliver messages or healing from God. *General angels* deliver lesser messages. *Warrior angels* fight in the army of God and include angels like the archangel Michael, and *thrones* are thought to oversee justice in heaven. *Dominions* are considered to be celestial housekeepers, regulating heaven's duties. *Principalities* are occupied with the welfare of nations or groups. Certain principalities are also called upon by God to create miracles for individuals. These miracles are performed so the individual concerned can better fulfill a destiny that will help many. The *virtuous angels* work miracles and dispense courage, grace, and the other virtues.

The *Thunder Beings* and *Cloud People* are particularly forceful archangels, delivering power to earth. The *Nephilim* are another type of archangel, briefly mentioned in Genesis; they could also be called Earth Angels. The Nephilim live in the material planes and are split into two factions: those that assist humankind, and those that serve personal and selfish ends.

There are other groups of helpful angels gathered to perform certain universal tasks; they include the *Healing Teams of Grace*, which deliver healing and restoration; the *Clean-up Teams of Grace*, which cleanse and purify; and the *Restorative Teams of Grace*, which bring entity parts and soul fragments into unity. These are terms used by Judith and Bill Baldwin, energetic healers who have an international practice working with entity releasement. More information is available in their book, *Spirit Releasement Therapy*.

Many people believe that we have personal *guardian angels*. This idea is supported by the Christian Bible. In Matthew 18:10, Jesus says, "Take heed that you despise not one of these little ones, for I say unto you, that in heaven their angels do always behold the face of my Father." But Jesus did not introduce this concept to the world. Before his time, the idea of personal angels was already well established throughout the ancient Semitic world and continues to be popular today.

Demons or Fallen Angels

Demonology is a system that believes that a plethora of evil spirits causes everything negative, from illness to lost objects. Many animist, spiritualistic, and shamanic-based cultures assert this belief. According to most cultures that believe in evil spirits, demons can even possess people by occupying their thoughts, minds, or bodies. These spirits must then be exorcised or driven out by a holy person.

Many individuals believe that demons are the *fallen angels*. Fallen angels supposedly followed Lucifer (Satan, Beelzebub, the Enemy), himself once a high archangel, in rebellion against God. Christians often believe that these fallen angels are now demons that work for Satan. Actually, all animate sources have independent thought and can serve "bad" or selfish as well as "good" or Divine ends. Some angels simply serve themselves, not simply one certain entity such as a Lucifer. The concept of a single devil embodied in a being like Lucifer or Satan is a bit simplistic and might best be considered as a metaphor for the "demon" or aspect within each of us that can choose whom or what to serve. Having said this, I again assert that there are beings that choose to work toward evil ends; therefore you can consider fallen angels to actually be angels of any type that were once of grace and now seek to interfere with Divine plan. Some individuals believe that some fallen male earth angels (Nephilim) committed the sin of copulating with human women and imparted some of their qualities to their descendants.

Islamic angelology holds that the *jinn* or *genies* can be either benevolent or malevolent. Some genies are similar to the ally spirits we previously discussed, in that they will grant people wishes to reveal true character. According to Islamic legend, God created genies two thousand years before making Adam out of fire. Therefore, they can be visible or invisible and appear in any form they so desire.

There is also discussion in virtually all cultures about the existence of an *Angel of Death*. The oldest idea probably originated in polytheism; more recently, the concept describes a figure connected to sin and condemnation, as is Satan. In an eastern European folktale, the Angel of Death is married to Lilith, a satanic female who does everything from eating babies to harming pregnant women. Other cultures, however, believe Lilith to be the first woman created by the Divine and a representative of the feminine side of God.

Other Spirit Sources

An *entity* is a being with its own unique spirit and a soul. Through its soul, an entity traverses time and space to gather experiences. You are an entity in that you have a soul that connects to an operating spirit.

A *ghost* is an entity that was once alive and is now dead. Ghosts have a spirit and a soul, although these are seldom integrated. A *phantom* can be either a ghost or a holographic projection from an entity that is alive or dead. Technically, a projected phantom is inanimate, though these projections always emanate from some sort of animate being.

People often confuse phantoms and ghosts. Ghosts haven't released the emotional charges holding them to life, so their etheric bodies are heavy and solid. Emotional charges are electrical in nature, which is why ghosts often disturb electrical circuitry; for example, causing lights or televisions to flash. Phantoms have discharged their emotional charges. Lacking the dark frequencies, phantoms are lighter appearing or invisible.

A *visitation* is a ghost or a phantom seeking to scare, control, or inform the living by visiting. A *haunting*, introduced in the chapter 5 section "Breaking the Energy Laws," is an entity that seeks to steal life energy from a victim. Ancestral ghosts often haunt their progeny, as the life energy is similar.

Poltergeists are ghosts or phantoms that use electrical energy to move objects. Sometimes a disturbed individual can produce the same effect as can a poltergeist.

A *succubus* or an *incubus* is a sexually preying entity that is not alive.

Projections are organic or inorganic entities or energies that project or cast images of themselves through time and space. Many sources considered to be channeled entities are actually projections of one aspect of the channeller.

A *walk-in* is a soul or soul fragment that agrees to "walk into" or occupy a deserted body. In doing this, a walk-in soul accepts the unfinished karma or problems of the departing entity while carrying out its own spiritual destiny.

A *master* is an entity that was once alive and excelled in bringing his or her spiritual truth to light. Many masters represent power forces, as they excel in the use of them when living, but they can also reflect truth from any pathway, such as the divine truth of grace or love. Masters often continue their life path after death and guide those who need their instruction. An *avatar* is a master with full command of his or her area of expertise who wields power as well. Avatars are like warrior spirits. Many masters teach but don't do; avatars are always instruments of change. An *ascended master* is a master who transcended to other planes while in the body.

Saints are the elect of the Catholic Church. The Church basically votes upon who or what might be a master based on certain standards. Catholics are then encouraged to call upon these deceased entities to help with particular problems.

Sorcerers, as discussed in chapter 5, manipulate energy or imagination delusions to bring about their own ends.

Spirit guide is a universal term given to any or all entities that provide wisdom, guidance, or protection. Many individuals source their spirit guides for information about healing. Two lifetime guides always accompany you; others arrive as needed. Usually you have one female and one male guide for balance of instruction. These can be of any sort of source or dimension. Many people have one spiritual being and one deceased relative. One of my sons, for instance, is guided by his deceased grandfather and a female shaman, as well as Jesus.

Extraterrestrials (ETs) are beings from other planets or dimensions. We discussed ETs as natural beings already, and are now introducing them as spiritual beings as well. ETs affect people as incarnated beings, therefore qualifying as natural beings. They also interact with people as discarnate entities, therefore operating as entities. In other guises, they either guide or interfere with humankind. ETs can be at the bottom of severe trauma, including abductions and sexual manipulation. Because ET experiences can also mirror early childhood abuse, you must be careful in determining the exact nature of post-traumatic stress syndrome.

Allies are neutral beings, neither good, bad, nor evil. By challenging someone, allies force the development of spiritual gifts and skills.

Forms are beings that have become so brilliant at their dedicated craft and purpose that they actually transform into a representative of that ideal. The idea of the Forms is inherited from Plato, who described a cave, far from the living, in which Ideals like Justice and Truth dwelled. Here are the most common Forms:

- **Shining Ones.** Beings of love and light that infuse this energy into the material plane. Shining Ones bring a little more heaven to earth.
- **The Powers.** Beings of power and darkness that enlighten this energy for spiritual purposes. The Powers convert earth to heaven.
- **Archetypes.** Beings that evolve into representative types or ideals and hold this modeling for others.
- **Muses.** Beings that hold vital source energy for different and inspired ends, such as art, writing, or music.
- **Ideals.** Beings that exemplify standards we all try to achieve, such as the ideal of mercy, mothering, or kindness.
- **The Virtues.** Beings that actually administer or deliver the spiritual virtues, energies of active love.
- **The Forces.** Beings that are experts at commanding and directing certain forces and can be called upon to select or direct forces as needed.

Sources on the Level of the Human

We often source other humans, alive or dead, for healing, inspiration, and information. The energy of any of these sources can also, however, cause disease or problems. For example, deceased ancestors can interact as many forms, including entities, phantoms, ghosts, and spiritual guides. They can offer healing or hauntings, help or harm.

We can also be our own source of inspiration or of problems. There are many subaspects to the self, each of which might vie for attention or power by causing difficulties. Most mental health therapy involves seeking within to find the "self" that wants attention. Therefore, we can source ourselves by looking for the origin of an issue in the following:

- Body aspects, subaspects, or body energies
- Spirit, soul, and mind aspects, or subaspects of any of these
- Group consciousness

The Body

Your body is the collection of the sensory-based parts of your human self. These typically vibrate at a speed slower than the speed of light. Your body also has energetic parts that can vibrate faster than the speed of light; these allow it to respond to psychic or sensory healing energy, and to all the energetic languages, if it knows how.

People source their bodies or aspects of their bodies all the time. Have you ever felt someone else's pain as your own, felt others' feelings instead of your own feelings, or intuited a disease empathetically? Then you've sourced the body. Here are a few aspects of the body that affect well-being.

The Physical Self There are many subaspects to the physical self, including:

- **The personality**. Reflects a blend of spirit, soul, body, mind, and interjected energies from other sources
- **The ego.** A soul-mind function allowing a current-life identity to incorporate earlier lives and the spirit self
- **Inner children.** The popular name for the subaspects of personality fixated in time due to trauma
- **The innocent child.** The child you would have been if completely united with your spirit self
- **The God self.** The self you would be if united with spirit for all your life
- **The primal self.** The aspect related to the reptilian brain, which functions on passion fed by fear or by love
- **The master self.** The already developed human-divine self

The Heart The **High Heart** links love-based concerns and relationship matters with spiritual truths. This changes the actual rhythm and function of the heart toward health. High Heart can link either with spirit or with soul.

The **Middle Heart** networks group principles—familial, ethnic, cultural, religious, or national—to the individual. Terms such as honor, faith, justice, or truth are therefore encoded into personal relationships and relationship decisions.

The **Lower Heart** links species-based programs and fundamentals to individuals, thus supporting survival.

The Mind Your mind is a collection point of thoughts, thought forms, beliefs, intelligence, charges, consciousness particles, and consciousness waves that connect soul with body with spirit. Here are the differences among the parts of the mind:

The *Higher Mind* contains all the concepts needed to fulfill spiritual destiny. This is the Mind most capable of accessing the Primary or Star-Point Grid and the divine pathway—but also most susceptible to being manipulated by imagination. The Higher Mind runs your higher brain, primarily through the pineal gland.

The *higher brain* is the learning and teaching part of the brain; it includes all the higher learning organs and glands, including the temporal lobes and the pineal-related endocrine system. The most conscious aspect of the brain, the higher brain is capable of all forms of communication, including sensory, psychic, intuitive, and spiritual, and can achieve full consciousness. Neurologically, it relates to your *amplification system*, which interconnects you energetically to everything else in the universe. This system is difficult to track in the human body. Its presence can usually only be tracked through the appearance of certain chemicals emitted by highly evolved individuals from the right temporal lobe and the pineal gland, such as the molecule DMT.

The *Middle Mind* governs relationships, emotions, and reasoning and is the primary link between mind in general and the brain. It links to the *mammalian brain*, the relational section of the brain and central nervous system that includes the limbic and the pancreatic endocrine system. The various glands in the mammalian brain control storage of memory and beliefs and the connection between thoughts and feelings, and they run your *unconscious*, the aspect of the self that directs relationships. Neurologically, the Middle Mind dictates the *digital system*, which regulates the classical nervous system, which in turn runs information as electrical impulses from one point to another. A Secondary Grid system, the digital involves using thoughts to create change. This area can understand the elemental and the power pathways. The *technological center* is located in the Middle Mind, but it is able to link with all three sections of the brain to process technological data for personal or humanitarian ends.

The *Lower Mind* runs physical survival through the *reptilian brain.* This is the fight-or-flight section of the brain; it includes the brain stem, parts of the hypothalamus, the amygdala, and the adrenal functions. The reptilian brain is connected to the *subconscious*, which governs the deepest and inherited desires and behaviors. The subconscious runs the *analog system*, the neurological system that works in waves. More ancient than the digital, the analog system can help manage instinctive injury repair, react to geomagnetic fields, control growth and rejuvenation, and help in achieving a hypnotic state.[2] The analog can access the Secondary or Primary Grids, but is highly susceptible to the imagination pathway.

The Self   The **Higher Self** is a reflection of the spirit or the soul's view of the body. Higher Self can access guidance and healing when needed.

The **Middle Self** reflects the layer of personality governing daily decisions and determining attunement to the mind.

The **Lower Self** is similar to the ego. It links history with memory and uses the past to project into the future.

Connections between the Mind and Body   The Higher Mind, Self, and Heart, and the higher brain can potentially link with spirit or soul. If they are connected to spirit, the pineal gland dominates the body and can access the unity language and the Primary Grid. If they are connected to soul, the pituitary gland runs the body and operates out of the analog system, where it can manage the "spaces" and the "lines" independently in the Secondary Grid. At the highest level, they can then use the language of light; at the lowest, the shadow language.

The Middle Mind, Self, and Heart, and the mammalian brain can run on consciousness waves or patterns rather than just thought forms. The middle levels can develop access to the analog or digital system and use the language of light, heart, matter, or shadow, depending upon the beliefs encoded within the system. The middle levels operate in the Secondary Grid but can potentially seize control of the power levels and achieve free will. The more spiritually based the principles dominating the Middle Mind, the cleaner the unconscious programs in the body.

The Lower Mind, Self, and Heart, and the reptilian brain merge to directly control the body and its physiological responses. The lower layers employ the digital system through the language of matter or shadow and employ the analog system through the languages of shadow, heart, and, potentially, unity. The lower aspects run the body through chemicals responding to communication. The lower levels focus on the power levels in the Secondary Grid. If aligned with spirit in matter (such as the seed of destiny), the subconscious can be freed from the electrical energy surrounding it, thus magnetizing spirit into the actual physical body. This is the process underlying ascension and miraculous cures.

The Soul

Your soul is the aspect of self that moves through time and space, carrying the results of your experiences and generating learning and love. It can be reborn and also linger in the netherlands between lifetimes.

There are several parts to the soul, including *soul fragments*, individual and often independently operating parts of the soul. A soul might fragment due to trauma. These fragments are unified by an *oversoul*—a parenting body usually desiring to unify the fragments. All soul parts have a *soul etheric body*, a charged casing that protects a soul and connects each fragment to the others. A unified soul, one that has never fragmented, has its own etheric body, which can separate from the soul and hold it, the mind, or the spirit's consciousness and thus travel through time and space.

Recession describes the sublimation of a soul or a soul fragment from yourself or someone else within your body, mind, or soul. A soul fragment is a splintered part of the soul. For instance, you might die and leave a part of your soul behind when returning to life, as it is too afraid to try life again. This splintered aspect of the soul remains energetically linked to the remainder of the soul, but can't add its powers to the larger unit. *Possession* occurs when a soul or soul fragment takes over someone else or part of someone else, like the mind, soul aspect, or body.

Soul Relationships Souls are grouped into *soul families*, based upon soul purpose, legacy, cords, and karma. Typical soul-to-soul relationships include the following:

- **Soul mates.** Souls that share similar spirit harmonics, prior soul experiences, or spiritual goals. You'll probably share a lot of past-life experiences and issues with soul mates.
- **Companion souls.** Souls that assist each other in meeting life tasks. Some companion souls become life mates, lifelong friends, or even solid business partners. They might also be members of the same physical family. These are typically positive and friendly relationships.
- **Causal souls.** A causal relationship forces you to become more real and solid in your life and focused on the here and now. Many

troublesome in-laws, difficult marriages, and challenging parenting relationships are causal situations.

• **Cosmic souls.** A cosmic relationship usually carries a high sexual charge and, paradoxically, forces you to examine your spiritual purpose. The explosion of sexual energy activates your first or second chakra, which forces the rise of the serpent kundalini and the transference of the seed of destiny into the physical body. These relationships seldom make it beyond the first volcanic rise of feeling.

• **Twin souls.** Your twin soul is your double or your exact complement. Twin souls often end up trying to become life partners or at least sexual partners. The situation is always a lesson in seeing the self in the other, or in seeing your opposite qualities mirrored elsewhere.

• **Spirit mates.** Here's the ideal relationship and the ultimate goal for personal and sexual companionship. Your spirit mate is the person who totally and completely supports your spiritual destiny and vice versa.

Soul Travel There are a variety of soul techniques for gathering information and healing energy. *Soul journeying* involves traveling via the body etheric, the soul etheric body, the soul itself, or a soul fragment. It could also involve the *Merkabah*, a five-pointed star within the spirit body that traverses all dimensions and planes in order to obtain information, meet with guides, transport to another time or space, or gather healing energy. *Lucid soul journeying* involves conscious spacetime travel; the soul's journeying while the body is sleeping or in a trance state is called *dreamwalking*. When dreamwalking, someone on a lucid soul journey could conceivably interact with a person physically in the room with them, while at the same time the dreamwalker's soul is out and about. This means that a healer can be working on a client while soul journeying to a different plane for energy or information. *Dreamstalking* best describes journeying while entranced in order to accomplish a task. Traveling through the sixth chakra is called *remote viewing*. Remote viewing is like traveling with a camera; you're using visual abilities to look into another zone. You can conduct remote viewing several ways. The basic method involves exiting the body through the sixth chakra to journey elsewhere and, once there, transmitting images back to the physical body. This is not nearly as safe a procedure as projecting your consciousness into a desired situation and accessing while you remain "in your body." *Consciousness journeying* is the safest form of travel and involves expanding your conscious awareness, best done through the divine pathway, into a selected region, dimension, or plane. Better known is *astral travel*, which involves travel on one particular plane of existence called the astral plane. The astral plane is like the center point of hundreds of spiritual and interdimensional highways. Here, you can meet just about any type of being, entity, soul, or consciousness, which must appear in its correct representative form. Someone who is "nice" on the job, for instance, might look like an ogre on the astral plane. In general, the astral plane is a shadowy realm full of mixed beings and thus can be highly dangerous. If you alter your shape or form while traveling, you're working through the eighth chakra—the place of the shaman—in a way called *shapeshifting*.

Some illnesses or problems occur because of soul journeying. *Disassociation* occurs when your soul, after traveling, cannot fully integrate into the body again. You are integrated when you jerk awake out of sleep; that's the sign that your soul has returned. If you continue to feel light-headed or not present, or experience a recurring obsession after a particular evening, head trauma, or surgery, your soul might be disassociated. *Soul entrapment* involves the capture or partial capture of your soul when journeying. *Soul damage* can also occur through journeying, either in flight or at the journey's destination. Nightmares sometimes indicate the result of soul fights, fright, or attacks; other signs include new or renewed problems, illnesses, fears, or issues.

Soul Healing There are many types of soul healing. Shamans usually use *soul retrieval*, which involves rescuing, repairing, and restoring lost or entrapped soul fragments; or *exorcism*, which involves exhuming a soul or soul fragment that is not your own.

The Spirit

The purest expression of self, the spirit is composed of creative source energy and enlightened or illuminated consciousness. It is the whole self, which mirrors the Divine and expresses eternal truth. It is the only part of you that cannot be damaged or destroyed; it merely expands into new lessons about love, power, and grace.

The *overspirit* is the most unified aspect of a spirit. The spirit manifests in material reality through four main parts. The *seed of destiny* is a concrete energy that encodes the spiritual genetics into the body through the subconscious. While physical genes are composed of chemicals and amino acids, which link in chains to determine psychological and physiological characteristics, the spiritual genetics fashion geometric shapes forged from spiritual energies like faith, truth, and hope. The *spirit star* connects one's personal spirit to the unfolding divine plan and is opened once the seed of destiny is unfolded. The spirit star is attached to *star crystals* that tie the material to the spiritual reality, or the Secondary to the Primary Grid. The *spirit body* is the etheric coating within and around a materialized spirit and is responsible for interfacing with the energy system.

The Relationship between Spirit and Soul A soul always has a parenting spirit, but a spirit doesn't always have a soul. Some spirits never reduce into a soul state. In their original states, angels have spirits but not souls. Humans have a soul and a spirit.

A natural being, such as an animal, bird, or plant, might be a spirit or one aspect of a larger spirit but it will not necessarily have a soul. Commonly, for instance, an individual bird is an extension of a unified spirit, which can appear as thousands of individual birds—or just one. The conglomerate spirit could be called a *group spirit.* When the single spirit-bird dies, it reconnects to the larger bird spirit.

Some natural beings are part of a *group soul,* which is similar to an oversoul. This soul group might be connected to its own overspirit. Sometimes, but rarely, a number of individuated spirits might share one or several souls and merge into a single group soul; they would not then share an overspirit. Of course, some natural beings have a soul and a spirit of their own. Included in this group are many members of the faery realm, certain trees, animals including dolphins, and other entities.

Consciousness

There are several consciousness paradigms that can create conditions for illness, mental confusion, financial problems, and spiritual distortions. These paradigms can also engender positive effects when positive and life-enhancing information is shared along the consciousness waves that compose a particular paradigm.

Another word for a conscious collective is *group consciousness.* "Group think" happens when entities merge their energies around a consciousness paradigm. The established collective is very powerful in that it works like a black hole. Free thoughts and beliefs are absorbed into the created paradigm.

There are several key types of group consciousness, each based in the various energy centers:

- **Group mind** describes the network of thoughts and ideals held in common by a certain faction. Group mind usually involves the third and sometimes the sixth or ninth chakras.

- **Group heart** comprises a collective of shared ideal feelings. Religious orders sometimes use group heart to motivate care. Group heart links through the heart chakra.

- **Group spirit** is created when common spiritual beliefs coalesce into a unified philosophy. Group spirit always involves individuals' seventh chakras and frequently the sixth, ninth, or even tenth as well.

- **Group identity** is created when individuals merge values and other identifying factors, such as economic desires, cause-based ideals, or survival drives. Group identity always involves the first chakra, at the least.

The Divine Source

There is only one Great Spirit. The Supreme Being, the Holy Spirit, White Light, God, Goddess, the Divine, the Almighty, the Christ—the names for it go on and on. The Divine is both formless and form, entity and consciousness.

Whatever your own idea of a Higher Power, most religions and spiritualities agree on one important distinction: God is the Creator. God is the One that was never created, a being and a consciousness that goes beyond male or female, here or there. We are talking about the I Am That I Am—the being of Oneness, the One Consciousness, that connects us all through the Divine.

As we've seen, there are infinite sources, but only one truly safe and dependable source: this Great Spirit. When we source the Spirit we have nothing to fear. By sourcing the Divine, we create an upward connection that provides us with downward protection. When we actualize the divine, we are at one with the Creator. This way of being is poetically described in the words of Ygrane, a character in a book, who, like us all, desires to find the treasure of the psychic in this mundane world. In her time, the representative of all Truth is the Holy Grail, or the chalice of Christ.

"Is this chalice yet in this world—or have the angels taken it away?"

"...It is not our work to know, Ygrane." Miriam rose and held forth the nun's veil. "The temporal powers contend in a world of things that cannot last, a world of darkness where objects can be hidden and lost. Come back to the world of things that can never be lost. For I tell you, everything hidden shall be revealed.... There is nothing for us to do, except to open our hearts and relieve the suffering of those around us."[3]

Once everything is revealed, we will realize the Oneness in all things, and by doing so, we cannot help but want to serve others. In the meantime, we must know that there are infinite sources of help—as well as sources that can harm. Only our hearts can tell the difference.

Energy *on* the Pathways

Pathway to Pathway

All pathways interconnect and all move toward Wakefulness in the One Consciousness. What isn't of the One is, over time and through experience, gradually sheared and pruned before becoming the One again. But in the meantime, we're in this space called reality and we're doing this thing called living.

The real movement toward the One involves moving inward. While shifting in, we look out and then around ourselves by interacting with and caring for others. On each pathway we wear different clothes, and so we get to experience new ways of being and doing. We get to see with different eyes.

In this chapter, we're going to compare the four pathways energetically, using the same categories as in chapters 4 and 5.

Elemental Pathway

Here are descriptions for how energy works on the elemental pathways.

Energy Particles and Charges

On the elemental pathway, protons create light matter and reveal physical reality. Electrons compose dark matter and reveal the substance underneath reality. Neutrons can attract dark and light matter for manifesting.

Life Energy and Kundalini

The elemental pathway runs on basic life energy, which feeds the serpent or red kundalini process and activates the managing energy bodies. Basic life energy involves both quarks and tachyons.

Energetic Communication Methods

These are sensory and psychic; when advanced to power, also intuitive.

Energy Languages

In the natural elemental state, these are matter, feeling, and heart.

Energy Bodies

These are the managing energy bodies that are introduced in chapter 2. Methods for working with them are covered in chapters 11 and 12.

Energy Packages

Thoughts direct beliefs, but beliefs also direct thoughts. In the evolving person, the soul uses consciousness waves to oversee the body and the mind. Usually the mind uses thought forms, or paradigms, and runs the body. Most people are trapped in mental and emotional consciousness. Group consciousness is also very strong in the elemental reality. An advanced elemental person operates under the spirit with pure consciousness.

Beliefs Beliefs govern the elemental body, mind, and soul. These are almost always perceived dualistically in correspondence with power levels and power fields. The spirit will hold only basic, or not-charged, beliefs.

Feelings On the elemental pathway, feelings are energetic and physical. As shared by Dr. Herbert Benson, feelings are "dispatches of the brain as it interprets the body's experiences in everyday life."[2] Energetically, feelings are frequencies that receive, decode, and send messages, usually through the second chakra and auric field. Without feelings, you cannot make logical or reasonable choices. You cannot function.

But feelings can also cause injury. On the elemental pathway, feelings can create disease in body, mind, or soul. One of my chiropractor friends says that up to 93 percent of all physical problems are emotional in nature. Stored, repressed, or unexpressed feelings actually alter physical pH balance and chemicals. In fact, feelings can kill. Dr. Stephen M. Oppenheimer at Johns Hopkins Medical School has located a spot in the brain called the insular cortex, which seems responsible for deaths due to extreme fright and "broken hearts."[3]

Elemental-based feelings are usually generated in reaction to memory. Memory is information that we store to help us make more effective decisions. Memory is laid down in the physical body, the soul, the chakras, and certain other energy bodies. Patterns produced by memory are programmed into the mind, the nervous system and brain, the soul body, and the managing energy bodies. Memory can be helpful; it can lead to feelings that give you a necessary message, such as "fire is hot, so don't touch it." Memory can also be damaging, if it causes you to create destructive patterns or strongholds. Healing on the elemental pathway almost always involves dealing with feelings.

Feelings such as happiness and calm can heal, creating the positive attitude that makes life worthwhile. Most of the research on spiritual healing suggests that people who are loved or hold a positive attitude recover from illness sooner, are less depressed, and live longer.

One elemental consideration is to discern whether a feeling is your own or not. Feelings as energetic frequencies can be absorbed into your physical, energetic, or soul bodies from outside sources. You can't deal with or heal from a feeling that wasn't generated from your body. A feeling frequency that doesn't harmonize with your body creates an energy charge—a congestion or disturbance that irritates your system. Left in place, it can create an illness, issue, or problem ranging from slight to life-threatening.

I remember working with a woman who had spent five years in a wheelchair. The medical profession couldn't see anything physically wrong with her. I determined that she had an energy charge blocking her lower spine, which was a feeling that was not original to her. Upon clearing the energy charge of the feeling, she attended physical therapy and could walk again within six months.

I've been asked if positive feelings can lodge in your system, and if this is helpful or not. Yes, joy, happiness, and other exciting feelings can be stored within your system. The truth is, any repressed feeling causes problems, whether or not the feeling is typically considered positive or negative. Feelings are meant to flow freely, carrying toxins and truths out of your system. Anything stuck makes you stuck.

Mental Strongholds Mental strongholds are part of almost every illness, life challenge, and relationship problem and almost always originate on the elemental pathway. The beliefs causing a mental stronghold can come from the following elemental points:

- Family-of-origin
- Geneolgy and legacy
- Past lives
- Cultural, religions, or gender-based sources
- Fields and forces, especially the morphogenetic fields

On the elemental pathway, there are morphogenetic fields around your cells and intercellular bodies; every organ or system of organs; the body itself; the energy bodies; you and your family of origin; your genealogical group; any strong grouping, such as community, ethnic, and religious organizations, an overall religious denomination or type, social club, political groups, or school; your soul and your soul family, groups, or strong relationships; mind groups; consciousness groups; countries; earth planes; and more.

Emotional Strongholds Emotional strongholds can and will cause elemental-based life challenges and relationship problems, distorted feelings, and blockages to power or divine pathways. Emotional strongholds or charges also harm the relationship to the other pathways in these ways:

- Preventing you from accessing your psychic attributes
- Distorting psychic energy or messages
- Twisting or deflecting spiritual energetic forces
- Making you vulnerable to psychic interference
- Locking you into imagination delusions
- Preventing you from accepting divine truths

Patterns, Boundaries, and Habits All elemental healing involves breaking energetic and physical patterns that don't work for health and well-being, as well as establishing the appropriate boundaries. Good habits establish preventive care.

Forms of Energy

On the elemental pathway we are highly responsive to waves, frequencies, vibrations, and harmonics. A low-functioning elemental person will operate mainly on frequencies generated by negative beliefs and strongholds, which will attract negative life issues that match. These destructive frequencies challenge the elemental self's ability to generate his or her personal harmonic. The inability to access or complete spiritual purpose leads to many disorders, including depression and anxiety.

Unless your harmonic is fully invested, your warped energy will attract or distort your position in the Secondary Grid. You will easily get trapped on power levels; the mental or emotional strongholds presenting difficulties will prevent ascension within the power fields. Most individuals get stuck in one particular power field, like that of relationship, and play it over and over. This creates difficulty in positively accessing the power pathway and certainly the divine pathway, though the delusionary imagination becomes more and more attractive the more depressed or stuck you become.

Times and Places

The elemental pathway occupies the first through fourth dimensions, although mind, soul, and spirit can all achieve greater heights. The energy bodies are often used as vehicles for conscious travel to the higher dimensions. The soul achieves the higher planes by following the development of the Planes of Light, reincarnating to complete learning that cannot be accomplished without form.

Energy Laws

These are the laws governing the play of energy on the elemental pathway.

Natural Laws The elemental pathway follows the same natural laws of science as altered by quantum theory's explanation of the Unified Field Theory. Basically, there are laws of motion and field laws. The laws of motion explain how matter moves in certain fields. The field laws explain how the different fields spread through time and space, depending upon the material that composes the field.

Conversion Laws These assume a balance of information-energy exchanged. What is taken must be replaced; what is positive must be balanced by a negative.

Spiritual Laws The ethical application of forces is determined by a being's or object's innate order. This means that if you try to change a pencil into a frog, you are breaking the elemental spiritual law of balance in the universe. However, if you shift a pencil into a frog from a divine perspective that allows it, you are creating more balance in the universe.

Energy Shapes

All shapes affect outcome on the elemental pathway.

Spin and Energy

All spins affect outcome on the elemental pathway.

Sourcing

You can source anything and everything in the five levels of reality from the elemental pathway. Many elemental problems are caused by or can be cured by dealing with sources.

Power Pathway

Here are ways that energy works on the power pathway.

Energy Particles and Charges

On the power pathway, protons hold spiritual forces and ideas, electrons command forces and ideas of power, and neutrons serve as pedestals from which to command.

Life Energy and Kundalini

The power pathway functions on life spirit energy, which carries all frequencies of matter and spirit, plus the spiritual energetic forces. This spirit-based energy joins with basic life energy and allows you to access and move the spiritual energetic forces necessary to free the vital source energy trapped within the body. Upon reaching a certain intensity of spin, you activate the golden kundalini process, which arouses all the power bodies.

Energetic Communication Methods

On the power pathway these are intuitive and spiritual gifting (charismatic gifts).

Energy Languages

On the power pathway these are light and feeling (which is incorporated in light in advanced states), as well as elemental languages when operating in elemental reality.

Energy Bodies

On the power pathway these are the power bodies introduced in chapter 2. Methods for working with them are provided in chapter 13 .

Energy Packages

Consciousness directs the beliefs that run the body and the mind. The power pathway often relies on your access to consciousness waves to command spiritual energetic forces. Based on your consciousness paradigms, you can access any of the sources that are conscious.

Beliefs Only the six primary beliefs exist on the power pathway, although power energies being transferred to the elemental pathway must be stronger than the elemental charges, or the elemental pathway will convert the basic beliefs into positive or negative.

Feelings Feelings are composite material woven into the spiritual forces available on the power pathway. If, from the elemental perspective, we reject a certain feeling, a power force will weaken within our system. If we only allow a certain feeling or set of feelings, the power spiritual forces containing that feeling will become stronger in relation to the other power spiritual forces, and we will be imbalanced.

Here's an illustration. Imagine you've sliced open an electrical cord. Inside are multicolored wires each carrying a different frequency. On the power pathway, a spiritual force like Abundance might contain a yellow cording of fear to frighten you away from bad investments, and a pink strand of happiness to encourage moneymaking activities. If your elemental self believes it is evil to desire happiness, you'll reject the pink part of the Abundance force and greatly weaken your manifesting abilities.

As said earlier, there are degenerative as well as generative spiritual forces. Repressed or interjected elemental feelings can attract degenerative spiritual forces from the power pathway. Instead of attracting abundance, a cache of sadness might attract the Poverty spiritual force.

Feelings often link between the elemental and the power pathways. Strong feelings force us to search for answers outside of the elemental pathway. The Christian Bible, for instance, instructs us to pray with all our hearts.

On the power pathway, the heart's three sections may act as follows: Outreach from the Lower Heart may attract injurious spiritual energetic forces or repel helpful ones. Prayers from the Middle Heart draw practical power help but may reject the most powerful assistance as being not pragmatic enough. Petitions from the High Heart can potentially link us to the divine pathway, through which we're always provided the correct spiritual energetic force for a situation.

Mental Strongholds The power pathway itself does not encourage the formation of mental strongholds, but someone really stuck in elemental strongholds can consciously or unconsciously use the power pathway to strengthen the strongholds.

From a power perspective, spiritual energetic forces are just swirling energies. When brought into the elemental pathway, however, those forces turn us into a version of King Midas, so that "everything we touch turns to matter," as author Brian Hines insists is possible through quantum physics. [4] When a degenerative spiritual force pulled in by a negative stronghold continues to "prove" that life is miserable, the stronghold is enhanced.

A clear example of this dynamic in action was Gladys, who was raised during the American Depression of the 1930s and consequently believes that money is scarce. Gladys wears threadbare clothes and lives in a studio apartment furnished with only a sofa. Well, Gladys won a $400,000 lottery, and within two months she had spent all but $50,000, with nothing new to show for it. She hadn't gambled away the money, but she couldn't account for the expenditures, so she came to me for help. Looking through the power pathway, I perceived a significant Insecurity spiritual force controlling Gladys's first chakra, the energy center in charge of safety, security, and finances. Because Gladys had assumed that money was insecure, she had attracted a spiritual energetic force that supported this decision. Often we're only aware of what spiritual energetic forces are impacting us when we look at what we're manifesting. As Gladys couldn't recall what she had done with the other monies, I helped her shift her beliefs on the elemental pathway while moving in both the Abundance and Security spiritual forces. I then linked Gladys with a financial adviser whom I trusted. After two years, Gladys has increased her banked money to $300,000 and lives in her own house. She also wears new clothes.

Emotional Strongholds Emotional strongholds can distort the feelings in the spiritual energetic charges as they move into the elemental pathway, weaken the needed force, or deflect the necessary forces. I have a young client who, at age twenty-five, had never had a date—and he wanted one. Joshua held deep shame on the elemental pathway, inherited from his father, who had many affairs during his marriage to Joshua's mother. If working the elemental pathway, we would simply have dealt with the shame, extinguished the energy that was not Joshua's, and brought forth his natural shine. However, I didn't believe that this would suffice, as Joshua was such a sensitive person that he would only attract women who would shame his lack of experience. Working on the power pathway, we perceived that Joshua was lacking virtues in the back of his chakras. Believing his dad to be unvirtuous, he rejected a positive perception of himself. Joshua used his intuition to choose which virtues to attract.

I think he turned the corner with the plugging of the virtue of Clarity into his third chakra and Discernment into his first. Suddenly, Joshua made great strides in separating his own issues from his father's, and in seeing himself in strength. He lost his immobility and today is engaged to a great young woman, with whom I can presume—seeing their glow together—he is enjoying a fulfilling sex life.

Patterns, Boundaries, and Habits As on the elemental pathway, we can develop patterns on the power pathway that keep our lives stuck and miserable. Spiritual energetic forces often respond to elemental-initiated issues, although it is possible for bad patterns to develop on the power pathway. Usually, this involves a carryover from a past life, as when we once learned how to use power energetics to command energy and now continue the patterns to our own detriment. I often see abusive individuals actually accessing power abilities unconsciously. In a past life, they used their powers to hurt or manipulate others, and they have continued this pattern unknowingly. Some very sensitive children begin, when young, to experiment with power forces, and can easily trap themselves in spiritual energetics that are too big for them to handle.

I worked once with a six-year-old who, every time she went to bed, was awakened by toys flying around her room. Her parents thought it was telekinesis or a poltergeist, the unconscious application of her own powers or those of entities. I determined that she had been a very powerful shaman in a prior life and that these power-based attributes only awakened when she was sleeping. After I gave her conscious tools to use, she quieted the abilities and settled into the here and now.

Given these and other examples, I recommend that individuals initiated on the power pathway work intuitively to establish good boundaries and habits so that they control the power forces, not the other way around.

Forms of Energy

The power pathway is actually part of both the Secondary and the Primary Grids. The power bodies occupy the Secondary Grid, but they are able to access the spiritual energetic forces of the Primary Grid, such as the spiritual forces, powers, virtues, and rays. Your ability to fully command these energies depends upon your conscious management of thoughts, thought forms, consciousness waves, and the like. In general, the more integrated your spirit is and, accordingly, the stronger your harmonics are, the greater is your power strength. Because the power pathway is so evenly positioned, you can increase your access of the power strength by maximizing your power field percentages.

Times and Places

The power pathway can stretch from dimensions one through six. As the soul progresses through the planes of light, you gain more conscious control of the spiritual energetic forces and natural forces available on all six dimensions.

Energy Laws

These are the laws that regulate the power pathway.

Natural Laws The power pathway follows the laws of the various dimensions and planes of existence. In the first dimension, for instance, you usually can use only points or particle-based forces. The exception is when you're accessing the power pathway through the imagination, in which case it's tempting to draw in three-dimensional energies, for instance, and gain increased power. While this is a valid access to power, it must be conducted carefully, so you don't end up with bigger than life problems, rather than a healing!

Conversion Laws Information is exchanged in accordance with the energy containing it. You can't, for instance, force a paradigm into a thought particle. Energy must contain the information that aligns with it.

Spiritual Laws The power pathway follows the stricture that force follows frequency; the higher vibration of your harmonic, the greater and more intense the force used.

Energy Shapes

Shapes determine the entry point of spiritual energetic forces between the power and the elemental pathways. Shapes also influence the nature and effects of these forces. You can see these shapes on the seals—the chakralike lenses we'll cover in chapter 8.

Spin and Energy

All power energy bodies and spiritual energetic forces have spin, which often determines functioning and effect. Through spin, you can actually convert a natural force to a spiritual energetic force.

Sourcing

The power pathway, like the elemental pathway, is available to energies and entities from several spacetimes. Healing often involves determining whether you are sourcing helpful or harmful sources, and calling upon only those that can be useful.

Imagination Pathway

Here are the ways that energy functions on the imagination pathway.

Energy Particles and Charges

On the imagination pathway, protons create illusions, electrons create delusions, and neutrons make up the place of nothingness. In the anti-world of the imagination, elemental-based electrons are called positrons.

Life Energy and Kundalini

There is no energy on the imagination, therefore there is no form of life energy. Imagination does effect change through belief, desire, sorcery, and intention on any of the pathways, however, and can convince you into a kundalini process.

Energetic Communication Methods

On the imagination pathway, you can use projections of any communication style except spiritual.

Energy Language

On the imagination pathway, the language is Shadow.

Energy Bodies

There are none of these on the imagination pathway, although you could consider the mirrorlike energy between the antiworld and the world to be an energy body of sorts. I use the term the *imagination mirror* to describe the lens centered in a chakra.

Energy Packages

If you hold intent strongly (through imagination) on the elemental pathway, you will exchange "nothing" from the elemental pathway for a "something" from the antiworld through the imagination pathway. Now you've created from your imagination. Fantasy involves believing strongly that the "nothing" in the elemental pathway is already real. Because you're clutching a lie, you don't allow an exchange of matter and antimatter through the imagination pathway and so you continue feeding something that wasn't—and never will become—real. The strongest imagination is fashioned knowingly or unknowingly from consciousness paradigms or consciousness waves, and affects everything and everyone on a weaker frequency. However, a single thought, if untrue, can create a delusion, while a single true thought can form an illusion. Emotional or mental strongholds are often the basis for delusions.

Beliefs The six primary beliefs exist in antimatter on the imagination pathway, but no matter how you illustrate them, they affect you negatively. The imagination belief "I am worthy" will cause pride; the imagination belief "I am not worthy" will create despair. To deal well in the imagination pathway, you must force yourself out of duality and deal with what you want to become, rather than what is.

Feelings Feelings are a basis of imagination delusions. Does voodoo really kill? Does it really work? In a deluded state, the terror of believing in a binding can kill. We must be careful to recognize that "personal feelings can be mistaken for universal truth."[5] Just feeling bad doesn't make us bad.

Mental Strongholds The imagination pathway will mirror your most intense strongholds, creating illusions and delusions from them. The positive advantage is that with consciousness you can direct mental energies to create more supportive strongholds or eliminate the ones that you have.

Emotional Strongholds *Emotional charges stimulate many of the delusions and illusions on the imagination level.* Remember, there are no material energies on the imagination level, but there are charges in that there are anticharges. These charges collect and form the apparitions that we think are real.

Patterns, Boundaries, and Habits The imagination pathway is equivalent to a blank slate. It will mirror the patterns portrayed on the elemental or the power pathway. However, you can read for patterns controlling your life by perceiving your issues in the imagination mirrors between the antiworld and the world. These lenses can be seen in the chakras. The only boundary in the imagination pathway is the lens dividing the "there" and "here." It is dangerous to eliminate this boundary, unless you are fully embracing the divine pathway. Many individuals in mental institutions are imagination experts but have torn the lens in frustration at wanting to see "real reality." Our brains must be trained and our spirits in charge before we can remain sane when merging with the insanity of existence.

Habits are behaviors that maintain certain information-energies in the antiworld versus the regular worlds.

Forms of Energy

There are no energies on the imagination pathway, so there are no real energy forms; however, the imagination pathway is able to duplicate the appearance of any and all energies. A common imagination deception, for instance, is to use a nonvirtue rather than a virtue to create confusion.

Time and Places

The imagination pathway can project onto any dimension, one through eight, and convince people that the others don't exist.

Energy Laws

There are no imagination laws, although anything done in the imagination pathway has consequences according to the laws of the pathway within which the act is done.

Energy Shapes

Lacking energy, there are no forms in the imagination pathway. You can easily perceive the shapes affecting energy on the elemental and the power pathways, however, by reading the imagination lens (called the *imagination mirror*). By changing these shapes with your imagination, you shift energies between the two sides of the imagination pathway and thereby shift reality.

Spin and Energy

The imagination messages convince you to change the shape and spin of particles or waves to conform to illusions or delusions.

Sourcing

Since there are no energies on the imagination pathway, there are no natural or innate sources. Anything and anyone, however, exists as potential on the imagination pathway. Because of this, beings of any sort can project upon the imagination pathway and either help or harm. You can visit the imagination pathway yourself and, by changing energies, make effective changes in 3-D reality.

Divine Pathway

Energy Particles and Charges

On the divine pathway, protons carry the energy of love. Electrons add movement to the stillness of love to create power, and neutrons function as the center point of grace, which is love plus power and the basis for cocreation with the Divine.

Life Energy and Kundalini

Divine initiation speeds up the red and gold kundalini processes and completes both through a process called *radiant kundalini*. Only on the divine pathway are you able to face the deepest human issues, metaphorically contained in the seven bowls representing the seven deadliest human pains, which are described in chapter 8. By drawing upon divine truths, you access the strength and wisdom needed to support the final kundalini process of transmuting pain into love. As I pointed out earlier, this ultimate conversion can take a few months to years, as it is stressful on the body. The illumined self doesn't deal in harsh and complicated healings.

Energetic Communication Methods

On the divine pathway this is numinous, which is spiritual.

Energy Languages

On the divine pathway this is unity, as well as all other languages when needed.

Energy Bodies

On the divine pathway these are the incandescent energy bodies I'll describe in chapter 8.

Energy Packages

The divine pathway packages truth in any or all forms of energies, although they never form a stronghold. Information actually changes form as needed, then disappears into formlessness when not needed.

Beliefs All six beliefs—in natural, positive, or negative form—commingle in the seven bowls of existence, but are not considered true to the fully illuminated. There is only one belief, held in the statement in the Old Testament that describes God: "I Am That I Am." You are a self that can do what needs to be done to express the full self.

Feelings Contrary to popular spiritual opinion, feelings are the most vital and potent of energies available on the divine pathway. Consider the New Testament story in which Jesus raised Lazarus from the dead. It is clear in reading Scripture that Jesus knew that he could and would revive his deceased friend Lazarus. He did not hurry home, despite the fact that Lazarus had fallen ill. Upon finally arriving at Lazarus's bedside, Jesus did not immediately perform the miracle of restoring Lazarus to life. What did he do instead? Jesus wept.

On the elemental pathway, feelings release chemicals that cleanse and produce a positive attitude. On the power pathway, sadness is a component part of all the love-based spiritual forces. Sadness, from a spiritual point of view, is recognition of love. On the divine pathway, feelings link us to the source of all healing: Divine Love.

The divine pathway functions within the elemental pathway because of feelings, thus allowing the entire elemental self to eventually convert the content of the seven bowls of existence to truth. Here's how.

1. You accept your divinity (or original self) on the divine pathway, along with your humanity.

2. Your spirit is activated in each and every core of your being, from cell to soul. Your spirit is able to recognize all needs.

3. In reaction to a need, your spirit generates a feeling.

4. This spiritual feeling causes a reaction. If the need is intracellular, for instance, the spiritual feeling stimulates a biochemical reaction.

5. These changes (as in biochemical) activate the superluminal or generating body.

6. The superluminal body opens to the needed power energetic forces, or releases those not needed.

7. Through the hypersonic waves, the superluminal body ripples messages or healing energy all the way through the elemental self (and power, if necessary). An intracellular reaction will eventually link a chakra to a seal to a divine wave, and an auric field to a power gateway to a spiritual gateway wave. These waves work in reverse through the imagination inversion, also bringing needed energies into each reality-based self.

8. On most pathways, you must sort feelings to determine which are yours and which are not. On the divine pathway, everyone else's feelings are already your feelings. In unity, we share everything.

On the divine pathway, everything is healed before it's a problem, so feelings are merely enjoyable energies used for change and growth. After generating a healing from the divine pathway on the elemental pathway, your spiritual feelings not only heal your own issues, but ripple out to heal others'. This includes healing of and from emotional issues.

Mental Strongholds The seven bowls contain all the falsehoods forming mental strongholds. As you go through the twelve spiritual gates, you are invited to dispel or eliminate these falsehoods for your self and others. When the lies are gone, there are no strongholds.

Emotional Strongholds If occurring on the elemental pathway, emotional strongholds greatly diminish someone's ability to illuminate. The divine pathway can also heal these.

Patterns, Boundaries, and Habits What might a pattern look like on the divine pathway? They do exist, developing from the swirl of all that "could be" when something needs "to become." I often come from the divine pathway to help myself and others break negative patterns from the other pathways and then advance the boundaries and habits that become "good patterns" when locked into place.

For instance, I worked with a woman with loose joints, osteoporosis, and rigid bones. On the elemental pathway, she was caught in fear and her body didn't know how to be rigid and flexible at the same time. This same issue on the power pathway reflected a mix of degenerative and generative spiritual forces; the degenerative were supporting the decaying bones and loose joints, while the generative were solely making the bones unyielding. I worked first from the imagination pathway, to help her see that the fears weren't real. She was then ready to move onto the divine pathway and accept the flow of life, along with her own personal strengths. Within one month, her bone structures tested within the normal range.

Forms of Energy

The divine pathway can use any energy form necessary to accomplish a given task; however, it doesn't need to do so. The divine pathway doesn't exist on any grid system, although it can center itself within either and reflect a truth that will actualize the correct components of a grid to accomplish goals.

Time and Places

The divine pathway operates on all thirteen—and any other—dimensions. It supersedes the need for development on the Thirteen Planes of Light, as the divine pathway involves the absorption and full healing of the soul into spirit, eliminating karma.

Energy Laws

Here are the laws governing the flow of energy on the divine pathway.

Natural Laws On the divine pathway, being the I Am that you are is your most natural state. The divine pathway will support all natural laws that intensify the true self; it will ignore the other laws, or support you in doing so, as they aren't seen as real if they don't help the real self. This is why miracles seem to occur on the divine pathway. If it's not in your highest purpose to die of cancer, natural law through the divine pathway will simply eliminate the cancer. Natural law isn't bent or changed, merely applied.

Conversion Laws On the divine pathway, all knowledge is already known but can only be transferred with truths. Truth based on need dictates what may be converted or not, not logic.

Spiritual Laws These laws adapt to the pathway. On the elemental pathway, the divine will follow the Ancient Laws of the Universe, upon which the universe was created; these include the following:

· **Protection of the Innocent,** guaranteeing that all innocents, such as children and the humble, are to be protected from evil.

· **Law of Clarity,** summoning the correct truth to every situation so that lies are exposed and illusions are illuminated.

· **Law of Abundance,** stating that everyone shall be provided what he or she needs to fulfill his or her spiritual destiny. Children are automatically provided for in parental abundance.

· **Law of Forgiveness,** insisting that the forgiveness was granted before the mistake. Upon owning Divine grace, you accept forgiveness and simultaneously allow the Divine to clear the strongholds underneath your errors.

· **Law of Healing,** stating that the healing has already been done. Through the Divine there is only good, no errors or evil; therefore, by accepting that the Divine has already provided for healing before the illness or problem, you can either erase a problem before it exists, or heal the part of the self that incurred the problem and thereby help the problem disappear.

- **Law of Choice**, maintaining that all beings have the right to choose Divine precepts or not.
- **Law of Consequences**, reflecting the very interesting allowance that there is no punishment; rather, there are consequences that can be delivered before the crime is actually committed, thereby releasing the criminal of the perceived need to perform the crime.

On the imagination pathway, the divine will only show or carry forth truth. Through the power pathway, the divine accesses only the *Wakened Force*, the single thread unifying all power forces. If you're on the divine pathway, all healing or manifesting must be done through willingness and merging of Divine and personal will.

Energy Shapes

The divine pathway will change or hold energy or information in the shape that fits truth.

Spin and Energy

The divine pathway will spin information-energy according to truth and need. Stillness has its own spin, which is maintained.

Sourcing

Everything and everyone is connected on the divine pathway. You could say that simply acknowledging your own illuminated existence automatically acknowledges the existence of everyone else. This means that you are always sourcing others while on the divine pathway. You can, however, decide which energies of others to access or activate within yourself or not and which to leave dormant.

Energy Bodies
on the Pathways

*Healing is similar to
singing a beautiful note
in a chorus and coming
to the note that requires
a sustained tone while
the other singers are
singing other notes in
the background.* [1]

—*Shannon Peck,*
Love Heals

Information-energy is stored, transferred, and translated by the energy bodies that are parts of the human energy system. They are subtle energy structures that vibrate at a slightly higher rate than do your physical organs.

As stated by medical doctor and energy medicine expert Richard Gerber in his book *Vibrational Medicine,* the physical universe is really composed of "orderly patterns of frozen light." Energy bodies, or energy organs, are relatively fixed organs of light that work like prisms. They attract certain energies and convert them into different beams of energies. [2]

This chapter describes the major energy bodies you'll need to understand to work the process of the Four Pathways. For our purposes, the chakras are the connection points between all the pathways. They link the physical and the psychic on the elemental pathway; they open to the seals on the power pathway; they are affected by the illusions and delusions of the imagination pathway; and they are transformed into their healthiest state through the kundalini process finalized on the divine pathway.

Major Energy Bodies:
The Elemental Pathway

There are countless energy bodies serving particular causes on the elemental pathway. The primary ones are:

- The chakras
- The spiritual points

- The auric fields
- The morphogenetic fields
- The physical body

The secondary energy bodies include the causal, mental, emotional or blue, pain, gray, tar, Christ, silver, and physical etheric bodies.

Your energy bodies are encased in the *energy egg* and function with basic life energy.

Primary Elemental Energy Bodies

These are the most important energy bodies on the elemental pathway to use when working the Four Pathway process.

The Chakras These circling units of light regulate your internal body. Across time, most cultures have visualized these energy bodies as spinning wheels of light that transform energy. Chakras are really subtle organs that transform one type of energy into another. Says Gerber, "Subtle energies at the etheric level are merely at a higher octave than the physical."[3]

Contemporary studies at learning institutions such as Duke University and UCLA are actually documenting the existence of chakras. Dr. Valerie Hunt of Stanford University, author of *The Science of Human Vibrations*, has produced striking documentation. Applications of her work are described by healer Rosalyn Bruyere in *Wheels of Light*. Bruyere explains that chakras aren't simply New Age or mystical phenomenon, but actual organs, the sounds and locations of which can be located within the body.[4]

The following chart provides the core information needed to energetically work each of the basic chakras; My first book, *New Chakra Healing*, provides additional in-depth analysis.

Chakra	Location	Color	Overall Mission
First	Genital area	Red	Security and survival
Second	Abdomen	Orange	Feelings and creativity
Third	Solar plexus	Yellow	Mentality and structure
Fourth	Heart	Green	Relationships and healing
Fifth	Throat	Blue	Communication and guidance
Sixth	Forehead	Purple	Vision and strategy
Seventh	Top of head	White	Purpose and spirituality
Eighth	Just above head	Black	Karma and universal linkages
Ninth	A foot above head	Gold	Soul programs and plans
Tenth	A foot below feet	Brown	Legacies and nature

Eleventh	A film around hands, feet, and body	Pink	Forces and energy conversion
Twelfth	Around the body and thirty-two points in the body	Clear	Ending of human self, access to the energy egg

The Spiritual Points These prisms of energy are similar to the chakras, but lie outside of the human field. They link spiritual energy with physical matter. Each point connects to the body via a vertebra of the spine.

Point	Spinal Area	Vertebra
Point 13: Yin	Lumbar	Second
Point 14: Yang		First
Point 15: Balance of Polarities	Thoracic	Twelfth
Point 16: Balance of Similarities		Eleventh
Point 17: Harmony		Tenth
Point 18: Free Will and Freedom		Ninth
Point 19: Kundalini		Eighth
Point 20: Mastery		Seventh
Point 21: Abundance		Sixth
Point 22: Clarity		Fifth
Point 23: Knowledge of Good and Bad		Fourth
Point 24: Creation		Third
Point 25: Manifestation		Second
Point 26: Alignment		First
Point 27: Peace	Cervical	Seventh
Point 28: Wisdom		Sixth
Point 29: Enjoyment		Fifth
Point 30: Forgiveness		Fourth
Point 31: Faith		Third
Point 32: Grace and Divine Source Consciousness		Second
Principle of Love		First

The Auric Fields These graduating layers of light manage the energy outside of your body. Auric fields connect to the chakras, creating a symbiosis between what happens inside and outside of you.

Field	Location	Color	Function
First	In and around skin	Red	Protection of life energies
Tenth	Outside first	Clear/brown	Mirrors programs, serves as a second self
Second	Outside tenth	Orange	Screens feelings and emotions
Third	Outside second	Yellow	Filters ideas and beliefs
Fourth	Outside third	Green	Attracts and repels relationships
Fifth	Outside fourth	Blue	Attracts, repels, and sends guidance
Sixth	Outside fifth	Purple	Opens to choices; projects decisions
Seventh	Outside sixth	White	Connects with spirits and Spirit; broadcasts spiritual decisions
Eighth	Outside seventh	Black or silver	Broadcasts karma and absorbs powers
Ninth	Outside eighth	Gold	Connects with others based on soul issues
Eleventh	Linked with eleventh chakra	Pink	Commandeers forces
Twelfth	Linked with twelfth chakra	Clear	Links with the energy egg; connects human and divine selves

The Morphogenetic Fields These fields of energy surround every animated being, body, organ, or cell on the elemental pathway. (Refer back to chapter 5 for more information.)

The Physical Body The physical body is an elemental pathway body. It is the plane through which we achieve Divine Love in action.

Secondary Elemental Energy Bodies

You will find information for most of these energy bodies in esoteric and energy-based texts. I have indicated which energy bodies became revealed to me as I was unfolding the Four Pathway system.

The *causal body* regulates the physical body.

The *mental body* processes thoughts and beliefs.

The *emotional* or *blue body* holds feelings.

The *pain body* records your relationship with pain and holds the energy of pain itself.

The *gray body* connects you with beings from this dimension and others. I first observed this energy body when working with the gray zone.

The *tar body* holds the codes of your spiritual purpose and spiritual destiny. These and the three energy bodies associated with it became obvious as I worked the Four Pathways, though there are similarities to my observations and those in the *Book of Enoch* regarding spiritual

energetics. These are imprinted upon your *spiritual genetics*, a complex weaving of spiritual principles that support your spiritual truth. That web of spiritual principles includes a *seed of destiny* and, over time, a *star seed of destiny*, which evolves with illumination to serve as a primary source of guidance.

The *Christ body* or *etheric mirror* reflects your essence as human and divine and is a template for physical health and function. This energy body became transparent to myself and a professional colleague, a holistic chiropractor, simultaneously. On the same day, we explored the use of this etheric body to heal clients' physical illnesses. We coined the two names for the body; both are interchangeable, because they describe the two functions of the energy body. The Christ energy marries the human and divine into a seamless whole, as is possible through use of this body. Structurally, the etheric mirror is located in the etheric realms, and mirrors the Christ energy unique to you.

The *silver body* attaches to your *Akashic Records*, the memory of all that you've ever done or said. I observed the silver body when working with a client's *silver cord*, which connects the soul to the body through the fifth chakra. The Akashic Records are available through your eighth chakra and the *Hall of Records*, a universal system of information storage. The *Shadow Records* also can be obtained through the Akashic; these cover what you didn't do, say, or become, though you had the opportunity. The Shadow Records connect to the imagination pathway through the eighth chakra and eighth auric layer, which is why shamans so often work both the elemental and the imagination pathways.

The *physical etheric body*, the layer actually next to your physical body, holds all the energetic programs affecting your health and well-being. This etheric body is the same as the tenth auric layer; it lies just outside of the first auric field, which includes the skin. There are etheric or double bodies around all of your cells, organs, tissues, energy bodies, soul, and soul fragments.

The Energy Egg

The energy egg encases your managing energy bodies and relates to the seventh auric field, then ripples outward to enfold your twelfth auric field. On one side of the twelfth, the energy egg functions as an elemental body. On the other side, it is capable of reflecting all other pathways. It is like the ectoplasm found in the cytoplasm of a cell, with the managing energy bodies paralleling the cell components. This is why it is a useful tool for all cancers, which always involve compromise of physical, cellular walls.

On the elemental pathway, the egg has leaders or threads connecting it to the thirty-two secondary chakra points in the body encompassed by the twelfth chakra, a set of smaller energy centers regulating systems such as joints and muscles. The egg is also linked to the spiritual points lying outside of the physical dimension, and to the power system with tachyon-based threads that connect the managing energy bodies with the power systems.

The egg is a contact point for all four pathways:

- Elemental: Available inside of the egg
- Power: Available inside the casing of the egg
- Imagination: Can be formed out of parts of the egg, specifically through the middle layer of the energy casing
- Divine: Available outside of the egg, especially through the outer layer of the casing

Major Energy Bodies: The Power Pathway

The power bodies link to the energy bodies of the elemental pathway so you can access the spiritual energetic forces, including the spiritual forces, powers, virtues, and rays described in chapter 5.

The primary power bodies are the seals.

The secondary power energy bodies include the *twelve doors*, the *gold body*, the *life spirit body*, the *platinum body*, and the *superluminal body* (also called the *generating body*). I determined the existence of all these energy bodies primarily when working the power pathway. The concept of the twelve doors mirrors text describing the same in esoteric literature including Gnostic and Christian scripture. The gold body was hinted at by a Costa Rican shaman, with whom I briefly interacted. He informed me that something was wrong with my gold energy, which first sent me to search for a gold body. Both a colleague and myself observed the generating body when working with sonic energy for client healing. I describe later in this chapter the origins of platinum body.

The power energy bodies are explicitly connected to the power pathway and are fed by life spirit energy. They also work with the vital source energy of the divine pathway and can transform the basic life energy of the elemental pathway into life spirit energy.

The power bodies are located outside of the fourth dimension of spacetime, so they can't be pictorially described.

Primary Power Energy Bodies: The Seals

The power bodies are designed to contain, manage, and transmit high-intensity energies and forces, but the typical human body is not prepared for them. You are born with boundaries on your chakras that keep you from fully engaging the spiritual bodies and energies until you are energetically ready. These boundaries are the seals.

The seals connect with your chakras and are available through the chakras. They are similar to lenses or protective coatings set over the chakras. Convex or pointed outward until activated, they become concave and able to act as receptacles for the spiritual energies of the universe when activated.

Here are the essential functions or overall missions of the seal for each chakra. (The following information on seals is in part attributed to J. Z. Knight's presentation in her book *A Beginner's Guide to Creating Reality*.) [5]

Chakras	Seals
One: Physical	One: Sets spiritual into matter
Two: Emotional	Two: Social compassion
Three: Mental	Three: Consciousness of self
Four: Relational	Four: Bridge of self to others
Five: Communication	Five: Place of truth
Six: Vision/Choices	Six: Divine choices
Seven: Purpose	Seven: Spiritual purpose/Oneness
Eight: Karma	Eight: "Hereness"
Nine: Soul	Nine: Harmonizing
Ten: Natural	Ten: Universal
Eleven: Commanding	Eleven: Conversions
Twelve: Mastery of Human	Twelve: Fully Divine

When you have fully engaged your conscious self with the Divine, the seals are activated or "set." See the chapter 13 power section about setting your seals and the circumstances that automatically begin the setting process. Only when your seals are activated are your chakras fully engaged on the elemental pathway to manage the spiritual energetic forces available through the power. Setting your seals allows you to access other power bodies and to focus and direct spiritual energies at will.

The seals are much easier to set after you have completed your serpent kundalini process; once set, they enable you to enjoy the benefits of the golden kundalini process. Because they are attached to the Christ body or etheric mirror on the elemental pathway, the seals can potentially be used to direct spiritual energetic forces that will "force" your physical body into its correct design. The etheric mirror duplicates your spirit's standard for your body.

The seals have been described by people since ancient times. References to the seals, usually in association with the chakras, are found in esoteric literature, including the Bible. Upon baptizing Jesus with the Holy Spirit, God speaks and informs the crowd that He has "set his seal" upon his Son. In the Revelation of St. John, the seals are referenced as coverings that, when broken, release beings that cause strife on God's behalf. In Revelation 7:2, an angel arises "bearing the seal of the living God." This angel says "stop" to the four angels about to cause great injury. It says that first it will "set the seal of the living God upon the foreheads of his servants" (Revelation 7:3). In these passages, we see at least two entry portals for the seals: the top of the head and the forehead. More illumination is provided in Revelation 10:4. Here, John is told not to write down what he is seeing, rather to "put under seal what the thunders have said."

It seems that the Divine connects our spiritual purpose to the seal point on the top of the head; protection to the forehead; and communication to points elsewhere. These points are illustrative of the seventh chakra and the pineal gland; the sixth chakra and the pituitary; and perhaps the fifth chakra and the back of the neck or throat.

These three illustrations suggest a seal as a protective coating that has at least three functions: illumination (at the top level), protection, and keeping of wisdom. But there are more chakras and more seals.

In her book *A Beginner's Guide to Creating Reality*, J. Z. Knight, who channels an entity named Ramtha, explores the connection between the seals and the chakras. According to Knight, the digital or binary mind is in charge of what I am calling the elemental pathway. In the digital system, and thus on the elemental pathway, we believe ourselves separate from God. The digital neurological system is considered the linear one that regulates our learned reactions to the world. Through the digital system of our body, we are only active in the three seals of sexuality and survival, pain and suffering, and victimization and tyranny.

But, Knight says, when we allow the analog mind—the mind that is in charge of the power pathway—to come forward, the rest of the seals become animate. The analog neurological system is considered the more ancient and intuitive of our in-body processing. The "bands spin in opposite directions, like a wheel within a wheel, creating a powerful vortex that allows the thoughts held in the frontal lobe to coagulate and manifest."[6]

Knight ascribes the following colors and energies to the seals:

Seal	Color	Energy
First	Rust/brown	Hertzian
Second	Red	Infrared
Third	Yellow	Visible light
Fourth	Ultraviolet blue	Ultraviolet
Fifth	Gold	X-ray
Sixth	Pale rose	Gamma ray
Seventh	Golden rose	Infinite unknown

In general, I agree with Knight; however, I see the coloration a little differently, and I perceive colors for the higher seals. This may simply be a personal rather than universal difference; I encourage you to figure out what color *your* seals are.

Seal	Color
First	Rose-red
Second	Orange-red
Third	Yellow-gold
Fourth	Gold-white
Fifth	Blue-rose
Sixth	Purple-gold
Seventh	White-gold
Eighth	Silver-purple
Ninth	Gold-cobalt
Tenth	Bronze
Eleventh	Rose and gold
Twelfth	White/light

Secondary Power Energy Bodies

Just as your chakras link to your auric fields, so do the seals link to the *twelve doors*. The doors connect with spiritual spheres and dimensions inside and outside of yourself. The doors are not available until your seals are activated. After the seals are set, these doors become various planes of consciousness and they are available via the auric layers. You access doors via auric layers, just as you access seals via chakras. Like the chakras, they serve to protect, filter, and emanate messages. Just as the seals protect us (our elemental selves) from spiritual, power energies until we're ready to handle them, the doors close us off to these higher planes of consciousness until we're ready to be aware of them.

Seal/Door	Plane of Consciousness
One	Subconscious
Two	Unconscious
Three	Consciousness of self
Four	Consciousness with others
Five	Superconsciousness
Six	Hyperconsciounsess
Seven	Ultraconsciousness (opening to divine pathway)
Eight	Inversion consciousness: Ability to be conscious without awareness of consciousness
Nine	Olympian consciousness: Awareness of God within self
Ten	Christ consciousness: Awareness that human and divine are same
Eleven	Mastery consciousness: Awareness of total free will
Twelve	Unity consciousness: I Am/You Are/We Are (human completion of divine pathway); the One Consciousness or Wakefulness

The *gold body* links your soul to others' souls. It is mainly accessible through the area in back of the neck, between the fourth and fifth seals, and allows your soul to harmonize with your spirit and with other beings.

The life spirit body connects with the universal *Book of Life*, a spiritual point of view covering all existences of all spirits. Mentioned in the Christian New Testament, in Revelation, the source of the Book is the Divine, and it is "written" with vital source energy. Everything any spirit has ever done, thought, said, or considered for the fulfillment of its destiny is recorded in the Book. There is a "chapter" on your own spirit within this larger Book of Life. This is your *Personal Book of Life* and can only be accessed by your own consciousness or another person with your spirit's permission. Your personal book is located in your *spirit body*, the etheric body that wraps your spirit into form. Through the eighth seal, you can access others' Books of Life and see how their books impact your own.

The *platinum body* is available through the seventh seal and chakra, the location of the pineal gland. The platinum body can be activated only on the divine pathway. After activation, the pineal has "total control over what will and will not transmit" in the body, leading to a "simple state of knowing," says Laurence Gardner in *Genesis of the Grail Kings*. Through the pineal, we make universal truths real and attainable on the power and on the elemental pathways.[7]

My naming of this body comes after working with it for a while. I chose its name based on research that has found fine granular particles, like crystals in a wireless receiving set, in the pineal/pituitary area.

These particles are linked to findings in a hidden repository of the King's Chamber in the Great Pyramid, where researchers have found a platinum-based powder. Laurence Gardner, in his studies of the Templars and ancient Egypt, relates that this white powder of spun gold has a "stunning effect on the pineal and pituitary glands." He reveals that this powder is comparable to residue from a "Paradise Stone," which, in ancient times, gave youth to the old. If the stone was weighed before being converted into dust, it registered physical mass; afterward, it was said to hold no weight. This stone is proposed not as a stone but a powder produced by striking metal with a high heat, which would establish a certain spin. After spinning, 44 percent of the weight disappears—as pure light, "translated into a dimension beyond the physical plane." What's left can be "made to disappear completely from sight, moving itself into another dimension." What's left? A platinum base. Moreover, it is said that in the right circumstances, the powder can "transpose its own weightlessness to its host."[8] There is science suggesting that the means for accessing the higher planes and miracles is available through a consciousness shift right in our own bodies.

The *superluminal body* or *generating body* uses hypersonic waves to translate energies from the spiritual plane into your physical self. Dolphins, for example, have a sensitive and active superluminal body, which can transmit spiritual energies that can alter feelings and therefore perspective through loving intent.

Major Energy Bodies: The Imagination Pathway

The imagination pathway doesn't have true energy bodies; it exists in a state between form and formlessness. However, the chakras are the basis for imagination work; your major healing tool is the lenslike mirror in the center of each chakra and managing energy body. This lens, which I call the imagination mirror, is often light on one side and dark on another. In most people, the light exists in this world and the dark in the antiworld, although this can be reversed depending upon your personality and purpose. Certain individuals are known as *heyoke*, a Lakota term describing shamans and other individuals who move opposite of everyone else in a community. *Heyokes* bring balance to the whole. In between these two sides lies a no-man's-land comprising the void. You can diagnose or perform healing by looking in either side of the lens or by operating in the center space.

Major Energy Bodies:
The Divine Pathway

The main energies on the divine pathway aren't really organized as energy bodies, only as composites of truth. However, I will refer to these truths as energy bodies so we can better understand them.

When activated, the incandescent bodies of the divine pathway use vital source energy to motivate universal laws and principles for use by anything and everyone. Vital source energy carries illumination rather than information. Energy in information form separates particles and waves. Even on the elemental pathway, a wave can transform to a particle and vice versa, yet these two forms are considered distinct. Illuminated energy melds particle and wave, so that the knowledge carried energetically is both particle and wave at the same time. Hence, a thought like, "I am Cyndi," which is a particle form on the elemental pathway and the power, is wrapped with a wave consciousness, such as, "Women are divine and human at the same time," on the divine pathway. Through the divine pathway, I can energetically be a separate entity called Cyndi, and reflect all human and divine characteristics of being a woman simultaneously.

Consider the application of this melding for healing. I can be a person with a tumor and yet have access to all human and divine healing wisdom, gifts, and properties at the same time. I could move a tumor out of existence before it even exists; or I could accept the tumor as being part of the human race and access divine wisdom through the healing from it.

Energies used on the divine pathway level are formless and timeless and include the *body of the eternal* and the *body of the infinite*. These are related to the seven bowls of existence that are available through the chakras and the twelve spiritual gates available through the chakras, auric fields, and doors of the power. I call these energies *incandescent*, which means glowing as a result of being heated at high temperatures. Divine energy is extraordinarily intense, so much so that it is still and therefore radiates. This is why people who have undergone near-death experiences (NDEs) describe having been met by a conscious, bright white light. Love is so intense, it becomes light.

Energy "Bodies" of the Divine

The body of the eternal is outside of the spacetime dimension and cuts across space. It therefore acknowledges the truth that space both doesn't exist and is also endless. With this knowing, you can create anything needed and in accordance with Divine Truth in any dimension. You could call this body the seed of formlessness. If you can shift into formlessness, you can destroy or create any form.

The body of the infinite also lies outside of all existence and represents the truth of "no time." While time isn't real, within time everything is possible. In timelessness, you can shift away something that currently exists; bring the future into the present or the past; or bring the past forward. The key for working the body of the infinite is shift healing into the here and now as this eliminates the strictures of linear time.

The seven bowls of existence are acknowledged in Revelation in the Christian New Testament. Called the seven bowls of God's wrath, they contain these plagues:

Bowl	Plague
First	Evil
Second	Death
Third	Judgment
Fourth	Power
Fifth	Suffering
Sixth	False miracles (the delusion of imagination)
Seventh	Endings

In my work on the divine pathway, I have come to see these seven bowls as representing the seven delusions we must each individually face—and erase.

These bowls are linked to the *seven lamps*, called the seven spirits of God in Revelation 4 and in Zechariah 4:2–6, which are equated with the one Spirit of God. In Zechariah, each of the seven lamps is seen connected to "seven channels to the lights." The seven lamps represent the seven faces or aspects of the Creator that heal the seven plagues of existence. This means that there are seven "stages" on the divine pathway for healing from all of life's pains. The labels of these stages or channels of light are not provided in Revelation; rather, John is instructed to "put under seal what the seven thunders have said; do not write it down" (Revelation 10:4).

The *seven channels of light* that open to the stages of truth are really the seven primary chakras. A complete and divine-based kundalini process, which combines the red or serpent with the golden, will evolve the chakras to the point that while you're alive and in-body (living in the elemental pathway) you will be able to transmute the plagues in the seven bowls of existence. Thus, you will be assured of the following:

- Complete security through knowing there is no evil (first chakra)
- Continuance of life by understanding that the Creator only creates, so there is no death (second chakra); when the final curtain falls, death is only a means of creativity
- Clarity of knowledge, through release of judgment or belief of the Divine as judgmental (third chakra)
- Unconditional love through understanding of Divine love as the only true source of power (fourth chakra)
- Provision of receiving and providing only godly guidance, for knowing of the delusion of suffering (fifth chakra)
- True vision, for discernment between imagination and reality (sixth chakra)
- Spiritual joy for acceptance of beginnings in the endings (seventh chakra)

In Revelation, the elimination of the seven lies or plagues is followed by the appearance of the "Holy City," seen as encompassed by a great wall with twelve gates. Three gates are found in each of the four main directions; they are labeled according to the twelve tribes of Israel. All the gates are made of pearl.

The Holy City's twelve spiritual gates are the evolved twelve auric fields, just as the seven basic chakras serve as the illuminated seven channels of light.

The wall of the Holy City also has twelve foundations, each made of different stones and of different colors. Through the city flows the water of the river of life; at the banks grows the tree of life. The nations will be healed; there will be no more curses, nor need for light, for all shall be given light by God. Here we see the final conclusion of Wakefulness, the enlightenment from within available to all who choose to serve the "Lamb," the one who showed the way to love God and to love thy neighbor as thyself.

All mystical insight points to the potential transformation available to us all, the state of Wakefulness, at which point our consciousness evolves so as to transmute our problems. We do not lose our human consciousness and knowledge, nor must we die to life to become holy. Our individual selves become holy and sacred spaces, the compilation of all the truths that remain in the human consciousness after we have dispelled the seven bowls—the seven illusions—that we all face and battle.

The Evolution of the Chakras and the Auric Fields

Following are descriptions of how the chakras and auric fields evolve over time, and pathway to pathway.

Chakra Progression

The chakras are the prisms of light that energize you in life. As they pulse, they unite with your elemental-self, creating an interchange between your cells and your mind, your thoughts and your feelings, your needs and your spirit. What seem to be simple instruments are now seen as complicated designs, a testimony to the existence of a Divine Creator.

In learning about the complex workings of the chakras, the self within the self, you begin to understand that perhaps you are more than you seem. There is more to you than meets the eye of the "other," and now you must look within to comprehend the grandeur of being human. Looking within, you unearth the mystery you've always known. You are a reflection of a Greater Mystery. Within this understanding, you see even more of the self than previously assumed.

The existence of the seals is one of the best-kept secrets of the esoteric societies. Look beyond the physical, and you will see what is looking at you. The opening of the seals advances you into the previously unknown universe, the power pathway.

The stellar nature of the power pathway invites you into a playground of power. You could spend forever, as some do, mastering the movement of spiritual energies—spiritual forces and rays, virtues and powers, colors within colors, a kaleidoscope of possibilities. Now, you have the means for forging possibilities into three-dimensional reality.

As chakras open to the seals, so do the seals invite you into nothingness. Advancement into the imagination pathway can seem like a step backward, until you learn the power of accessing the chakra-centers to move dreams between nonreality and reality.

The person set in power thinking must now overcome the greatest challenge of all: Access to all-power. Imagination maestros can do anything they want, and at will! A quark "there" is a tachyon "here." The flick of a thought, you can create what you desire. Another blink of an eye, you can take away what someone else has. Only by learning compassion do you evolve to a greater challenge: the sublimation of your will to Divine will, the entry pass to the Divine.

As you conform to Divine will, your chakras begin to illuminate your Awakened state. As you entrust the Divine with your life, so does the Divine begin to trust you with divine powers. The basic seven chakras are now known as the seven channels of light—conduits for coping with the seven bowls of existence, the representations of human suffering. Gradually we realize that we must heal from not only the evils done unto us, but the evils we've done unto ourselves. We must heal not only the self, but also others. By serving others, we serve the self.

Major Energy Bodies

Elemental Pathway	Chakras	Auric fields
Power Pathway	Seals	Doors
Divine Pathway	Channels of light	Gates (of the Holy City)

What's the exact formation of the chakras, in relation to the Four Pathways? The chakras and the seals are corresponding but separate energy bodies. However, the setting of the seals enables the chakras to operate at a higher functional level than when working only for elemental purposes. The seals can be pictured like lenses that "plug into" the chakras in their centers. At this center is the convergence point for all pathways through the chakras. Here is the chakra center of the elemental pathway and the interface between the seals and the chakras. Here also lies the lens of the imagination, allowing exchange of antiparticles and particles. Through this center point, the truths of the divine transform the chakras into channels of light. These channels completely integrate physical and spiritual matter into perfect balance. In each chakra, you find the exact needed amounts and types of minerals and elements, forces and energies, particles and waves, truths and learnings. This balance allows you to operate as a full human and divine being while in your body.

Likewise, the auric fields conform and develop with each consciousness and pathway shift. The power doors are actually a higher and evolved state of the basic auric fields. When evolved, the auric fields still psychically look similar from an elemental point of view, but they glow with new shades and colorations. When changed again through divine understandings, these fields-doors become incredible walls of light. The lesser qualities of the elemental-based auric field are transmuted to allow inspiration of spiritual truths into the elemental self.

Ancient societies understood the transformation of the chakras, and the transcendence available through the chakra passageway. I like the ideas set forth by Elizabeth Haich in her book *Initiation*. She explains that the human being radiates seven octaves of vibration through "nervous centres corresponding to the seven octaves of transformed and untransformed creative power." Haich believes that these centers remain latent until a person becomes "conscious on a given level."[9] These centers are the in-body chakras.

Haich lays out an evolutionary path for human development by explaining that most humans learn how to vibrate to what she calls the fourth level, which is equivalent to the elemental pathway. More advanced individuals access the chakras to gain a fifth level—which she terms the place of genius, and which I call the power pathway. The prophet reaches the sixth level, which I call the imagination pathway, but the "God-man"—the person fully conscious of Divine self—can radiate all seven octaves and transform, change, or transmit higher energies into lower energies at will. Haich's "God-man" is the illuminated self, now using the chakras as conduits of Divine Light so as to serve the Divine will for humanity.

Auric Field Progression

You begin life chiefly associated with the elemental pathway. Though you won't be taught about your twelve auric fields at school, your personal development requires learning about them, for they constitute the self outside of the self. This learning may or may not be conscious learning. The development of the auric fields is something every human goes through naturally, as part of the human development process, although not all are aware of it or label it as such. As you struggle to gain control of these energies—and therefore of your elemental self—you evolve to higher powers and goals. The twelve auric fields, when set through the power seals, translate into the twelve doors, corridors for the spiritual energetic forces needed to seize command of your life. You now explore the power pathway and learn how to run your own life, rather than be a victim of circumstances.

Inevitably, you hit a wall. No matter how hard you apply your newfound and developing powers, one or all of your gifts seem to stop working. You begin to feel that nothing is as it seems. Seeking insight, you are welcomed into the imagination pathway, and find yourself suddenly swirling in a sea of confusion. It's really true that nothing is as it seems! As you learn on the imagination pathway, everything emerges from the state of nothing, and no matter how many spiritual forces, virtues, or commands you access, it's now finesse that counts, not strength. You graduate to the lesson of the imagination pathway, the creation of something from hope.

If you understand shadows, if you can endure the imagination pathway, if you can accept ambiguity and the reality of what doesn't exist, you gradually learn how to invert reality, how to summon what you need from the void, and how to send what you don't want back into the void. There is no form in the imagination pathway. Now you learn to know yourself as formless.

But formlessness isn't the only truth. Pinch your skin. Analyze your auric fields with Kirlian photography. There is also form! And so, you reach onward, attempting to find a way of knowing that incorporates all sides of duality, the truths of form and formlessness, speed and stillness, noise and silence. You transcend into the divine pathway.

On the divine pathway, the twelve doors serve as portals to the twelve spiritual gates. These spiritual gates, the foundation of the Holy City of the Wakeful self, still function as did the originating twelve auric fields. The gates are part of the wall that surrounds the self. What does a wall do? It protects. It screens. It filters. It keeps out what is not yours, and keeps in what is good for you. The spiritual gates are the doors, the auric fields.

A long time ago, I was intuitively instructed as to the existence of the twelve spiritual gates and provided the names and logic of each. I consider this information reflective of the twelve spiritual gates on the divine pathway, which reflect the evolved auric field. Each gate is instructional, which means that we must learn the lesson of the gate to advance to an Awakened state. As you know, the everyday life provides more than enough learning opportunities. You don't have to search them out.

The following table provides an outline of the twelve spiritual gates of the divine, compared with the auric field powers enhanced by the power pathway and the basic purpose of each auric field on the elemental pathway.

Physics speaks truth in theorizing that certain particles exist only when you see them. Only the artist within, however, asks the pertinent question: where are these particles, these waves of consciousness, these telltale truths, when you're not seeing them? The imagination master has an answer: they exist, they linger, on the other side of reality, through the mirror of the imagination pathway.

Auric Field	Elemental Function	Power	Divine Truth
First	Assures security	Gives or takes life	Forgiveness
Second	Regulates feelings	Directs the feelings in forces	Manifesting
Third	Obtains knowledge	Analyzes knowledge for Truth	Illusion
Fourth	Orders relationships	Creates and dissolves relations	Completion
Fifth	Processes communications	Manages communications	Light
Sixth	Screens insights	Creates future	Relationships
Seventh	Filters spiritual energies	Directs spiritual destiny	Infinite Faith
Eighth	Regulates elemental forces based on karma	Manages spiritual energetic forces	Creation
Ninth	Screens energy based on soul programs	Connects and directs soul energies	Choice
Tenth	Adjusts to nature	Accesses and directs natural and nature-based spiritual energies	Grace
Eleventh	Screens forces	Summons and commands all forces	Renewal
Twelfth	Maintains human boundaries	Connects human with divine	Freedom

part four

Energy Mapping Tools »
Getting in Gear for Health and Healing

The Crystal Ball for Psychic Mapping

"You're still not moving slowly enough," Hank insisted. "You're still not feeling the dark. Did you ever watch the way a blind man knows an obstacle's in front of him, even if he doesn't have his cane? It's because he's so used to living in the dark that he can feel the air bounce off his surroundings. He can sense things around him, almost as if they give off vibrations. And that's what you've got to learn to do."[1]

—David Morrell,
The Fraternity
of the Stone

Y̲ou have a crystal ball inside of yourself: your psychic ability. It's the key to making a healing diagnosis, mapping energy, obtaining guidance, manifesting, and moving around the Four Pathways. To energy map for healing, you will need to figure out your major psychic gift and learn how to access it.

We're all born with innate psychic gifts; they are necessary for our survival. In years past, these attributes told our ancestors which herbs to pick for healing and when to shelter from an impending storm. Throughout the ages, most cultures taught the individuals who showed the most talent with these gifts to access and use them for tribal benefit—most cultures, that is, except our contemporary one.

Psychic means supernormal, but this term does little to explain the real nature of the gifts. *Psychism* is the ability to convert tachyons to quarks and back again, to change fast-moving information-energy into slow-moving information-energy and vice versa.

The first step in working the Four Pathways is to own your psychic gifts. To do that, you must determine which are your strongest gifts, because those are the ones you'll want to use when working the pathways. This quiz will help you begin pinpointing your specific gifts.

» Psychic Sensitivity Quiz

Directions: Circle the number that shows how strongly you agree with the statement. Zero means you don't agree at all, five indicates that you strongly agree. You will score and tabulate your results at the end of the test.

1. When someone tells me about a gruesome event or a physical trauma, I feel the physical sensations of the event in my own body.

   0 1 2 3 4 5

2. I feel others' feelings as if they are my own.

   0 1 2 3 4 5

3. I know information that I have no reason to know.

   0 1 2 3 4 5

4. I would be a good matchmaker. I know who should and should not be with whom.

   0 1 2 3 4 5

5. I sense that my words are guided, that they come from a "higher place."

   0 1 2 3 4 5

6. I get visions or pictures that tell me what to do.

   0 1 2 3 4 5

7. I know how God or the Divine would think about a certain situation.

   0 1 2 3 4 5

8. I know that there are other worlds and that I visit them.

   0 1 2 3 4 5

9. I run my life on ideals.

   0 1 2 3 4 5

10. Nature sends me signs and omens to guide me.

    0 1 2 3 4 5

11. I can command natural and supernatural forces.

    0 1 2 3 4 5

12. I can pick up an object and sense the mood, personality, or appearances of people connected with it.

    0 1 2 3 4 5

13. I know what others are feeling, even when they aren't visibly showing emotions.

    0 1 2 3 4 5

14. I get "gut senses" that are accurate.

    0 1 2 3 4 5

15. I seem to know who is ill and what will help.

    0 1 2 3 4 5

16. I hear words or messages that don't come from any outside tangible source or from my own mind.

    0 1 2 3 4 5

17. I see images of the future that often come true.

    0 1 2 3 4 5

18. I know what God or the Divine would do in a situation.

    0 1 2 3 4 5

19. I like to learn about power and powers.

    0 1 2 3 4 5

20. I can sense what's going on in someone else's soul.

    0 1 2 3 4 5

21. I would like to help people to access the healing properties of nature.

    0 1 2 3 4 5

22. I would like to be able to change the weather at command.

    0 1 2 3 4 5

Review the following statements; choose for only the one that you relate to most and circle the five for that one. Circle a number from one to four for each of the other questions.

Complete the statement "If I had one wish, it would be…"

23. To snap my fingers and make something concrete appear

    0 1 2 3 4 5

24. To take care of everyone's negative feelings

    0 1 2 3 4 5

25. To eliminate prejudice

    0 1 2 3 4 5

26. To wake up in the happiest relationship imaginable

    0 1 2 3 4 5

27. To hear the Divine speak to me whenever I need guidance

    0 1 2 3 4 5

28. To see all my choices and their results clearly whenever I needed

    0 1 2 3 4 5

29. To know what the Divine wants done in any given situation

    0 1 2 3 4 5

30. To access any world, spirit, or power to get something done

    0 1 2 3 4 5

31. To cure the world of just one of its major problems, such as poverty or hunger

    0 1 2 3 4 5

32. To cleanse the environment of all chemicals and pollutants

    0 1 2 3 4 5

33. To use any force, such as moving objects or changing weather, to get something done

    0 1 2 3 4 5

Scoring and Interpretation

Fill in the numbers you chose for each of the following sets of questions and add up your points for each.

All the gifts are transferred into the body through the chakras, which are each paired with a corresponding auric field. Each question set corresponds to one of the chakras and the basic psychic gifts associated with it. The question sets with the higher total points indicate which chakras house your strongest gifts.

Questions	Total Points	Chakra	Psychic Gift
1, 12, 23		One	Physical sympathy
2, 13, 24		Two	Feeling sympathy

3, 14, 25	Three	Mental sympathy
4, 15, 26	Four	Relational sympathy
5, 16, 27	Five	Verbal sympathy
6, 17, 28	Six	Visual sympathy
7, 18, 29	Seven	Spiritual sympathy
8, 19, 30	Eight	Shadow sympathy
9, 20, 31	Nine	Soul sympathy
10, 21, 32	Ten	Natural sympathy
11, 22, 33	Eleven	Force sympathy

Read through the following descriptions of the chakra gifts to determine your most available abilities.

Chakra Psychic Gifts

Chakra One. Physical sympathy. You are highly physical, and your own body will feel what's going on in others' bodies. You can pick up objects and get information about them and their owners. You can trust what your body tells you about the world and other people.

Chakra Two. Feeling sympathy. You are feeling-oriented and sense others' emotions as if they are your own. You easily read others' emotions and often communicate through feelings.

Chakra Three. Mental sympathy. You interpret psychic data and are good at categorizing this information. Follow your "gut sense"—also called clairsentience or clear sensing—for accurate perception.

Chakra Four. Relational sympathy. You easily sense what's going on relationally for yourself and others, and you can often intuit others' heartfelt healing needs. Trust your inner wisdom around healing and relationship issues.

Chakra Five. Verbal sympathy. You are able to receive psychic information as tones, or as verbal or written messages. Use this verbal gift to source auditory messages. This gift is often called clairaudience, or clear hearing.

Chakra Six. Visual sympathy. You can picture psychic information in pictures, symbols, colors, or shapes. This gift is often called clairvoyance, or clear seeing.

Chakra Seven. Spiritual sympathy. You can sense the presence of spirits or of the Divine Spirit. You can learn to know God's will.

Chakra Eight. Shadow sympathy. You can walk among dimensions and the various worlds of existence, calling forth powers, energies, and information. You can read the Akashic Records and look for curses, bindings, and other control techniques. This gift is shamanism.

Chakra Nine. Soul sympathy. You can read what is best or ideal for the world, as well as for individual souls. You can interpret the patterns and symbols that support souls' purposes and understand relationships as soul relationships.

Chakra Ten. Natural sympathy. You can work with the psychic information that is in the environment or provided by ancestral entities. You also can interpret the signs and omens of earth, sky, and planets and can call upon power animals, totems, and natural spirits.

Chakra Eleven. Force sympathy. You can read the signs of forces and powers, such as the elements, winds, and spiritual forces, and summon these at will.

Psychic Styles

The chakra gifts are organized into *psychic styles*. Most individuals have more than one strong psychic gift; these interact as psychic styles. A psychic style is similar to a learning style. For instance, there are individuals who academically learn most easily through movement; others, through hearing; and still others, through seeing. In the same way, individuals will access psychic data in a particular way.

There are four basic psychic styles:

The physical kinesthetic style. Chakras one, two, three, ten, and eleven work with a lot of sensory information as well as psychic information. You can feel, touch, or sense the world through these chakras and use the energy of these chakras to produce physical change.

The spiritual kinesthetic style. The gifts of chakras four, seven, eight, and nine also provide kinesthetic or sensory-based information, but of the spiritual nature. Psychic messages here lead to understanding that can be used for action and are ideal for accessing power energies.

The visual style. Chakra six is the source of visual psychic information and can be used for psychic seeing. You can also see through the eighth chakra and the pineal gland, which when illuminated is a highly evolved psychic organ.

The verbal style. Chakra five is the source of verbal psychic information and the channel for words, tones, and noises. The third chakra often provides information for the fifth, as do the eighth and the tenth.

You may have one or many strong chakras and more than one psychic style. When energy mapping, you want to use your most potent abilities, yet still consider the psychic and sensory information available through your less strong chakras.

Safety and Psychism

Most psychic processes, including prayer, meditation, contemplation, and energy mapping, are best performed using basic safety techniques. These techniques keep you immune from interference, centered in your own personality and space, and clear about the information received. You conduct psychic safety procedures a little differently on each pathway, but the process will typically involve following these five steps.

Five Steps for Safe Psychic Use

1. **Grounding and centering.** Grounding involves anchoring your consciousness in a secure and trustworthy substance, such as the

earth itself, a place of knowledge, a natural or spiritual force, or a spiritual quality. Centering involves locating your full conscious self where you can access all your gifts and truths. You can center in a part of your body, an energy center, a concept, or a truth.

2. **Establishing parameters.** Boundaries keep us inside of ourselves, and keep what could harm us outside of ourselves. There are different forms of boundaries for each pathway. On the elemental pathway, you must set physical and psychic boundaries to stay intact and to screen data. On the power pathway, you establish boundaries made of various forces and energies, so that you always work with ones that harmonize with your spiritual self. On the imagination pathway, boundaries separate the antiworld and this world and help you decide which realities you want to create and where. On the divine pathway, boundaries involve radiating from your center point, thus illuminating truth. What isn't truth is encompassed in something greater so that it can't hurt you. You can establish correct parameters on each pathway by using the principle of each pathway. Use intention on the elemental pathway, commanding on the power pathway, imagination on the imagination pathway, and petitioning on the divine pathway.

3. **Conducting the goal.** Proceed with your objective, whether it involves healing, manifesting, obtaining information, achieving peace, or striving toward any other goal.

4. **Release energies.** In the course of achieving your goal, you may have freed energies that now need to be released. In the chapters on each pathway, there are exercises for getting rid of energies that aren't your own, processing feelings, and doing any other such tasks that may be necessary.

5. **Center, ground, and reestablish parameters.** Return to your center as a way of returning to your everyday self. Ground in the appropriate energy and then set parameters for everyday functioning.

You will find it easiest to perform psychic maneuvering in certain chakras rather than others. Most of us have a single psychic center that allows us to best access our psychic gifts.

Your Psychic Center

I have developed the following exercise to help you define your *psychic center*, the chakra that will mirror your spirit's interpretations of psychic data. This exercise is conducted in several steps. It helps you to (1) select the most ideal chakra for your energy mapping, (2) help heal and spiritually infuse this chakra to ensure accuracy, and (3) use the chakra to screen and assimilate all chakric data.

Step One: Selecting Your Psychic Center Chakras gather sensory and psychic information, so your psychic center will relate to both your everyday world and your spiritual world. No matter which is your strongest psychic chakra, I recommend that you use your third, fourth, fifth, or sixth chakra as your psychic center, for several reasons. First, your in-body chakras must be represented if you are to work the elemental or power pathways. The elemental pathway is entirely physical; many power and even imagination techniques will incorporate body energy. Second, the kinesthetic nature of these chakras allows for the sharing of feeling, sensation, knowing, vision, and verbal insight. Third, it's easy to bring your full spirit and complete set of psychic gifts through any of these chakras.

You may already have a sense of your psychic center. Do you intuitively use one chakra rather than the others on a regular basis? Would you say that you are a stomach, heart, throat, or eye person? A logical way to select a psychic center is to consider the types of information most easily processed by these four chakras.

Third chakra. Mental processes, thoughts, beliefs, fears, and judgments. Ideal for individuals who are physically kinesthetic.

Fourth chakra. Relational concerns, feelings, ideals, and values of healing and love. A good choice for people who are spiritually kinesthetic.

Fifth chakra. Communication processes, verbal ideas, tones, words, or knowledge. Best for individuals who are verbal.

Sixth chakra. Visual procedures using images, strategies, long-term thinking, and clarity. Ideal for people who are visual.

Select a psychic center and prepare for the next stage of this exercise.

Step Two: Ordering Your Psychic Center With knowledge of your preferred psychic center, you are ready to prepare it for full psychic functioning. Use the "Five Steps for Safe Psychic Use" as a baseline for performing this exercise.

Settle into a meditative state. Now connect with your psychic center. If you are using the third chakra, you will sense your connection with your solar plexus. If accessing your fourth chakra, breathe into your chest and heart. If devoted to your fifth chakra, use language and words to bring yourself into your throat; tell yourself that you are now centered in your fifth chakra. If linking with your sixth chakra, visualize yourself standing in the middle of a bright purple light in your forehead.

You have now placed your consciousness in your psychic center. To transform this chakra into a meeting ground of accurate information, simply permit your spirit to fully infuse itself into this chakra. Give permission for any needed healing and then ask your spirit to structure the chakra for full psychic functioning. Sense, watch, or ask to be informed of the results. You will find that all your chakras are now able to advance knowledge into this single chakra, which screens for applicability and accuracy before assembling the information into usable data.

Step Three: Using Your Psychic Center When energy mapping, you will be using your psychic center to feel, sense, hear, or visualize the data you need to perform pathway healing. Regardless of the specific pathway, your psychic center will admit only spiritual truth and, therefore, useful information.

It will be helpful to engage your psychic center before you start learning how to energy map. Here are a few brief ways that you can practice in your everyday life. You can use "The Five Steps of Safe Psychic Use" to perform any of these exercises.

Prayer. Communicating to God. Linking with your spirit, which is fully invested in your psychic center, think of a question or a concern you would like to send to the Divine. Know that a response might come now or at a different time.

Meditation. Receiving answers from God. Establishing your consciousness in your psychic center, set forth a question of the Divine. Breathe deeply and allow a response to come to you.

Contemplation. Experiencing God's presence. Simply experience the nature of this psychic center and your own spirit within it. Remain in this state of openness until you completely realize the vibrant relationship between your own spirit and the Divine Spirit.

Diagnosis. Request a first-level or brief diagnosis of a particular problem by first centering in your psychic center. Now relate to a presenting problem, making sure you give permission to feel, sense, experience, and accept the problem as having merit and a gift. Ask to better understand the cause of this situation. Instead of concentrating on a solution, work on accepting the validity of the concern.

Problem solving. After doing a diagnosis, open to input from your own spirit and the Divine. What actions, attitudes, thoughts, or energies will alleviate your concerns? What will bring you back into balance? What would help you reassert your innate condition of being whole?

Decision-making. Think of something as simple as selecting a grocery store. From your psychic center, ask yourself which store carries the food that is healthiest for your body. I recommend that you work your psychic center for the most seemingly normal of issues to gain confidence in your abilities.

Psychic Mapping

Accessing information from all the chakras is called *psychic mapping*, an invaluable and necessary process for accurate energy mapping. Psychic mapping involves using your spirit to gather, screen, and assimilate psychic information from all chakras through a single chakra, in order to energy map for healing.

Although you will naturally depend upon the psychic data that is available through your strongest chakras and organized through a psychic style, all of your chakras busily communicate psychic information. At any given time, your first chakra is perceiving data to inform you about your physical body and the physical universe. Your second chakra happily processes your own and others' emotions, while your third chakra gathers and disseminates thoughts, fears, and judgments. Each chakra spins in its own orb, sorting and sending, attracting and aiming psychic information, independent of the other chakras. Yet getting a good energy reading depends on the sharing of all chakric information.

To be accurate, psychic data must be valid, applicable, and complete. To ensure this, you must gather information from all the chakras and screen it for accuracy. It does little good to know what your first chakra says about a cold if you don't also consult your other chakras. Nor is it useful to collect data unless it is useful and correct.

I'll give an example from an age-old fable. As told, six blind men surround an elephant from six different sides. Each touches a different part of the elephant to draw his own conclusion of the beast. Do you think the man in the rear arrives at the same conclusion as the man near the tusk, or on one of the elephant's sides? Perhaps our front man will decide that the animal needs a nose reduction, and our rear guard will set about happily swinging on the "string" he has discovered. None of the ideas are wrong, but none of them provide a fully accurate illustration of "an elephant." You must create a composite of all views to establish a complete picture. To gather complete psychic input, you must be informed of every chakra's point-of-view. All the chakra perspectives must then be woven together in a unified and correct whole. The easiest way to achieve this goal is to assemble psychic data into a single chakra. You must select a chakra for this task, one that is healthy and able to accurately weave a summative picture. This means that the chakra must be converted to a spiritual center, fully infused and aligned with your spirit—the only part of you absolutely able to see and share truth.

Your Psychic Gifts and Pathway Change

But I'd forgotten one of Father Ruley's maxims— Change is good. It's necessary. It defies evil. [1]

—Cathy Maxwell, The Seduction of an English Lady

Psychic mapping is the key to working the pathways for healing. As you develop your psychic mapping ability, you will find that it enables you to perform two very important tasks:

· Gathering information

· Making changes

Most psychic practices concentrate on collecting and interpreting information. Of course, it's imperative that you understand the core of an issue. It's important to know what you can do to solve problems. If you stop here, however, you are shortchanging the gift.

The psychic sense can be used not only to see reality, but also to change it. I worked with one highly visual client who was a whiz at predicting the future. Clara received nightly dreams that suggested events of the next day, and she was smart enough to use the insights to her advantage. If her inner sense suggested a stock-market fluctuation, she decided whether to sell or buy. If she'd dreamed of dark and stormy skies, she brought an umbrella to work, no matter how sunny the day started.

But Clara wasn't happy with her gift, because of the revelations of a more tragic nature. Every so often, she would envision a disaster. Once, she imagined that her friend was in a car accident. The accident occurred and her friend died. Another time, she awoke screaming, sensing the thud of a plane while picturing a flaming ball falling from the sky. That was the evening of September 10, 2001—the evening before terrorists hijacked airplanes and flew them into the World Trade Center in New York City and the Pentagon in Washington, D.C. So Clara was periodically afflicted with insomnia. She didn't want to perceive a reality that wasn't kind.

Most psychic development experts would do as I first did for Clara. I taught her the basics of psychic boundaries. Over time, Clara learned how to screen incoming and outgoing data so she could select the type of information she wanted to know. This conscious management of psychic data is called intuition rather than psychism.

I came to realize that simply monitoring information wasn't enough. Clara had a gift. Why not fully use it? Once Clara excelled at intuitively managing her psychic abilities, she moved on to exploring the dreamlike qualities of imagination. It took her awhile to discern the differences between being imaginative and creating fantasies. Finally, Clara was ready for the leap into the divine—the access of all gifts simultaneously as a whole. Understanding the numinous evaded her at first, until she realized that there are no limits on the divine pathway. (You don't have to receive revelation and then figure out an interpretation; you can actually first understand a truth and then fashion a vision, sense, or word that applies.) As Clara began to read herself and the world around her through the numinous, she decided she needed to incorporate her gifting into her work as a physician. In essence, she transformed her intuitive abilities into an advanced state of spiritual gifts. She now asks patients if they would like "feedback" in addition to medical tests, providing this input in an office separate from her medical one to distinguish the work for herself and her clients.

As you can see, psychic information can be gathered and used differently according to the various pathways.

Psychic on the Pathways

On the elemental pathway, the psychic sense is most easily used to receive and send information. If you want to create pathway change, however, you must learn how to consciously direct the psychic sense for higher ends. This involves evolving the psychic sense to the intuitive. An elemental-based healer now evolves into self-management.

Here is an example of how a problem might be addressed on the elemental pathway. Joe Blow might be poor because he lacks financial skills. No one taught him how to balance a checkbook, pay his bills on time, or show up for work. A solid psychic reading or energy map will highlight these and other issues on the elemental pathway. With this data in mind, Joe can construct a plan for change. He can meet with a banker and learn how to use a checkbook. He can attend job training classes and buy a watch. The plan involves the use of the psychic sense, or the gathering and interpretation of data.

Pathway healing, however, can provide Joe with other answers. Intuition is available on the elemental pathway. By thoughtfully managing his psychic processes, Joe can decide to perceive helpful psychic data and ignore the opposite. He can "tune into" others' positive and supportive thoughts and reject others' judgments and criticism. Thus feeling better about himself, he will be more likely to perform well at work and gain financial stability.

He shouldn't skip the use of the psychic sense and the practical elemental actions, but why not speed the process, perhaps by learning to use power resolutions in addition to elemental solutions? The intuitive also opens the door to the power pathway.

On the power pathway, Joe might perceive an entirely new way of working toward prosperity. Now his psychic sight might spy the degenerative force of Poverty blocking an Abundance force. His intuitive sense will enable him to select which forces to allow into his energy field and which to block. An intuitive consciousness will help him select Abundance over Poverty.

On the power pathway, Joe will awaken to yet another use of his evolved psychic gift. Devotion and training can expand each psychic gift into a spiritual gift.

Spiritual gifts can create new energetic options. They are transformative in nature and so are able to transform energy into new shapes and forms. Intuitive gifting enables Joe to switch off the Poverty force and contact the Abundance force. Using the psychic sense spiritually allows Joe access to any or all subaspects of either force. He can potentially snip a little of the Poverty force and merge it with a section of the Abundance force and thus create a "new force" altogether— one customized to himself and his needs!

The creative process actually opens the doorway to the divine pathway. In between are other forms and uses of the psychic sense. On the imagination pathway, the psychic sense transforms into phantasm giftings, a means of discerning between fantasy and imagination. An excelled imagination worker can use imagination to change reality from one state to another. An evolved divine master uses all psychic gifts simultaneously and can instantly alter reality at will, if the changes are supported by the Divine. I call this process the transformation of the psychic sense to the numinous.

These amazing, life- and reality-changing applications of the psychic sense all begin with the simple acceptance of your psychic self. By working through your psychic center, you gradually learn how to advance your powers ethically and practically. Thus, the basic energy mapping technique of psychic mapping is a pathway unto itself, preparing you for the Wakefulness state that some call enlightenment, others higher consciousness, and still others the God State.

The Psychic Pathway

Know that evolving through the pathways will automatically advance your psychic gifts from one state to another. The opposite is also true. As you advance your gifts, you stair-step onto different pathways. In allowing these changes, you become better and better at performing shift healing and the move into Wakefulness. Here is a snapshot of the evolution of the psychic sense, pathway to pathway.

On the elemental pathway...

1. Develop psychic sympathy into intuitive empathy through management of the chakras and auric fields.

2. Open to the power through intuitive inspiration.

On the power pathway...

1. Use the intuitive to manage and choose between forces, powers, and energies for your own and others' well-being.

2. Allow the divine to transform your intuitive abilities into spiritual gifts. As you use these gifts to help others according to Divine will, you access aspects of the divine pathway while still on the power pathway and can begin serving as a conduit for Divine change.

3. From the power pathway, you can open to the imagination or divine pathways.

On the imagination pathway...

1. Use the phantasm gifts to choose the imagination pathway instead of fantasy. Now you can create something that has never been and make something that exists disappear.

2. Evolve onto the divine pathway having grasped the fact that all dualities are interwoven; i.e., the imperfect is perfect, and vice versa.

On the divine pathway...

1. Apply the spiritual gifts to learn the differences and similarities between your will and Divine will, and so transform your spiritual gifts into numinous gifts.

2. Use the numinous gifts to assist yourself and others in meeting everyday needs. At this point, you have achieved living Wakefulness. While you are still fully human and therefore are guaranteed to make mistakes, the Divine corrects these mistakes into expressions of Divine will. You are now the "enlightened master serving tea to his servants"—a Zen Buddhist analogy to

describe the normal, everyday nature and behavior of the truly Awakened.

Here is a model of the potential evolution of the psychic gifts.

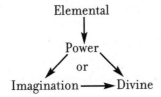

Psychic Pathway Evolution

The following describes what occurs to and through your psychic gifting as you cross from pathway to pathway.

From the Elemental to the Power Pathway: The Journey of Control On the elemental pathway, your psychic sympathetic gifts enable you to sense, feel, know, see, and hear fast information-energy. The sympathetic nature of these basic psychic gifts helps you absorb external energies and forces into your body. This helps your body relate to others and understand the nature of physical reality.

Psychic sympathy requires psychic boundaries—filters that keep out harmful energy, retain your basic life energy, and emanate psychic messages so you can attract what meets your needs. These psychic boundaries evolve over time through your energy system.

The most important psychic boundaries are established through your chakras and your auric fields. As you become able to consciously monitor these energy bodies, your psychic sympathy evolves into intuitive empathy.

Intuition is the managed and conscious process of using psychic data for defined goals. Intuition uses the mind rather than the brain and involves making conscious rather than unconscious choices. It is an *empathetic* process rather than a *sympathetic* process in that it allows you to relate "to" instead of "with" information-energy. Through empathy, you can read and understand information-energy without absorbing it, thus forming stronger psychic boundaries. The more intact you are, the easier it is to objectively evaluate psychic information and the world around you.

Empathy is a protective mechanism for yourself and others. One of the hazards in psychic absorption is the vulnerability to being manipulated. It's difficult to always know if you're acting for yourself or for someone else. Empathy keeps you from absorbing others' energies, prevents you from being manipulated, and helps prevent you from becoming manipulative.

Being intuitive is a key code to opening the power pathway. Intuitive rather than psychic perception invites you to perceive beyond the digital system and the language of matter. Intuition welcomes the mystical, ushering in the whispers of the language of light. The slightest hint of mystery and powers beyond the physical alludes to a world vaster than that perceived through the elemental pathway. Through the chakras and the auric fields, you are now able to perceive the seals and the power gateways.

The Power Pathway and Intuition: Sharpening Your Powers To "enter" the power pathway, you must be able to command energies. You must be not only psychic, but also intuitive; you must be able to sort and filter, not just read and gather. As you evolve onto the power pathway, your natural psychic gifts are honed into keen instruments of perception. While you will receive less information, you also receive a lot less static, so the data you do gather and disseminate is much more reliable.

To make true power change, however, you must advance the basic psychic gifts even further. Once you learn to manage your gifts, you must use them to create. In this way, your intuitive gifts become spiritual gifts. When fully developed, this honed intuitive faculty will be able to cut and shape reality like a fine sword.

Intuition through empathy safeguards against the unethical use of power forces. Power forces can generate great and constructive changes. These same forces can cause equally imposing evils. Using power forces before you're ready is like handing a machine gun to a six-year-old fan of Rambo.

The problem isn't the increased power, but the temptations of power. The power pathway doesn't "cure you" of your problems; rather, it magnifies and intensifies. Through this magnification, you can further personal healing and follow the impetus for spiritual development. You can achieve exponential growth and be a true source of inspiration for others. But what about your inner wounds and those unkempt soul issues? Past-life resentments, repressed feelings, and hidden desires? Add these to your strongholds, negative beliefs, and the all-too-human drives of revenge, power, greed, selfishness, and lust, and, well, let's just say the monster is unleashed.

Here's where you have to make a choice between two options:

1. Convert intuition to spiritual gifts via the power pathway, which in turn opens you to Wakefulness on the divine path.

2. Access the imagination, where you evolve the gifts either to create with imagination and therefore ascend to the divine, or to further a delusion and thus destroy your integrity.

From the Power to the Divine Pathway: Ascending in the Spiritual

When you commit to extending from the power pathway to the divine pathway, once you reach into the divine pathway and begin to care about "Thy Will" instead of just "My Will," your intuitive/psychic abilities transform into the spiritual gifts. These are also called *charismatic gifts.* (Charisma means "in the spirit.") The transformation of the intuitive abilities into the spiritual gifts is the first stage of Wakefulness.

Your gifts transform when you are dedicated to infusing your physical body with your eternal spirit. This enlightening occurs as your spirit animates through the seals, then into the chakras, and then into the physical body. Spiritual truths also transfer from the twelve spiritual gates into the power doors and then into the auric fields. Eventually, the star seed of destiny atop the body in the pineal gland engineers the unfolding of the spiritual genetics and your seed of destiny. You are readied to fulfill your spiritual mission.

At this point, you might not qualify as fully Wakeful or enlightened from a worldly point of view, yet in the eyes of the Divine you are entirely embraced as perfect in your human imperfection. You have not developed the numinous or divine-level ability to fully realize all psychic gifts simultaneously, but your strongest innate gifts are powerful and dynamic. You can now use your gifts to change reality in alignment with your spiritual purpose.

A fully awakened spiritual gift can be directed to help others in addition to yourself. A power master can use a highly developed spiritual gift to change reality for someone else. Spiritual gifts are correctly and ethically used in alliance with the spiritual truth that underlies your spiritual mission. This spiritual truth determines whom you help, as well as when and where. Your intuition will inform you when to summon particular powers and the reasons for doing so.

This unfolding of spirit into body isn't an overnight process. It accompanies the completion of the red and golden kundalini processes, which must be gentle to accommodate the physical body's limitations. By the time you're called to power, you'll be prepared. Remember, the spiritual gifts are natural expressions of the intuitive empathies and psychic sympathies you've been using all of your life!

The Imagination Pathway: Making the Self in the Mirror

There are two faces in the imagination pathway. One is illusion, which is the real you. The other is delusion, which is the artificial you.

The imagination pathway is as real a place as any other pathway, except it's fashioned from antienergy. This means that the imagination you is the "real you," except in reverse.

What we deny in the other pathways is made solid on the imagination pathway. The issues and problems we refuse to face on the elemental and power pathways and, yes, even on the divine pathway are transferred into our mirror self, the self in the imagination pathway.

There are two uses of the imagination *phantasm gifts*. When you use psychic or spiritual gifts with your imagination, you can potentially transfer data from one side of the imagination pathway to the other. How would you like to imagine a tumor out of this reality and tuck it safely away on the other side of the "looking glass," the world of antiparticles? You can use your innate psychic gifts conjoined with imagination to do this, as long as you're willing to exchange the tumor for energy previously housed in the antiworld. It would be best to swap a tumor for healthy body tissue instead of a new disease.

Through the imaginative application of phantasm, what you dream can be created. On the imagination pathway, you cannot transform the intuitive gifts into the spiritual gifts without imagination. You must *imagine* someone as miraculously cured to allow it to become so. You must *imagine* love for an enemy to give that love. You must *imagine* yourself to be a writer in order to write.

Fantasy involves believing that you can create what you want by believing enough in what is already here. Fantasy is also an application of the phantasm ability, but it supports the establishment of delusions instead of illusions. Fantasy does not require the exchange of energy between chakra doors. Given no switch, the two sides of the imagination world become imbalanced, and you are increasingly forced to devote your energy to believing in what's not real or true.

When I was studying for my English major in college, I read *The Picture of Dorian Gray* by Oscar Wilde. Dorian is a painter. Brilliantly, he creates a self-portrait and hides it away. To the world, Dorian appears ever-young. We wonder at the secret of his immortal visage until, peering through the shadows, we see that Dorian has closeted the self-portrait. There in the portrait is the aging, miserable, and despicable Dorian, the self he has refused to own. The beautiful Dorian is not an illusion; he is a delusion. The painted Dorian is the illusion—the real self, honestly immortalized. Dorian has tricked himself into thinking that he can hide from reality and hide reality away. We are all capable of using our imagination phantasm skills to fool the world and ourselves.

This is the test of the imagination pathway: How are you going to use your phantasm powers? Will you hide your inner demons by creating delusions, or will you face and transform them by making illusions real? Will you use fantasy to hold onto the artificial you, or will you use imagination to own the authentic you?

If we hide our demons in the shadows of delusion, they will prevent us from accessing our full, divined truth. We might be powerful, but shallow. We might be religious, but not righteous. We might be rich, but not enriched.

The gift of illusion is that it forces you to face yourself truthfully. If you peer into the illusion, you will see all the lies, deceits, and evils you still need to conquer in your self. And that means that in due course you will face each of the seven universal delusions that everyone must face and overcome—the seven bowls of existence described in chapter 8. Illusion and imagination help you transmute these negativities through the only true reality—love.

The imagination pathway provides the key to destroying the seven bowls of existence. The imagination pathway forces you to ask, "What *is* really real?" Illusion will show you that if love is real, then the contents of the bowls—including evil, death, judgment, and suffering—are not real. These understandings transform the phantasm gifts into early-stage numinous gifts, and this invites further movement onto the divine pathway.

Some people ask me if they can skip the imagination pathway altogether and jump from the power to the divine pathway through the spiritual gifts. The answer is yes and no. At one level, there is no higher versus lower or more sacred versus more profane pathway. We all have the potential to achieve Wakefulness through a single pathway, without ever landing on the other three. The reality of being human, however, would encourage most of us to evolve step-by-step.

Few of us were encouraged to develop and use our natural psychic gifts when we were young. Youngsters who *are* encouraged to are seldom taught psychic ethics, boundaries, laws of management, and capabilities. It's very difficult to activate the psychic gifts fully without learning how to translate information from the world to the antiworld and back again. The imagination pathway forces us to face the self in the mirror and to confront the dilemma of the ethical use of power. You must be able to accept yourself and others completely before the psychic sense transforms to the numinous.

The Divine Pathway: The Channel of Love The gradual emergence of the numinous from the psychic sense depends upon leaping from being a vessel for love to being love itself. Upon making this leap, which is truly nothing more than an inspired awareness, your psychic gifts combine into a unified whole. You can see, hear, touch, know, sense, and hear all sides of a single truth in the eternal Now. You know yourself as being everywhere all at once, in the infinite Here. You can gain any knowledge that you need, eliminate knowledge that should not exist, and determine what does not need to be known. You will be as Christ; at one with the Divine and human at the same time.

The core psychic gifts are the same on the divine and the elemental pathways. The elemental pathway forces us to acknowledge the secret self. This is the psychic self, capable of lightning-speed deliberation and action. Applying the psychic sense invites us to look beyond the norm and consider questions that push us beyond the three-dimensional self. On the divine pathway, however, the separation between self and others drops away. When accessing psychic information for the self, we're accessing it for others as well. When psychically communicating to a friend, we're psychically speaking with the All.

The power pathway requires using our abilities as spiritual gifts. The master power healer is an instrument for the Creator. The spiritual power healer not only is capable of directing forces and energies, but must do so if called. Your strongest spiritual gifts are channels for powers that must be used to sculpt earth into heaven. This is the nature of living according to spiritual purpose.

The numinous is a natural outgrowth of the spiritual gifts, with a few differences. Through Wakefulness, the spiritual gifts combine into a unified whole. You can use any or all at the same time. But the main distinction is philosophical. The psychic sense becomes numinous rather than spiritual through this understanding:

- We are one with the Creator and therefore, creators ourselves.
- You are not "God." Being a part in the whole doesn't make you *the* whole. But it does make you whole.

On the imagination pathway, we confront the true power of the psychic sense. It can change reality. It can eliminate what currently exists and create what has never been. The imagination pathway deals us the most intense test yet: the test of power.

Are you content with using the psychic sense in a balanced and ethical way, applying your imagination to manufacture only good? Or are you tempted with the notion of establishing a world that suits your fantasy? Wouldn't it be nice to pretend anything you want into existence? Few of us comprehend the true lure of the fantastic until given the opportunity to create glamour instead of truth.

When converted from phantasm to numinous, the psychic gifts can never be used to sugar-coat reality. What's ugly must remain ugly. What is false must be left as false. You don't change something from "bad" to "good" through make-believe, only through choice.

Someone with highly evolved numinous gifts will not erase what's not pretty. Rather, he or she will reflect truth. Then others can make their own decisions. Divine love necessitates acceptance of the imperfect and allowance of free will. On this level, the psychic sense is seldom used to establish change, only to enhance the light.

In I Corinthians 12:4, the Christian apostle Paul discusses the interconnectedness of all people. While each person is gifted in a different way, he asserts that all gifts come from the same place.

"There are different kinds of gifts, but the same Spirit." The evolution of the psychic, intuitive, spiritual, and phantasm gifts to the numinous requires an acknowledgment of this fact. We all share through the same Spirit. If one child is hungry, you are hungry. If somewhere a woman is being beaten, then you are beaten. If a man in China carries a burden, so do you. You don't change these situations by ignoring, overpowering, or erasing them, or by pretending them away. By being a being of love, you help others—as you help yourself.

The Elemental Pathway: Where Physical and Finite Unite

I did not see
That lie of trees
Along the hill
Until today…
They seem to be
A curtain
Waiting to receive
A moment to be seen. [1]

—*Roger Cooper,*
Impressions

The elemental pathway is the most physical of the pathways, reducing to a series of moments that led to the present time. When working this pathway, you have only enough time to catch your breath before you move into the future. By working the chakras to figure out the elements that created a present situation, you can shape the future into something more desirable than the present you live within.

We will discuss the elemental pathway in two chapters, this one and chapter 12. Because it is composed of the most basic of factors, it is the most complicated to work with, and there is more material to cover than involved on the other three pathways.

In this chapter, we will cover fundamental issues of the chakras on the elemental pathway, including the major concerns of each chakra, cultural differences, physiological touchstones, age development, physical issues, chakra infrastructure and points about chakra shape, spin, speed, color, symbology, and tones. We will then discuss matters related to energy particles and charges, kundalini, and energetic communication. Throughout this chapter, you will be provided information helpful for performing energy mapping on the elemental pathway.

While the elemental pathway is the most concrete of all the pathways, it is no less magical than the other pathways, as experienced by my client Bridget.

A Case Study on the Elemental Pathway

My client Bridget serves as an example of benefiting from wholeness-based elemental healing.

When I first met Bridget, I was amazed at her ability to cope with her rapidly degenerative multiple sclerosis (MS). From her wheelchair, she was still able to command a bevy of kids, five in all, and as a single mother. The family lived on welfare, food stamps, and the good graces of Bridget's neighbors.

Bridget had a sense that the cause of her MS lay in the past. I conducted a soul regression, helping her into a meditative state so she could become conscious of an event or experience that might have created the conditions for MS. Bridget immediately walked into old Ireland, seeing herself as a woman attempting to keep her children alive during the potato famine. With nothing but moldy potatoes to eat, she and the children of that time eventually died. Hunger and infection rendered them unable to move.

Bridget was sure that she had actually lived this life. It is also possible that she was recalling an ancestral soul memory, an experience lived by her this-lifetime Irish ancestors. Then again, her psyche might have created this story to demonstrate the existence of a yeast infection and allergic condition that could underlie the MS. Regardless, Bridget began to change the environment holding the MS in place. She figured out the beliefs garnered from that lifetime and altered them to be more positive. She expressed the feelings still held in her tenth chakra—powerlessness, immobility, and other fears. Pinpointing fear and the power field of Survival, she searched her morphogenetic and tenth auric fields for miasms, energetic disease patterns that run in families, and other fear-based patterns. She found several that seemed to create MS symptoms.

I knew that fear also relates to bacteria and heavy metal and so Bridget agreed to work with a holistic physician to alter her biochemistry and undergo heavy metal detoxification. This revealed an underlying layer of yeast, common in MS. Bridget now had to deal with incredible amounts of sadness, from the other lifetime but primarily from this one. As she did so, she changed her diet from the sticky carbohydrates so loved by Candida (a yeast infection), to a much healthier vegetable and protein-based eating plan.

Bridget and I did minimal symbol work, except to help her access her "soul purpose" symbols in her ninth chakra. They added up to work along the lines of interior or home designing, actually a common skill base for individuals with a lot of tenth chakra strengths. Bridget began to study design.

She was now healing from the inside to the outside. Having changed her attitude toward herself, she decided she needed to be self-focused. Daily, she focused on the integral physical alterations she could make, but more important, she changed from an "I'll do it all" attitude to a "can do" one.

And her MS has been in remission for five years.

Elemental Healing, Chakra Healing

The chakras are utilized in every elemental operation, from intracellular tasks to daily decision-making. This means that the most complex chakra functions occur on the elemental pathway. As we've discussed, on the elemental pathway, your chakras convert slow energy to fast energy and back again. Through the chakras and the spiritual points, you use psychic information-energy to read and sense the world around you.

These energy bodies also act as doorways for energy on the Secondary Grid, helping you to not only adjust to the world but also change it. Prisms of light, chakras can spin energy into existence from another plane and then, just as fast, spin energy out of existence. Each chakra has its own vibration and therefore regulates a different set of life concerns. The lower the chakra, the lower the vibration and the more physical the job performed.

The chakras, spiritual points, and auric fields can be checked to diagnose almost any concern. Diagnosis can involve tracing a problem back to the chakra it relates to, or psychically examining the chakra for color, symbols, shapes, spin, and so on to see what problems errant energies might be causing. The types of concerns usually regulated by particular chakras are as follows:

Chakra	Issues
One	Physical health and lifestyle
Two	Creativity and emotions
Three	Self-esteem or work
Four	Relationships
Five	Expression and communication
Six	Decision-making and self-image
Seven	Spiritual belief and purpose
Eight	History or power
Nine	Soul or "life meaning"
Ten	Nature/environment, housing, or ancestors
Eleven	Taking charge or being commanding
Twelve	Questions about being human versus divine

Other charts and lists throughout this chapter and the next will help you track presenting symptoms back to the originating or key chakra.

Remember that an issue in a chakra will also appear in its corresponding auric field; a first chakra issue will also be reflected in the first auric field. You can then work chakras or auric fields for healing on any of the pathways.

The elemental energy bodies are also sites for setting your healing intention, the goal you hope to accomplish. All elemental change occurs through action, which can be managed physically, chemically, or energetically. To heal, you usually need to perform several healing steps simultaneously. The advantage of adding a chakra-based method is that chakras can unify all healing energies and potentially increase the effectiveness of other therapies.

The following are some cultural, ethnic, and/or national chakra tendencies that I have perceived. The chakras are listed in the order of strongest to weakest in terms of cultural tendencies.

Culture(s)	Chakras	Emphasis
American	First/Third	Materialism and thought
African	Tenth/First	Environment, ancestry, and physicality
Norwegian	Third/Seventh	Rules, rightness, beliefs, religion
German	Third/First/Seventh	Rules, productivity, purpose
British	Third/Fifth	Rules, communication
Japanese	Eighth/First/Tenth	The past, materializing, ancestors and the clan
Mexican	Second/Fifth	Feelings and communication
Russian	Third/Tenth	Rules, the land, the clan
Chinese	Third/Sixth	Rules and power, vision
French	Fourth/Second	Heart, feelings
Italian	Fifth/Second/Seventh	Communication, expression, beliefs
Spanish	First/Second/Fifth	Physicality, creativity, and sensuality; communication
South American	Second/Eighth	Feelings and sensuality; heritage and magic
Native North American	Fourth/Ninth/Tenth	Nature and ancestry, heart, connection, and ceremony
Australian	Tenth/Twelfth	Ancestry and earth, maturation into spiritual completion
East Indian and Pakistanian	Sixth/Ninth	Spiritual vision, harmony; following spiritual insights
Jewish	First/Third/ Seventh/Ninth/Tenth	Family, knowledge, spiritual values, the soul, the clan; achieving God's purpose for the people

Chakra Development and Age Regression

In chapter 12, we will look at ways to apply this information for elemental healing, as described in the section, "Development and Age Regression."

Most chakra problems originate in the past. You can use techniques such as regression, EMDR, mental-health therapy, bodywork, or energy healing to unlock the issue and memories and prepare for healing. Since the chakras develop one step at a time throughout your life, you can go directly to a particular chakra if you know the age at which a trauma happened. Or, by knowing which chakra is malformed or malfunctioning, you can figure out the age at which the wound occurred. The following table presents the developmental stages of the chakras.

At age fifty-seven, you enter the twelfth chakra and also begin recycling at chakra one.

When chakra seven begins its development at age fourteen, the first seven chakras start a second development pattern in which a single chakra is recycled every year. This means, for example, that while a seventeen-year-old is in the middle of her chakra seven development, she is at the same time recycling through chakra four—so while she is addressing her spiritual beliefs and purpose, she is also reconsidering relationship issues.

» Cultural Differences

BEFORE ASSUMING A problem, know that there are personal as well as cultural chakric differences between people. No two individuals are alike, but there are tendencies. One of the significant distinctions is in countries or ethnic cultures, all of which shape the morphogenetic fields and therefore the chakras. For instance, it would be easy to assume a first chakra problem in someone from South America, because his or her first chakra is faded and less intense in comparison with that of someone from the United States. People from South American countries tend to have more developed second and eighth chakras than do people from the United States. Therefore, chakra diagnosis must be adjusted.

Such differences can make diagnosis challenging, because so many people reflect multiple national and cultural influences. A Chinese-American client can be affected by the influences of two very different cultures. Two people with the same ethnicity might also run their chakras differently if raised in different countries. A German born and raised in Frankfurt, Germany, will have stronger Germanic tendencies than someone of German descent living in Frankfort, Kentucky. Because of these and other personal differences between people, I recommend that you perform chakra diagnosing with a number of techniques before arriving at a final conclusion.

Chakras	One	Two	Three	Four	Five	Six	Seven	Eight	Nine	Ten	Eleven	Twelve
	Womb to 6 mo.	6 mo. to 2.5 yrs.	2.5 to 4.5 yrs.	4.5 to 6.5 yrs.	6.5 to 8.5 yrs.	8.5 to 13 yrs.	14 to 20 yrs.	21 to 27 yrs.	28 to 34 yrs.	35 to 41 yrs.	42 to 48 yrs.	49 to 56 yrs.

At First Glance
Chakras and Physical Health

The simplest way to figure out a chakra-based concern is to examine your physical health. If you can pinpoint the damaged chakra, you can more easily determine elemental-based healing methods. This chart summarizes the types of bodily concerns that affect particular chakras.

Chakra and Location	Physiological Touchstones
One: Sacral area	Genital organs and adrenals; coccygeal vertebrae; affects some kidney, bladder, and excrement functions; skin
Two: Abdominal area	Affects part of adrenal endocrine system; intestines; parts of kidney function; some aspects of reproductive system; sacral vertebrae and the neurotransmitters determining emotional responses to stimuli
Three: Solar plexus	Pancreas endocrine system; all digestive organs in stomach area, including liver, spleen, gall bladder, stomach, pancreas, and parts of kidney system; lumbar vertebrae
Four: Heart	Heart and lungs; circulatory and oxygenation systems; breasts; lumbar and thoracic vertebrae (Note: According to many recent studies, the heart is an endocrine organ; beat and rhythm regulate other hormone-producing glands.)
Five: Throat	Thyroid endocrine gland; larynx; mouth and auditory systems; lymph system; thoracic vertebrae
Six: Forehead	Pituitary endocrine gland; parts of hypothalamus; visual and olfactory systems; memory storage; some problems with ears and sinus; left eye
Seven: Top of the head	Pineal endocrine gland; parts of hypothalamus; higher learning and cognitive brain systems; parts of the immune system
Eight: One inch above the head	Thymus (immune system); memory retrieval functions; aspects of central nervous system; right eye; thalamus
Nine: One foot above the head	Diaphragm; pineal gland; corpus callosum and other higher learning centers, including the cortex and neocortex
Ten: One foot under the feet	Feet, legs, and bones
Eleven: Around the body, especially the hands and feet	Skin, muscles, and connective tissue
Twelve: In 32 points on body	Secondary chakric sites: includes the knees, elbows, palms, and organs; this layer connects to your energy egg

Different body parts relate to certain chakras. By linking the body part to the chakra, or by looking up the symptoms you are having, you can determine the meaning of the illness. The following chart shows common physical issues and/or symptoms and the chakras they are linked to.

Body Part(s)	Meaning	Symptoms	Chakra
Genital organs	Life	Poor memory, blood issues, depletion, suppression, addictions, loss of life energy	One
Bones	Structure	Lack of control, bone disease, spinal problems, rigidity	Ten
Muscles	Connections	Relationship issues, inability to connect	Several
Adrenals	Ability to respond	Inability to be responsible, over-responsibility, greed, burn-out, self-hatred, mood swings, sluggishness, eating disorders	One
Ovaries	Nurturing	PMS, female disorders, emotional imbalances, infertility, creative issues	Two
Prostate	Strength	Prostate problems, weak will, inflexibility, lack of success or drive for success	One, two
Bladder	Release	Irritation, indecision, timidity, anger, inefficiency, blood issues	One, two
Small intestine	Feelings	Insecurity, emotionalism, feeling lost or overwhelmed, wheat and gluten problems, need for comfort through food, digestive and absorption issues	Two
Large intestine	Action	Rigidity, "stuckness," denial, emotionalism, compulsive neatness, digestive and waste issues	Two
Kidneys	Fear	Memories, desire to run, terror, compulsion to work (i.e., making up for "past sins"), guilt, kidney disorders	Two, three
Gall bladder	Self-expression	Inability to accept self, indecision, repression, depression, anger, resentment, and digestive issues	Three
Liver	Power	Power issues, anger, rage, hatred of authority, aggression, inability to be assertive, stuck in victim or victor role, liver, heart, blood, digestive, and circulation issues	Three
Stomach	Ideas	Self-disgust, egotism, confusion, stifled self, caffeine or soda addictions, obsession, and digestive complaints	Three
Pancreas	Joy	Worry, mistrust, inability to accept sweetness, indulgence, low self-esteem, blood sugar and food issues	Three

Spleen	Protection	Defensiveness or offensiveness, lack of control, excessive control, hopelessness, addictions (can include crack), blood and immune disorders	Three
Heart	Love	Poor relationships, emotionalism, shock, love addictions, heart or blood disorders, sugar addictions	Four
Lungs	Spirit	Lack of self-love, sadness, loneliness, grief, hiding of true self, cloudy thinking, despair, sorrow, unmet desires, breathing problems	Four
Thyroid	Energy	High or low energy, stress, paranoia, extreme highs or lows, weight issues, mood swings, always being rushed, energy issues	Five
Teeth	Fundamentals	Abused in past, cracked foundational beliefs, betrayal, issues with money, functionality and "getting it together," mouth and jaw problems, some heart disorders	Ten
Ears	Learning	Mistaken beliefs, inability to hear clearly or separate self from others, psychic stimulation, constant replaying of "old tapes," hearing problems	Five
Eyes	Visioning	Indecisiveness, dislike of self, poor body image, food issues, self-deception, inability to see choices, overplanning or inability to plan, pituitary and sight problems	Six
Pineal gland	Purpose	Lack of focus, lack of meaning, fanaticism, depression, anxiety, exhaustion, SAD, heavy metal toxicity, weakness, racing heart, endocrine problems	Seven

Basic Life Needs and the Chakras

Here are examples of chakra and energy-based elemental healing you can perform in relation to basic life needs. These basic needs are regulated by particular chakras.

- Shelter: Tenth (environment) and first (clothing)
- Breathing: Tenth (environment) and fourth (lungs)
- Water: First (skin), fifth (drinking), and all other in-body chakras
- Touch: First (skin and sexual entry points) and fifth (eating)
- Movement: All
- Food: All

Elemental Chakras and Shelter

Your home energetically reflects your inner self and, most particularly, your tenth chakra, which regulates genetics, your relationship with your surroundings, and the foundations of life. Does your environment match your true self or not? Do the colors, textures, and symbols inhibit or support your natural expression? When your environment echoes your true self and whole, healed state, the energy will support your body toward reflecting the same.

Clothing, too, is a form of shelter, specifically for your physical body. It communicates your true self to the world and serves as a natural protection and buffer. If your clothing is self-expressive, it assists your auric field in manifesting and protection. If it doesn't, it will inhibit your realization of self.

Elemental Chakras and Breathing

Many physical conditions are actually related to environmental sensitivities carried on the air, including chemical toxicity from glues, paint, carpets, pesticides, secondary smoke, air emissions, power lines, and the like. Breath is a reflection of our spirit. In Greek, Hebrew, and Latin the word for *spirit* is one and the same as the word for *breath*. Working with the fourth chakra to clear strongholds and the tenth to purify the entire system can help you breathe deeper and naturally cleanse your body.

Elemental Chakras and Water

Since over 75 percent of the body is made of water, water is a highly important healing tool. Water is a crystalline structure that can be programmed to create results on all levels. You can program water by blessing it with your thoughts or a crystal. I also recommend writing a wish or desire on paper, then putting the paper underneath your drinking water overnight and drinking it in the morning. Internalizing your desire via the water prompts your body's energy system to attract what you desire. Many healers also recommend oxygenated water.

Elemental Chakras and Touch

Touch is a first-chakra drive and need. If you don't meet touch needs, you'll be prone to physical illness, addictions, shame, and sexual and monetary problems. If you can't get touched, even through hugs, use other first-chakra modalities such as the following to love yourself: wear clothing that feels good; touch your food before you eat it; buy a cozy or an infrared blanket; sleep in silk. Even eating is a touch-based endeavor, as the food "touches" the inside of your body. Many alternative modalities are effective because they involve touch.

Elemental Chakras and Movement

All movement or exercise creates specific energetic responses in the body. Moving actually changes the spin of the energy organs, physical organs, and individual cells. Here are examples:

Walking. Creates fluidity and aligns the chakras. Establishes rhythm between the inner and outer chakras. Helps integrate the physical with the spiritual, and therefore provides healing openings for issues related to chakras one, two, three, four, seven, and ten.

Running. Excites forward drive and speeds up all the chakras to work uniformly toward desired goals. Motivates the lower chakras to healing, especially chakras one, three, and ten.

Biking. Allows the lower chakras to receive external assistance to move forward. Excellent for chakras one and ten.

Swimming. Allows the buoying nature of the Divine to support you. Ideal for all the chakras and the integration of spiritual points in the spine.

Tennis or racquetball. Helps you practice fun partnership and healthy competition to hone skills for work success. Especially helpful in coordinating the first, third, fourth, and sixth chakras.

Downhill skiing. Teaches "flow." Surrendering to life's process allows the chakric instincts and the lower brain, mind, and heart to guide your survival.

Weight lifting. Provides empowerment for challenging times. Excellent for all the in-body chakras; provides the means for the eighth, ninth, tenth, and eleventh chakric strengths to integrate into the body.

Yoga. Accesses the higher chakras to balance the lower chakras. Especially integrates the seventh and ninth chakras into system.

Martial arts. Accesses the higher chakras to increase discipline over the lower chakras.

Dancing. Complete expression of spirit through the body.

Elemental Chakras and Food

Food is a vital elemental need, and food-related physical issues are fast becoming one of the most tragic problems affecting both men and women today. You can figure out the origin of many food issues on a chakra basis. Look up symptoms in the list below and see which chakras pertain to them. You can use regression techniques—such as "eye movement desensitization and reprocessing" (EMDR), hypnotherapy, and guided meditation—to return to the age or event that originated the food issue. (See "Chakra Development and Age Regression" earlier in this chapter and "Development and Age Regression" in chapter 12.) Then continue healing with pathway techniques and other elemental-based modalities.

Chakra: One

Primary Functions: Survival and security; general health of body, blood, sex drive, and health of finances

Types of Food Issues: Substance addictions, including hard drugs and alcohol; food cravings or behaviors relating to sexual relationships; food issues threatening life, such as anorexia, and those involving beliefs of worthiness or deservedness, including cravings for or repulsion to milk products and meat; obesity to reject sexual advances of others; some chocolate cravings in relation to a drive for, yet a fear of sex.

Chakra: Two

Primary Functions: Creativity and feelings

Types of Food Issues: Food behaviors that stifle or prevent feelings; foods that cause digestive disturbances; issues stemming from emotional needs to be comforted and loved; most common problems involve gluten and wheat products; frequently site of originating problems for binge-purge and sometimes bulimia; may result in obesity to hide need for love and sensual touch or anorexia to gain perfect body and so earn affection; some chocolate cravings relate to the need for sensual touch and originate in this chakra; high-fat foods tend to relate to this chakra as well, as they cover up shame yet provide fullness and comfort.

Chakra: Three

Primary Functions: Personal power; self-esteem; center of beliefs, fears, drive for success, and organizational abilities

Types of Food Issues: Food behaviors affected by self-esteem and self-confidence; often involves attraction to foods that provide quick energy, such as caffeine, colas, and other stimulants; often involves food compulsions or allergies related to corn (the man's "success" food) and beer (a way to disguise one's softness with machismo); craving for crunchy foods may indicate an anger at someone seen as being in an authority position.

Chakra: Four

Primary Functions: Center of love and relationship

Types of Food Issues: Food issues related to need for love and companionship; cravings and food-related problems often involve sugar as a substitute for needed love or tobacco as a "safe friend"; most food disorders are at least partially heart related.

Chakra: Five

Primary Functions: Communication and sharing of needs

Types of Food Issues: Food issues related to need to express oneself; results in need to compulsively eat or fill the mouth to stifle emotions.

Chakra: Six

Primary Functions: Vision for future and self-image

Types of Food Issues: Food issues related to poor body- or self-image; almost all anorexics are affected in this chakra, as well as anyone with distorted body image; many chocolate addictions or cravings relate to issues sitting in this chakra, especially in regard to self-image.

Chakra: Seven

Primary Functions: Purpose and spirituality

Types of Food Issues: Food issues related to beliefs about God and one's place in the world; determines relationship with foods affecting the pineal gland—the "feel good" hormone producer; drive for carbohydrates, often a substitute for connection with God and indicating a lack of clear spiritual purpose; obesity can become an excuse for not fulfilling one's destiny, as can any food addiction; connections to negative entities or spirits can exacerbate any shame-related food issue.

Chakra: Eight

Primary Functions: Relationship with the past; alternative presents and possible futures

Types of Food Issues: Food behaviors carried over from negative occurrences in one's own past or in past lives; here is the connection between food disorders and associations with negative spirits, dark forces, nightmares, and other evil influences.

Chakra: Nine

Primary Functions: Seat of the soul; place where soul touches others' souls

Types of Food Issues: Food issues resulting from over-connection to other individuals' souls, their issues, or global concerns; if you always eat after watching starving children on the television, for example, you are dealing with a ninth-chakra issue.

Chakra: Ten

Primary Functions: Environment and home

Types of Food Issues: Cravings or allergies regarding root vegetables; issues and beliefs about ancestors, home, and the environment can cause chemical sensitivities or allergies.

Chakra: Eleven

Primary Functions: Transforms negative energy into neutral or positive

Types of Food Issues: Food issues resulting from an inability to see the positive in the negative or to transform negativity into something positive; issues of powerlessness, depression, or anxiety, can cause you to eat like you did in childhood.

Chakra: Twelve

Primary Functions: Completion of human maturity

Types of Food Issues: Issues involving the refusal to grow up, such as cravings or addictions to exercise, extreme dieting, obesity (if it keeps one looking immature), smoking, or substance abuse (if it prevents intimacy or maturity).

You can also strengthen a chakra by eating the foods associated with it, provided you aren't allergic and don't go to extremes. All foods carry frequency-based messages and change vibration. Here are examples of chakra-based foods and the energetic messages they provide. When eating the foods, I recommend that you repeat the spiritual messages to yourself, and so form new and positive beliefs.

Chakra	Foods That Fuel	Spiritual Messages
One	Red foods like meat, beets, grapes, strawberries, and cherries.	You deserve to be alive, safe, strong, and passionate.
Two	Orange foods like yams, salmon, sweet potatoes, papaya, and wheat.	Your feelings are good; you are desired and desirable.
Three	Yellow foods, especially corn; also grapefruit and squashes.	You deserve success, you are intelligent, you can learn what you need to know, you can be powerful.
Four	Green foods like vegetables and sauces.	You are loved and lovable; you deserve healthy relations.
Five	Blue foods like berries, and foods of intense flavors (salty, sweet, bitter).	You can be honest and have integrity; you can manifest your needs; it is safe to communicate.
Six	Purple foods like grapes, and vision-inducing substances like wine, and organic cocoa.	You are acceptable as you are; you are made in the Creator's image; you deserve to make healthy choices.
Seven	White foods like parsnips, white asparagus, fish.	You have a unique destiny; you are connected to the Divine; there is divine destiny.
Eight	Black foods (carbon based) such as alcohol, coffee, white flour, and sugar; past-life foods of meaning—often these foods trigger issues; also colloidal silver.	You can draw on the past for guidance and power; you deserve to be freed from the past; you can choose a new future.
Nine	Gold colloidal, bee pollen, honey, foods symbolizing your soul.	You are seeded for greatness.
Ten	Earth foods: nuts, grains, potatoes, herbs; water.	Your body is the meeting ground of the Divine and nature.
Eleven	Vibrational substances, such as homeopathic treatments, tinctures, teas, and blessed water.	Negativity can transmute into something positive; you are an instrument of divine force.
Twelve	Minerals, vitamins, higher metals such as platinum and titanium and substances such as frankincense and myrrh as provided in tinctures.	You are fully human and divine.

Chakra Infrastructure

Each chakra has a back and front side. In general, the back side regulates your unconscious, primal programs, and spiritual matters, while the front side oversees your conscious and day-to-day needs.

Inside the chakra is an inner wheel, which should move in harmony with the outer wheel. The inner wheel links to your subconscious and, potentially, your Higher Self and even your spirit. On the elemental pathway, this inside wheel processes tachyons or antiparticles, which can move faster than the speed of light. When illuminated, this inner wheel transforms your brain and Higher Self, Heart, and Mind into capacities of pure white light, which in turn heal your Middle and Lower selves and align you with your spirit. The outside wheel runs on quarks and creates demonstrated action.

The following is a chart of the issues that affect these chakra infrastructures.

Chakra	Chakric Part	Areas Regulated
One	Back:	Unconscious security issues; how others' security issues affect you.
	Front:	Interface with everyday life; how you carry yourself into the world.
	Inner Sphere:	Is regulated by your soul's relationship with the Divine. If your soul thinks that God abandoned you in this life, you will refuse Divine grace and power. You might over-function and motivate yourself through worry and doubt, or under-function, which can cause radical judgmentalism/fundamentalism or lack of concern about your behavior. If spinning properly, your spirit, versus your soul, will help you align your will with Divine will.
	Outer Sphere:	Regulates your movement in the world. Overfunctioning causes harried and hyperactive behavior. Underfunctioning creates sloth and laziness.
Two	Back:	The feelings you unconsciously carry; your unconscious response to the feelings of those around you; decisions about which feelings of others you will pick up and hold onto and which you won't.
	Front:	How you express your feelings into the world; your ability to translate your feelings into creative responses.
	Inner Sphere:	Do you believe that God has feelings? Your response sets the rhythm of this wheel, with a "yes" establishing the healthiest spins. Your judgments and your beliefs about God as a feeling God set the rhythm about feelings as reflecting spiritual messages. If you disregard the spirituality of feelings, you will be judgmental, closed, and unsympathetic to others. If you fail to translate the spiritual messages behind the feelings, you will be emotional, hypersensitive, and codependent.

Chakra	Chakric Part	Areas Regulated
	Outer Sphere:	Establishes the ways you act as a feeling person in the world. Repressed feelings will attract people who exhibit these feelings to you or cause illness. If you hold feelings that are not yours, you will feel crazy and out of control. You cannot process an issue that isn't yours.
Three	Back:	Your unconscious beliefs about power, success, and your worthiness.
	Front:	Your ability to succeed in the world.
	Outer Sphere:	Frequency is established by your internalized beliefs about your place in the world. Do you believe the Divine has special work for you and that you have unique gifts? If you do, you'll feel healthy and balanced. If you don't, you'll feel strained and continually disappointed in yourself.
	Inner Sphere:	Maintains your boundaries with the world. If you believe your work is divinely guided, you will perform well and command respect.
Four	Back:	Your unconscious beliefs about relationships; keeps you connected to people you have not let go of.
	Front:	Your major and minor relationships; your ability to give and receive.
	Inner Sphere:	The relationships within: self to self; Divine to self; self and Divine to all aspects of the self, including the inner child, dream self, soul self, and the essential self (or spirit).
	Outer Sphere:	Balance: relationships between self and all aspects of self with the world and others in it.
Five	Back:	The type of guidance you are willing to receive, which can be from lower or higher planes.
	Front:	Determines which tapes or messages regulate your communication— those that are healthy or those that are not.
	Inner Sphere:	What you're willing or unwilling to say or express. How others will perceive your communication. Your ability to manifest your desires based on courage and truth. The speed and frequency should match that of your spirit. If it's too fast, you aren't listening to the Divine. If it's too slow, you are listening to lower-ordered beings.
	Outer Sphere:	Responds to your intention. If your true intention is to be loving and kind, your communication, or silence, will match; if your intent is the opposite, your communication also will not be loving and kind.

Six	Back:	Potential futures. All choices enter through the back-side chakra. Your inner ability to see these choices is dependent on your self-image.
	Front:	The path chosen. If you train yourself, you can look ahead from this place in time and see what choices you still face.
	Inner Sphere:	Place of your spirit's image of you and of your life. If you allow your spirit or the Divine to set this image, it will be of truth and will help you make the right decisions in life.
	Outer Sphere:	Projects your self-image, which tells others how to respond to you.
Seven	Back:	The types of spirits and spiritual beliefs programming your belief system; sometimes these hold you hostage.
	Front:	How you project your image of the Divine and spiritual self into the world; the religion you follow and the values you live.
	Inner Sphere:	If healthy, your spiritual beliefs and discipline will match your purpose and God's desires for you. If not, there will be discord.
	Outer Sphere:	Reflects how you carry out your spiritual beliefs.
Eight	Back:	Patterns or parts of your past that guide your decisions.
	Front:	How you express these patterns through life choices—decisions about a mate, friends, work, use of your spiritual gifts, and more.
	Inner Sphere:	Reflects ability to forgive self for past mistakes; you can release all karma and have a clear inner sphere if you're able to forgive. Connects directly to the imagination pathway; you can perform healing depending upon what you send through here.
	Outer Sphere:	If unforgiving of self or of others, every aspect of your life will reflect prior decisions. You will live the life you were fated, not destined, to live.
Nine	Back:	Beliefs held in your own and others' souls about universal love, global needs, and care for others.
	Front:	Ways you express care for others in everyday life.
	Outer Sphere:	Can serve as a portal for spiritual truths that, if entering, assist your spirit in integrating in your body.
	Inner Sphere:	Shows how you've carried spiritual truths into action.
Ten	Back:	Which aspects of the natural world you draw upon or bring into your life.
	Front:	How you interact with nature and the things of nature. Will even show whether or not herbs or natural healing will work for you.
	Inner Sphere:	Place in nature that can hold the seed of your spirit if you allow yourself to be grounded in physical reality.
	Outer Sphere:	Reflects how well you live as a physical being, a product of nature, the world, and your ancestry—not just of divinity.

Chakra	Chakric Part	Areas Regulated
Eleven	Back:	Beliefs aiding or impairing your ability to alter and transmute energy.
	Front:	How you impact the physical and energetic worlds around you; which beings of energy and spirit you draw into you, as aid or foe.
	Inner Sphere:	Place of contact through which your spirit can draw upon energetic powers and forces.
	Outer Sphere:	Reflects proper or improper use of supernatural power.
Twelve		This chakra does not have a front or back side. The inner sphere concerns your divinity; the outer sphere relates to how well this divinity is reflected in your everyday, human existence.

Chakra Shape, Spin, and Speed

Here are important points about chakra shape, spin, and speed.

Using a Pendulum

The easiest way to check for general chakric shape, spin, and speed is to use a pendulum, an object on a chain or a string. When allowed to swing freely, a pendulum when held will respond to the electromagnetic frequency from a chakra, back or front side. When holding a pendulum over the front or back side of you close to the chakra area, you are primarily evaluating the outer wheel of the chakra. If the outer wheel is counterclockwise, the inner wheel is probably running the same. It is difficult to evaluate the inner wheel with a pendulum, which is best done with psychic means. See the following section for tips on checking outer and inner wheels with a pendulum.

You can make a pendulum assessment by having a partner stand over you, holding the pendulum six inches to a foot over the center of a chakra. Record information about the shape, direction, movement, and apparent speed of the circling pendulum. Now you can determine what this information might mean.

Evaluating Shape

The shape of a chakra can be misshapen or distorted. In general, a shift of the shape toward the right side of a chakra (from the subject's perspective) indicates issues of the masculine nature, such as domination and power, action and behavior, logic and rationality. If the shape shifts toward the left side of the chakra, the person may be dealing with feminine issues, such as receiving and responding, learning or healing, creating or feeling.

Here are some basic meanings of the general chakra shapes as perceived with the pendulum or through psychic vision.

- **Round.** Healthy and balanced.
- **Lacking substance on right.** Oriented toward unconscious programming, emotions, right-brain creative, but lacking action and follow-through.
- **Lacking substance on left.** Geared toward consciousness behavior and actions, left-brain analytic, but lacking creativity and intuition.
- **Lacking substance on bottom.** More spiritual than practical.
- **Lacking substance on top.** More practical than spiritual.

Correct the situation by shifting energies until the chakra is balanced. Use a symbol to hold this new shape; a cross of equal lines always works.

Evaluating Spin

Ideally, a chakra should hold a solid, even spin. Both the front and back sides ought to move the same direction. A clockwise pendulum spin usually indicates health. A counterclockwise spin often shows a blockage or a misperception.

However, the chakras spin counterclockwise when clearing or detoxifying. For women, this occurs right before and often during menstruation. For all, the chakras will spin backward under severe trauma, such as after an accident, after birth, just before death, when abused, during post-traumatic stress recovery, or after a medical procedure. Certain medical drugs will force the outer wheels to spin backward. Whatever the direction, a healthy spin should appear round, even, and about one foot in diameter.

Whatever the direction, a healthy spin, as reflected in the pendulum, should appear round, even, and about one foot in diameter. The inner wheel should move about twice as fast but in rhythm with the outer wheel. It usually moves in the same direction, but, like the outer wheel, will switch direction as needed. Sometimes it will go in reverse to clear negative information-energy or to provide balance. The inner wheel of the eighth chakra goes counterclockwise most of the time to create connection with the imagination pathway. When the eighth inner wheel spins fast and hard, it often forces the outer eighth chakra wheel to spin backward, too.

Following are the meanings of outer wheel spins; this also correlates to inner wheel spins. It can be difficult to use the pendulum to differentiate between the inner and outer wheels of a chakra. I check on the inner wheel by holding the pendulum in the very center of a chakra and close to the physical body. You will see tight spins if you've hit your target. To test the outer wheel, hold the pendulum two to three inches offcenter and farther away from the body. I recommend starting at least a foot away. Know, too, that you can use visual psychic senses to track chakra wheels. Knowing these meanings can help you work on the issues involved.

- **Round, uniform, and even swing, clockwise.** Healthy and functioning.
- **Round, uniform, and even swing, counterclockwise.** Attempting to create health or balance by processing or clearing negative energy.
- **Nonuniform or uneven swing, counterclockwise.** Chakra is blocked and unable to clear itself.
- **Elliptical or straight line in a vertical direction.** Developed but impractical spiritual views, closed to real-life perspective or won't take action.
- **Elliptical or straight line in a horizontal direction.** Practical but lacking spiritual perspective, closed to the big picture or divine assistance.
- **Elliptical or straight line, swinging to the right (of the subject).** Oriented toward action and the day-to-day, known as the masculine perspective, but lacking the emotional or spiritual, known as the feminine, perspective.
- **Elliptical or straight line, swinging to the left (of the subject).** Geared toward inspirational, feminine, or intuitive but lacking practical, grounding action.
- **Not moving or nearly still.** Indicates a closed chakra, shut down in functioning. A good place to look for a block or cause of a presenting issue.
- **Large swing.** Usually means very open, healthy, and functioning, but if too large and imbalanced in comparison to other chakras, it means the chakra is overstrained and overfunctioning. Figure out which chakra this one is compensating for.
- **Small swing.** Underfunctioning; must be cleared and opened.

In general, you want all chakras spinning about the same. This indicates a balanced system.

Evaluating Speed

How do you know how fast or slow a chakra or its component part should go? You can often assess the proper speed of a certain chakra by comparing it with other chakras. If it is out of synch with others, something is wrong.

In general, the lower the chakra, the slower both wheels should be moving. The other rule of thumb is that the inner wheel usually moves at exactly twice the speed of the outer wheel and, except for the eighth chakra, in the same direction. Here are a few diagnostic tips for inner or outer wheels:

- **Wheel too slow.** Indicates damage from previous overuse, exhaustion, fatigue, blocks, strongholds, and probably repressed memories or feelings.
- **Wheel too fast.** Indicates current overuse; overstrain; acting to compensate for a weaker chakra or chakra wheel; or a desire to escape certain life events, people, feelings, or issues. Could be an attempt to release negative energy.
- **Outer wheel fast, inner wheel slow.** Lack of spiritual, emotional, intuitive, or creative drive or perspective; underdeveloped beliefs, feelings, or spiritual sense; excessive concern with physical or appearance.
- **Outer wheel slow, inner wheel fast.** Lacking action, commitment to follow-through, physical drive, or energy; excessive concern with spiritual or psychic matters; fear of moving into the world; exhaustion in the physical.
- **Out of synch.** Inner beliefs and needs don't match with outer reality or action.

Healing Infrastructure with Shape, Spin, and Speed

Once you figure out which chakric infrastructure might be disturbed, you have many healing choices. First, consider the extent of the chakric damage. If severe, use traditional or alternative medical or therapeutic means to work on the issue. Critical chakra disturbance almost always mirrors challenging life issues. If you don't have a presenting problem, consider obtaining medical tests to make sure you don't have a hidden illness.

Once you've covered your medical bases, the easiest way to heal a chakric infrastructure issue, and improve the correlating elemental issue, is to directly change speed, spin, or shape. Here are means for doing this.

- **Infuse with color.** Taking out discoloration and incorporating the correct color can change speed, spin, or shape.
- **Use symbology.** In the center of each chakra is a symbol representing the elemental program of the chakra. You can see this psychically through the elemental or the power pathway. You can remove negative symbols, repair injured yet accurate symbols, or insert supportive symbols.
- **Use toning.** Tones can spin out a problem or help infuse a solution.
- **Examine power levels.** A damaged chakra is almost always linked with a negative power level. Figure out the imbalance and process the issues involved.
- **Assess beliefs, feelings, and strongholds.**

The following sections describe the use of color, symbology, and toning in more detail. Power levels, beliefs, feelings, and strongholds are addressed later in the this chapter under "Elemental Energy Assessment Healing Techniques."

Chakra Diagnosis by Color

Particularly if you access any of the psychic visual gifts, examining the chakras for colors and discolorations can help you pinpoint an unhealthy chakra and therefore the root of a disease. You can then add and mix colors to encourage chakra healing. The following table outlines the healthy chakric colors.

Chakra	Color	Meaning of Color
One	Red	Passion
Two	Orange	Feelings and creativity
Three	Yellow	Wisdom and power
Four	Green	Healing
Five	Blue	Communication and guidance
Six	Purple	Vision
Seven	White	Spirituality
Eight	Black	Karma: the effect of the past
Nine	Gold	Soul purpose and unity with others
Ten	Earth tones	Relationship to the environment
Eleven	Pink	Transmutation (of negative to positive and vice versa)
Twelve	Clear	Link of human with Divine

Here are a few steps to take on the elemental pathway for checking colors.

Color and Generic Diagnosis

The color of a chakra indicates the health of an individual and the current state of spiritual integration. A clear-colored (or attuned) chakra is at least fairly aligned with the Divine, thus enabling a connection with the Spirit and increasing access to higher spiritual truths and powers. Discoloration, markings, muddy or black tones, or off-key colors indicate imbalance or disease. Very black or condensed areas can show entry points for energetic contracts or bindings, possessed energies, an influx of information-energy, or even aspects of someone else that don't belong within the system. Consider the color that is off, too slight, darkened, or overly potent. What's the color? Link it to the chakra colors, and you'll have a jump start in figuring out the chakra or auric fields in trouble.

The color and shape of a chakra reveal balance issues. If all the coloration is on one side of the chakra, you are missing half of the picture, indicating a stronghold. Keep in mind that the strength and intensity of certain colors may vary according to a person's ethnic or cultural background. (See "Cultural Differences" earlier in this chapter for more information.)

Correct the situation by shifting colors and energies until the color is balanced throughout the chakra.

Missing Colors and the Missing Self

What if you perceive empty spaces where there ought to be color, shape, or form? In all probability, some aspect of the self is fragmented and held either in another aspect of the self or elsewhere. "Elsewhere" can include another lifetime, a dimension or Plane of Light, free space, or even another person or entity. Or it may indicate recession—sublimation of an aspect of the self in another entity. If recession is occurring, you will psychically spy an energy binding of some sort around the empty space. Use the elemental techniques for owning the missing self and to renew the strength and power of this self in "Finding Your Fragments and Reclaiming Yourself," later in this chapter.

Coloring Your Healing

Using the following color charts, add colors to discolored or malformed chakras to create the necessary hues and configurations. Test the healing by reviewing the change the next day. If the coloration or shape is off again, review the list of harmful colors. You can determine the possible rationale for a chakric disturbance and then use other means to work out the issues. For instance, you might detect a black, brackish spot in the first chakra. You instill the red energy of life, but the next day the discoloration has returned. Black represents issues of violation or evil. Now you can search for an originating cause to this disturbance.

You can fill missing or tilted areas with colors, and then fasten these colors with geometric symbols to keep the healing in place, much like using a bandage. Tones can deliver the healing and help the chakra accept the change. For more information on which symbols and tones might be useful, refer to the "Healing with Symbology," below, and "Tone Diagnosis," sections later in this chapter for more information on what symbols and tones might be useful.

Spirit-Enhancing Colors Each color represents a different type of energy. This is my understanding of the meaning of a few of the basic colors:

Red	Life energy
Orange	Creativity and feelings
Yellow	Intellect
Green	Healing
Pink/Rose	Love
Blue	Communication
Purple	Vision, clarification of choices, and results of decisions
White	Divine will, spiritual destiny
Black	Power for movement, force behind change
Gold	Harmony
Silver	Transference of energy from one place to another
Brown	Practicality and grounding

Harmful Coloration By altering colors, you can create negative effects or bring someone under your power. The following colorations have these effects when done inappropriately and out of pathway law.

Added red tones	Overstimulates passion, anger, ego, or survival fears.
Added orange tones	Creates emotionalism or hyperactivity.
Added yellow tones	Overemphasizes certain mental ideas or beliefs to create falsehoods or judgments.
Added green tones	Overstimulates drive for relationships, codependency, and perceived need to heal what doesn't need healing.
Added pink tones	Can cause a sense of love where it doesn't exist.

Added blue tones	Causes perceived need to obtain more and more guidance or overexplain oneself.
Added purple tones	Causes compulsive planning or difficulties in seeing or sorting choices.
Added white tones	Overstimulates sense of spirituality and deemphasizes the need for power and action.
Added black tones	Imbalances spiritual energies with an emphasis on power; can cause power-lessness, emotionalism, or greed.
Added gold tones	Causes excessive idealism and a resulting loss of hope.
Added silver tones	Creates susceptibility to psychic sources.
Added brown tones	Muddies the waters and results in confu-sion, excessive practicality, and mundane obsessions.
Added gray tones	Shadows or covers an issue, causing lack of clarity; a symptom of smoking is too much gray in the fourth chakra.
Neutralizing	Erasing intensity creates emptiness and powerlessness; voodoo and mind control use these methods.
Imposing	Forcing a color over someone else's, thus achieving control of the other person; this is also called creating an *"overlay."*
Blotching	Creates inconsistency, making it hard for a victim to rely on him- or herself.

Healing with Symbology: Geometric and Number Symbols

There are two ways to accomplish symbol diagnosis. By far, the easiest is to examine the center of the chakra. Look to the middle of the chakra and ask to see which symbol is determining the current state of disre-pair. Refer to the number and geometric symbols charts to figure out the causal symbols.

Then return to the spirit-enhancing lists to figure out which sym-bols to substitute for the broken ones. Sometimes you'll want to choose an equivalent symbol, such as a right-side-up pentagram for an upside-down pentagram. (A pentagram is a five-pointed star.) Other times you'll need to provide an entirely different symbol. The easiest way to select an appropriate symbol is to harmonize with your spirit, using the exercise on personal harmonics in chapter 13. Then allow your spirit to choose the right symbol.

For instance, let's say the presenting symptom is overspending and the inner wheel of the first chakra is spinning four times too fast. You might find a broken circle in the chakra, indicating an early childhood "broken" relationship. You can repair the circle energetically, set the wheel at the correct speed, and then insert a pyramid to keep it in place. You may also want to conduct feeling and belief system healing as well.

Geometric Symbols

Here are generic meanings of major symbols, described in their healthy and spirit-enhancing states, and unhealthy and harmful states.

Spirit-Enhancing Symbols

Circle	Wholeness
Square	Foundation
Rectangle	Protection
Triangle	Preservation and immortality
Spiral	Creation and cycles
Five-pointed Star	Alchemy and movement
Six-pointed Star	Resurrection
Cross	Human-Divine connection and spiritual protection

Harmful Symbols

Altered Circle	Causes hurt, injury, damage, or separations
Altered Square	Used to overthrow or topple systems
Altered Rectangle	Imprisons or exposes to danger
Altered Triangle	Creates illness, disease, imbalance, and death
Altered Spiral	Forces abrupt endings, cessation of cycles or rhythms
Altered Five-pointed Star	Stifles, contains, suffocates, makes base
Altered Six-pointed Star	Causes stuckness, despair, and depression
Altered Cross	Accentuates ego or causes extreme dejection
"X" Formation	Evil or anticonsciousness

Number Symbols

Here are the twelve numbers most important for energetic healing work, with brief descriptions of their meanings when used appropriately and inappropriately.

Spirit-Enhancing Number Symbols

One   Beginnings. Represents the Highest Form, the Creator.

Two   Pairing and duality. Reflects that everything in the material universe is made of opposites, which are the same. A two splits unity but also holds two ones in unity.

Three   The number of creation, which lies between and emanates from a beginning and an ending.

Four   Foundation and stability. The number of complete balance—consider the four-legged stool.

Five   Direction setting. Space for making decisions. Represents the human figure, able to go in every direction at once or to travel at will.

Six   Choices. The presence of light and dark, good and evil, and gifts of love, as offered through free will.

Seven   Spiritual principles. The Divine. The number of love and action that produces grace. Key number of the third dimension.

Eight   Infinity. Recurring patterns and karma. Path of recycling. The number of knowledge.

Nine   Change. Elimination of what was. Ending of the cycles of the eight. The highest single-digit number, nine can erase error and evil and bring us to a new beginning.

Ten   New life. Release of the old and acceptance of the new. This number of physical matter can record the heavenly on earth.

Eleven   Acceptance of what has been and what will be. Release of personal mythology. Opening to divine powers.

Twelve   Mastery over human drama; becoming okay with being fully human and seeing the power in it. Mystery of the human as divine.

Harmful Number Symbols

Altered One   Prevents you from reaching a conclusion.

Altered Two   Forces unhealthy liaisons and keeps victims stuck on powerless side of the power levels.

Altered Three   Causes chaos.

Altered Four   Imprisons or creates craziness.

Altered Five   Creates trickery or delusion.

Altered Six	The number of the lie. Causes confusion and disorder, convincing the victim to choose evil.
Altered Seven	Establishes doubt about the Creator's very existence.
Altered Eight	Stifles learning and forces the recycling of harmful patterns.
Altered Nine	Instills terror and fear about change; keeps victims stuck in the eight.
Altered Ten	Prevents new beginnings and seeks to make victims continue the old ways.
Altered Eleven	Obliterates self-esteem and seeks to keep victims from accepting their humanity.
Altered Twelve	Disavows forgiveness and casts shadows over human goodness.

Geometric Symbol and Number Combinations

Certain geometric symbols derive extra power from their connection with a particular number. For example:

Number	Geometric Symbol(s)
One	Dot or a circle
Two	Horizontal line
Three	Triangle
Four	Cross with arms of equal length; an equilateral quadrangle
Five	Pentagon, also a pentagram
Six	Equilateral hexagram
Seven	Equilateral septangle; also a rainbow
Eight	Equilateral octagon
Nine	Three equilateral triangles
Ten	Circle with a cross of eight arms; a square with a circle in the middle
Eleven	Parallel lines
Twelve	A corona or rising sun with twelve lines; the lotus

More Healing Tips
through Chakra Symbology

By psychically seeing, repairing, and changing a chakra symbol, you can conduct elemental healing work. Here are some pointers:

· Find out if the current symbol is correct for a particular chakra. Compare with the symbols in the ninth for this chakra. If it's correct, leave it as is.

· Examine the symbol for discoloration, misshapenness, or breaks. Incorrect or damaged symbols will cause chakra disease and therefore life problems. (Ironically, they are usually damaged because of life issues.)

· Repair the symbol with intention, color, tone, or other means, or add a new symbol to create a desired outcome. You can connect the two individuals with three circles—the circle representing wholeness or return to wholeness, and the three calling the Divine into the union. If you want the relationship to assume its destined form, then color the circle white. If you want direct healing, the color green is appropriate. If you desire harmony, use gold; and so on.

Here are two examples of how to use geometric symbols and numbers for diagnosis and healing.

Relationship Problems

Broken or misshapen circles indicate inability to connect with the self, others, or the Divine; triangles indicate triangulations; misshapen squares reveal lack of safety. Disconnected lines with arrows show inability to connect with certain persons.

A 1 in the heart could reveal selfishness or fear of intimacy; a broken 1 in the first chakra might show a lack of self-acceptance. A 2 in the heart, especially a glowing or radiant 2 with a circle, reveals a healthy attitude toward partnership; a 2 in the first chakra, especially a dull or misshapen one, could indicate an unhealthy relationship attachment that is causing damage. If you see a 1 present inside a broken circle, you might simply substitute a 2 within a completed and pink or love-colored circle.

Mental or Emotional Depression

Depression is almost always indicated by a square holding muddy energy or a representative symbol. As with all symbols, you can analyze all aspects for diagnostic assistance. Consider the outside of the symbol. A black-lined square indicates a severe stronghold and can be tracked onto a power level. A white-lined square indicates a spiritually based stronghold. A square that is choppy or frayed can indicate a slight depression or indicate confusion about the reasons for being depressed.

Next, deal with what's inside the symbol. Let's look at the square. If empty, you're dealing with recession—you are depressed because you are missing a part of the self. If the box is full, analyze the insides to figure out which energy of the self is repressed. Red, for instance, might indicate repressed anger, an aspect of the first chakra (as in the infant self) or part of one's power. If the inside has a number, consider the meaning of the number. A 1 could indicate loneliness. A 9 might reveal problems with endings. An 8 might show karmic issues.

Consider also the placement of a geometric symbol. You could find the symbol inside the chakra, but the chakric configuration is usually mirroring another energetic or physical area. For example, a fourth chakra–based depression can be visualized in the chakra's center, but its causal box can be found outside the chakra—say, in the left shoulder. Picture a white-outlined box with a red 7 inside of it in this shoulder. This means that the depression is a relationship-oriented issue caused by a spiritual misperception, as white reflects spirit. A 7 is a spiritual number and, if causing difficulties, relates to a question about the Creator's existence. The red coloration could indicate a number of ideas. Perhaps the issue is causal and relates to the first chakra and therefore one's parents; or perhaps it creates a great deal of pain and anger. By continuing the analysis, you can more easily figure out the root of the depression and move on to using symbols and shapes for healing.

Want to release depression? Get rid of the box and "speak with" the energies that have been repressed. What does this hidden self need? What type of color, tone, symbol, or form will help him or her heal? Make these changes in the chakra and be willing to continue processing feelings that arise.

Tone Diagnosis

The auditory psychic sense can most easily use tone for diagnosis, but so can the more visual or kinesthetic. An auditory person can simply listen to a chakra and see if it's healthy or not, as well as tune in to the sound pattern of a problem. A visual person can envision a tone, by reading either a musical notation or chart, or a word ascribed to a note. A kinesthetic person can sense or feel music; off-tones will feel grating or heavy, and on-tones will create calm and happiness.

All musical notes hold a vibration and create different results. The human body is attuned to the note of A, as supported by academic research revealing "A" as the tone that started (and might end) the universe. This means that all of the body's physical and energetic systems will balance with "A" from the core of a chakra, outward. If we're dealing with overspending, for instance, you could play an "A" when repairing the circle to help the entire chakra accept its spiritual potential.

I've seen amazing results with tonal healing. A friend of mine listened to soothing tones every day for a month, and her arthritis disappeared. Over time, the tones cancelled out the patterns or spin of disease and replaced them with the body's natural order.

Although tones can assist in healing, they can also harm. There is, for instance, a Tibetan cult that hires out its members as assassins. They kill their victims with toning, reading the energy patterns of the victim and then deliberately emanating grating and counterproductive tones to stop the flow of basic life energy. This type of manipulation takes practiced skill, intention, and the ability to warp the spins of individual notes.

Tonal Baselines

In order to reap the benefits of tonal healing, you must decide if you want to use generic information or personalize the process.

There are several types of tonal healing. One of the most popular Western systems is based on the Chaldean system, which works with a "C"-based system. This means that "C" is the core tonal baseline. In the section, "Core Tones," I will present the basics of this system, as well as the version I developed for the Four Pathway approach, which is based on an "A"-baseline. Both processes are fundamentally Western and are best used by people descended from European and certain other northern continents. Certain cultures operate on atonal or chromatic scales, which would fix the core baseline as more sharp or flat, and perhaps operating in fifths rather than octaves. If you know the musical baseline that correlates with your primary ethnic background, I encourage you to use it as your tonal healing baseline.

The sections "Whole Notes" and "Sharps and Flats" are oriented toward the Four Pathway approach, and are based on healings conducted by professional musical healers and myself. I encourage you to experiment with this system, and see if it works for you, before using it for all your healing processes.

Usually, I recommend that individuals figure out their personal baselines before performing tonal healing. Everyone has a personal harmonic, a set of chakra-based frequencies that coordinates with his or her spirit. You can arrive at your personal harmonic using the steps provided in chapter 13, in particular the section on "Keying Into Your Personal Harmonic." I then encourage you to explore ways of applying your harmonic in tonal healing, using the ideas listed in this chapter on "Tips for Tonal Diagnosis" and "Tips for Tonal Healing."

The following table depicts the meanings of the basic tonal vibrations in the Western music system.

Whole Notes

As developed for the Four Pathway system, here are the meanings of the seven basic whole notes, when used for tonal healing.

A	Of spirit	Attunes human to divine nature, your human self to your spiritual self.
B	Of mind	Attunes your Lower and Middle Mind to the Higher Mind.
C	Of feelings	Attunes your human feelings to spiritual feelings.
D	Of body	Attunes your physical body, condition, or material needs to your spiritual body, gifts, or manifesting abilities.
E	Of love	Attunes whatever is out of love to unconditional divine love.
F	Of miracles	Attunes any aspect of your being to the spiritual forces needed at that time, breaking through duality into the miraculous.
G	Of grace	Delivers grace, which is divine love and divine power, to the situation at hand.

Sharps and Flats

Sharps and flats will have different meanings in different cultures. This is the understanding of these notes in relation to the Four Pathway approach to tonal healing.

Sharps bring the spiritual into material reality. An F-sharp, for instance, will activate that part of your internal spirit that links you with the force you now require.

Flats cause release. A G-flat, for instance, which is the same as an F-sharp, pushes out any negative or evil forces preventing your spiritual destiny.

The difference between working with a sharp and a flat is intention. If you desire to get rid of something, think flat; to attract something, think sharp.

Core Tones

As already suggested, there is disagreement as to the core tones of each of the chakras. Several esoteric groups, including versions of the Chaldean, work with a "C"-based system. I point out that there are two versions of the scales. The first is octave-based, in which notes are repeated in eighths. The second counts in fifths and is the model I believe underlies the Primary Grid, alchemy, and the divine in the elemental pathway, as relating to the Fourth Pathway approach. I start fifths with an "A," and then merge the idea of the octaves into it for elemental-based healing.

Basic Chakra Tones

Basic Chakra Tones	My Theory	Esoteric Theory
First Chakra	A	C
Second Chakra	B	D
Third Chakra	C	E
Fourth Chakra	D	F
Fifth Chakra	E	G
Sixth Chakra	F	A
Seventh Chakra	G	B
Eighth Chakra	A	C
Ninth Chakra	B	D
Tenth Chakra	C	E
Eleventh Chakra	D	F

As suggested, a more personalized way to figure out tonal healing is to establish your own baseline. The next two sections offer tonal healing processes, some of which involve using your personal harmonic as the baseline. Please see chapter 13—in particular, the section on "Keying Into Your Personal Harmonic"—for more information on this.

Tips for Tonal Diagnosis

You can follow these steps when using tones to diagnose an issue.

1. Figure out your basic or personal chakric tones.

2. Assess your chakras or those you believe are healthy to establish the accuracy of your baseline.

3. If you want to figure out the chakra containing the core problem, listen to the center of each chakra to see which is most out of tune. Consider whether the tone is flat or sharp in relation to a well-tuned instrument, such as a pitch pipe or tuning fork. If flat,

the causal issue is most likely on the physical plane, subconscious, and involving negative and depressed energies. If sharp, the causal issue is probably spiritually oriented, relates to the unconscious or conscious, and involves positive and anxious energies.

4. Every disease or problem is an aberrant tone. If you suddenly sense an out-of-tune energy in your body, quickly assess for incoming issues.

5. Refer to the meanings of the notes to see which issue might be affecting you. If an "A"-based chakra is off, for instance, you might ascertain the issue as one of balance, or consider that your basic assumptions of life are off.

Elemental Energy Assessment Healing Techniques

There are several ways to assess and direct basic energies for healing on the elemental pathway. Here are a few.

Energy Particles and Charges

For health on the elemental pathway, you must have a balance between positive and negative charges and protons and electrons. Here are tips for determining where you lack balance.

Depleted Negative/Electrons (overly positive/protons)	Depleted Positive/Protons (overly negative/electrons)
Anxious, scared, can't settle down	Tired, depressed, lackluster
Managing energy bodies disconnected	Managing energy bodies stuck
Fear-based beliefs, feelings, and power levels	Shame-based beliefs, feelings, and power levels
Chakras never spin in reverse; too "wired"	Chakras consistently spin in reverse
Auric field too thin	Auric field too thick
Coloration too light, won't hold substance	Coloration too dark or muddy, sticky
Chakric tones too high	Chakric tones too low
Issues future-based; fear of what's coming	Issues past-based; shame and fear because of what's been
Overly psychic	Psychic sense too low

All elemental techniques are basically a way to balance the electron-proton energies in the body. However, there are a few unique methods for using electrons, protons, neutrons, and charges to actually accomplish healing.

Electron-Based Healing Electrons are electrical in nature. What's interesting about their attachment to atoms is that sometimes they are simply not attached. You can find an electron for a chair, for instance, possibly a football field's length away from the rest of the chair.

Electrons store what we often consider to be negative feelings and beliefs. Why not work with the nature of electrons when healing? Here are three techniques for doing this.

Regressing to the Past. Electrons will congest in the place and time originating an issue. Let's say your food issues started at a birthday party when you were two years old. Feel the issues of today. Concentrate on the negative effects listed in the table under "Energy Particles and Charges" on page 202, and then follow the energies and feelings on the "electron highway" to the anchoring electron base. Now you can recall the original trauma and subsequent self-defeating decisions. This information can be useful in understanding your issues or illness. Making a new decision can also transfer the change all the way into the present and reorganize the electrons you're currently working with so that they work for you.

Expanding the Present. Electrons follow logical pathways. If you're experiencing electrical-based issues, it's because you've taught your electrons to stay in a pattern. Breathe deeply and imagine that your current problem has transformed; healing has occurred. Use your visual psychic sense to watch the movement of the electrons that are holding this "new life." Use intention to establish your chosen solution as true in the here and now. Ask inside which behaviors you need to adopt

» Tips for Tonal Healing

THERE ARE MANY ways to use musical notes, even for the most unmusical of us. Once you have diagnosed your situation energetically, you can use an instrument, toning, or singing to create single-or multi-noted healing tunes. Here are a few ideas:

• I recommend that you begin and end any sequence with an "A." A high "A" can open your system, and a lower "A" can close it.

• Place the note signifying your healing need before the note you think will assist you in owning the healing. For instance, if you have a cold, you could open with an "A" followed by a "D" for the physical system. Do you want a miracle? Play an F— or, if you want your own spirit to activate more fully along with the miraculous forces required at this point, play an F-sharp. You can follow with an "A" if your objective is this simple.

• Trust your intuition to guide you in selecting notes, instruments, and songs. Many spiritual songs—including ballads, old Christian hymns, Hindu chants, Buddhist mantras, African-American soul music, cultural folk tunes, and inspired classical pieces such as those written by Mozart, Bach, and Beethoven— are coded with musical sequences for healing.

• For general balancing, align your chakras with the various notes.

• For personalized balancing, figure out your own harmonic. (See chapter 13.) Everyone is attuned to his or her own composition or harmonic. You can work with a professional to figure out your own soul or spiritual arrangement, or simply select a song that sings to you. Most likely, your favorite melodies are those that best match your personal self.

Use music for intuitive purposes. I often hear songs that indicate divination information or healing instructions. If a song pops into your head, pay attention!

to permanently effect this change. See elemental physical solutions earlier in this chapter for ideas.

Owning the Future. There are many potential futures, and in the psychic world these possibilities already exist. Select the one that you want and that harmonizes with your spirit. What beliefs are operational in the future? What feelings keep you happy? Lock into these fresh feelings and beliefs and download them into your brain circuitry through intention. Ask what behaviors you need to perform to secure this resolution.

Proton-Based Healing Protons encourage love and highlight our spirit's dreams. Light particles within the protons can also move faster than the speed of light. Here are ways to work your protons for healing.

Changing the Past—a Regression Technique. What if your spirit had managed your past? Think of how different your life would now be, mainly because you would have seen situations differently at the time and perhaps made different choices.

Protons don't move the way electrons do. They are attracted to neutrons or electrons and disappear elsewhere when there is nothing to keep them in place. Look backward at a difficult time, one that you believe may have caused a current problem. Now ask where the protons "lived" before they gathered around the causative situation. What if they had never joined their brethren to light up the difficult event? If they had had their choice and if they represented your spirit, what would these protons have chosen to enlighten instead? Let them do it! Let the protons of your own spirit change what happened back then, and see what occurs now.

Creating a New Present. Concentrate on a current problem, especially one causing you anxiety. Imagine that all the protons involved in the situation are centered inside of the issue. Now enlighten them. What spiritual beliefs underpin your current issue? What spiritual idea would alter the situation into a more positive one? Allow a switch of either protons or the information coded within them, and see what radiates forth.

Bringing Brightness from the Future. Ask to see the best potential outcome for a current state of affairs. The protons in this possible future will shine. See what you might need to do right now to create this reality and possibly even transfer it into the here and now.

Neutron-Based Healing Neutrons are neutral charges and hold the key to healing issues such as cancer. Here are several neutron-based healing techniques.

Get What's Going On. Want to know why things are the way that they are? To get beyond judgments to the truth? Imagine that you are standing on the neutrons holding a situation in place and ask to psychically perceive the energetic reasons for this situation.

Going for the Pink. Neutrons can emit a "pink" charge, the energy of love that can heal electric issues. Think of the issue and ask what discharge (or anticharge) you can intentionally release from your neutral self that will "love" a healing into place.

Going for the Gold. You can also access "gold" charges through the neutrons, which are magnetic energies that create forceful change. Think of the situation and ask which types of magnetic energies need to come through your neutrons to remedy it. Are you willing to allow the potential transformation?

Blending the Best. It's important to integrate the magnetic and the electrical aspects of yourself or an issue. I commonly come across individuals in fundamentalist religions who have been "saved" or "healed" by the Holy Ghost or their religion's equivalent. The healing involved in spiritual settings usually involves an opening of gold, magnetic energy, which often heals spiritual issues and ideas about love. But what about the electrical side—the one holding the life wounds, pains, and agonies? These don't feel good to the spiritualized self, and so the psyche splinters the dark, electrical shadow side from the light, magnetic spiritual side. The wounded, inner-child aspects are now abandoned, left behind in the mundane while the profound flies. The self hasn't healed, only split. The magnetic side becomes anxious and stretches toward the future, while the electrical side becomes depressed and cries to be rescued from the past. The issues are still there, but are now projected onto other people who are seen as bad or evil if they don't meet one's spiritual standards.

It's equally dangerous to remain entrenched in the electric and deny the magnetic. This is the story of materialism and excessive emotionalism. Without a link to spiritual meaning and love, the power-based drive of the electrical turns money, sex, alcohol, or other material resources into gods. If not transformed by spiritual energies, feelings remain body-based and it's difficult to discern their true meaning. What we deny flies in our face.

Neutrons provide an ideal perspective for blending the best of the other two sides. After healing an electrical or a magnetic issue, "stand" in the place of the neutron and link the two energies. Envisioning the healed state, you can picture dark matter or electrons within the image and light around the image. Now emanate pink and gold energy from the neutron and connect the different energies. Once they blend, you have integrated and exponentially increased the healing effect.

Dealing with Charges Sometimes the information causing a situation departs, but the positive or negative energy charges don't leave. A negative charge will be psychically dark and cause electron-based issues. A positive charge will appear light and cause proton-based issues. Charges are held by elements. Figure out which element is holding the charge in place and call for the contrary element. For instance, water drenches fire and air can move water. Figure out how to bring these elements into your physical self through elemental means such as diet, exercise, and breath work.

Life Energy and Kundalini

Most often, the kundalini on the elemental pathway is either under- or overfunctioning, usually due to ignorance. Here are signs that could point to kundalini dysfunction, although these problems could obviously indicate mild to serious medical disorders and must be considered by a professional.

- **Underfunctioning.** Lack of energy, low adrenal, thyroid, or other hormone usage, sense of hopelessness or uselessness. (See other signs under "Depleted Positive/Protons" in the previous section.)
- **Overfunctioning.** Oversexualization, wild behavior, out-of-control thoughts, blown-out chakras. (See other signs under "Depleted Negative/Electrons" in the previous section.)

If these energies are underfunctioning, consider concentrating on the red energy in your first chakra. Remove blocks—especially cords, bindings, and attachments. Now build the kundalini energy. Kundalini is nothing mystical, although esoteric literature would have you believe it so. It is simply basic life energy.

Work psychically to perceive which elements are needed to increase the intensity. Fire? Wood for the fire already there? Air to fan the fire? Do you need to get stone off the fire?

Check the chakra spins. You want the inner and outer wheels balanced; if you lack kundalini, one wheel or the other wheel, or both, is going in reverse either so slowly you're "killing the fire" or so fast you are whipping it around. Establish a rhythmic spin in the first chakra (women can start in the second chakra if preferred, pulling energy up from the first chakra) and when you've built enough fire, weave this energy from chakra to chakra. If it gets stuck, work on the issues in that chakra and set the spin there before continuing. This technique is ideal for weight issues—as it will raise your metabolism—as well as for lack of financial success and low libido.

If your life energy is overfunctioning, it's for one of two reasons. First, you might not be controlling the energy in your first chakra, which means it is probably getting displaced horizontally instead of being used vertically. This is an anxiety-producing situation and it's a good one to get under control. First figure out the reasons for this situation, using psychic viewing and regressions if needed. You can use most elements to structure the basic life energy for full use. Stone can surround and contain the fire, directing it upward. Air can draft it upward, and metal can deflect the fire to keep it contained. Now follow the energy upward chakra to chakra; in the upward direction, you'll probably find a problem in one of chakras, which is one of the reasons the kundalini wasn't moving up.

The other typical reason for kundalini overfunctioning is a pull into the future. Highly anxious people (or chakras) want to escape the present so badly that they fan the flames toward the future. So what if the self of today needs a boost? Today isn't any fun. Let's go for tomorrow. If you are actually dealing with an illness, see Part Five to figure out how anxiety might play a part. Otherwise, figure out why you so badly want to avoid today's problems or opportunities, and then start the serpent going.

For more information on kundalini, see the activation of the golden kundalini process described in chapter 13.

Energetic Communication Methods

Sensory and psychic abilities must be balanced for healthy participation in the three-dimensional world. Signs that these are off include the following:

- **Too Sensory.** Receives little to no psychic or spiritual input, can't obtain spiritual guidance when needed, has depleted positive/proton energy charges. You need psychic and spiritual insight to reach other pathways for exponential healing.
- **Too Psychic.** Can't deal with real life, lacks psychic control, is manipulated by external sources, has depleted negative/electron energy charges. You need grounding in senses for life performance.

Dealing with being too sensory or too psychic is actually the topic of another book that I have written, which is only available over my website at this point. It is called *The Intuitive Development Bible.* These are major life issues and deserve more than a few words. And yet it's vital to achieve a healthy state of sensory and psychic information usage. Here are some quick pointers.

If you are too sensory, you're probably entrenched in the past. So make it work for you. Use regression to return to the situation that's causing you to "turn off" your psychic sensitivities. Opening the psychic sense in a healthy manner can help alleviate depression, give you needed insight to improve your current life situations, and help you relate better in relationships. Studies even show that psychic individuals are better at making stock-market decisions; you can follow "gut instinct" even when reading a balance sheet.

Being overly psychic is potentially dangerous; it can lead to a strange sort of vampirism—a sort of psychic codependency. Gathering others' psychic data into yourself clogs the lymph system, which processes physical and psychic wastes; this can create an inordinate amount of problems. I would say that up to 75 percent of all issues in sensitive people are caused by absorbing others' energies.

You can take on just about any energy from any of the five levels of reality. The following are the most commonly absorbed energies:

- Feelings
- Beliefs
- Illnesses and diseases
- Patterns
- Energetic charges
- Energetic contracts
- Fragments of others' souls, of mind or body aspects, or of group consciousness

These energies can be absorbed partially or fully, which is a means of possession. You can be possessed by an energy that is animate or inanimate. If it's strong enough, it can overpower your own natural sensitivity or ability. Quite often, energy absorption occurs through an exchange. You give someone else your energy and receive his or her energy. If someone or something else is holding your energy, you are affected by recession.

There are many reasons we might take on or give away energy. The first is security and safety. We consciously or unconsciously soak up others' energies because we believe it will guarantee our survival. Usually, we begin this process in the womb or early childhood. For instance, a newborn might sop up Mom's rage, fearing that otherwise, her anger will overtake her and she might kill her own child. A five-year-old might adopt Dad's belief that the world isn't safe, in an effort to feel close to Dad.

I once worked with a woman with high cholesterol and hypertension, for instance. I knew that both conditions are blood-related, which typically involves the first chakra. I also sensed that they related to feelings, which tend to run through the second chakra. Through a chakra-based elemental analysis, I determined that the cholesterol was caused by her adrenals, located in the first chakra, where she was holding her mother's fear of her husband. The spinning anxiety raised the cortisol to such levels that my client's liver was unable to keep up with the overdriven hormones and clean the body of harmful fats. The hypertension was created by my client's hatred of her abusive father; she stored the hatred in her kidneys, which are in the second chakra. The hatred affected the cell salts and ultimately, her blood pressure. The body didn't care which feelings belonged to whom; they affected my client as if the fear and the hatred were self-oriented.

Know, too, that unless you clear to wholeness, the spinning energy will repel elemental-based healings, from energy work to supplements. My client was on Lipitor, a drug for cholesterol, as well as natural supplements. Neither had worked. As soon as she diagnosed the origin creating the lack instead of fullness in the body, both long-term conditions cleared up within a few weeks. Conscious recognition of the situation allowed her mind to let go of the reasons for holding onto symptoms. All along, the symptoms were messages to point the way to wholeness. Once the message was finally received, my client could alter her intentions and the body, tune in with all other aspects of herself, and allow the drug and supplements to work.

Here are ways you can tell if you've absorbed energies from others:

Feelings In a current situation:

- A feeling hits you out of the blue and you can't figure out why.
- Your feelings suddenly swing from more to less comfortable when spending time with a certain person. His or her undesirable feelings dissipate when with you.
- You're off your game all day, until you come in contact with someone whose life circumstances explain your previously unexplainable feelings.
- You're suddenly overcome by a surge of energetic colors, sensations, symbols, tones, or other feeling indicators.

Over time:

- You try but can't get to the bottom of a challenging feeling.
- No matter what, you can't ever feel a certain feeling. This might indicate an exchange of feelings, or that you've recessed a feeling somewhere outside of yourself.
- Certain situations trigger an unexplained emotional reaction, and professional assistance hasn't helped you figure it out.
- You find energetic contracts between you and someone else; feelings will probably be involved.

- You stay in a negative situation, relationship, or environment even though you know it's bad for you, because of a strong emotional reaction when you try to leave.
- When using psychic means to evaluate the elemental pathway, you notice the presence of a too-intense coloration or a strong form in your feeling-based bodies, such as the second chakra or auric field or the emotional body. Or you spot off-orange colors in any of the managing energy bodies.

Beliefs You may have assumed a belief that is not your own if:
- You keep acting a certain way and can't seem to stop, despite constant work on the issues.
- Thoughts run through your mind; you aren't mentally ill, and you can't figure out where they come from.
- There's a certain thought process that just doesn't seem "you," and you can't shake it.
- You know that Mom or Dad used to think a certain way; you don't agree, but you act as if you do!
- You seem stuck in a prior time period that has nothing to do with today. For instance, you want to be "taken care of" despite being a modern-day feminist. The belief is perhaps left over from a Victorian lifetime.

Illnesses and Diseases Center in the chakra with the presenting problem. Visual psychics should think of a presenting illness and ask it to form into an image. Now ask to see the source of this image. If it's not you, you'll know. Verbal psychics can ask to speak to the illness and demand that it honestly share its source. Kinesthetic psychics might first move into the state of the pure self and then imagine the illness dwelling as a contained energy within the first chakra. They can demand that a personal illness remain within the chakra but that anything not of the pure self be expelled.

Patterns You've likely absorbed someone else's pattern if:
- You can't explain certain of your repetitive actions or behaviors with your own life story.
- No matter how hard you work on breaking a pattern, you can't.
- You feel like you are "under a spell," as if compelled into certain repetitive ways of being.
- You keep acting just like Mom or Dad, and you don't want to do so.

See the write-up under "Energy Bodies" in chapter 12 for important ways to use the tenth chakra and auric field. All patterns can be seen through these energy bodies.

Energetic Charges You can assume energy charges from other people, places, and time periods. For instance, have you ever walked into an empty room feeling fine and left feeling depressed or fearful? There might have been a lingering energy charge from another person in that room. Anything that has weight carries information. Information can be stored in all elements, physical properties, foods, substances, and so on. You can eat bread and actually tell if it was baked with love or hate. Any sudden change in mood, disposition, or even health in reaction to a person, place, or time could involve assumption of an energy charge. (For healing suggestions, see "Energy Particles and Charges" earlier in this chapter.)

Energetic Contracts We form many energy contracts, bindings, and attachments ourselves. What about those that we inherit? What about those we're born into? Think of the American story of the feuding Hatfields and McCoys. If you were born a Hatfield, you had to hate the McCoys, and vice versa. These types of agreements are assumed, sometimes along with forces. Refer to the "Energetic Contracts" section in chapter 5 to learn how to psychically detect these inhibiting contracts. The "Transpersonal Process" in this section will work for healing energetic contracts, and there are additional healing methods under "Energy Contracts" at the end of chapter 12. The tenth chakra write-up in the "Energy Bodies" section of chapter 12 also includes tips for healing contracts.

Fragments You can review chapter 6 for a thorough overview of the types of fragments of self and others you can assume. Here are the most typical situations that I see:

Others' Soul Fragments. This problem usually carries over from a prior life and is often guilt motivated. My client Harold, for instance, had appropriated an aspect of his daughter's soul from a previous incarnation. Having caused her death back then, he felt he needed to carry her now. Indications of an internalized soul fragment include an inability to free yourself from a relationship, an intense pattern with a particular person, hauntings or visitations from the same being, and an inability to release someone after he or she has died. Some people even continue to hear the deceased speaking from inside of themselves.

Mind Aspects. You can assume any part of an animate being's Lower, Middle, or Higher Mind through the particles or consciousness governing that being. This is even more catastrophic than absorbing a belief, because you could absorb a pattern or consciousness paradigm of beliefs. If you can't shake a belief, check for a mind subaspect that will cause the type of interference symptoms discussed in chapter 6 and use the tools provided to locate absorbed beliefs.

Body Aspects. It's very common to take on others' body aspects. It's usually done out of care and love; the negative form, however, is called *caretaking*—which literally means to "take in" and "care for" parts of others.

- *Caretaking of an inner child* is the practice of guarding, protecting, or tending another person who can take care of themselves. You, however, can't stop seeing them as too little or wounded to self-care.
- *Caretaking of an innocent child* creates the incessant drive to see someone else as good or innocent despite evidence to the contrary.
- *Sublimation of a personality aspect* gives you a sense that you're uncontrollably acting like someone else, copying the person's mannerisms or attempting to live the person's life.
- *Absorption of an ego aspect* means you've taken on a way of thinking about yourself that doesn't seem natural. For instance, you find yourself reaching for fame when you really don't desire it.
- *Caretaking of a primal self* involves an overwhelming and instinctual drive to follow base nature, such as in sex addiction, violence, personal neglect, refusal to bathe, or other self-degrading behavior. If professional help isn't working, consider checking to see if you've sublimated someone else's primal self.

Group Consciousness. Group consciousness is extraordinarily powerful; it is often at the bottom of unexplainable, erratic, or fanatical behavior. Check the consciousness section of chapter 6 for the various types of group consciousness if you see these signs:

- Zealous adherence to a negative, destructive, or controlling person, group, idea, or force.
- Inability to escape the leaders of a fanatical group or a person caught in a strongly discriminatory belief system (such as a wife beater, religious fundamentalist, or tax evader).
- Inability to fit in or follow normal societal mores; inability to prosper or thrive even though you have the obvious skills and drives.

Freeing Yourself from Others' Energies: The Transpersonal Process
If you think that you're dealing with assumed energies, you can conduct an elemental-based healing process called the Transpersonal Process, which will also work for any of the eight types of assumed energies discussed above.

1. Center yourself in the issue and ask the Divine to separate your own from any others' energies. Ask your own energy to step aside and wait awhile. You will communicate with it shortly.

2. Command that energies not your own create an image that can speak and communicate with you.

3. Demand that the energy now present itself in a representation that shows its truest form or nature.

4. Ask why this energy joined with you. What did it want to receive by this action? What did it receive?

5. What did it take from you?

6. Now ask the energy of yourself, which has been separated out, what you received from joining with the other energy. What was your payoff? What did you expect to receive? What did you actually receive?

7. Ask yourself what you need to do, own, know, feel, learn, or experience to release the energy that is not your own.

8. Ask the other's energy what it needs to do, own, know, feel, learn, or experience to be willing to leave.

9. Release the energy that is not your own. If it doesn't want to go, ask for Divine assistance. This is your right.

10. Cement your chakric and auric field back into place, first repairing any damage. Ask for Divine assistance and healing, now and as you integrate this change.

11. Commit to acting in a whole way for yourself.

Finding Your Fragments and Reclaiming Yourself Not only do we implant others' energies, but we also give our own energy and parts of ourselves away. Ever feel, for instance, that a part of yourself is missing? Maybe it is. Life energetic cords keep us attached to a part of ourself that lingers in the past. Can't stop thinking about a former girlfriend or boyfriend? You might have done an exchange. You might have given a part of your heart and are holding a part of his or her heart. Sometimes we can't recover from an illness, relationship, or job loss because an aspect of ourself has been recessed.

Here is a method of calling back recessed energy.

1. Ground and center yourself.

2. Track the recessed energy to its location. You can look for cords, bindings, filaments, energy lines, and attachments; follow the flow of neutrons; or simply ask to see where the missing self or energies are at this time. If you are verbal, you can attune with your heartbeat and listen for the rhythm of the missing self in the universe.

3. Acknowledge the presence of the Divine in and around you for safety.

4. Psychically look at the situation. Are you caught or trapped? Willingly somewhere else? What aspect of the self is externalized and why? How is your life affected by the lack of this self, energy, or gifts?

5. What needs to occur to integrate this self or energy again? What do you need to know, understand, do, or learn? What does this self or energy need to know, understand, do, or learn?

6. When it and you are ready for integration, ask the Divine to bring the healing or release teams of angels on the scene, and other guardians of the Divine to assist. Allow this self or energy to be fully purified, cleansed, and transformed for integration, and that room be made inside of you for it.

7. Ask the Divine to deal with energies that are not your own—whatever or whoever was holding the externalized self—and to completely sever and heal you from any energetic attachments.

8. As you allow integration, ask that you be told anything you must do to be supportive of a safe and easy incorporation.

9. Cement your chakric and auric field back into place, first repairing any damage. Ask for Divine assistance and healing, now and as you integrate this change.

10. Commit to acting in a whole way for yourself.

Energetic Cleansing with Physical Properties Repairing after an energetic release can take some time. Here are some elemental-based measures that can speed the process, aid in recovery after possession and integration work, and take care of cleansing from others' energies on a daily basis.

White Wash. Picture the Divine's white energy flooding your body like a fountain, flowing from above, through your body, then down through your tenth chakra. Ask that all energies be transmuted by the earth, which will recycle them.

Black Tea Bath. Boil five to six black tea bags in rapidly boiling water for five to ten minutes. Add to a full bath. Set the intention of flushing feelings and toxins that are not useful. When done, add colloidal oatmeal to the bath or rub baking soda on your skin to restore your skin's pH.

Implements. Select a rock, amulet, or other tool. With intention, use it to absorb others' energies. Cleanse the tool weekly in the rain, in Epsom salts and water, or through intention.

Shaman Techniques. Use candles, incense, drumming, or burning sage to cleanse yourself or your home of others' energies.

The Elemental Pathway: Where the Finite Becomes Infinite

While most of us are attuned to the physical substance of the elemental pathway, the elemental bridges to places and spaces beyond that which we typically imagine as "real." In this chapter, we will continue exploring the fundamentals of the elemental pathway, in addition to the spacetimes that take us into the Great Beyond.

In chapter 11, we examined the major areas governed by each chakra, cultural differences, physiological touchstones, age development, physical issues, chakra infrastructure, and points about chakra shape, spin, speed, color, symbology, and tones. We then discussed matters related to energy particles and charges, kundalini, and energetic communication. In this chapter, we will continue with our discussion of the elemental pathway, covering issues regarding energy languages, energy bodies, power levels and fields, energy packages, forms of energy, times and places, energy laws, and other forms of elemental healing.

Our thoughts form what we believe to be reality,"
he said.

"At this moment, my mind is creating a very deep crevasse, master,"
the prince murmured.

"And my mind is creating a very strong bridge," the lama replied. [1]

—Isabel, Allende,
*Kingdom of the
Golden Dragon*

Energy Languages

As discussed in chapter 7, each pathway has its own energy languages. Those languages work together to maintain health, but imbalances can develop when our fears or issues prevent full use of a certain language. We might, for instance, be afraid of certain feelings and so ignore the language of feelings altogether. We will then inaccurately perceive others' feelings and react inappropriately in emotional situations. Here are signs of elemental language imbalances:

Matter. If you rely solely on matter, you will be too sensory, depressive, and unable to heal from repressive illnesses. Lacking feeling, you won't understand why you feel depressive or stuck. Without heart, your relationships will appear empty. Illnesses and stresses will be material-based, such as those involving lower chakras.

Feeling. If overusing feeling, you will be overly emotional and suffer from emotional strongholds and emotion-stimulating traumas. A lack of matter can cause severe life stresses, including monetary issues. Without enough heart, feelings cause disrepair rather than bonding in relationships. The second and sixth chakras will be especially affected.

Heart. Too much heart leads to codependency, caretaking, and heart issues, usually because you take on others' energies. You will be heavy and despondent and never feel "good enough." Lacking matter will keep you ineffective, though well intentioned. Too little feeling ensures that you feel only others' feelings, not your own. Signs include boundary issues in any chakra or auric field and a distended or overused fourth or sometimes seventh chakra.

For imbalances, you must first figure out why you are too scared to use an elemental energy language. Use electron-based regression if you're missing matter or feeling; use proton or neutron for more heart. Make the shifts by doing the following:

To increase matter. Practice your psychic sensing through the first chakra. Meditate while exercising. Hold objects and see if you can read their energies or those of their owners. Flush out all extra psychic information with white light.

To increase feeling. Exercise your psychic sensing through the second chakra. First, make sure you always know your own feelings. Then begin to sense others' feelings. Turn feelings into colors and read others for their colors. Flush with white light to release extra energies.

To increase heart. Work your psychic senses through your heart. Attune to the nature of your relationships and analyze which energies you pass back and forth. Study the relationships between all else, including those in the natural, supernatural, human, and Divine. Get in touch with your inner children and, most important, your innocent child. Flush with white light.

Energy Bodies

Here is a chakra-by-chakra analysis of healing you can perform in each chakra and their attached energy bodies.

Through the First Chakra

Do you have money, a healthy sense of sexuality, meaningful work, close companions, an active lifestyle, and good health? Any imbalances in your daily physical life indicate a first-chakra imbalance, usually caused by a sexual, financial, or physical trauma and often originating during the chakric development stage from womb to six months. Energetically, I often check the first chakra (and all others) for energetic contracts. These have a very strong effect on your well-being. Removing these contracts can make an instant difference.

When dealing with life-threatening addictions, genetic illnesses, cancer, and other traumas, I check the power levels fixated in the first chakra. *Any* severe and especially life-threatening pattern usually involves a fixated, first-chakra power level, which, in turn, inhibits the first power field development for security.

The first chakra is highly affected by any sort of womb or birth trauma, past-life difficulties, adoption, or abandonment situations. When the tiny child isn't nurtured, wanted, accepted, or physically tended, even in the womb, the first chakra is inhibited. Basic life energy won't flow evenly or correctly, and the outcome is physical disease later in life. If the first auric field doesn't fully unfold by the time the child is delivered, the other auric fields will be stunted as well. The child then won't develop what's called the *light body,* a secondary impression of the auric field that allows power infusion. The energy egg will retract from the power bodies, leading to an inability to later perceive a reality greater than the elemental one. This easily leads to hopelessness and inhibitions. It also can potentially lead to either an inability to believe in a God or, ironically, a fanatic religiosity, which also indicates an inability to believe in God or goodness. If the egg implodes, so will the cytoplasm of the cells themselves, leaving the person vulnerable to disease processes, including cancer.

You can often determine first-chakra issues by examining the skin itself, which is part of the first auric field. Is it healthy and glowing? The first chakra probably is, too. Sallow or weak? Yellow? Full of lesions and breakouts? That's exactly what you would see in psychically mapping the first chakra. By treating the first chakra, you can treat the skin and vice versa.

First-chakra solutions are too numerous to list, but they always include taking practical action in addition to energetic work. Don't like your job? Get a new one. Overweight? Join Weight Watchers and start walking.

On the elemental pathway, the first energy bodies are linked to the causal body, as are the tenth energy bodies. The causal contains codes for the distribution of basic life energy and the access to vital source energy. Any energy, chronic, or terminal issues should be examined through the causal body. Is the causal programming helpful or not? Does it match one's physical or spiritual genetics or not? Sometimes the programs in the causal are ancestral or interjected and need to be changed.

The pain body can also be fused with the first energy centers. This body is supposed to float freely, so as to collect and clear pain or allow the power pathway to transform the energy within it. We humans like our pain, however. We mistakenly think that if we hold onto it, it will protect us from attracting more. The pain body consequently becomes filled with the pain, shame, feelings, and beliefs about pain, and, in turn, attracts the same types of frequencies and situations. Clearing the pain body can sometimes eliminate repetitive situations.

Through the Second Chakra

Here, feelings are king and queen. This center physically houses dozens of neurotransmitters, which must all be operational for good health and well-being. You can psychically overview these neuro-transmitters to make sure they are clean and pure, much like performing a car engine overhaul. Then ensure that this chakra is plugged into the first chakra. The first chakra sends basic life energy into the second chakra, which floods the *feeling bodies*—units of the five basic feeling constellations—with this life energy. In turn, the feeling bodies transform basic life energy into *chi*, energy needed to express yourself physically and psychically. If this process gets gummed up, the lymph system, for instance, becomes clogged with psychic toxins and eventually physical waste.

Here is where you check for feelings that aren't your own but assumed from others. Others' feelings will psychically look like energy clogs, congestion, and shadows. They will often be attached with fila-ments to energies or people outside of yourself. Others' feelings will supplant your own, and you'll see empty spots in the second chakra and auric field where you've given up your own self. In women, empty spots can also reflect abortions, miscarriages, or children desired but never conceived. Abortion issues include a mother's wish or attempt to abort us; the abortion of our own child; or a desire to abort ourselves from life.

Smudges or discolorations can indicate judgments against certain feelings and, sometimes, feelings we've used to manipulate others or ourselves. Black spots reflect victimization from abuse, such as in physical, sexual, emotional, or verbal abuse by others, or self-abuse, which can involve self-hatred, anorexia, bulimia, or substance addic-tions. Spinning spots often cover repressed feelings, and deadened areas reflect agony and apathy. The key is figuring out if the smudged, discolored, or heavily colored areas hold our own or others' feelings.

You can't heal a feeling that isn't your own. On the elemental pathway, such feelings must be released.

One way to work feelings on the elemental pathway is through the blue or emotional body. This body is supposed to access higher spiritual points or power forces to energize feelings into creative drives. Usually, however, it's treated like a suitcase. We stuff uncomfortable feelings into it and pull them out when it's convenient. Usually, the blue body attaches to the second centers, although it can latch onto any of the chakras. Like a bucket, it gradually becomes full until it slops over. Indicators of this include emotionalism, feeling-based cancers and illnesses, bowel and intestinal disorders, anxiety, and attraction to negative relationships.

Through the Third Chakra

Governing the digestive organs, the third chakra is an ideal stomping ground for energy, work, and power issues. This is the first place I check for energy leaks. With issues such as chronic fatigue, hyperactivity, and hypoglycemia, you'll probably see holes, splotches, and misshapen power fields in and around the third chakra and auric field. By mending these, you can greatly improve daily functioning. You might also find energy blocks—stuck energies lodged either in or between the actual physical and energy organs. By examining these blocks for their payoff, the body can rebalance itself.

I examine third-chakra organs for general health and specific organs if a life condition seems to correlate. Look at the liver and gall bladder for power issues or anger at men. Confusion? Look at the stomach. Unhappiness? The pancreas. If I know I'm dealing with mental strongholds, I check all organs to see which might house a related misperception, then continue to work with the third auric field. This field is like a net into the universal library, rather like Carl Jung's collective unconscious. Through it, you can access beliefs, thought forms, and consciousness waves that can change thinking—and thereby change a life.

Want to run freely through the known universe? Exit energetically through the pyramid-shaped indentation just under your rib cage. Each rib connects to a different dimension, all of which can be reached by flying through this indentation. If entity interference, including ETs, is a possible issue, I check for cordage in this space. The interconnection to other dimensions can open the susceptible to all sorts of influences.

The third energy bodies are your connection point to the mental body—that finely meshed series of consciousness waves fused to the third auric field, several of the morphogenetic fields, the mental plane, and the power fields. The mental body will store information that you acquired in the past and information you might need in the future. It also peruses others' mental bodies for pertinent data, sometimes accessing knowledge that isn't useful or could even be harmful. Prejudice, self-criticism, and judgments frequently impede the effectiveness of this body and can lead to fear, phobias, uncertainties, rigidity, ignorance, and learning problems.

Sometimes I work through the third chakra to access the *technology center*, an energy body able to link all three sections of the brain through the Middle Mind. This center processes technological data for personal or humanitarian ends. If someone has difficulty organizing, structuring data, or working with technology, they might not even have a technology center—a necessity for joining the Information Age. You can template this center from the Christ body or etheric mirror if necessary.

Through the Fourth Chakra

The heart connects to all dimensions involving relationships. Many health, monetary, and relational issues involve the heart and can be diagnosed or solved through this chakra. For instance, the back of the heart chakra houses beliefs about relationships—with finances, the Divine, your body, objects, and other living beings, dead or alive, from this life or previous lives. I frequently check the heart chakra for cords and miasms, working the tenth chakra simultaneously. Feeling and emotional charges are commonly lodged inside of the heart or translocated in the shoulders, elbows, wrists, or knees; joint problems can be tracked back to the heart and relationship causes. Other chakras may also be involved. Joints are also linked to the twelfth chakra.

All six primary beliefs impact how open the front heart chakra is; if energy moves through from front and back, you'll know or receive your heart's desires. If there are blocks, you won't be open enough to receive what you want.

The fourth auric field can link to any or all dimensions or planes. If nightmares or fears are common, I usually check to see if the fourth field is vulnerable to the astral plane, a level open to any and all characters, living or dead. Hauntings, incubi, succubi, and negative creatures of all sorts can creep into our energy system through the astral plane.

One of the primary ways to work the fourth chakra is through the Low, Middle, or High Heart. Depression and anxiety almost always involves Low Heart issues, as well as other energy centers, whereas manifesting problems can involve the Middle Heart. Issues including lack of courage, low self-esteem, self-hatred, victim-victor relationships, battering and abuse, and codependency may result from an inaccessible High Heart. Fundamentalism and fanaticism almost always stem from the High Heart's being invaded or controlled by group consciousness.

The fourth chakra is an ideal place to conduct inner child work or the healing of the personality self that has developed because of life trauma. Your inner children are really fragments of the self, fixated in certain time periods by the terror of the trauma. Because they are reliving the same tragedy over and over, they are linked with life energy cords, and your current self serves as the battery charger. Basically, your inner children are draining you of basic life energy and holding you in terror. I often recommend uncovering the innocent child, who is similar to the God self, except very here and now. This is the self you would have been if not abused or traumatized. By integrating this self into your heart, you allow a full healing of the inner children, with the added benefit of the wisdom and compassion emerging from experience.

Through the Fifth Chakra

This verbal center is perfect for gaining guidance and input, and necessary for commanding change. Before working from it, check for cords, bindings, or other interference in the back. Use intention and verbal commands to get free, as these "old tapes" can distort or block information from your own higher self or spirit. You can also use tones, chants, or music to clear the back-side chakra. Once cleared, you can use this chakra to source higher guidance from any of the five levels of reality.

I usually establish a gatekeeper—a guide appointed by the Divine—to prevent interference and to ensure that I correctly understand messages. You can also gain insight from others' guides through this chakra.

The front side of this chakra expresses various forms of consciousness to manifest the reality held by the front-side sixth chakra. If these two energy centers are in conflict, the stronger one wins—usually the reality charged with emotional or mental strongholds, or the one most intensely bound on a power level or field. If you're not getting what you want in life, check the alignment between both sides of your fifth, sixth, and seventh chakras, concentrating on the front-sides of the fifth and sixth.

A powerful manifesting technique is to link forces through the eleventh chakra with the back side of your fifth before expressing your intention through the front side of your fifth. Make sure you're clear about what you want, because you'll get it. You might also energize unspoken and unconscious desires, which might not be that great, so consider first working the divine pathway before using this technique.

Another important dialogue occurs between your fifth energy bodies and the gray body—the tunnel-like body that connects you to the beings of various dimensions and planes. This body can be directed toward any source, including your own aspects and subaspects, for information. If you frequently find yourself prey to incoming voices or obsessive-compulsive thinking, you should check the location of this body and learn how to intuitively manage it.

Through the Sixth Chakra

This place of sight is ideal for visualizing causes and solutions. The best technique is to center yourself in this chakra to examine all other chakras. When energy mapping, keep this center open; then, no matter what your psychic gift, you'll be able to picture or draw your map. When healing, link your strongest energy center to the sixth; as you visualize change, your main center can follow your visualizations and create energy shifts.

I often look through the back of the sixth auric field to access potential choices. Don't like the choices? Access your seventh chakra to create new ones. Then examine the front auric field to see what choices have been selected. This is your *manifesting screen*, a visual portrait of what's coming into focus and reality. Don't like what you see? Center in your sixth chakra and create a link to your fourth chakra, the holding place of heart's desires. Then ask what's causing resistance to your inner dreams and work from there.

Through the Seventh Chakra

What an invaluable center for conducting preventive and spiritual care! My first suggestion is to use the seventh auric field to check for potential illness. A future illness or calamity often enters the auric field most visibly through the seventh chakra; it is often seen psychically as a gray shadow beam pointing to its final destination. Potential breast cancer, for instance, will appear in various colors but will always shoot toward one or both of the breasts. Keep in mind that with this and all chakras, you can use any means to work energetically. If you're not visually psychic, ask for guidance and input, or use your senses to "feel" your seventh chakra.

Check and work the seventh chakra for causes related to depression, anxiety, seasonal affective disorder, spiritual ailments, brainwashing, and just plain stress. I also like to clear heavy metals in and around the seventh chakra. These often armor the seventh chakra and the pineal as a defense against spiritual negativity, but can become a problem if there is too much of them.

The seventh chakra is a vital psychic resource. Access your main psychic gift—let's say it's sight. Now, read a presenting problem through the seventh chakra. You'll determine the nature of the consciousness or intelligence creating the issue. By figuring out the belief-based cause, you can change beliefs, unlock strongholds, and erase the structure of the issue. Do the same through your pineal gland, the main doorway to the divine pathway. Through the pineal, you link all psychic abilities so they function in unison. You'll be able to hear, sense, know, touch, smell, and understand anything, all at once.

Another important information source connected to the seventh auric field is the energy egg, which encases your managing energy bodies. This egg has leaders connected to all the secondary chakra points and the power system. The secondary chakra points are available through the twelfth chakra and auric field and include the knees, ankles, organs, cranial bones, and other structural, muscular, and connective-tissue functions. If you have an issue with these body parts, it can be helpful to check for energy egg leads to make sure they are present and in working order.

A note on the development work done through the tenth in regard to the tar body: as the star seed of destiny activates in your seventh chakra, you free the master self—the aspect of your Higher Self that has mastered the human existence and finds joy in the everyday. By putting the master self in charge of your daily life, you can achieve great and small things.

Through the Eighth Chakra

A trained and gifted healer can accomplish thousands of tasks through the eighth chakra. The most obvious skill is reading the Akashic Records, to source the soul's historical record, and the Shadow Records, to unearth regrets. These can tell you if a presenting problem started in the past and why it might now exist. I specifically read these records for issues in the Zones, the Planes of Light, other dimensions, and other spacetimes.

The eighth chakra is the access point to all the dimensions and planes of existence. Together with your eighth auric field, it serves as a walkway between all worlds, including the natural, spatial, interplanetary, and more. It's an ideal place to center yourself if you want information. Simply "stand" in the core and ask for help! You can also ask for healing energy or information to be delivered directly to you.

When needing to release certain energies, such as cancer, it's helpful to set this intention in the center wheel of the eighth chakra, which frequently spins in reverse. You can also deliberately spin the points within the eighth auric field—or the entire field—backward for a set amount of time. This counterclockwise spin can spin the disease out of your system. You can channel higher forces or use symbols to establish a more intense or directed reverse spin, thus adding more power to the process. For instance, using a spiral shape will increase your success; a reverse spiral emanates energies out, a clockwise spiral brings energy in.

Frequently, I check the eighth chakra for the same types of cords as I do the first. The nice thing about working cords out through the eighth energy bodies is that you can direct numerous universal energies to aid you in your task.

The eighth chakra and auric field are ideal for soul journeying to other places, dimensions, times, and universes. You can remote-view by linking to your sixth chakra or lucid dream through the heart chakra to connect to guides and other people. Or you might dreamwalk through the first, tenth, or eighth chakra and produce physical changes through the administration of force. When doing any of these, be sure to protect your silver cord, as well as your physical body. The silver cord links your soul to your physical body, as well as to the silver body. The silver body processes information from the Akashic Records. Based on your beliefs, the silver body determines what issues, gifts, and weaknesses from the past you should activate in the present. If you don't like what's in your life, check the silver body and make a new decision.

As with all journeying, it's best to set stones or other infused protections around yourself for added safety. Journeying is the easiest way to examine for recession or possession issues, to gather soul fragments, and to battle negative energy predators.

Through the Ninth Chakra

The ninth chakra is ideal for working with symbols. It is rich with the symbols, numbers, shapes, and patterns that determine your soul nature and purpose, as well as your link with the extended world. Here you can search for broken or interjected symbols and forms. Correcting the symbols that cause disease can sometimes cure problems. As well, you can channel various natural (and power) forces through the healthy symbols to increase health and well-being. By spreading forces first through the corrected ninth chakra, then to the ninth auric field, you extend the healing through all worldly aspects of yourself.

I also check the ninth chakra when someone is experiencing repetitive relationship challenges with either a specific person, a group, or a behavior. Soul relationships lock in and can be corrected through this chakra; look for energy cords, bindings, and all the other energetic connections discussed in the first chakra description.

I sometimes have people work their ninth chakra to find the God self. The God self is an idealized version of the human self—the self that any human would or could have been if life had been easy. The God self isn't the same as your pure spirit; it will still have issues and problems. It will, however, have experienced unconditional love from another human being and so be better able to accept Divine and human love. You can access the energetics of the God self and correct anything from attitude to physical malformations by simply transmitting part of the God self into your elemental self. Be careful to not exchange "that life" for "this one"—an imagination delusion fantasy. Here, you have free will; in the God life, you don't.

Through the Tenth Chakra

The basis of tenth chakra work is working with nature. A traditional practice in indigenous communities is to call upon environmental beings and energies for diagnosis or change. Plant, animal, faery, elemental, and other nature beings are available to pinpoint the causes of physical disease. Many medicine people form ongoing relationships with natural spirits that serve as personal helpers, providers of vision, or sources for healing energy.

I often check the tenth chakra to determine the source of someone's grounding—that is, how they obtain, process, and use earth energy and the basic life energy available through matter. Many people don't ground into nature in any way; this is a common source of problems, including spaciness, dizziness, disassociation, low energy, environmental allergies and illness, and even mental illness. Others ground into negative energies, from either this life, past lives, or ancestral sources. Chronic or serious illnesses can arise from improper grounding. If you're too deeply grounded into the center of the earth, for instance, you become a channel for the fire beings. A few fire beings can burn blood toxins; too many result in viruses that cause diseases such as arthritis.

I psychically examine the tenth chakra to check for ancestral or environmental causes of disease. The entities involved in hauntings or *latent interference* will always cord through the tenth chakra and then secondarily through one or more other chakras. The term latent interference means the same as hauntings. My physician friends usually use the latter term. Soul fragments from previous lives or from ancestors also link through the tenth, as will negative connections from entities, such as familiars or ETs.

You can determine the nature of all natural and ancestral relationships by analyzing the types of cords in the tenth energy centers. Search for cords, energy marks, holds, curses, and bindings.

As well, peruse the morphogenetic field for *miasms*, which are family or soul patterns decipherable in the tenth chakra. Miasms often carry family disease traits and tendencies. Multiple sclerosis and other autoimmune diseases often run on miasms. To check for a miasm, psychically look at the tenth chakra for smudges, dark places, or empty areas. Then trace these distortions to the tenth auric field and inspect for distorted grid marks. The tenth field is like a net that plugs into the Secondary Grid lines. A miasm presents as a clear and distinct change in grid patterning. It's usually tied to one or more power levels. You can actually follow the miasm to its origin—the person, place, or experience that started the patterning.

The other key tenth-chakra elemental work involves working natural energy fields and forces. The tenth chakra is your key lock-in site to the following.

Ley lines. Chronic or persistent problems should be checked for ley-force involvement. Many individuals, for instance, hook into an earth or a planetary ley line when being born, and it keeps them locked into a familiar but unhappy pattern. This may show up on an astrology chart, but not always. If a therapist suggests that life issues originate in childhood problems, such as moving homes a lot, I try to uncover which ley line the adult is fixated to. Then I help the client instead connect to a current geographic site—or even to a spiritual energy. I also evaluate the present connections for shape, coloring, and flow to see if they are healthy.

The Vivaxis. You can spot the Vivaxis between the inner and outer tenth chakra wheel and also in the very center of the tenth auric field. It looks like a net latticed to various earth and sky energies. Work it as you would for all ley-line examination, detachment, and repair.

Morphogenetic fields. These are all imprinted in the tenth chakra and auric fields. Many organic, chronic, lifelong, or terminal illnesses are marked in the morphogenetic fields, and therefore in the tenth energy bodies. These fields can be intracellular, cellular, organic, systemic, or energetic. However, it's too complicated to check every organ or diseased physical site for field damage, so I work through the tenth energy bodies. The easiest way to do this is to picture the vertical lines in the tenth auric field. The ones closest to the center (where the

Vivaxis is) are intracellular; those farthest away are fields connecting to the spiritual points (and global energies). You can assess the various lines for health and thickness and thus determine which morphogenetic fields may be in disarray.

Power levels and fields. Want an easy—okay, somewhat easy—way to assess power levels? These appear as the horizontal lines in the tenth auric field. Each power level continuum connects to a power field and then onto the Secondary Grid. Power levels and fields repeat in patterns up and down your body. It's very helpful to map your own power levels and fields, using psychic visualization and obtaining help from your spiritual guides. You can then check your tenth auric field for problems and conduct repair work. You can also correct emotional and mental strongholds by repairing the power fields, since strongholds wrap into the power levels, then the fields, then the Secondary Grid. All of this can be checked through the tenth auric field.

Through the tenth centers, you can also check two other bodies. The Christ or etheric mirror body holds the correct template for your tenth auric field and therefore your physical body. Want to skip a lot of diagnosis steps? Create a template or model health for your physical body? There's a slight psychic space between the outside walls of your tenth auric field and the Christ body. This is an aspect of the imagination pathway, where you must imagine yourself whole and complete to access the Christ body. Make this leap and you will land in your physical template in the Christ body. From there, you can access full power and divine energies through the imagination capability of pretending, and translate these into your tenth auric field. It usually works best to transfer energy through the power fields.

The tar body is also connected to the tenth energy centers. It is located beneath the tenth chakra in an aspect of the subconscious. This body holds not only beliefs, but also the seed of destiny. The spiritual genetics the seed contains will, ideally, unfold within the body through the chakric development until you reach full maturity. These spiritual genes help convert the chakras into channels of light for the divine pathway and manage the physical genetics to reach spiritual destiny. As they unfold through the various enlightenment and kundalini processes, they actualize the star seed of destiny in the seventh chakra, which converts the pineal into the master of spirituality. The tar body is a good lens for checking the primal self—the reptilian-based self that is able to access natural energies. This self reflects the analogue way of moving in the world and, if healthy, can keep you in flow with the rhythms of the universe.

Other significant diagnostic and healing methods available on the tenth are soul journeying and *consciousness journeying*. When soul journeying, you are traveling in your soul, a soul fragment, or soul etheric. When consciousness journeying, you put yourself in the middle energetic field or, even better, the Christ body or etheric mirror, to consciously project into different worlds, in order to gain information and healing energy. This type of journeying and others were briefly described in chapter 6.

Through the Eleventh Chakra

The primary technique of eleventh-chakra elemental work is to command forces for diagnostic setups and to clear negative energy. You can command natural forces—for instance, wind, water, and sun—to move anything from others' feelings to a blood clot out of the way so that you can use other psychic techniques to check what's really going on. These and other natural forces can also be used to perform healing. Colds and flus, for instance, often respond to increased wind or water—whichever force will wash them away. Fungus, yeast, and molds are sticky and can sometimes be eliminated with fire.

The following can intensify natural force healing: adding various colors; using spin; shaping the forces geometrically; or filtering the forces through numbers, geometric shapes, or symbols. You can also pull natural forces through the spiritual points to add spiritual energies; this is extremely useful in spinal healing. As well, the eleventh chakra and interlacing auric field are a perfect place for filament healing. Filaments are energy strands that connect the elemental, imagination, and power pathways. By moving filaments out of the way, such as around a tumor, you can potentially free basic life or vital source energy and allow the body to balance itself.

Through the Twelfth Chakra

The twelfth chakra connects to thirty-two secondary points in the body. If you think connective joints and tissues, you have this chakra. All of these points are connected; therefore, if you work on your knee, for instance, you're also working on your elbow. To find the center of the twelfth chakra, look in the center of any of the secondary points, which are all listed in chapter 8 and detailed in my first book, *New Chakra Healing*. You can work a secondary point as you would a regular chakra and thus repair all other aspects of your body.

Power Level and Field Diagnosis

Power levels are obvious in everyday life. You can use the chart in chapter 5 on power fields and levels in several ways for diagnosis. First, consider the presenting symptoms. Do you have a terminal illness? You are facing a survival issue, which qualifies as a first power level and a first power field. Use the following section, "Energy Packages," to help determine the types of feelings or beliefs holding you in stronghold; you can then determine the nature of the issues causing your problem.

You can also link the power levels and fields with corresponding chakras. The first power field and level link to the first chakra, power field and level two link to chakra two, and so on.

For a quick assessment of your relationship with other energy fields, consider the following:

Ley-line involvement. This is often present when you're unable to change focus or geographic areas or to free yourself from natal chart issues pinpointed in astrology.

Morphogenetic fields and lines. This is a probable factor if your issues repeat common family patterns—including genetic, relational, financial, or emotive—or reflect another strong group membership, such as cultural or ethnic.

The Vivaxis. This is an issue if you are constantly "hit" by natural or spiritual forces.

Energy Packages

All elemental issues involve misplaced or misinformed energies holding information comprising beliefs or feelings.

Beliefs, Emotions, and Spiritual Themes

For substantial change, you often must process the beliefs or feelings holding you in strongholds. This may very well take professional counseling. When preparing, you can make progress by figuring out which chakras are blocked or problematic. This can be done by assessing the mental, feeling, or emotional issues, or by looking up which chakras relate to a corresponding issue.

The easiest way to perform elemental-based energy mapping is to figure out which chakra holds the originating issue. The following table outlines the mental, emotional, and spiritual themes associated with each chakra.

Chakra	Beliefs	Emotions	Spiritual Themes
One	Beliefs about security and safety. Beliefs about our sense of worth; whether or not we deserve to be alive or to be the gender we are, or deserve to have a body at all.	Initiator of primal feelings, such as rage, joy, terror, sorrow, grief, despair, guilt, and shame. Holds others' feelings and opinions about our existence and perceived value.	Is the body good? Is it of the Divine? Will we run on divine power or on our own power? Will we follow divine will or our own?
Two	Beliefs about feelings and creativity. Beliefs about sensuality and your right to enjoy your body.	Processes the softer feelings, like fear, frustration, sadness, happiness, and disappointment. Determines how you will respond to your own or others' feelings.	Do you know God as a feeling God? Do you know your feelings are messages from your own spirit, telling you how to respond to events and people?
Three	A collection of beliefs, usually fear-based. Beliefs about power and success that affect your self-esteem, self-confidence, and behavior in the world of work. Place where you can be held in bondage to the "group mind."	Runs the feelings that determine self-esteem and self-confidence; stores fears and judgments about yourself, others, and the world.	Are you living your life purpose on a daily basis, especially at work? Do you know you deserve to be treated with respect, as well as to have and maintain boundaries?
Four	Processes beliefs about love and being worthy of it; how you should treat people and be treated in kind. Here you can be affected by "group heart" and beliefs bonding people through relationships.	Deals with all feelings related to relationships. The place to heal emotions that have caused you pain.	What is your relationship with the Divine? Do you know you deserve divine love? Here is the place the Greater Spirit can integrate with your spirit; place of the lotus symbol used in East Indian philosophies to illustrate the blending of human with divine through love.

Five	Beliefs regarding your right to say "yes" or "no." The place where "old tapes" enter. Back of throat receives guidance from higher- and lower-plane spirits. Front of throat is regulated by issues of self-responsibility.	Stores words you haven't said and the feelings behind them; the place to add power of feelings to your words.	Do you know the Creator began it all with a Word? Do you know that the Divine will give you words? That the Divine will tell you what to say? The place of manifesting your own desires through thoughts, writing, music, and speaking.
Six	The place where you store your self-image, which determines what futures you can see. Here is where you are programmed by culture, experiences, family, and your own soul. Group visions designed to benefit the group or a cult figure, rather than yourself, can also manipulate you.	Holds feelings about how others imagine you. Can access feelings that will create you in body as in spirit.	Can you see yourself through Divine eyes? If you can, you can view life choices through the back of the chakra and their results through the front of the chakra.
Seven	The place where you interject religious or spiritual ideas about the Divine and your humanity. Source of "group soul," if you are forced to follow a cult figure or fundamental beliefs limiting free choice and God.	Holds judgments about feelings as either spiritual messages or cause of problems.	Do you know you have a spiritual purpose and a destiny, and that the Divine provides the insight and power you need to meet them?
Eight	Holds beliefs gathered from the past—past lives or beliefs affecting you from other times, people, planets, or places. The notion of karma rules unless you undo it: an idea must make up for all past sins.	Storage of all repressed feelings from all lifetimes' experiences. Place where lack of forgiveness can rule.	Do good and evil exist? Is evil stronger than good? Can the evil you've done ever really be forgiven? There is a need here for the consciousness of the Buddic philosophy, which would ask if there is even a need for forgiveness.

Chakra	Beliefs	Emotions	Spiritual Themes
Nine	Illuminates beliefs held in soul groups and your own soul.	Holds feelings you have never felt about your purpose and soul-based relationships.	Do you know your soul has followed a path and is unique? Where is that path headed?
Ten	Holds beliefs about your ancestors; life experiences and conclusions; nature and your relationship with it.	Can carry feelings of your ancestors and of nature, including animals and plants.	You are a product of all who came before you. As a child of the earth, do you take care of your body and the environment?
Eleven	Programmed by beliefs about good, evil, and power.	Acts as a screen to emotions. Allows some emotions and energies in and not others. Ideally, here all feelings can be transmuted into healthy energy.	As a part of nature, you can command peace. You can transmute negativity into goodness.
Twelve	Shape and function are a result of beliefs about humanity and divinity.	Separates "good" from "bad" feelings unless you are accepting of them all.	Do you know we have a new model—one that blends the human with the Divine?

Review the chakra-by-chakra analysis under "Energy Bodies" earlier in this chapter to see which healing techniques are available with each specific chakra.

Here are a few general tips for healing after diagnosis.

Beliefs

Look at the lists of elemental-based beliefs versus feelings in the chapter 5 section "Energy Packages." Which draws you? Do you center on a belief or a feeling?

Belief-based issues usually cause rigidity, inflexibility, and either a severe inability to act or an overuse of action to solve problems. This usually results in an adherence to idea-oriented power levels, such as victim-victor, ignorance-knowledge, and bad-good, as well as an inability to achieve 100 on power fields one, three, five, seven, and nine. (Power levels and fields are outlined in chapter 5.)

On the elemental pathway, you usually attempt to heal a belief by working with its opposite on the continuum. For instance, if you believe that you are powerless, you would substitute that energy for a belief that you are powerful. There are several other successful ways to boost healing of beliefs on the elemental pathway.

Substitution of Beliefs The quickest way to start belief healing is to consciously decide that you are going to live as if you believe the opposite of the negative belief. Get used to thinking and acting positive. Then practice a method that I call *choosing voices*. We've internalized hundreds of voices that tell us what to do. Ask to hear which voice is overriding all others and causing your presenting issue. What core negative belief is this voice supporting? Pinpoint the chakra that holds it. What belief should be substituted for the misperception? Make sure that the belief you select mirrors a spiritual truth, not simply a belief opposing the one in charge. Selecting a contrary message only furthers the tendency to run power levels and create internal discord. Now transform this spiritual truth into a voice, giving this new voice permission to command all other voices (and beliefs) that have caused your current problem.

Continuum Belief Healing Pinpoint the causal belief of the six major negative beliefs and the chakra that houses this controlling misperception. Ask yourself where this belief is positioning you on a power field. For example, does your third-chakra powerlessness inhibit you at 30 percent on the third power field? Use internal mediation to ask what it would take to reach 100 percent. At 100 percent, you won't be stuck on a power level—you won't be sliding between "powerful" and "powerless." You will be your own source of power in carrying out your own life plan. The goal is to get *off* the continuum. So write a plan. Remember the power of intention on the elemental pathway. If you strive for your goal, you can get there.

Choosing a Quality When we assume a negative belief, we're testing this belief through life experimentation. We're trying on a way of perceiving ourselves. Unfortunately, we get used to negative thinking. In this healing method, don't worry about the core negative belief or its opposition. Instead of substituting another belief, try replacing a negative belief with a quality, such as faith, honesty, assuredness, or joy. One of the "genes" on your spiritual genetics will work best. Visual psychics can also picture colors, flowers, symbols, or gems to lock in the substitutions.

Feelings

Feeling-based issues often create emotionalism, inability to self-determine, inability to act effectively, and confusion. The results are an adherence to feeling-oriented power levels, such as holding-sending, fear-love, and innocence-guilt, as well as problems on power fields two, four, six, eight, and ten.

An important point to remember about elemental feelings is that the body can't distinguish between feelings about yourself or someone else, or your own feeling frequencies and those of others. See the "Energy Particles and Charges" section in chapter 11 for a list of signs that you've absorbed another's feelings. As I've said, feelings hold messages, but you have to get to the spiritual message to really work your feelings. Read the section labeled "Feelings" under the "Energy Packages" section in chapter 15 on the divine pathway and then fill out this chart to assist you in feeling healing. Think of your presenting issue. Now follow these steps:

1. Is this mainly a mental or an emotional stronghold? If mental, work on beliefs. If emotional, separate belief from feeling. Work on the beliefs and then proceed to feelings.

2. Feel the feeling. Use your pendulum or psychic sense to see which chakra holds the original feeling. Check psychically to see if there is any shame involved; if so, separate the shame, just for now, by envisioning it as a gray, blobby energy and putting it in a psychic box. Stay with your core feeling and transform it into an energy. You can perceive this energy as a color, sound, sense, symbol, or sensation. What is the message of the information-energy?

3. Deal with the message. What is it telling you to do, become, or show? Forgive yourself for not having listened before, and then deal with the belief, if you've been in an emotional stronghold. (Step one has you work on the belief prior to doing this, so presumably you have already dealt with it.)

4. If you've set aside shame, you are dealing with denial. You have denied a truth about yourself and covered it with shame. You must get to the truth and its message. Use regression, if necessary, or chakra-based analysis. Go onto the divine pathway and unpin the basic need. Shame will burn away if you figure out your core need and decide how to meet it.

Elements

You can work elements physically or psychically on the elemental pathway. After testing for missing or superfluous elements, work physically with a naturopath or nutritionist to remedy the situation. Work with a pH expert if possible, as elements alter pH. Psychically, it's easiest to work chakra by chakra to rebalance elements. After pinpointing the chakra holding the core problem and figuring out your elemental imbalances, connect your spirit into the center of the chakra. Now fill out the following chart.

Element	Percentage Too High	Percentage Too Low
Water		
Earth		
Fire		
Air		
Metal		
Wood		
Stone		
Ether		
Star		
Light		

You can ask what electrical or magnetic charges, feelings, beliefs, bindings, cords, or attachments are inhibiting the automatic balancing of your body and energetic system. Work these issues and the elements will shift. As well, you can use your psychic senses to shift elements inside and outside of a chakra core. This core will then release unnecessary elements through reverse spin (usually through the inner wheel) through your auric field, or distribute needed elements into your body through a clockwise spin (again in the inner wheel).

The pH Balance and a Unified Approach to Energy Packages

One way to measure for general and specific issues is by checking your pH balance. pH is a measure of the acidity or alkalinity of a solution; the term actually refers to the acid-base balance. In reference to the body, the pH of your blood, saliva, urine, and vaginal fluids is easiest to measure to check one's health and test for specific health issues. The ideal pH measures 7.0 on a scale of 0 (strongly acidic) to 14 (strongly alkaline or basic). Acidity rises when there are too many acidic compounds in the body, either through increased intake or production of acid substances, through decreased elimination of the same, or when the alkaline compounds fall. The reverse can make your system become too alkaline.

The body uses many mechanisms to control pH. Carbon dioxide accumulation increases acidity and so lowers your blood scores. Adjusting the speed and depth of your breathing can quickly regulate pH. The kidneys excrete balancing compounds, but it can take days to make a difference. There are also pH buffers that work chemically.

Severe pH imbalances underlie or indicate almost all elemental-based disorders. A too-acidic condition lays the foundation for diabetes, lowered immune response, lung problems (including pneumonia and asthma), fatigue, premenstrual syndrome (PMS), yeast infections, and more. Too much alkaline can cause panic attacks, hyperventilation, anxiety, cirrhosis, and fevers.

I don't believe that pH fluctuations are the cause of an elemental problem, but rather the response to emotional, spiritual, mental, or physical factors creating an imbalance. Respected pH expert Dr. Mark Cochran suggests that the saliva pH measures the emotional imbalances causing physical maladies, and that urine pH assesses straightforward physical causes for problems. By using medical means to

» Working with pH Balance

THIS IS A picture showing the continuum of acidic to alkaline pH measurements. Many experts recommend achieving an overall balance that is slightly alkaline, such as 7.0. Following are descriptions of the different measurements as developed for the Four Pathway process.

0	7.0	14
(acidic)	(balanced)	(alkaline)

0–3.0. Particles or thoughts too negative, electrical-based, and emotionally charged. Severely depressed energy and spin. Trapped in the past and lower dimensions. Ruled by subconscious; the Lower Heart, Self, and Mind; causal, emotional, black and silver bodies; lower chakras including tenth, first, second, plus the eighth. Possible bindings in the ninth chakra, as well as hauntings, bindings, or latent interference affecting other energy bodies. Probable recessed or possessed soul issues. Probable life energy cords, spells, curses, and similar bindings. Pain and gray bodies need work. Tar body inclusions (like seed of destiny) and spiritual genetics not accessed at all. Decisions made through Akashic Records. Probable capsized energy egg, often leads to cancers, major heart disease, or autoimmune disorders. Probable collapse or near-collapse of auric fields. Insufficient tenth, first, second, and third auric fields. Higher fields probably not activated. Probably too entrenched in the Languages of Matter or Feeling. Probable influence of a group consciousness, often from past life, ancestral bed, or a life in between lives. Consider working the Zones described under "Times and Places" later in this chapter. Any or all of the power fields are functioning at a mark under 25. Must immediately deal with power levels and fields one through three.

3.1–5.0. Particles or thoughts negative and electrical-based, but not as severely as with a pH under 3.0. Depressed energy and spin. Emotional strongholds for certain; possibly also mental strongholds. Affected by both past and present, lower dimensions and the third dimension. Ruled by unconscious; Middle Heart, Self, and Mind; emotional and mental bodies; lower to mid chakras. Possible presence of hauntings and latent interference, likely energetic cords from present-day times, some recessed or possessed soul issues. Affected by black body and Shadow Records, and maybe also the same energy bodies listed for lower pH. Energy egg rigid or partially collapsed. Partial rigidity or collapse of auric fields; run by programs affecting second, third, fourth, and possibly fifth auric fields. Insufficient energy in tenth and first auric fields, plus those fields above the fifth. Too entrenched in Language of Matter and insufficient in use of Languages of Feeling or Heart. Possible influence of group consciousness; compared to lower pH, this consciousness most likely from the present-life family of origin, rather than a past life or time in between lives. Consider lifting to higher dimensions or Planes of Light for help. Any or all power fields are functioning at a mark between 25 and 50. Must immediately deal with power levels and fields numbered three through five.

5.1–6.6. Slight effect of negative and electrical-based issues; person is probably dealing with many of the emotional or mental strongholds. Slightly depressed energy and spin, sometimes masquerading as anxiety. Affected by the present with overtones of the past, and third and fourth dimensions. Run by fluctuating consciousness and Higher Heart, Self, and Mind, which dip under current stress. Some negative influences in and from mental, emotional, black, or silver bodies and from Akashic and Shadow Records, most likely affecting chakras two through seven, but especially the fourth chakra. Possible bindings or hauntings. Energy egg wobbly or too inflexible. Auric fields too rigid or insufficient, especially two through seven. No use of eleventh chakra or auric field and insufficient activation between tenth energy bodies and the Christ body or etheric mirror. Insufficient but growing use of Language of Heart. Fear of complete breaking from a group consciousness or full activation of tar body inclusions and serpent kundalini. Any or all power fields are functioning at a mark between 50 and 75. Must deal with power levels and fields numbered five through seven. Possibly, there is one power field that is very low or damaged, and others are sufficient.

6.7–7.3. Balanced or in good shape.

7.4–9.0. Particles and thoughts too positive, magnetic-based, and spiritually inclined. Energy spin tends toward anxiety. All aspects of being are affected by consciousness waves that seem positive but lack substance and realism. Person is future-driven, as are problems and diseases caused by fear of unknown. Devotion is to the future, as in the fourth dimension, not the here and now. Incomplete links to Planes of Light. Chakras five, six, seven, and nine will be healthier than others, leading to difficulty in effecting change. Ruled by one's own consciousness; Higher Heart, Self, and Mind disconnected from Middle and sometimes Lower layers. Susceptible to group consciousness, especially through seventh chakra, as in spiritual brainwashing. Check higher chakras and spiritual points for energetic bindings and cords. Decisions often made to avoid the present. Ineffective boundaries for any or all auric fields. Energy egg loose. Overemphasis on Language of Heart. Any or all power fields functioning at a mark between 50 and 75, with the higher ones functioning better than the lower ones. Affected by power levels in the very lowest and the very highest fields.

9.1–11.0. Particles and thoughts too positive, magnetic-based, and spiritually inaccurate. Energy spin is anxious. Soul affected by inappropriate consciousness waves. Person is future-oriented, as are problems and diseases. Incomplete connection to three-dimensional reality, though appearance is of spiritual development and a link to higher dimensions, chakras, and spiritual points. Without grounding in lower dimensions and chakras, self is fragmented, disassociated, and easily disillusioned. May be stuck on a Plane of Light. Issues originally caused by others' inaccurate spiritual assessments or severe abuse. Ruled by own unconscious; Middle Heart, Self, and Mind; and a form of group consciousness from the past. Check gray body and higher chakras for energetic bindings and cords. Decisions often made for others' higher good, not own, or to avoid issues in the present. Ineffective or collapsing middle auric fields, such as third, fourth, fifth, sixth, and seventh. Rigid or too flexible energy egg, often connected to others with bindings. Too heavy emphasis on Language of Heart, too unconnected to Matter and Feeling. Any or all power fields functioning between 25 and 50, with the higher ones functioning better than the lower ones. Affected by power levels in the midlevel fields.

11.1–14. Particles and thoughts too positive, magnetic-based, and charged with incorrect spiritual perceptions. Highly anxious energy and spin. Stuck on consciousness waves. Consciousness or aspects of self projected into the future and shadows of higher dimensions, although seldom is the person actually locked into a particular dimension. Often a link to a Plane of Light that is stuck and negative. Often completely out of touch with reality. Ruled by others' consciousnesses and own subconscious; Lower Heart, Self, and Mind; and definitely some form of group consciousness. Can be affected by or through all managing energy bodies. Look for bindings, especially life-energy cords, through chakras seven, eight, nine, eleven, and spiritual points. Especially check White and Black Zones for stuck aspects. Decisions often made from others' Akashic and Shadow Records. Illegible energy egg. Undetectable or completely collapsed higher auric fields, with tight and heavy lower fields. Control of spiritual points by other entities or energies. Self in reality best compared to that of a phantom—where is the "real person"? Schizophrenic tendencies of soul. Can't access Languages, except through others. Any or all power fields functioning at a mark of 25 or below, although one or more of the higher fields is probably working at close to 100, which gives the presentation of developed spirituality.

assess your pH, you can determine whether your main issues are physical or emotional-spiritual.

See the sidebar "Working with pH Balance" (pages 236–37) for my idea of the basic sorts of determinants measurable by certain pH tests.

Healing through pH is best done with a professional to monitor diet and allergies, but you can also follow these general tips:

- Use breathing. As I've said, carbon dioxide accumulation increases acidity in the blood. Deep, intentional breathing when performing regressions, healings, or energetic shifts can actually shift your pH.

- If your pH is too acidic, use electrical healing methods and regressions. You must free yourself of entrenched feelings and beliefs, and possibly cords, bindings, and attachments. Face issues about power and control. Various light-based and computer therapies, if frequency-based, can assist, as well as acupuncture and concentration on odd-numbered chakras and power fields with energy work.

- If your pH is too alkaline, use magnetic healing methods and regressions. You must face embedded spiritual beliefs and issues with love. Deal with your anxiety and perceived need to live in the future by performing energy work on the even-numbered chakras and power fields.

Patterns, Boundaries, and Habits

Figure 1 shows major energetic differences between patterns, boundaries, and habits. Patterns look like crisscrossed lines that hold problematic charges both within the lines and inside of the spaces. This net keeps you stuck in self-defeating strongholds and behaviors. Boundaries are flowing energy waves, based upon decisions that ideally mirror one of the truths held within your spirit. They might be shaped in different forms outside of your system, to instruct the world how to treat you. Habits are internalized thoughts that then emanate as waves, which enable you to develop behaviors that reflect a life-enhancing decision.

The easiest way to work on a pattern is through the power fields. First figure out which power field relates to your pattern. Think of a pattern as a conglomeration of energy filaments keeping you stuck on a certain place in a power level continuum. Get to the power field through chakra diagnosis. For instance, first-chakra patterns, such as those involving sexual addiction or sexual fears, will relate to the first power field (and a power level on that field).

You must be willing to release the payoff for keeping yourself stuck in a pattern. Ask yourself these questions to unlock your payoff.

- Am I capable of achieving 100 percent on this power field?
- For what reason am I keeping myself on a lower frequency?
- If I achieve 100 percent, what will happen in my life?
- Am I willing to accept these changes? If so, what technique will best serve me to break the patterns keeping me from reaching the optimum field level?

Once you receive an answer, do the work. Psychically, you'll know you are done with a pattern when you perceive the power level filaments releasing and you can easily pull them off. Now you're ready to raise your percentage of function on the power field. You may have to release certain other energies and increase others. Intensify the healing property by setting an intention stating that the release or attraction work is conducted to the "correct power of ten." Ten is the number of new life. When you multiply a negative number by ten, you perform healing by reduction. You can eliminate tumors, growths, or problems or get rid of an overabundance of electrical or magnetic-based feelings, beliefs, elements, and charges. When you multiply a positive number by ten, you manifest that which is desired.

Numbers can greatly assist you in pattern work. Numbers can measure the level of power achieved on a field, as described above. Perhaps you've reached the 80 mark on a power field and want to go higher. You can also use numbers (or other symbols) to initiate or lock changes in place. I might use a 9 to access energy for individuals seeking to break bad habits. By placing a 9 in the center of the chakra originating the pattern, you can gather energy and strength to evolve into a 10, the symbol of new life. You might find an 8 in the center of a chakra that is symbolically keeping you in a patterned response and then replace it with a 1 to establish a brand-new viewpoint or fresh start.

On the elemental pathway, patterns must be replaced by boundaries and good habits. You usually must replace a pattern to completely defeat it, or else under pressure you will revert to the tried and true and have to break the pattern all over again. Ask yourself what emotional, mental, spiritual, and physical boundaries will keep you from returning to an old pattern. What good habits must you adopt? It generally takes twenty-one days to establish a new habit, so get going as soon as possible!

Forms of Energy

All natural energy forces can be used on the elemental pathway for healing. If you are failing to use these well or at all, you might see any of the following:

- Frequency, wave, vibrational, or harmonic disturbances
- Electromagnetic imbalances
- Gravitational imbalances
- Strong nuclear force issues
- Weak nuclear force issues

Frequency, Wave, Vibrational, and Harmonic Disturbances

All diseases can be measured by energetic disturbances. Each elemental body functions on an optimum set of frequencies, waves, and vibrations, both as input and internally, and emanates its own set of energies to maintain health for the entire system. Disease disturbs and warps these energies, and off-energies cause disease. When the entirety of a cell, subaspect, or system is down, the harmonic is completely wrong. If a problem isn't responding to help at any level, you must work harmonically. The most important broad diagnostics to consider are these:

- Does the disturbance come from inside the crippled chakra (or a cell, organ, or other energy body)?
- Does the disturbance come from outside of the crippled entity?
- Is the disturbance meant for this person or not?
- Is the disturbance desired by the affected person's subconscious or spirit, or not?
- Here are tips for healing each of these types of issues.

Internal Disturbances Consider physical causes and remedies. Interstitial parasites and bacteria such as *Chlamydia pneumoniae* that function like a parasite, as well as other invaders, cause many problems and disturb internal cellular functions. Use electron- or proton-based regressions to pinpoint the issue or futuring to help heal. Internal chakra problems are often caused by fragmentation, including recession or possession. The quickest energetic technique is to access the spiritual genetics through guided meditation, then "download" the correct light-based genetics into the affected organ or body.

External Disturbances Always check for physical invaders like a virus, bacteria, or fungus (see Part Five). Also check for energetic cords, bindings, or attachments. Source for entities, rejected aspects of the self, consciousness waves, and thought forms; release any connections you find.

Many physical energy techniques, such as the electrodermal screening computer (EQ4) and hands-on healing work by "canceling out" the frequency flow of the invader. For instance, a virus will ride a certain consciousness wave; if you send a counterwave at it, it can potentially cancel out this flow. Homeopathic remedies also work on vibration. A homeopathic remedy contains a frequency duplicating the actual problem, which then stimulates immune reactions in the system to force the body to release the issue. The problem with many frequency or vibrational remedies is that on the elemental pathway "might is right." You must send a stronger frequency or vibration to effect change, and then replace the "empty space" with a new energy so it doesn't attract the same problem again—or a different one. It's much more effective to send multiple frequencies or vibrations—some to cancel out the invading energy and others to replace the information you're eliminating with information that will work for you. It's like multitasking, or performing several jobs at the same time, instead of single-tasking, which leaves room for new or renewed problems. The best way to do this is to attune to your personal harmonic when using energetic techniques and send in multiple strands of needed energies through the star seed of destiny. (See the "Keying Into Your Personal Harmonic" section of chapter 13.)

Personal versus Impersonal Disturbances We can hook into issues, energies, and frequencies that are not ours. To deal with this, use the exercises on "Energy Contracts" later in this chapter, or the techniques outlined under "Energetic Communication Method" in chapter 11.

Spiritually Appropriate Disturbances You will never clear an issue that your subconscious doesn't want clear. Nor should you clear an issue that your spirit doesn't want clear. The subconscious and spirit may be holding the disturbance in place until a particular time or circumstance, at which point they will work together to clear the issue themselves. The power of working the subconscious and the spirit together can be miraculous. I once worked with a client diagnosed with metastasized breast cancer. I didn't do a thing to help her. She simply decided in front of me that it was going to go away. I watched as her spirit expanded throughout her entire body. It was a lovely blue color with rainbow touches. It touched her subconscious through the tar body, which unlocked a brilliant seed of destiny that transcended into her seventh chakra area. Her pineal burst into light. She called a week later saying that the cancer had disappeared.

Electromagnetic Imbalances

These imbalances reflect all chakric or physical organ imbalances. Excessive electrical charge causes symptoms related to the presence of too many negative/electrical particles; it eventually leads to depressive/reverse spins of cells and physical and energetic bodies. This attracts traumatizing circumstances. Too much magnetism relates to too many positive/proton particles; it eventually leads to anxiety and feeling out of control, or ununified spins. You can be clinically depressed but have too much magnetism and anxious spins. You can also be hyper or have ADHD but have too much electrical and depressed spins. If you're too electrical, electrical ley lines or energies will severely deplete you; if too magnetic, magnetic ley lines or energies will severely deplete you.

Work with the techniques at the beginning of chapter 11 to deal with electrical or magnetic imbalances. You can lock in a change with a symbol inserted into the center of a chakra.

For severe imbalances affecting your body, you can sometimes make use of certain ley lines or Vivaxis energies to remedy the situation. In Sedona, Arizona, for instance, there are strong vortexes of electrical, magnetic, and combined vibrations. The body's chakras will spin in reaction to these strong energies. The core of an issue might suddenly clarify when the body shifts even for a short while; the body itself could establish a new and healthy neurological pathway to maintain energetic healing. I once spent two weeks crossing England, visiting different ley-line areas and sacred sites. After crossing two fields and stepping all over sheep waste, I found one of the many wells attributed to the sorcerer Merlin. It was a magnetic vortex. During the search, I had cut myself on a fence; the cut healed before my eyes when I waved my hand over the well.

You can access energy vortexes in any geographic area. You can also establish vortexes in your own home using toning, feng shui, and intention. Using and wearing programmed gemstones can help establish energy shifts, as can "tuning into" astronomical and other Vivaxis changes. If you are in the days approaching a new moon, concentrate on releasing old energies and goals. If close to a full moon, move a project to completion or fill in the empty spots in your energy field. Holding energetic qualities in your heart can also create an energy shift in the body, as shown by studies conducted by organizations like the Institute of HeartMath in California. Energies like faith can actually change the DNA and RNA of material on a petri dish. When assessed through the pathways, these energies might represent any of the spiritual energetic forces or a divine truth.

Gravitational Imbalances

You are a force for gravity, much like a planet, emanating your own field, and therefore you have the ability to attract objects and forces. Gravitational imbalances create difficulties with attraction—either you fail to attract serendipitous opportunities, or you attract only negative occurrences. Either can indicate that you don't relate harmoniously with time and space.

To resolve the problem, work the neutrons to strengthen your resolve, goal, or intention, and then psychically attract protons (light images) and electrons (feelings and ideas about materialistic needs) to the neutron-based intention. Now infuse this image with your own spirit. With this core intention in place, expand your spirit through your auric field, beyond your system, and into the universe.

Strong Nuclear Force Issues

Each cell and physical and energy body emanates this fusing force. If it is not present, you're susceptible to degenerative diseases and problems, from connective-tissue disorders to empty relationships. Remember, if you're dealing with degenerative problems, you can access this force for fusion. Envision this force in your own mind. What color, depth, and breadth does it hold for you? Now emanate it from a chakra containing the core degenerative issue.

You can also use this force to help integrate a previously fragmented self or perform physical healing, such as healing a broken bone.

Weak Nuclear Force Issues

If this fission-oriented force is not present, you cannot disconnect. This inability can affect all aspects of life, including too-strong relationships with other people, disease patterns, and certain behaviors.

Use this force to assist with energies that need to disconnect, such as a tumor or a bad relationship. Envision what this force looks like to you and insert it wherever there is something you must disband.

Gender Differences in Energy Processing

When working with energy forms such as vibrations, it's important to know that men and women process energy slightly differently. Notice the difference between the energies emanating from center between men and women. Core energy extends first through the physical and then emotional and mental planes for both men and women. Men then express electrical and then magnetic energies, while women next continue into magnetic and then electrical. In general, this means that men will first process practical thoughts, stored feelings and beliefs about power, and next take action before turning to spiritual ideas and thoughts about love and issues of relationship, while women will do just the opposite. The core elemental psyche is physical for both genders. But these energies expand out in a circle, like waves rippling from the center, in slightly different ways. Here are the different frequencies that men and women use. Basically, all energy first ripples from your core human self as physical, then as emotional, then mental, and so on.

Men	Women
Core: Physical	Core: Physical
Emotional	Emotional
Mental	Mental
Electrical	Magnetic
Magnetic	Electrical
Vibrational	Vibrational
Harmonic	Harmonic

The energetic differences between men and women are mirrored in the brain differences between the genders.

There are two sides of the brain, separated by the corpus callosum. The right brain processes more randomly, and is known as creative and visual. The left side processes logically, and is known as verbal and rational. Traditionally, men are considered more left brained, while women are more able to access the right as well as left sides of the brain.

This statement is supported by several scientific studies. A large majority of women use both sides of the brain under observed conditions, while men mainly use the brain hemisphere that is dominant, according to handedness. Because men are most frequently right- handed, as a group, they most frequently rely on the left side of the brain.[2]

While verbal abilities are more frequently associated with the left hemisphere, there are other parts of the brain responsible for language —a gift most usually ascribed to women. Researcher Jenny Haraty and her colleagues at the University of Sydney, Australia, have shown that the Broca and Wernicke areas of the brain, known for language, are 30 percent larger in women than in men.[3]

Other major differences between men and women's brains include differing sizes of the corpus callosum, a thick bridge of tissue that separates the brain hemispheres. This tissue is 23 percent larger in women than in men, according to Roger Gorski and Laura Allen, neuroscientists at the University of California, Los Angeles. This increased capacity for information exchange might account for why women can process quicker between brain hemispheres. In everyday life, this ability is called "multitasking."[4]

Women are also known for being more emotional than men. Several studies revealed that this capacity, too, is supported by differences in brain activity. Studies discussed by Dr. Deborah Sichel and Jeanne Watson Driscoll in their book *Women's Moods*, show that the paralimbic cortex is more advanced in women than in men. Even when at rest, this part of the brain acts as an emotional register to the environment. In fact when women are asked to recall sad experiences, this part of the brain showed eight times more activity than men asked to perform the same task.[5]

Many current researchers are connecting these brain differences to hormonal and other biochemical equations, at least in part. Brain chemistry is highly affected by hormones. Studies by Dr. Barbara Sherwin, a research psychologist from McGill University in Canada, show that women who are lacking in estrogen experience a lessened ability to recall recently learned information.[6] Other studies reveal similar findings—but the female estrogen hormone isn't the only determinant of brain chemistry!

Many scientists are proposing that exposure to testosterone in the male embryo leads to the development of masculine traits, usually defined as aggression and spatial skills, while the lack of this hormone results in the development of feminine qualities in the female embryo, usually characterized as empathy and interpersonal skills.[7] Furthermore, prenatal testosteone affects sexual differentiation of the brain and subsequent behavior.[8] There are many similarities between the scientific claims made on the differences between men and women and those I am making in regard to energetic differences. Esoteric knowledge usually points to the left side of the body as more feminine, relating the spiritual and emotional concerns, and the right side of the body as more masculine, governing action and logic. These ideas reflect those of hemispheric differences, in which the left side of the brain is more masculine in orientation and the right side typically considered more feminine in characteristics. The left-brained approach to life matches the descriptions of electrical, negatively charged vibrations, summarized in the concept of "power." The right-brained approach to the world synchronizes with ideas ascribed to magnetic, positively charged vibrations, coined within the ideas like "love" and "spirituality."

As shown in the charted energetic differences between male and female processing, men orient first with electrical and then magnetic energies, understanding the world through left-brained processes that propel their ideas into the world through acts of power. Women's thoughts, beliefs and ideas are first relayed as magnetic energies, and evaluated through the lens of love and spirituality, before they are moved into the world in demonstrations of power. While women's brains are capable of simultaneously processing linear and creative, logic and intuition, the energetics of the Four Pathways approach would support women as first orienting through magnetics and then through electrical. Research showing the continual attention of brain organs like the paralimbic cortex supports the view that foremost, women entertain the importance of emotion and feeling, nurturing and maternal qualities accessed best through right-brained activities—and the magnetic sphere around the body.

Consider also the differences pointed out in regard to processing kundalini, in chapter 4. Men begin the serpent kundalini process in the first chakra, an electrical-based center. Women start the serpent kundalini process in the second chakra, a magnetic-based center. Each gender is generically oriented toward one approach over another, one set of concerns rather than another.

It's important to understand these differences in Four Pathway healing, especially on the elemental pathway. Women will be most concerned with the emotional, creative, and intuitive reasons for changing. Men will be convinced of healing if appealed to through logic and practical reward. These are generic differences, upheld by science and esoteric knowledge. All people differ. A left-handed person will already be more magnetic in orientation, as his or her right brain is dominant. When seeking for causes or solutions, search first for personal differences, but use the generic guidelines to assist the healing process.

Times and Places

Most elemental issues, especially those that affect chakra spin, involve being anchored in the past, failing to see all current choices, or attempting to escape into the future.

Depressive, negative, or electron-based issues usually reflect being stuck in the past. Staying glued to past issues keeps old feelings, especially shame-based feelings, fixated in the body; slows down spin; and dampens the immune and hormone systems, among other issues. This keeps aspects such as the Lower Mind and Heart in charge. Souls that remain stuck in the past often relive the negative memories from the Akashic and Shadow Records. Memories aren't bad, but clinging blindly to them without using them to make beneficial changes is counterproductive.

Anxiety-related, positive, or proton-oriented issues intimate fears of the future. Focus on the future causes slippage in the present, making it difficult to access the power and strength necessary to make change and, therefore, create a desirable future. Souls that push toward transcendence through fear often flit from one dimension or Plane of Light to another, without learning a thing anywhere.

Change is only really possible on the elemental pathway when you can bring yourself into the here and now; then the chakras can act like doorways for all universal energies. Used correctly, the records, dimensions, and Planes of Light can be used to clarify your current choices.

When it comes to the records, other dimensions, and other planes, your most important elemental diagnostic techniques are going to involve regressing, projecting, and futuring. You can use these basic psychic techniques on any of the pathways, but they are most helpful on the elemental pathway, the pathway most anchored in time and space.

Regressing

Regressions involve looking back into the past or reconnecting with a part of you stuck in the past, in order to gather data regarding a current problem. You can also potentially use regression to free yourself from the past and to change the past so the present can be different.

Regressions are especially helpful with electrical-based issues, which tend to cause slow and reverse chakra spins and depression. You can regress into a past time period, an earlier point in this lifetime, a past life, or an in-between life; a different time and space, such as a Plane of Light or a zone; into the Akashic or Shadow Records; or even into somewhere that you have never been, if the visit will provide you with needed data or healing.

For serious or scary issues, I suggest that you work with a professional to conduct a regression. Certified hypnotherapists are trained to work with the issues and feelings that arise, as are licensed psychologists who use EMDR, a particularly helpful form of regression. For lighter issues, here is a process that you can use:

1. First, ground and center yourself. Think of your causal issue. After asking for Divine protection and guidance, ask which chakra is key to this causal issue. (Sometimes you will regress through a different energy body, such as a managing energy body. To deal with pain, for instance, it can be helpful to journey through the pain body.)

2. Now ask the Divine to fully open your psychic senses and to allow only loving use of your gifts. Now sense or see the chakra center. There you will spot a door, mirror, or opening of some sort. Ask the Divine to guide you through this portal and into the situation that created your current predicament.

3. Once in the situation, ask to see, hear, know, and experience everything necessary to obtain the information or healing that you need. State that your conscious self will remember all that you are experiencing. Then ask to understand what decisions you (or someone else) made during this time period that are still affecting you today.

4. Ask for clarification. Why did you make these decisions? What other choices were available? What did you need to learn? What do you still need to learn? What healing and forgiveness is necessary? Is it appropriate to change the circumstances of that time? If so, is it appropriate to bring these changes forward so as to affect the present? Remain in the situation until you feel complete and whole with what happened and who you were at that time. Ask the Divine to return you to the present and to bring with you the learning, energy, wisdom, and information you need to make today a better place. Ask the Divine to internalize all appropriate learning or healing through you at all levels in a way that will be safe and easy for assimilation.

5. Reground and center and ask for Divine protection and guidance as you integrate this information.

Projecting

Projecting is a form of shamanic journeying. When journeying, mystics send an aspect of themselves or their consciousness in search of wisdom, data, or healing energies. There are dozens of ways to journey. The Kalahari Kung, for instance, use drumming during group ceremony to enable a select few to exit their bodies when in a trance state. When out of body, these few battle the dark spirits for the health of the community. In Peru, I have experienced journeying deep inside of my body with the assistance of Sachamama, an aspect of the Divine Feminine, in order to better understand my own issues.

Journeying can take you near or far, into the past, present, or future, but it isn't always easy to do without guidance. I use the term projecting to describe journeying into only the present time.

On the divine pathway, all healing occurs through expansion. Projecting is an elemental-based way to expand into the corners of reality that may hold data or healing that you need:

1. Using the steps of grounding, centering, and protecting, ask the Divine to connect you fully with your spirit-self. Breathe deeply and imagine that you are fully invested in your spirit, which is inside of your body and also able to expand fully around you. Encompass your body in your own spirit and then "feel out to the edges."

2. Now push further. Sense the presence of your spirit, which continues to envelope your body, as it swells into the room and then outdoors. Notice that nothing hurts you; everything simply is what it is. Your spirit is inviolate and remains its own pure self no matter what it touches or surrounds.

3. Now think of your causal issue. Simply expand your consciousness as your spirit enters a place or space that contains everything you've yet to learn about this issue. Perhaps you're someplace three-dimensional, perhaps you're in the netherlands, perhaps you're in heaven. Fully embrace this place as "here and now" and learn what you came to learn.

4. When you feel complete with this situation, return on your spirit as it enfolds into your body again. Reground and center yourself. Allow yourself to keep resonating with and as your spirit; that is, after all, the only protection really needed.

Futuring

The future is really a net of possibilities that surrounds your current self. You don't have to "go anywhere" to access the future. The lines of the future are being drawn around you as you sit and read this book!

By accessing future potentials, you can see the possible outcome of the path that you are on. Let's say you are undergoing chemotherapy for cancer. Where can this possibly lead you? You can also obtain ideas for bettering a possible future. What might you do in the here and now to allow chemotherapy to heal you from cancer? And you can transfer energy or information from the future into the here and now to make changes in the here and now. When envisioning the self healed of cancer, you can figure out how you got there and perform these activities now. You can also "download" this healed self into your current self and make more effective decisions, or allow this healed self to serve as a template for quicker healing.

When futuring:

1. First ground, center, and resonate with your spirit-self. Then attune with the energies of the future that are around you already. You'll see that it's like being surrounded by a grid of Christmas

lights! These are magnetic, proton-based timelines that link to possible futures. What do you desire to see? The most likely path? The best path? The healed self? Watch the line enlighten those threads to the requested future or future self.

2. Instead of sending your consciousness into the future, pull the line as if you are fishing. Reel it to the front side of your heart and ask to perceive it with True Vision, the vision of your own spirit. What do you perceive? Ask the Divine to guide you to respond to this imaging. Are you to learn from it? Own it? Magnetize this potential so it occurs, or do the opposite?

3. When finished with your task, assume a position of gratefulness for the knowledge received and allow the future web to reshape around you. Close your eyes and connect again with your body. Ground, center, and resonate with the decisions that you have made. Ask the Divine to help you continue to integrate your choices safely and with love toward self and others.

Organic Spacetime Distortions

There are a few important points to make about the past, present, and future.

On the elemental pathway, the past is fixed in stone. However, it's possible, using the records, to change the information of the past—to rewrite it, if you will—and so to change the structure of the past. Change the structure of the past and you can potentially shift the present.

Regarding the present, on the elemental pathway you are stuck in the here and now. But there are other here and nows. There are selves that could be, if the past had only been different. Side-stepping into the present allows you to find ideas or energies that could heal, but that lie outside of your everyday existence.

On the elemental pathway, the future hasn't happened—it's only possibilities. The future isn't actually in "front" of you, because until you step forward, you haven't chosen any one of the hundreds of future potentials. Rather, future choices are like independent selves on both sides of you, each connected to your current self with filaments. Some filaments are strong. They connect to the selves that you are most likely to choose into being, usually because you are so comfortable with the issues that they represent. Other filaments are weak. These connect to potentials that you're probably too scared to choose. If you want to choose a future that doesn't include your current maladies and problems, you have to select one that you've never chosen before. You then have to "insert" that future before you and walk into it, so that you are stepping into a different now.

I once worked, for instance, with a woman who wanted to meet the man of her dreams. The problem was that she didn't have any self-esteem. She sabotaged every relationship, because she put herself down so much and the men tired of her negativity. Finally, she selected a future self that was an outgrowth of a potential current self—a woman who liked herself. She made the choice, envisioned the future self in front of her, and imagined walking into this self. Within a week, she met a great man to whom she is now engaged.

The Records

Through the Akashic and Shadow Records, you can obtain information about the past, present, and future that you need for many elemental healing processes. Both sets of records can be used for regressions, checking out current situations, and projecting into possible futures.

The Akashic shows you exactly what occurred and is most useful for clearing the issues resulting from time-specific events; for pinpointing the exact energies causing current concerns in the present; and for checking for future information useful for specific applications. You might use the Akashic Records to evaluate a past life causing low back pain, check on what pain clinics exist right now that might be helpful, or project into tomorrow's pain clinics to find techniques that might work today.

The Shadow reveals what was never said or done. It is more a magnetic than an electrical body. It is most useful for looking at lost opportunities to love, which is why I call it the house of regrets. The Shadow will show the origin of today's patterns, ways that we could be more loving in the present, and future ideas that could inspire a healing today. Taking our back pain issue, it would show why we're "beating ourselves up" with pain; what we didn't do but should have in the past; ways we can use comfort and love to help heal the pain today; and a spiritual self who doesn't have back pain in the future, because he or she adopted better beliefs.

Here are ways to use the Akashic Records information.

Means of Accessing

• The shaman path allows actual projection of the soul, soul etheric, physical etheric, or consciousness directly into or onto the Akashic Records through the eighth chakra. If you enter the Akashic Records directly through the core of this chakra, you can immediately access the event or time period that you need without having to journey and leave your body.

- You can access the Akashic Records through any of your chakras or endocrine glands, using the intuitive skills associated with these points. For instance, use mental sympathy through the third chakra, visioning through the sixth chakra, or physically move while working through the adrenal glands—a first-chakra organ.

- Many people access the Akashic through the *Hall of Records.* The hall is a set of energy paths that move through spacetime and branch into the past, present, and future. It's relatively easy to walk into a past event by searching through the hall for the portal or entry point related to a question.

- You can use the pendulum to determine which chakra might be the best for accessing the Akashic Records. State that you want a response from the chakra that is most open for the journeying, then have a partner wield the pendulum over all your chakras, front and back. The one that emanates the largest circle may be the best doorway.

- You can project onto the fields. After determining which field is shy of complete, envision yourself into the situation that caused a problem. Technically, you are now accessing the Akashic Records.

- Guided meditation, dreamwalking, hypnosis, age regression, storytelling, and intuitive assessments are all ways of deliberately accessing the Akashic Records for yourself or for others.

There isn't a right or wrong way to gather Akashic data. As with all psychic and journeying methods, you will receive information and revelation according to your personal style. This means that you might see an event through your current body, through a conscious state, or as a viewer in the past. You might completely relive an event from the past, as if you were there. You might hear information regarding the past or how it applies today. This information might come from your self of the present, the self of the past, or a higher guide. You might feel, sense, or just plain know what's going on.

Applications

- Research the origin of a problem or a disease. Ask questions to determine the origin of the issue.

- Determine the history of the problem. By checking how a problem has played out in the past, you can assess the past for specific causes.

- Assess the reasons for relationship, financial, or health-care problems in the present and look for current solutions.

- If you don't know the diagnosis of a current problem, compare current symptoms with problems of the past or future for ideas.

- Change events from the past. If you rewrite or rewire history, you alter the perceptions that you are currently working from. New perceptions create new choices, and among these are choices that will help you create a better life. Through learning from and potentially altering the Akashic Records, you can:
  - Free repressed feelings and desires
  - Change negative beliefs into positive ones
  - Own needs that you have denied and decide to make them real
  - Activate imprisoned psychic, spiritual, and worldly gifts
  - Release unhealthy relationships and relationship patterns
  - Establish supportive and loving relationships
  - Access the powers and strength needed to achieve goals
  - Get rid of others' energies, including bindings, cords, and feelings
  - Forgive yourself and others

- Project to the future to see what's probably going to happen if you continue the way that you are, or what would happen if you make certain changes.

- Project to the future to a time when your problem is solved (or the disease you have is resolved). You can potentially bring this "healed energy" back into today's form and system.

Note: The Akashic Records are set in stone, but your interpretations are not. When assessing them for yourself or others, you must be careful about how you spin the data. Judgmentalism often clouds perspective. It's easy to feel so guilty about an event in the past that it haunts our current assessment of self. You should only approach the Akashic Records using the virtues of Forgiveness, Clarity, and Love as tools. These spiritual forces are available through the power pathway.

Here are ways to use the Shadow Record information.

Means of Accessing the Shadow

- **Through the Akashic Records.** Once in the Akashic, ask to see the record of what could have been. Ask that it appear as a doorway. Enter the doorway and now work with the Shadow.

- **Through the eighth chakra, in the space rippling around the chakra's center.** This is the "space" side of the eighth chakra. It contains everything not said, done, or thought, among other space issues.

- **Through any of the other chakra centers, but most easily through the fourth or seventh chakras.** Once in a chakra, look for a shadow near the back side of the chakra. This is one entryway into the Shadow Records.

· **Through the imagination pathway.** The easiest way to do this is to picture the Shadow as a two-way mirror. This mirror centers in each of your chakras. By walking through the mirror from the front side of a chakra, you enter the antiworld side of the imagination pathway and can see what has never been.

· **Through peripheral psychic vision.** Imagine any life situation—fix it in your mind. Visualize it and the main people or components. Now, instead of gazing directly at the situation, "look to the side" and ask to view what did not occur. This is the Shadow present in and around all life events.

Applications

· Sometimes we remain locked in the past, re-creating the same issue or pattern over and over, because we never did what we knew we should have done. Ask to lock into the originating pattern of what should have been, but never has been. Sometimes we can change the present—and therefore the future—by seeking other choices. The Shadow holds all choices that we ignored. Some of them might work for today!

· If you want to know an unknown diagnosis, enter the Shadow of the future. Ask to know what is currently unknowable, but known to the future self.

· For healing purposes, ask to see what you could be doing (that's different from what you're doing) that would heal today's problem.

Planes of Light

Sometimes we can enter a Plane of Light and gain the perspective needed to diagnose. Here is an exercise for doing this:

Attune your consciousness with your soul self. Know that your soul's goal is to graduate from all Planes of Light through death, but that it doesn't need to wait until death to enter these planes. Give permission for your soul to access its personal mastery to enter each of the planes through the chakras themselves.

Chakra	Corresponding Plane of Light
First	Plane of Rest
Second	Plane of Evaluation
Third	Plane of Healing
Fourth	Plane of Knowledge
Fifth	Plane of Wisdom

Sixth	Plane of Truth
Seventh	Plane of Peace
Eighth	Plane of Momentum
Ninth	Plane of Love
Tenth	Plane of Power
Eleventh	Plane of Charity
Twelfth	Plane of Mastery
Spiritual Points	Plane of Consciousness

All your soul must do is enter each plane through its corresponding chakra. You will see a doorway in the center of each chakra, through which you can enter a Plane of Light and ask for information to diagnose problems and disease.

There are two main ways to use the Planes of Light for healing. First, figure out if you're stuck on a certain plane. If so, gain the learning and energy of this plane, and move on. Present-day projection techniques are the easiest to use. Second, figure out if an energy or data from one of the Planes of Light might be useful. Do you want to be a better parent? Visit the Plane of Wisdom.

My client Mark serves as an example of someone who benefited from working on the Planes of Light. His major life issue was gaining love. No matter his behavior, women never stayed with him longer than a few months. Working with me, he perceived an in-between life in which he had graduated from the Plane of Peace but was too scared to enter the Plane of Momentum, which meant he'd never reached the Plane of Love that follows. Using hypnotherapy, he regressed to the moment at which he averted entering the Plane of Momentum, and he dealt with his fears. During the session, he quickly accepted the learning of momentum, graduated, and entered the Plane of Love. Shortly thereafter, he met a great woman and is getting married.

The Zones

Sometimes you must determine "where" you're stuck to figure out how to get unstuck. There are certain problems connected to linkages to each of the four zones, which are each most easily accessible through particular chakras.

White Zone Issues

White Zone issues arise when life doesn't meet our innermost expectations. Sometimes we have a deep sense that something has gone wrong—that Mr. or Ms. Wonderful was supposed to have married, not deserted, us; that we weren't supposed to lose our child; that we were supposed to have been a newscaster instead of a homemaker; or that we are supposed to be disease-free.

Regressions into the White Zone can determine whether we're on the original plan or not. Use regression techniques through the first, seventh, ninth, or tenth chakras to work with the guides that helped you draw up your life contract and figure out what you were trying to learn. This assessment can sometimes inform you of the higher purpose of a specific complaint, and you might decide to learn the lesson a different way. I had a client who had entered into a life contract to marry a man who turned out to be her first cousin, and such marriages aren't allowed in the United States. She spent twenty years fantasizing about him. We changed her White Zone plan, and within three months she had met another great potential partner. I've seen one woman become free of arthritis within months of changing her lifetime soul contract.

Gray Zone Issues

In the hurdle between death and life, there is the Gray Zone. I call it this because most souls become amnesiac about their past lives and White Zone contracts through this stage. Sometimes too many memories are erased, and you can regain past-life memories through regression to the beginning of the erasing process. Certain detrimental energetic bindings are established here as well; some of my clients have reported interference from ancestral spirits, past-life soul relationships, and the Grays, a set of cruel extraterrestrials. Nightmares and disturbed sleep, especially during infancy and childhood, can indicate Gray Zone problems.

Use either regression or projection techniques to uncover Gray Zone issues, Akashic Records to remember the events of the Gray Zone, and decording processes to release entity attachments.

Red Zone Issues

People too attached to life or afraid of death can enter the Red Zone before birth and use basic life energy to hold onto life. You sometimes find this circumstance among the elderly who linger beyond hope, coma victims, and Alzheimer's patients. The soul needs to use the red life energy as a rocket uses propulsion to take off from life, not to escape death.

Use futuring techniques of the magnetic and spiritual nature to figure out if it's best to assume more or less basic life energy at life's end.

Black Zone Issues

Most of us have returned from another life. Sometimes aspects of the soul linger in this in-between land and cause indecisiveness in our current lives. Some problems are caused by energetic bindings between ourselves and a being dwelling in the Black Zone, as in a loved one who refuses to enter a tunnel or Plane of Light. I had one client who was plagued by her deceased husband, to the point that she would feel him enter her body; she would then wear his clothes and drink gin, as he had done in life. We sent him through the Black Zone to the White Light, and she was released.

Use regression techniques to return to this zone of the afterlife. You can also travel through the first, eighth, or tenth chakras to this zone. Electrical techniques work best for regressions or healing.

Development and Age Regression

Obviously, not every spacetime issue is going to lie on a different plane, Zone, or in a past life! We incur a lot of strongholds as we move through life (as well as positive learning). Current life issues often mirror past-life or interdimensional and cross-zone issues. If you work on the strongholds and patterns reflected in this lifetime, you automatically heal the issues carried over from other spaces, places, and times.

Reference the chart in the section "Chakra Development and Age Regression" in chapter 11. You can use the information about chakra development to track the source of this-life issues and heal them at their source. There are two main ways of applying chakra development information. You can figure out the physiological origin of an issue, track it to the lead chakra, and determine the probable age at which you incurred an issue. You can also work directly in a specific chakra if you already know the age at which an issue originated.

Consider the client with high cholesterol to whom I referred in an earlier section on elemental-based feelings. I knew that she was dealing with blood issues and that these correspond with the first chakra. I pinpointed her adrenals, and my client's discussion of her infancy confirmed the origin of her block. Her mother was unwed at the time of her conception and my client unconsciously assumed her mother's shame about an unwanted pregnancy. My client in turn "sped up" her own adrenals to attempt to ensure her survival.

Since the chakras develop one step at a time throughout your life, you can also go directly to a particular chakra if you know the age of a trauma. I worked with a client who was going deaf and imagined hands around her throat. I asked her if she had ever seen or experienced strangulation. She replied that her father used to choke her when she was seven and eight. I already knew that deafness was related to the fifth chakra, but her age at the time of the abuse confirmed my theory. The fifth chakra develops at these ages. I asked this client to work with a therapist and perform regressions to clear the feelings and regain her memories before we returned to our own healing work.

Energy Laws

You have to obey elemental laws in order to work the elemental pathway without a boomerang effect. Here are signs that you've tampered with the laws:

» Dimensional Diagnosis

SOMETIMES IT'S DIFFICULT to diagnose the causes of a problem that affects you physically because you lack perspective. If an issue has landed in the third dimension, you can get too tangled up with appearances to perceive its true nature. You can then enter one of the other dimensions to gain the perspective needed for accuracy. Reference information about dimensional healing in the section "Dimensions" in chapter 5 for backgrounding, then continue with these ideas of using the dimensions for pathway healing.

• The first dimension is a point. Enter the center of a chakra or a cell of a disease and ask to literally see the point or origin of a presenting issue. What's the one factor causing the problem? Put a symbol, tone, color, or another healing intention in the point; check to see if you need to add electrical, magnetic, or neutral energy in this structure.

• The second dimension is lines. Ask to see the incident or person to whom a presenting problem is linked. This is a perfect way to check for energetic bindings. Either erase this line or draw a circle between you and the other person for unification if you want to continue a relationship but in a healthy way.

• The third dimension is a cube; structure. You can enter the power and imagination pathways by shaping a cube into a pyramid or a cross. If using a pyramid, merge with the point on the top and ask for answers; if using a cross, center yourself in the middle and turn this center point into a circle. Now that you have this 360-degree view, ask questions. You can also access the divine pathway through symbology by shaping two tetrahedrons within a divine tetrahedron. Center yourself in the empty space and access the divine pathway through the types of techniques covered in chapter 15. Once there, pray healing qualities into the structure and allow expansion of these energies beyond all boundaries.

• The fourth dimension is a point outside the cube. Project yourself into the future by standing on the point outside the cube, and ask for a diagnosis from the future self. If you can't shift consciousness this way, ask the Divine for a guide that can stand in this spot and speak with you. Then transfer the healing energies or information into your "here and now" self.

Natural Laws

Do something foolish, you pay for it. I have a client who sprayed her house for fleas, despite my multiple warnings about the consequences of the poison. She smokes and her husband has multiple sclerosis. Not only did they spray, but they remained in the house. He almost died, and her nerves became numb. You can often track an elemental-based concern back to behavior. If you broke a natural law and are suffering for it, you must adhere to the law before you'll get well. On the positive side, whatever you do for healing can only help. If you set your bone, it will mend. If you cut out a lump, it is gone. The key is to accentuate natural law when using it for healing. Use the power field related to the issue and multiply your healing energies to the power of ten. Again, might is right on the elemental pathway. If you're going to effect

• The fifth dimension is a cube with lines outside of it. You can link with a power seal by following a line outside of one of the chakras and enter the power pathway, gain power ideas about the diagnosis, and then return with this data back into the elemental pathway. Access healing energies this same way.

• In the sixth dimension, the cube lines dissolve and leave only disconnected points. Each point is a point of creation. Select any one point and ask for a new idea regarding your diagnosis. You are now in the power pathway. You are also in the imagination pathway and will probably receive information about the antiworld. Use imagination-based techniques to shift diseased thoughts, feelings, or illnesses into the antiworld from this world and to accept helpful energy in return.

• In the seventh dimension there are no points and no lines. You are pure consciousness. Decide where and what you want to be; go there and become that, and ask for information and healing.

• The eighth dimension is nothing and everything; pure imagination. What do you want to know? You will know the truth of your diagnosis, but also the unimportance of this truth. Ask for higher truth to gain power through your problems.

• The ninth dimension is pure expression of love. Go into a loving state within the center of your heart chakra and from there ask the Divine for a diagnosis and healing.

• The tenth dimension is grace. Simply ask the Divine to share with you—anytime, anyplace—not only what you need to know and understand, but also what you need to do or receive.

• The eleventh dimension is purity with all. Ignore your desire for a diagnosis, and instead ask for wisdom.

• The twelfth dimension is unity with the Creator. Give the Creator your human lack and problems, understanding that the Creator is human and imperfect, as are we, through the sharing of love. This stance allows a transformation of the human into its highest states, and you gain awareness you thought never to get.

• The thirteenth dimension is cocreation. Allow the Creator to share divinity with you. Seize the force of being Divine and use it.

change, you need more energy going into the healing than is holding the problem in place.

Conversion Laws

All sorts of attitudes and actions break conversion laws and force consequences. Greed can make someone steal, and that calls for jail time. If you take something, you must give something. You take money, you give time. Conduct elemental healing with this in mind. If you "take" a tumor through surgery, what energy are you going to replace it with? Make a conscious choice, such as volunteering time for a good cause, or something you want might be taken instead.

Spiritual Laws

You must respect innate order, or you'll suffer some sort of breakdown. In the old Greek tale, Achilles, the son of a god, was raised like a girl by his mother as a barter with the gods for his immortality. She also dipped him in a special solution to guarantee him invulnerability; the solution covered every part of his body except for his heel, where she grasped him. As an adult, he was killed by an arrow that hit that vulnerable heel— hence the term "Achilles' heel" is used for one's point of vulnerability.

Achilles' mother tried to alter innate order by pretending away Achilles' male and human aspects. Spiritual law always catches up. Problems due to a refusal to obey spiritual law involve an inner knowledge that you've been lying about some vital part or way of self. If you think you've been wronged by someone or something that has broken spiritual law, call upon the divine pathway's spiritual law to effect justice. If you broke spiritual law and are suffering the consequences, forgive yourself and call for healing through grace. On the elemental pathway, spiritual law must run in tandem with conversion and natural laws. The exception is when you perform healing through your spirit and the Great Spirit; through these mediums, spiritual law takes precedence and miracles are possible. Elemental law is never broken, but time can be speeded up or turned backward. The tumor can disappear before it even enters your body.

Energy Contracts

Determining the nature of an energetic contract will help you choose the best method for removing it. To decipher a contract, respond to these questions:

- Am I one of the original creators of this contract, or is something or someone else?
- If it wasn't me, how did I come to receive it? Is there something I must do, say, understand, or express to release myself from this contract?
- If I did enter this agreement, when did I do so? For what reason?
- What type of contract is this? An energetic cord? Life-energy cord? A binding or an attachment? If one of the latter, who else is involved in or affected by this agreement?
- What is the nature of the contractual agreement? What am I giving? What am I receiving?
- How is this contract affecting me? The others around me or in the contract?
- What do I need to know to release myself from, to change, or to better use this contract? What feelings must I understand or express? What beliefs must I accept? What energy must I release or accept? What power levels must I free myself from? What power field must be brought to its optimum function?
- What forgiveness or grace must I allow myself or the others involved?
- Am I now ready for this healing? If not, how or when can I be?

There are three main ways of exorcising energy contracts; these methods also work for hauntings. They differ from a cord or binding release in that they rely on your power to command and hold intention, rather than a healing process. Here are the methods:

- **Rejection.** To reject a contract or interference, you must use 100 percent intention to refuse the contract and repel the energies attached to it. Might is right: if you command with more energy or intelligence than what's used against you, you will win. Request Divine healing for all concerned.
- **Containment.** You have the divine right to isolate yourself from negative sources. Simply command that the Divine immediately protect you. If you are mightier than your foe, you can also demand the containment of any energies, forces, or entities that have been plaguing you.
- **Transformation.** By giving the energy of forgiveness, you are directing "white light" at the energy or entity that is bothering you. This energy offers grace to the interference or contract partners. If they accept the forgiveness, divine love offers healing, and they automatically release you. If they don't, the "white light" pushes

them out of your boundaries and deals with them. Any personal energy that the other forces have been holding is automatically returned to you when you request transformation for all concerned.

Beyond the Chakras: Other Forms of Elemental Healing

Although this chapter and chapter 11 focus on chakras and energy work, these are not the only forms of healing available on the elemental pathway. There are thousands of ways to address elemental concerns through traditional and complimentary health-care modalities, including the following:

Allopathic medicine, for all physical concerns and certain mental health problems, such as clinical, biochemical, or acute depression and anxiety, as well as major addictions. Allopathic is especially invaluable for front-line diagnostics, preventive health-care screening, prescription medicine, surgical treatments, and bone setting. It's important for holistic-minded people to respect allopathic medicine. For example, I had a client diagnosed with breast cancer; although I recommended an energetic process, I also supported her decision to have a lumpectomy followed by radiation. She was relieved to deal with the issue in a way that felt normal to her.

Vibrational medicine, including homeopathy, computer diagnostics and frequency-based healing such as the electrodermal screening computer (EQ4), toning, energy work, aromatherapy, feng shui, flower or essential oil remedies, hands-on healing, and radionics.

Naturopathic medicine, including naturopathy, nutritional consulting, herbalism, and plant and spirit-plant medicine; cleansing therapies such as colonics and detoxification; bodywork therapies such as various massage therapies, transpersonal emotional release, yoga, tai chi, qi gong, acupuncture, osteopathy, physical therapy, and chiropractic care.

Mind-based alternatives, including hypnotherapy, Holographic Repatterning, this- and past-life regression, psychic healing, astrological reviews, spiritual direction, guided meditation, meditation, guided imagery, shamanic journeying, and soul repair.

Mental health therapies, including the Twelve Step program, addiction treatment and recovery, counseling, psychiatric or psychological treatment, and methods like EMDR; coaching for problems in areas like finances, business, or home management.

Diet and exercise, for preventive and treatment-based health care.

You can combine chakra healing with any of these modalities. The diagnosis and healing methods in this chapter include means for using chakras to make decisions and supplement basic health care—but not to replace it. I would never advise a client to replace a suitable and professionally monitored program with chakra work alone. Often a combination of several therapies, including chakra work, is the most holistic approach.

chapter thirteen

Conduits of Light: The Power Pathway

Power Diagnosis and Healing

All elemental issues involve misapplied power forces. Until you set your seals and begin to consciously direct power energies, your chakras will automatically attract power forces that keep the elemental system stuck in place.

The seals are lenses on the chakras. As each chakra has a front and a back, so do you have seals attached to the chakras on the front and back. In their natural state, the seals are convex; that is, the rims of a seal cover your chakra, and the center of a seal does not. In this form, a seal is inoperable. It fails to portray the various spiritual energetic forces already affecting you, and cannot be consciously used to deflect or attract spiritual energies that might assist you.

It is desirable to "set your seals." I use this phrase to describe the process of flipping the seals so that they become operational. When set, the center of a seal connects with the center of a chakra, and the rims don't touch. When in this concave shape, a seal functions like a satellite dish. When working in a chakra center, you can peer through the lens of a seal and determine the various spiritual energetic forces already at play within your system. You can also direct these forces for your own benefit.

In this chapter, we will more fully delve into the subject of the seals, so you can see the purpose of the seals. We will examine the various reasons for setting your seals, as well as means of determining if any of your seals are currently set or not. Next, we will look at ways of setting your seals, with how-to instructions, before considering various ways to work with set seals.

The seals are the primary energy body on the power pathway. Setting your seals enables exponential healing on this pathway. All ingredients of the power pathway are involved in power healing, however, including understanding the various spiritual energetic forces.

Alcoholism, for instance, is a first-chakra elemental issue and can involve several first power levels on the first power field, which maintains the causative emotional strongholds. Alcoholism is also a depressive issue, held in place by spins that are energetically slow. The intensity of the alcoholic energies attract certain power forces, which inadvertently strengthen and maintain the negative elemental patterns. You can figure out, in part, which spiritual energetic forces are enforced based on the chakra involved. The first chakra is about survival, as is the first power level. Therefore, the power forces at play will involve the first chakra ray of Will, a degenerative spiritual force (like Depletion), and a lack of needed virtues (such as Discipline).

Healing on the power pathway is a matter of commanding the power forces to support or break elemental strongholds, power levels, and power fields. Power healing is much more direct than healing on the elemental pathway. There you establish a healing environment and suggest supports. On the power pathway, you more or less ignore the backdrop and concentrate on movement. You actually select energies and forces at will. You might substitute one spiritual force for another, move filaments around, or ignore one goal for another. You put yourself in charge.

Of course, selecting which forces to command is just as important as being able to move them. There are two questions that help you determine the best solution to a power problem:

1. What power forces are holding a pattern in place?
2. What power forces could enter to clear this pattern?

There are two ways of examining the power forces behind an issue. The first is to part the power curtains from the perspective of the elemental pathway. The second is to peer at the power pathway while actually on it.

For the novice, it's easiest to diagnose power issues from the elemental pathway. To do this, you align with a chakra, perform a chakra-based assessment, and then analyze the power pathway.

To diagnose from a power perspective, you associate with a seal rather than a chakra, and then search the power pathway for problems or imbalances. You stand in the power pathway and see exactly what's happening, rather than guessing from the elemental pathway. From the power pathway, you can determine exactly which rays, virtues, spiritual forces, and powers are causative and which are healing, and you can call upon various sources of spiritual strength for help.

My work with Mike provides an example of working from an elemental perspective and then jumping to the power pathway. Although he was only thirty-three years old, Mike was worried about dying. In his family, every man died of a heart attack at age thirty-four. I began with an elemental diagnosis. Knowing that there were genetic tendencies and psychological factors involved, I still wanted to know what had started the trend from wholeness to brokenness. We worked intuitively to trace the issue through Mike's tenth chakra, the place of genealogy. There Mike psychically uncovered a situation involving a family member alive in the 1300s. At that time, a Catholic bishop condemned Mike's ancestor to a "life of heartache" for crossing him politically. The energetics of the energetic binding, a curse, were passed in the morphogenetic field for centuries, felling son after son after son at the death age of the original recipient.

I could have ended our work by healing on the elemental pathway, perhaps by breaking the curse with a regression, symbology, stronghold release, or even herbal medicine. Instead, I decided to check out Mike's familial status on the power pathway. Since the curse was in the tenth chakra, logic told me to access the tenth seal and assess the power conditions.

On the power pathway, I perceived several foundational power forces attaching the original binding to Mike's tenth chakra, as well as his ninth or soul chakra. With Mike's permission, we stilled the interfering spiritual forces. Then we "asked" his ninth chakra for a list of spiritual energetic forces that would break the binding for himself and the generations above and below him, and reflect his true destiny. Mike, who had never done intuitive work before this, actually saw and heard his own answers and, with prayer, commanded an exchange of energies.

When last I heard from Mike, he was thirty-eight and his brother was thirty-six.

How Power Forces Work

Power forces don't really change elemental-based frequencies, waves, vibrations, harmonics, or natural force disturbances. Rather, they support or deter the power of these forms of energy. Here's how they do it.

Spiritual forces support either helpful or harmful elemental energies. They can also attach you to entities, group consciousness, or other energies that can be helpful or detrimental. You should assess all spiritual forces to see if they are attached to the Primary Grid, which is positive, rather than a detrimental external force or source.

Powers supplement a spiritual force and greatly increase its potency. These elemental energies are positive if they are supporting a helpful power force, permanently or temporarily. But they are a problem if attached to a spiritual energetic force that creates difficulties.

Make sure you test a spiritual force before you connect it to a power, because you don't want to aggravate the wrong force. It's like using a hair-coloring product. The box insists that you first test a sample before you color all your hair. I ignored the directions once and ended up very, very redheaded—not good on a blonde. Testing forces works the same way. Try a power force for a day and see if you get positive changes. Then summon a power to add to it.

Virtues can greatly enhance and speed a healing. A simple power solution for sex addiction, for instance, is to train the addict to work with the virtues. What happens if he plugs a virtue like Compassion into his system? He'd feel guilty misleading a potential victim. How about Clarity? He might become clear that his true intention is seeking intimacy. Staying with this thought can bring him to elemental healing as he struggles to figure out why he believes that sex is the only way to obtain love.

But virtues will create problems if plugged into an inappropriate chakra-seal. Imagine what would happen if Honesty were turned up too high when you were dealing with your interfering mother-in-law or much-hated boss. Alternatively, virtues can also cause problems if they aren't attached where needed.

Effectively using the rays depends on your ability to turn a ray's "volume" up or down. For instance, the third ray of Intelligence doesn't create smart thinking in the third chakra; it supports the intelligence already latent or active in the subject and programmed into the third chakra. You don't become smarter by turning on the third ray; you simply activate the intelligence already present. If the third ray of Intelligence is already animate but, in contrast, the second ray of Loving Kindness is inactive, you'll be overly intellectual and poor in relationships. When diagnosing a power issue, you should always check for the balance between active and inactive rays, and for equal volume among rays.

Activation of the Seals

Before I cover individual power diagnostic techniques, you should know all about the purpose of your seals, setting your seals, and the process.

Purpose of the Seals

Seals are the most important instruments for change on the power pathway. When set, you can accomplish the following goals:

- Consciously attract and deflect spiritual energetic forces
- Fully engage your chakras on the elemental pathway
- Initiate and complete the golden kundalini process
- Make intense and sometimes instant change in the physical world

Seals are lenses that attract and deflect spiritual energetic forces. When unset, they are ineffective. However, this doesn't mean that they aren't operational. Since conception, your seals allow spiritual energetic forces in and out of your body and energy system. Until you fully engage your mind with your seals, which occurs as you consciously set your seals, you are the victim rather than manager of the spiritual energetic forces at play within your system.

You are born with spiritual energetic forces already attached to your seals, therefore affecting your chakras. Most likely, the placement of forces will mirror your parents' placement of forces. Unless they were involved in a spiritual process that works with the seals, your parents were probably unconscious as to the placement of their own spiritual energetic forces. This leaves you copying the use of spiritual energetic forces that doesn't coordinate with your spiritual design. Because of incorrect usage of spiritual energetic forces, some of the unique gifts latent in your chakras have probably never been activated. As well, some of the spiritual energetic forces in your system are also disempowering certain chakras.

Souls also select forces before birth and inutero. Usually, they choose those that reflect past-life issues, and hold these frequently negative patterns in place. This means that most of the spiritual energetic forces engaged in your system will be unhealthy or detrimental, rather than healthy and life enhancing.

After being set, you can fully engage your chakras for pathway healing, creating powerful change on the elemental pathway and therefore, in your everyday life. You will be able to see which forces are currently operational, and get rid of those that aren't appropriate. You will be able to test various forces for fit, and use those that will support your healing goals. Your chakras will naturally balance and provide energies that will create optimum well-being.

Another reason for setting your seals is to enable the initiation of the golden kundalini process. Through the elemental pathway, you might already have increased the potency of your serpent kundalini. Red kundalini can only take you so far. Think of how much more powerful is your mind and your chakra capabilities when the red and gold kundalini combines!

When unset, seals cannot complete the loop of golden kundalini that infuses your system with spiritual powers. Your body must rely upon the serpent kundalini without the benefit of golden kundalini. Your basic life energy can still be potent, but it will lack the luster and brilliance of the more spiritual energies of the golden kundalini. Setting the seals boosts your understanding of power, the spiritual dimensions, and your capabilities of controlling spiritual energetic forces.

Access to the golden kundalini increases your ability to command spiritual forces for physical change. Do you want to eliminate a virus? Your overall life force, when supported by both serpent and golden kundalini, is already well on its way, as these two energies bolster all aspects of your physical system. As well, the perceptions available through a set seal can enable you to track the spiritual energetic forces supporting the viruses' existence, and to see the forces that can eliminate them.

As you peruse your system, you might find that some of your seals are already set. This is not unusual. Many people unconsciously set some of their seals, for reasons discussed in the next section.

The Unconscious Setting of the Seals

When a seal is set and centered, its fulcrum will point toward the center of a chakra. When unset, the fulcrum points the other direction. There are several reasons that you might discover set seals, despite the fact that you haven't consciously invited this process.

Seals might set or "flip" under intense stress, as your higher self might decide that you need the extra support of certain seals. Under pressure, the higher self will set those seals that benefit you situationally. If you have to lift a car off of your child, your higher self might set your first seal, which provides physical strength. The seal might remain active if it was completely set during the crisis.

Sometimes individuals are born with a few set seals. This can be a carryover from a highly advanced spiritual life, or a decision made by the soul if it determines that a certain chakra ability or gift will be necessary from birth onward. Children born with set seals will be highly evolved in the areas governed by the related chakras. For instance, a child with a set sixth seal, front and back, will display incredible gifting in the visual psychic senses. A child with a set seventh seal, front and back, will be unusually prophetic and might experience relationships with angels, entities, and ghosts. Lacking a full setting of the front and back sides of a seal, the child will still appear gifted, but not as overtly.

Years of devoted spiritual study, meditation, or prayer can flip certain seals. Often these practices invite the setting of the higher chakras, but not necessarily the lower chakras, which can lead to a progressive spiritual life that might lack substance in the material world. Commitment to areas regulated by certain chakras can also initiate the setting of the related chakras. For instance, a dedicated therapist might discover upon examination that one or both sides of her second seal are already set because of her constancy in working though emotional issues. People greatly altered by Near Death Experiences (NDEs) often return from death with some set seals. Their awakening on the other side encouraged an awakening here. And in rare cases, people who ignite upon the divine pathway often experience an automatic setting of some and perhaps all seals. This might have been the case for Jesus when he was baptized in the River Jordan, or for Siddhartha when he suddenly awoke to his Buddha state.

If upon perusal you discover that some or all of your seals are set, rejoice! Having a set seal, however, doesn't imply knowledge of how to use it. Some of your seals might be set, but the spiritual energetic forces moving through them are probably not fully supportive of your health and happiness. The reason you want to consciously rather than unconsciously set your seals and work with them is that this is the only way to personalize the management of the spiritual energetic forces.

How do you recognize whether or not it is time to set your seals? Here are a few indications.

Deciding On Your Settings

You can, at any time, decide to set any or all of your seals. Some people don't feel ready to engage all of their seals at the same time, but want the advantage provided by a certain seal. For instance, let's say you have breast cancer and are undergoing chemotherapy. You might simply feel too tired to learn how to cope with the new information that might flood your system upon full seal activation, but you do want to access spiritual energetic forces to battle the cancer. In this case, I would encourage the activation of the fourth seal, front and back, to disengage forces that are bolstering the cancer and to engage forces that will eliminate it.

Know, too, that setting a seal isn't a substitute for working the elemental pathway, especially in regard to dealing with deep feelings and issues. In fact, it's often problematic to set a seal before you process elemental concerns, because the set seal is going to accentuate rather than heal your problems. If you're a little depressed, you'll become a lot more depressed; if you're a little anxious, you'll become a lot more anxious.

One of the reasons why ancient and secret societies evolved initiation rites to set the seals is that the process ensured gentle advancement and the presence of supportive experts. These brief criteria will help you determine when to set a seal:

- You have gone as far as you can in processing an elemental-based issue.
- You are willing to use your gifts and powers to help others, not only yourself.
- You are at a loss diagnosing an issue or problem and it seems that peering through a seal might be the only technique remaining.
- Your seals have begun to set by themselves.
- You have so many set seals, you might as well benefit from completing the process.
- You know that you need to use your energy for more spiritual, rather than only physical, reasons.

To figure out if these conditions apply to you, you can ask yourself these questions:

- Have you devoted yourself to a spiritual pursuit, and find that it isn't taking you as far as you want to go in terms of achieving your sense of purpose?
- Do you believe that you have innate abilities that need to be summoned if you are to more fully embrace your destiny?
- Do you sense that no matter your spiritual studies or pursuits, there is wisdom you can't quite uncover?
- Have you relentlessly committed yourself to dealing with the beliefs and feelings that have caused you problems?
- Are you prepared to act as a force for good if your deepest gifts and abilities were to open?
- Are you willing to act but also to not act, in accordance with divine will?

I encourage you to set your own seals, or to at least be involved in your own process. Of course, it can be beneficial to employ the services of a spiritual adviser who understands the process. Power masters are able to set others' seals. In fact, I know how to set other peoples' seals. The benefit to allowing help is that an ethical power master can set another's seals so that he or she can access a full palette of power energies for manifestation or healing purposes. It's not always easy to

see how to do this for ourselves, or to figure out which spiritual energetic forces might best suit us. I seldom involve myself in someone
else's setting process, however, for it's all too easy to use this ability to
serve the wrong purposes, even unintentionally.

Some power masters intentionally manipulate someone else by
controlling the power energies in the other's field. They do this by setting another's seals and then accessing the spiritual energetic forces for
personal use. Voodoo also involves using spiritual energetic forces to
keep the victim unaware of his or her own higher self and behavior.
Because of the ability of misappropriate decision-making, never
assume an unconscious state when your seals are being set. The
exception involves situations involving near-death, comatose states,
and children. Intervention without conscious approval is sometimes
necessary under these conditions.

The Process of Seal Setting

The seals are set when you have fully engaged your conscious self with
the Divine. To make the transition to power awareness, we must shift
from the uncontrolled psychic to the mindfully managed intuitive.
The evolved brain is one prepared for advanced enlightenment and
ready to step beyond the perceived limitations of the elemental pathway through the awakening of the golden kundalini, a power process for
accessing higher powers.

The connection between the golden kundalini and the seals is a
chicken-or-the-egg question. Which comes first? Various life changes
can activate the golden kundalini process, as described in chapter 4. As
the golden kundalini unfolds, the seals can automatically open or set,
although this can be an inconsistent process. You can also set the seals
intentionally and, by doing so, start the golden kundalini process.
Either way, the golden kundalini energies are much more effective if
you've already been working the red serpent kundalini. As well, the
seals are more apt to set if you've devoted time and attention to clearing the issues that arise as the serpent kundalini rises. Energy must
match energy. You need a great deal of physical power to maintain a
well-established flow of golden kundalini energy. The seals are best set
when you've attained an awareness of the importance of the physical
plane and an enthusiasm for your spiritual destiny.

When your seventh chakra is linked through the red kundalini to all
the other chakras, three things happen. First, your pineal gland produces higher-order hormones, including dimethyltryptamine (DMT),
sometimes called a "spirit molecule" because of its presence during
transcendent states and moments of birth and death. Second, these

hormones awaken the platinum body, which coordinates the biochemistry of the evolved pineal with the elemental pathway's managing energy bodies. Third, the red kundalini hitting the seventh chakra/pineal also triggers the golden kundalini process of the power pathway.

You don't have to be of a certain religion, ethnic group, or socioeconomic class to experience power transformation. We are all physiologically programmed for Wakefulness. A study by researchers at the University of California at San Diego showed that probing the temporal lobe of the brain produces "intense feelings of spiritual transcendence, combined with a sense of some mystical presence." Michael Persinger of Laurentian University in Canada found that people undergoing this stimulation typically "reported a presence. One time we had a strobe light going and this individual actually saw Christ in the globe."[2]

Highly evolved persons exhibit a higher amount of certain pineal-gland chemicals, which seem to include melatonin, serotonin, and DMT. The DMT or a chemical compound containing it seems to spin at a rate so high that it can actually spin disease out of existence.

This transcendence or awareness of the power pathway can emerge through focused spiritual practices, or with a flash of inspiration. Most of us recognize the power pathway through spiritual discipline, as is shown in the study by Masters and Houston discussed in chapter 2. In their study of over two hundred subjects, the six who achieved the highest state of enlightenment were over forty, with mature brains and years of dedicated spiritual practice behind them.[3] Without such strong mental discipline, the fire of the serpent kundalini will sting and possibly hurt you.

Once in a while, however, a person's pineal gland erupts like a tornado, forcing a hormonal conversion. The most typical cause is a near-death experience (NDE), which involves someone clinically dying and then returning to life. NDEers, as they are nicknamed, often report seeing a great white light that consciously emanates love. Researchers have concluded that the white light creates a measurable physiological difference in brain chemistry, specifically to the right temporal lobe. The blast of energy alters the lobe, which, in turn, "has a profound effect upon the various structures of the brain and the electromagnetic field that surrounds the body."[4] NDEers are universally described as more altruistic and psychic than the average population. They aren't afraid of death—they are happy to be alive and of service.

When the pineal gland of the seventh chakra reaches this state of intense development, it in turn stimulates the platinum body. When this body "turns on," your seals activate or are set.

If you completely believe you must set your seals to more fully encompass your truest nature, you can consider taking these steps to setting the seals. Before starting this process, ask yourself if you want to set one, a few, or all of your seals. As already explained, it is perfectly appropriate to set just one or a few seals, although you won't engage the full benefit of the golden kundalini process. If you only want to set certain seals, decide this before you use the process described next. The steps are the same, but you will only concentrate on your selected seals.

Consider also the issue of setting the front and back sides of a seal. It is always best to set both sides of a seal, otherwise you run the risk of chakra imbalance. Just knowing what is occurring in relation to the spiritual energetic forces on one side of a seal doesn't mean that you know what is happening on the other side. Good work done through the front side of a seal, for instance, can easily be undone by what is occurring through the correlated back side.

1. Use your five-step method for safe psychic use covered in chapter 9 to prepare for intuitive work and focus yourself in your psychic center.

2. Cleanse each chakra, front and back, with your breath. Acknowledge that breath and spirit are one and the same. With each inhalation, you accept purification and sustenance; with each exhalation, you release waste and worry.

3. Evaluate the current state of your seals. An already-set seal will be concave (pointing inward), while a convex seal (pointing out) is unset. When your seals are set, they flip from the inactive convex to the active concave position, and the concave seal is then able to accept and focus power energies into you through your chakra centers. You might also note signs of seal-based problems. Indications include pictures or senses of strongholds or other negative factors causing disease. X symbols show interference or issues controlling chakra functions and creating disease and problems. At this point, ignore these signs. Many will disappear as you set the seals; those that remain can be addressed when conducting pathway healing. What should you do if you find that some of your seals are already set? I encourage you to act as if the seals appearing are not set, and complete the steps provided. Seals can be inappropriately or incompletely set, and this is your opportunity to complete the process. If a seal was correctly set, you won't damage the process by double-checking.

4. You will first set the seal of your psychic center. If other seals already look set, simply leave them as is to set your psychic seal. Accessing your full psychic gifts, visualize, sense, accept, and even hear the tones of your center's front seal. Which way is it pointing? What color is it right now? What shape is it? What symbology

is locking it into its current state, as perceived in the center of your chakra? Shift focus to the other side of the seal and examine it with equal precision. Then do the same for the seal on your chakra's back side.

5. You can set your seals in any order, but I usually encourage a logical progression. If you consider yourself a physically-oriented person, I would jump from the psychic center to the second chakra for women and the first chakra for men, then follow the path of the serpent kundalini. If you are more oriented toward your spiritual nature, follow the path of the golden kundalini, as outlined in the section "Tracing the Golden Kundalini Process" later in this chapter.

6. Choose *one* of the following methods for "flipping" or setting the seal.

- Ask the Divine to send a guide to set your seal. This divine being will accomplish the task for you, if it is appropriate, "flipping" the seal from convex to concave. Ask that this guide remain as a gatekeeper to teach you how to safely use the seals.
- Use your own visual sense to command the seal into its highest setting and correct placement. Watch the changes and then command that the seal continue safely adapting and opening to your system.
- Listen to the tones of the seal, as is, then ask the Divine to help you hear the tonality of the set seal. Holding onto these tones, shift your seal from convex to concave with the power of these tones. Then ask that it be established securely through ongoing musical sequencing.
- Ask your future self to help you sense, feel, and know what it's like to have a set seal. Now command that your spirit establishes this shift and continues to monitor it for your education, effectiveness, and security.

7. Set the safety of the seal, front and back, with a cross of equal arms. Establish this same image in the center of the corresponding chakra to allow that chakra's expansion into the power pathway.

8. At this point, you can practice working this seal for a few days, or continue on to set the rest of your chakric seals with the technique that has worked for you. Most individuals find that the seals set instantly, but it takes a few days to get used to the feeling that results. You will feel "different." It is not unusual to experience a rush of feelings or a series of feelings as the chakras unload repressed emotions when the seals are set. Sometimes people experience grogginess for a few hours or days, as depressive

spiritual energetic forces might spontaneously clear. Soon, you will begin to feel clearer than ever before, mentally and emotionally. Some people experience a spontaneous change in a physical condition. When your psychic abilities become more intense, know that you are well on your way to being able to consciously direct forces on the power pathway.

Within a few days of setting your seal or seals, determine your harmonic, using the technique provided later in this chapter. You will then be equipped with most of the fundamental tools you need to conduct power healing.

Healing through Seal Activation

As your seals settle, you emerge ready to heal on the power pathway. As already discussed, you might have already noticed that certain seals were marred with negative symbols, such as an X mark. Though you picture X marks and other symbols on a seal, they are energetically located in the very center of the spine. A full and complete X is not a good thing. An X keeps your front and back chakras working at cross purposes and creates vulnerability to evil: energies causing anticonsciousness—the crossing or X-ing out of life, creativity, and awareness.

When your seals are setting, the superluminal body, or generating body, becomes available to break feelings free from emotional strongholds and—even more important—generate your spiritual feelings throughout your body, allowing Divine Love to heal you at all levels. The superluminal body uses hypersonic waves to translate energies from the spiritual plane into your physical self. Sonic waves are sound waves. Sound waves can emanate light and dark energies; because of this, they can carry feeling frequencies much deeper and farther than any other wave pattern. Spiritual energetic forces established through a hypersonic wave can be shaped and formed into various symbols for protective and manifesting reasons. You can, for instance, surround an ill organ with a healing-based sound wave to support healing, or surround your seventh auric field with a protective shield to keep yourself safe. On the elemental pathway, you can access the superluminal body by mingling power energies with those from your motor and sensory brain. This can help you picture psychic images or obtain verbal messages through your thalamus and the nerves around it. You can also send power energies through your heart into your hands to convey healing through your motor system. The magic of the process is the way that the chakras network energy.

Another solid healing technique is to temporarily or permanently attach the seals to the Christ body or etheric mirror on the elemental pathway. The seals can potentially be used to direct spiritual energetic forces that will "force" your physical, elemental body into its correct design. The etheric mirror duplicates your spirit's standard for your body.

Know that setting your seals is like discovering the "stairway to heaven" in relation to the divine pathway. The power energies flooding your seals intensify all spiritual energies, and potentially initiate greater spiritual awareness. The divine pathway is one of spiritual awareness. Your intuitive gifts can transcend to spiritual gifts through awareness of Divine love and invite you onto the divine pathway. Set seals are natural to the human; however, it's as if we have collectively "forgotten" our universal heritage. By setting your seals, you allow yourself the mastership you were born to enjoy. We aren't here to be victims of the human condition, rather creators of it.

Chakra Changes after the Seals Are Set

This describes some of the changes that occur in the chakras after you set your seals, as well as energies available after the setting.

Seal One

The rust-brown energy of the first seal sets spiritual energy into matter. Over time, the first seal adapts your first-chakra abilities of physical sympathy and empathy into the spiritual gift of manifesting, so you can actually change matter at will.

When first set, the luminized seal converts your reptilian brain—your Lower Mind, Heart, and Self—into expressions of love. You stop being so afraid and become more loving. The flood of love alters your biochemistry, and you express more intensely the first ray of Will. On the elemental pathway, the tar body unlocks the seed of destiny and releases it into the first chakra via the tenth chakra so you can better manifest your life needs. (Eventually this seed will rise further in the system to become the star seed of destiny.) This

(Note: The energies of problems and diseases don't all hold a literal X shape. They may appear as malformed or misshapen geometric symbols, numbers, tones, colors, spins, or other representations of the program running your chakra and therefore its elemental functions. Their effect is the same as that of the X described above.) Once you set a seal, you can more easily read the core program of a chakra and therefore go about healing it.

emergence has the potential to alter your physical genetics and clear up certain genetic diseases.

In the meantime, the first power door activates the first chakra's full ability to protect, reducing fear and ensuring safety. Now the conscious initiate can better command the most primary of the power forces, including the basic generative and degenerative spiritual forces.

The generative spiritual forces are ideal for improving body chemistry and pH balance, renewing physical organs, and accessing life spirit energy to cleanse and intensify basic life energy. Degenerative spiritual forces can detoxify the body; wipe out fungi, viruses, and bacteria; cleanse the system; and eliminate cancers or unnecessary growths. Consider accessing the virtue of Self-Orientation to balance aspects of the self and unpin yourself from any group consciousnesses affecting your system. You are strengthening your resolve in the first power field of Survival. Emotional and mental strongholds about life and death, worth and worthiness, will probably rise to the surface so they can be addressed.

Seal Two

The red energy of the second seal infuses the orange of the second chakra, adding zip and zest to the chi energy pumping through the body. The Chinese believe in a form of chi called *ancestral chi*, which is really a form of vital source energy. By transforming the orange chi with the red life spirit seal energy, you are producing this special brand of vital source energy and boosting longevity, creativity, passion, and expression. Meanwhile, the second power door floods your second auric field with life spirit energy for cleansing and repair. This life spirit energy now washes your system free from others' feelings and your own repressed feelings. This bathing renews and transforms the feeling bodies so that they can automatically access, through the back of the second chakra, power energies needed for compassionate healing.

On the elemental pathway, feelings inform personal needs. On the power pathway, this kindness extends to others. Now your feelings—and therefore your creative expressions—expand communally. Mercy and compassion are the spiritual gifts housed in the second chakra. The second seal adds awareness of social needs, transforming the unconscious to rid you of selfishness, greed, envy, approval issues, and fear for self. This soothing heals the mammalian and middle brain, and the Middle Heart, Self, and Mind. You become more conscious and therefore better able to use the second ray of Love and Kindness, which actually enters through the sixth chakra and exits through the second in the elemental pathway. On the power pathway, this process converges and there is no entry or exit; you can directly access the second ray through the abdomen. What seemed to matter before suddenly doesn't, and you pull free certain feelings that were stuck in emotional strongholds. This also frees you from feeling-based power levels, like victim-victor and holding-sending. You are now more functional in the world, fulfilling your second power field.

Seal Three

Setting your third seal invites full consciousness of self through the visible spectrum of yellow. Your third chakra, with all its mental and learning capabilities, brightens and expands. Intuitive empathy provides information for yourself and others, eventually evolving into the spiritual gift of administration. You can now organize data, your thoughts, and your activities toward meeting higher spiritual goals.

This organizing carries over into your physical health as you gain the conscious ability to direct cells and their activities. For instance, cancer reflects disorganized cellular activity. By adding structure in your thinking, you structure all aspects of your elemental self. You could literally reorganize cancer cells by using the power capabilities through the third chakra. On another level, accessing power consciousness unlocks the thoughts, particles, and beliefs casting you in mental and emotional strongholds, particularly those on power levels like success-failure. As you continue, your third power field completes ego learning so the third ray of Intelligence, which enters through the third chakra on the elemental pathway, can help decipher energy intelligence. The virtues of Truth or Clarity are ideal for sharing knowledge through the third ray into the throat, so you speak and therefore manifest with conscience.

Seal Four

Ultraviolet light is an electromagnetic radiation that expands beyond the violet end of the visible light spectrum. This is the power energy accessed through the fourth seal and the fourth power door. Setting the fourth seal shifts the entire body from a physical to a spiritual base necessary for expanded consciousness.

This seal bridges us to others. The heart is the center of Divine Love. Setting the lower seals begins acceptance and maturity of self, but through the heart you move into the true call of love, which is to bond. Your heart-based relational sympathy and empathy are transformed into the spiritual gift of healing. By attuning to the High Heart, it becomes possible to break free of the fourth power field impediments to true relationships with self, others, and the Divine. This reaching out necessitates moving from soul-based to spirit-based relationships, therefore allowing healing to occur at the deepest level of the soul.

Soul healing is dependent upon inner-child healing. Your inner children, traumatized aspects of the self still trapped in the shock that created them, mirror soul fragments. By working through power levels such as together-apart and innocence-guilt, your innocent child can come out and play, healing the inner children and soul fragments and thus allowing an infusion of conscious waves that are joyful. Being conscious of others enables the complete shift from the Lower or Middle Heart to the High Heart. Once this is done, you can channel intense power forces; the love won't allow something in your body that might injure you. With love as motivation, conscious waves flow in harmony so you can safely work with more than one force at a time. Holding virtues in your heart helps you maintain boundaries while healing others. The fourth ray of Unity, which flows through the heart, assists your work. Now Divine Love can automatically bring your heart's desires through you.

Seal Five

Through the fifth seal, your fifth chakra moves from verbal psychism to empathy to the spiritual gift called Word of Knowledge. The third ray of Intelligence is finalized in this conversion, and now, through the application of Truth, you can verbally summon power forces.

The gold of the fifth seal is magnetic—it attracts. When set, the fifth chakra doesn't direct forces; rather, it summons them through attraction principles. If you're willing to receive higher help, things happen. Statements of need can attract what you need.

The power gateway through the fifth auric field connects you to beings on the Primary Grid, not just the Secondary. This assistance will help you break power levels such as self-other on the power field of Recognition. Recognition references your awareness of the Divine's power and personal access to the power. This recognition can be the final blast you need to finish with those worth-worthlessness issues. Now you can truly achieve harmony with others—the key in accessing the gold body, which allows full linkage from soul to soul. The "X-ray" energy channeled through Truth will help you sense, hear, and communicate Truth superconsciously.

Seal Six

Setting the sixth seal involves using the pale-rose gamma energy of the power pathway to achieve hyperconsciousness. Hyper- versus super-consciousness is a measure of speed or timing. The psychic images of the sixth chakra eventually become instantaneously available through the spiritual gift of vision. This process transforms the pituitary gland by releasing strongholds causing poor self-image and misunderstandings about femininity.

Misunderstandings about the feminine affect both men and women. When women reject the feminine, they lose touch with their vitality and their innate powers. When men judge the feminine, they forget about the importance of love and nurturing. All such judgments affect the function of the pituitary and the regulation of the feminine hormones. Even men produce estrogen! Considered on the physical level alone, these problems often result in weight gain, food issues, and low self-esteem.

A healthy pituitary will help you make spiritual-based decisions and present you with healthy choices. These decisions are translated onto the manifesting screen. When you command choices through an evolved fifth chakra, you set events in motion according to spiritually accurate time frames.

Vision helps you see not only what could be but also what should be. The sixth power door allows movement of the sixth auric field so you can tap any dimension with your vision and dreams. This assists in the manifesting and eventual illumination process. If you can see where you need to be, you can get there. Love and Kindness, the ray connected to this chakra, can ensure a positive outcome for everyone concerned—the true mark of cocreation. Virtues like Clarity can assist with the process. Ultimately, the power pathway transforms the definition of Transformation, the sixth power field. Transformation involves a balanced relationship between changing the self to fit the world and changing the world to fit the transforming self.

Seal Seven

Setting the seventh seal invites acceptance of human and divine as one and the same state. This is the seal set upon Jesus by the Holy Spirit through his baptism; after this, Jesus accomplished the miracles that he later promised us we could also perform. The seventh seal is considered gold-rose, a blend of magnetized gold and the rose color of love. It allows transformation of psychic spiritual sympathy into intuitive spiritual empathy and, finally, movement to the spiritual gift of prophecy.

A prophet speaks for the Divine. A prophet is more than a foreteller of what will or might happen; a true prophet is invested with the power to help others find spiritual purposes. In ancient times, prophets were often stoned and killed; not everyone wants to hear that they are ultimately responsible for their own lives and destinies. If a prophet can access the Oneness of Ultraconsciousness, however, he or she will be illuminated with Love and, from there, the ability to command others to do what is right. Consider Jesus when he was twice summoned by the Roman soldiers. He basically said, "Not today," and they left. Jesus knew his own destiny and therefore understood that these soldiers were not destined to arrest him on those particular days.

The seventh chakra is the ultimate place for working through victim-victor issues. What you see is who you are; what you are can shape what lies outside of the self.

Christ achieved spiritual power because he was attuned to divine will. We're back to the first ray: Will. Through the setting of the seventh seal, personal and divine will merge. Thus the seventh power field of Applied Power is fulfilled, and the disharmonic aspects of the universe are perceived as harmonic. The power forces previously known as dualistic can be seen as two sides of the same coin.

The seventh power door performs a unique function in and through the seventh auric field. Through the Christ body, this door (and the pertinent seal) links with the platinum body. When readied, this body opens to illumination and the finalization of the red and gold kundalini processes. This process actually begins when one makes ethical and appropriate choices on the power pathway, such as being loving instead of vengeful when someone is being cruel.

Seal Eight

The place of karma, of shadows and mysteries, is confounding on both the elemental and the power pathways. As you set your eighth seal, you move into a full awareness of the shamanic. You can still move dark and light energies, but now you become an actual conversion point for these forces. Through the power pathway, the willing can assume the transmutation capacity of the eighth power field: becoming an alchemist of emptiness.

Emptiness is a space. Being in emptiness requires linking into the consciousness of "here." The initiated shaman acquires full control of spin and is able to use zero point to capture an energy while moving the same energy forward. Picture spinning a particle in two opposite directions at once: by doing so, you cancel out reality, such as the reality of a tumor, a cold, or a stronghold. In order to fully grasp these abilities, it is important to work through power-level philosophies such as something-nothing and attachment-detachment. By knowing that something is nothing and that nothing is the same as something, you can set an intention, which involves an attachment to outcome, but you can also do nothing, which allows detachment and therefore movement. The space between attachment and detachment is zero point, where you can use spin to invert energies, even to the point of canceling out the anticonsciousness of evil.

The set eighth seal is an ideal place for accessing life spirit energy. On the elemental pathway, you can read the Akashic Records; through the power pathway, you open the Book of Life. By reading this book in the "here," you cancel karma, own the wisdom you've acquired through the ages, and finalize your use of the fifth ray of Knowledge. This ray now grounds you into material reality, not only the spiritual planes.

Another powerful eighth-chakra power tactic is to access two or more virtues simultaneously. Virtues, like all forces, move at different spins. Spin more than one virtue and you create an inversion process—the key to shifting space for exponential change and learning.

Seal Nine

Setting the ninth seal enhances your ability to harmonize soul energies for global change. The expanded effectiveness lifts your consciousness to what I call the Olympian—the knowledge of self as having godlike attributes. These available powers convert soul sympathy to soul empathy, the ability to sense what's true for others' souls.

They also challenge the ego to deal with the ninth power field of Truth. Typically, the power level of virtuous-not virtuous will force the initiate to decide whether to manifest from universal or personal truths for personal or community gain. It's easy to stay hooked into one's own harmonic and keep manifesting for the self, drawing upon power forces at will. It's less selfish but sometimes personally unsatisfying to use harmonics to generate energy for higher purposes. Good-bad, another commonly triggered power level, takes on a new meaning. If it's good for everyone but yourself, is it good? If for all but a few, is it good?

Figuring out the meaning of Truth evolves the ninth chakra into a vessel for the spiritual gift of harmonizing—the blending of oneself into the whole and vice versa. The sixth ray of Idealism, which exits through the ninth chakra on the elemental pathway, is transfigured into a glowing beam of gold light, which attracts goodness to you. The ninth auric field, linked to the ninth spiritual door, now attracts spiritual forces, powers, and virtues to you as needed. You are now given what you need to be selfless, including the full assumption of power.

Seal Ten

The tenth chakra impacts so much of elemental reality, you'd expect a significant shift upon setting the tenth seal. You'll get it. While you automatically move from being natural- to universal-based, you assume divinity through your human self. The Divine is formless. When you understand that everything in nature is simply a form of essence, you begin to understand Unity. You are free from power levels like one-all and can complete darkness in light, the bad in the good. Conceivably, you could pop off of the Secondary Grid and begin to move among the various dimensions, planes of light, spheres, and other realities.

Through this seal, the Christ body or etheric mirror more fully actualizes. The tenth door invites a blending of your Christ body with your tenth auric field. You can begin to truly control the substances in your body and, if you want, shape them in line with your Christ body. You can also assist others in this process by infusing the natural with its complementary power forces. An herb becomes a true healing force when merged with the spiritual forces, powers, or virtues that enhance its divine expression. The ray of Knowledge now finds its completion in the world around you. Literally, you can pick up a rock and hear the Creator; listen to a shell and summon the element of water. All is one; as above, so below.

At this point, you can start to see the tragic challenges of the natural with more kindness. You'll stop struggling against bindings, curses, and hauntings. A cord to a plaguing ancestor becomes a telephone line for knowing what he once knew. An energy marker reflecting a great sin indicates the greatness of your learning. By releasing the idea that form determines the nature of intelligence or information, you can reformulate information from bad to good, harmful to helpful, useless to useful.

Seal Eleven

We first connect to the eleventh chakra through the psychic ability of force sympathy. The power pathway invites us to empathize with natural energy forces. But we're now moving off the Primary Grid and potentially beyond the "1,000-plus one" power field. There are no power levels to hamper or contain us, but there are consequences. We must decide what to command—the spiritual gift possibly achieved through use of the power pathway—and take the consequences upon ourselves.

Here lies Mastery Consciousness: the knowledge that we can act as Creator and become a Creator if we so choose. We perform commands by converting one substance to another and channeling power forces through various shapes, spin, vibrations, or forms. If we act righteously, the sixth ray of Idealism can transform into the sheer energy of the Divine.

Seal Twelve

The twelfth chakra interfaces with the energy egg, the Primary Grid, and the Secondary Grid. Can you be human and divine simultaneously? This is the question that invites the illumination process and activates the thirty-two secondary chakras (the spiritual points) to evolve in line with the Christ body.

Keying Into Your Personal Harmonic

I find that the key to effectively and ethically using the power pathway for healing is to find and stay in your own personal harmonic. Your spirit runs on its own spiritual truth or harmonic. This harmonic reflects a spiritual principle and represents your spiritual purpose. By figuring out your major and secondary spiritual harmonics, you can better access the higher components of yourself and open to the miracles that are yours to receive.

The power pathway is harmonic-based. When you access an Abundance force, for instance, if you're in your personal spiritual harmonic, you can automatically pull in corresponding forces, powers, and virtues. You won't just attract money, but also better relationships and opportunities to share with compassion.

Your harmonic mirrors the frequencies of your spirit, spiritual truths, future selves, past spiritual selves, innocent child, healthy Higher Self, High Heart, spiritual genetics, and all other truth-based aspects of self. If you come from your harmonic, you'll also attract the "higher help" available on any pathway but necessary on the power pathway: the Powers, Forms, angels, master, and other beings here to instruct and guide.

Here is a list of the basic harmonics (there are thousands more):

Harmony	Peace	Justice	Faith
Honesty	Knowledge	Knowing	Healing
Manifesting	Compassion	Mercy	Sharing
Love	Loving	Joy	Happiness
Truth	Doing	Being	Supporting
Caring	Vision	Creating	Destroying
Making	Teaching	Showing	Beauty
Morality	Integrity	Birthing	Guiding
Charity	Power	Empowering	Grace

Identifying Your Key Harmonics

Here are the steps involved in defining your personal harmonics.

Step One Think of the happiest moment in your life, one in which you felt completely open and glad to be alive. Holding that event or episode in mind, speak each of the listed harmonics out loud. Cross off those words that don't seem to fit or match the situation; circle those that do. Continue this process until you have narrowed your choices to five. If another word pops into your head, add this to your list and test it as well.

Step Two Complete each of these statements with one of your five chosen harmonics:

1. During the best times in my life, I have felt....
2. I believe that I encourage people to be, act, or feel....
3. If there were one spiritual truth for which I would die, it would be...
4. The people who know me best would say that I am....
5. If I could help only one person, I would show them the truth of....

Has a pattern emerged? Is there a concept or word that stands out? If you have mixed results, you may be using more than one harmonic. One of these harmonics will be primary, however, and another secondary. To further narrow down your list, eliminate those harmonics that didn't appear on any of the Step Two statements and move on to Step Three.

Step Three Now you should be down to fewer than five harmonic choices. Try out each of them for one day. Pretend that you are "wearing" the harmonic. How do you feel, for instance, operating in Grace all day? Truth? A harmonic that you've named? Your primary harmonic will enable you to feel clear, act with integrity, receive clear intuitive information, withstand pressure, understand others, make effective and immediate decisions, remain compassionate without caretaking, genuinely like yourself, sense the presence of the Divine or your spiritual guides, and feel capable and deserving of commanding power forces.

Tonal Harmonic

Your personal harmonic tone is a single emanation of your personal harmonic. Remember that a harmonic is similar to a frequency that is vibrating and emanates overtones. You are more than just "one note"— you are a manifestation of all energies that come from one or more divine truths.

Secondary Harmonics

Most people have more than one harmonic, though it's rare to have more than one main harmonic. It's helpful to find and use your secondary harmonics. My main harmonic, for instance, is Happiness. My primary second harmonic is Love. What makes me happy? Being about love!

Specific Power Diagnostic and Healing Techniques

There are several ways to diagnose and heal through a power perspective. Specific healing tips will also be provided in each section, as applicable.

Assessing Spiritual Forces

By far the easiest power trick is to examine the spiritual forces, which are always locked onto the elemental causes of severe problems. Your intuitive sense will show you which spiritual force is supporting an issue. You can examine the entire power system or a specific chakra, checking to see which spiritual force is most potent or present. This will likely be the culprit upholding the problem.

Spiritual forces may be the key to problems, but they are also the key healing tools on the power pathway. They are usually centered in a chakra, but can also be attached to physical organs, systems, or cells; auric fields, which transform into the power doors when the seals are set; sources either helpful or harmful; and even invaders such as viruses, bacteria, and fungi, as well as the group consciousness controlling some of these organisms.

Spiritual forces can also attach to feelings. Remember, most spiritual forces are interlaced with feeling energies. These feeling energies will magnetize to the helpful or harmful feelings in the body. They can also connect with divine or spiritual feelings and so enhance any healing process.

In general, the generative spiritual forces increase the function and capabilities of the energy body using them, while the degenerative spiritual forces inhibit the function and capabilities of the energy body attached. Don't assume, however, that all generative forces are good and all degenerative are bad. A generative spiritual force can link with cancer cells and spread them throughout the body. Often we unconsciously connect the generative to feelings like shame, which then extends the shame until it plugs entry points for needed power energies. But imagine what happens when you connect a degenerative spiritual force to cancer or a fungus infection! Both generative and degenerative spiritual forces must be seen as instruments with the capacity for both harm and healing.

One of the keys in healing spiritual forces is a matter of spin. Again, if you spin a degenerative spiritual force counterclockwise, you will destroy the attached substance or energy and spin it out of the body. If you spin it clockwise, you might destroy the energy but spin the waste products into the body. The best way to work spin with spiritual forces is in tandem with the imagination. If you really want something to disappear and to then attract helpful energies, spin a degenerative spiritual force into the center of the imagination pathway through the imagination mirror. Reverse the spin so the "bad energy" is shifted into the antiworld; corresponding "good energy" will appear in this world. You can also use a generative spiritual force to spin "good energy" from the antiworld into this one, as described in chapter 14, on the imagination pathway.

I can't tell you which particular generative or degenerative spiritual forces to use when energy mapping, because each person's system, personality, and power needs are different. However, the list below and the examples in chapter 5 give you some specific spiritual forces to draw upon.

Generative	Degenerative
Accepting	Rejecting
Agreeable	Disagreeable
Attractive	Dismissive
Aware	Unaware
Balanced	Imbalanced
Believing	Disbelieving
Carefree	Careful
Cheerful	Sober
Confident	Insecure
Conscious	Unconscious
Defending	Attacking
Devoted	Unconcerned
Energetic	Contained
Erotic	Asexual
Excellent	Sufficient
Fertile	Sterile

Gentle	Rough
Helpful	Harmful
Humorous	Serious
Inviting	Rejecting
Learning	Unlearning
Liberating	Restricting
Mundane	Inspirational
Natural	Unnatural
Noticeable	Invisible
Open	Closed
Orderly	Disorderly
Patient	Impatient
Peaceful	Agitated
Principled	Unprincipled
Prolific	Barren
Purposeful	Irresolute
Respectful	Disrespectful
Serenity	Alarm
Spontaneous	Resolute
Suitable	Inappropriate
Tender	Violent
Timeless	Measured
Unifying	Dividing
Valuing	Devaluing
Warm	Cold

Perusing for Powers

Strong spiritual forces are supported by powers. A critical issue is probably established by a spiritual force or set of forces, intensified by a power. Look for the energy behind the spiritual forces. Those empowered by powers are probably the ones causing the most problems.

While the powers support disease and imbalance, they also excel at healing. Connect a fire power to a generative spiritual force like Creativity, and you'll be painting pictures all night! Structure a stone power into the energy egg to establish cellular walls, and those cells will hold their structure until kingdom come.

Here are two ways to figure out which powers to use:

• Evaluate elemental or pH imbalances and generate powers that will add what's needed or subtract what is too flush. For instance, fungus grows in water, so if you want to assist the release of a vaginal yeast infection, you would use a degenerative spiritual force with a reverse spiral and perhaps an air power to blow out the water. Once you've achieved vaginal balance, you could shift to a generative spiritual force to increase the chi and add a star power to initiate spiritual wisdom (ether) and kill any remaining yeast (fire). When fully stable, try a balance of the two types of spiritual forces and perhaps insert an earth power into the generative for solidity.

• If what's there isn't working, insert the opposite of what's present. Stone keeping you stuck? Then try air or water. Wood making you too flexible? Try metal or stone.

Using the Virtues

Call and implement the virtues that will help you with diagnosis, whether you're performing elemental, power, imagination, or divine pathway diagnosis. For instance, access the virtue of Clarity through the third-chakra seal to correctly intuit the cause of a disease.

Some virtues are similar to the spiritual forces, in name at least. The difference is that virtues end up activating spiritual qualities from deep within you. They enter the back side of the chakra system to shape your unconscious so you eventually act in accordance with your "innate" virtuous nature. Spiritual forces are external energies that can be directed by you, but at no time do you actually "become" the force. Correct use of the spiritual forces requires virtuous decision-making. The virtue of Creativity, for instance, will help awaken your own creative nature. The force of Creativity will help you stimulate the creative in any substance or person to which you direct that force.

The virtues aid in healing when they support the natural harmonic of a certain chakra and encourage you toward your destiny. As with the use of all power forces, you have to select virtues that meet your short- and long-term goals. This is an individual choice. Try following these tips:

• Evaluate for nonvirtues as well as virtues. Often we think we're employing a virtue, but we're really using a construct instead— usually so we can continue avoiding our real needs and feelings. Are we really being serene? Or are we stifling our desires so we don't rock the boat and get into trouble? A virtue is a quality: it will support honesty and authenticity and will not allow you to hide your true light.

• In general, decide whether you need an uplifting or a calming virtue. Some virtues, like Expression or Creativity, push you into the world. Others, such as Tranquility and Harmony, soothe. There are virtues more oriented toward healing; others, toward manifesting. Healing is a virtue, as is Release. The Release virtue is ideal when joined with a degenerative spiritual force to eliminate toxins, for instance. Manifesting virtues, including Prosperity and Expansion, will draw energies to you. These are best associated with generative spiritual forces.

• To select virtues, attune harmonically or assess via your spiritual genetics. That way you'll choose virtues that fit you.

Applying the Rays

As with the virtues, you can empower the rays to more effectively understand a problem. Try commanding the third ray of Intelligence to gain information when diagnosing. Try using the ray of Unity when you're talking with your medical doctor and want his or her best input. Rays can also cause problems—as with all power forces, they can be misapplied, broken, overused, or just plain ignored. Too much Will, for instance, will overpower the first chakra and shut down the first seal, thus supporting or causing physical or lifestyle imbalances such as money issues, sex addiction, alcoholism, or blood disorders.

Ideally, all rays should be in good working order and in balance. Here are some tips for ensuring this:

• Make sure that the rays in your causal chakras are working correctly. Check for lack of alignment, entry, and exit points with corresponding chakras; the health of the ray itself; and the balance between this and other rays. Rays enter in one chakra and exit from another.

• Check for cords and bindings and eliminate these.

• Connect a ray with a spiritual point or other power forces to increase effectiveness. Codependency, for instance, can involve a low first ray of Will. You may need to heal this ray and then possibly enhance it with a generative spiritual force to boost its power.

Energy Particles and Charges

Energy exists on the power pathway, as do neutrons and proton- and electron-based particles. In general, however, these particles transfer in energetic or consciousness waves on the power pathway. Here are tips for diagnosis and healing with this knowledge.

Protons As on the elemental pathway, too many proton particles, waves, or charges in comparison with the number of electrons indicates magnetic imbalance on the power pathway. The spiritual strength will overwhelm practical concerns, and there will be tendencies toward anxiety and using the future for escapism. Fungus is often attracted to overwhelming protons that contain certain information, and they can attract certain types of power forces to enhance their position in the physical body.

Proton power forces will encourage the spiritual beliefs and behaviors needed to allow healing. Proton-oriented forces include generative spiritual forces such as Fertility and Love, and degenerative spiritual forces such as Release and Seriousness. They also include healing or calming virtues and relationship-based rays such as Unity, Love, and Kindness. These power energies ensure the presence of love, safety, and inspiration in the chakras or organs that need healing.

Electrons As on the elemental pathway, too many electrons, electron-based waves, or charges carrying electrons indicate an imbalance of an electrical nature. You will find more depressive and regressive tendencies when electrical energies are present on the power pathway or enforced by power forces. Viruses, for instance, are carried on electron-based group consciousness waves and will attract generative spiritual forces that support their spread throughout the physical body.

Electrical power forces will enhance the powers needed to heal. These will typically include the power-based generative spiritual forces such as Strength and Power, and degenerative spiritual forces, including Agitation and Violence. They also include manifesting or uplifting virtues and strengthening rays, such as Will and Intelligence. These power energies will shove repressed feelings to the surface, muscle "bad energies" away, and increase the overall potency and vitality of any chakra or organ.

Neutrons Neutrons never present a problem; they should be used more often for both diagnostics and healing. They are neutral but use elemental forces such as gravity to attract electrical and magnetic energies. They also work through power laws, including the spiritual law of harmonizing, to shift power energies to match your spiritual self. You can access the neutral or "blank" area in any chakra or energy body to evaluate which power energies are in effect or not.

To heal, stand in the energy body's neutral area, then use harmonics to decide which power forces are beneficial and which are not. This is the best way to decide what to use.

The center of the neutral areas also contains advanced spiritual forces. These are completely unprogrammed and undirected power energies. It takes a lot of trust to access these energies. You can't control them. They shift the system and all other power forces into correct spiritual order. Lack of faith in our own spirit or the Divine inhibits a trust in this process; however, when employed effectively, they can be extremely powerful. Cancer in particular is very responsive to neutral spiritual forces.

Life Energy and Kundalini

To better determine where and why the basic life energy is stuck or depleted on the elemental pathway, you can evaluate where you are in your golden kundalini process. Accessing the golden kundalini increases the potency of power you can direct from the power pathway for healing. The steps below show how to trace the path of golden kundalini through the chakric seals.

Before examining the golden kundalini, look for red serpent energy in the seventh chakric pineal. The serpent energy stimulates the platinum body, which automatically activates seal setting. If red kundalini has not yet reached your pineal, the seals will not be set; there will also be a pinched, cold appearance to the pineal and metallic energies surrounding it. In this case, you can manually set your seals, following the exercise earlier in this chapter, or you can use the following golden kundalini process and include seal setting when you get to the pineal.

Tracing the Golden Kundalini Process

1. Begin in the highest spiritual point, the thirty-second, which is governed by Divine Love.

2. Ask the Divine to fully activate your thirty-second spiritual point, converting it to completely match your own spirit. Bring the energy of Love through each of the twenty out-of-the-body spiritual points, until it reaches the twelfth chakra.

3. The twelfth chakra and auric field connect with your energy egg. Completely infuse the egg and its walls inside the inner casing with Love. Ask the Divine to completely and permanently heal the egg and to translate the Divine energy through the leaders connecting the egg into the seventh chakra and your secondary chakra points (which are part of your twelfth chakra; some of the lower minor chakras feed directly into the tenth chakra).

4. Simultaneously, your seventh and tenth chakras will infuse with Divine energy. You may feel a slight buzzing or see an ever-brightening light. Ask for a full spiritual activation of these energy bodies and the organs or glands within them, according to your

spiritual programming and your Christ body or etheric mirror. At this point, your system can complete the rising of the seed of destiny. Contained by the tar body, the seed of destiny unlocks from this black cave when you set Seal One, releasing it into the first chakra by way of the tenth chakra. Depending upon your internal readiness, the seed of destiny might have already risen within your chakra system by the time you reach the activation of your seventh chakra in the golden kundalini process. Wherever this seed now lies, which can be within any of the chakras between one and six, it now completes its initiation into the seventh chakra, where it activates your spiritual genetics. These spiritual genetics will, over time, compel your physical genetics to adapt to your spiritual needs. Upon Wakefulness, this seed of destiny evolves further into the star seed of destiny and is able to activate others' destinies.

5. Writhing in the seventh and tenth chakras, the golden kundalini now uncoils from the twelfth chakra into the eleventh and then down farther into the body through the ninth chakra. (I'm attempting to explain this process in linear form, though it is closer to the movement of a snake undulating in several directions at once.) At the eighth seal, your system begins to activate the life spirit body and your ability to read the Book of Life.

6. When the golden kundalini reaches the fifth and fourth seals, the gold body is fully awakened. Your soul is now able to resonate with your spirit, which transforms the elemental silver body attached to the eighth chakra, so that the Book of Life overwhelms the Akashic and Shadow Records. The past is transmuted as if only good has ever occurred.

7. As the remaining seals are touched with Divine energy, the superluminal body is eventually activated. This body uses sonic waves to connect divine truths to the physical body; it also processes spiritual rather than body-based feelings. It continues to develop in power and intensity over time.

8. Gradually, your basic life energy is transformed into life spirit energy, and you begin to live in your spiritual rather than your physical nature.

9. As your seals set, your auric fields graduate into the power twelve doors, attracting and deflecting spiritual energetic powers.

Using the Golden Kundalini for Healing

Here are a few indicators that you should use the golden kundalini for healing.

- You're facing a terminal illness or a serious chronic problem. Your red serpent kundalini is obviously stuck and your chakras are probably running serious reverse spins.
- Your issues are obviously spiritual in nature or cause.
- Magnifying the red serpent kundalini or using any physical force on the elemental pathway is just causing more problems.
- The golden kundalini process has spontaneously started already.

Know that you can spread the golden kundalini development over a long period of time and so concentrate on elemental healing, chakra by chakra. This gentle process will help you heal in a safe and easy way.

Energetic Communication Methods

The golden kundalini and seal-setting processes invite full access to power pathway intuitive senses. Before these processes are initiated, or if they aren't done correctly or incompletely, you could experience the following energy communication problems.

- If you are not intuitive enough, you will be too psychic and lack boundaries, hooking emotional strongholds. If you are not spiritual enough, you will be too slow and mind-oriented, which will trigger mental strongholds.
- Although being intuitive is a good thing, it requires a great deal of mind control. If you concentrate too much on being intuitive or mind-based rather than spiritual or Divine-based, you will have rigid boundaries and tend toward mental strongholds. It will be hard to learn how to use imagination on the imagination pathway, and it will be hard to accept Divine love or joy. Attempting to use your psychic abilities only for spiritual ends without first gaining some intuitive control can lead to emotional strongholds and fantasies on the imagination pathway.

To heal from either of these conditions, return to the elemental pathway and work on the basics of psychic development and psychic boundaries. You must have a solid system in place to use intuition or the charismatic gifts correctly.

Energy Languages

The following are signs of power imbalances.

Feeling Lacking light, one can become too emotional and carried away with events of the day. This can result in evil or manipulative use of powers as a means of carrying out feeling-based desires.

For healing, first process your stuck elemental or body-based feelings therapeutically. You can then use the power superluminal body to free yourself of feeling charges and connect with the spiritual message contained in your feelings. Now start listening to your feelings. What are they really saying to you?

Don't use or shift any power force except soothing or uplifting virtues or love-based rays until you deal with your darkest drives and desires. A client of mine started accessing his power forces accidentally after he read a book on various powers and began to command. Within a few months, he had almost ruined his marriage with an emerging violence, lost his job because of temper tantrums, and was quickly losing his friends. He was commanding forces based on repressed anger and rage, and he needed to work with a therapist to deal with childhood trauma.

Light Lacking feeling, one can become too mind-driven and pedantic and can lack conscience. If never transformed by the Divine, one can lack heart and love.

Light is always good, right? Not necessarily. I once hiked through the jungles near Panama to meet a famous shaman who supposedly could heal everything. After hours in a rickety bus and a sloshy hike through a mosquito-laden, uncut jungle path, we arrived at this man's clinic. He was very spiritual. He seemed to glow. And he must have had fifty animals in various states of starvation inhabiting his front lawn— a product of too much light in relationship with feeling. If you are affected by this problem, you can heal by examining your "magnetic" beliefs. Ask why you think spirituality is separate from feelings, and see what repressed feelings you are denying for fear of the pain.

Energy Bodies

Here are indications that there might be something wrong with the following power bodies.

Seals If your seals are incompletely set, you will feel drained, tired, disempowered, and perhaps victimized by entities, dead or alive. You can reach the pinnacle of the elemental pathway through red kundalini, but life will lack meaning, purpose, and higher spiritual drive. The red kundalini energy will be stuck and causing havoc at certain chakras. (Setting the seal and initiating golden kundalini can heal the chakra and allow flow of basic life energy.)

To solve the problem, work the center of a seal to figure out which spiritual forces are creating a disadvantage. In it lie the pictures, symbols, or tones of the spiritual forces directed from the power pathway into the elemental pathway. You can also determine which spiritual forces are being rejected by the elemental pathway by checking for deflecting forces.

Power masters are able to set others' seals. This gift can be twisted to serve the wrong purposes, as the skilled can manipulate someone else by controlling the power energies in the other's field. On the positive side, when following divine will a power master will set another's seal so that he or she can access a full palette of power energies for manifestation or healing purposes. Think, for instance, of how much more effective chemotherapy might be if supported by spiritual forces that enhance the immune system's response. With the permission of the Divine, a power worker can enable this type of assistance.

Twelve Doors Lack of full consciousness indicates a failure to activate certain doors or auric fields. Check each door to see which ones are open, colorful, and healthy. Those with problems indicate auric field disturbances and issues about protection, vulnerability, or authenticity. Work as you would with an auric field or its corresponding chakra on the elemental pathway, or connect with the corresponding seal on the power pathway for further diagnostics and healing.

Life Spirit Body Trouble is evidenced when you access Akashic, Shadow, or others' records instead of your own; you'll know you're doing this because your "memories" don't pertain to you.

Spirit Body This is the clothing on your spirit and connected to your life spirit body. The main concern with this body is lack of activation.

Gold Body If this is not activated, you continue to attract people who trigger your emotional and mental strongholds and soul issues.

Platinum Body Until it is activated, your pineal may be coated with heavy metals, thereby impeding its effectiveness and leading to hormonal imbalances, insomnia, or depression.

Superluminal Body Unless this is fully active, body-based emotions will control rather than enhance your life.

Energy Packages

Here are ways to use energies available on the power pathway for diagnosing or healing.

Beliefs Check a presenting problem against the six primary beliefs. Intuit which of the negative beliefs is reinforced by power forces, or which positive belief is lacking power support.

You can reinforce needed or already-present positive beliefs by linking them with a generative spiritual force or a virtue; this linkage usually involves a connection to the chakra seal. You can decrease harmful beliefs by using degenerative spiritual forces and accentuating a helpful ray or virtue. It's sometimes helpful to perform this work through the imagination pathway so you can use spin to shift beliefs from here to the antiworld or back again.

Feelings Working feelings from the power pathway can be complicated yet effective. For diagnostic purposes, work first as you do with beliefs, evaluating for repressed, withheld, overwhelming, or denied feelings that are causing disruption; feeling charges; or feelings that aren't your own. This will help clarify whether or not problematic feelings (or the lack of them) are intensified through the power pathway.

You can also assess the feeling energies in spiritual forces and how those energies are applied on the elemental pathway. The feeling energies in the spiritual forces are already balanced, but the elemental self can split, derange, or ignore these energies in favor of retaining a problem. By learning to see into the spiritual forces emanating from the power pathway into your elemental system, you can evaluate for the use of the feelings contained within.

Yet another measurement for feelings is to evaluate them through the superluminal body, if it's been activated. Watch this body, which in most individuals is located near the front fourth-chakra seal. What spiritual feelings is it processing? Where is this body directing these feelings into the elemental pathway: an organ, cell, gland, chakra, or auric field? Your spirit sends spiritual feelings where they'll do the most good, usually to alert you to a message or to heal a problem. By following the flow of feelings, you can often pinpoint the origin of a current or upcoming issue.

Once feelings are recognized and felt on the elemental pathway, the best technique for processing them is working the power superluminal body, as follows:

1. Recognize the elemental-based feeling. Feel it completely in the physical body.

2. Imagine the superluminal body. You can imagine it anywhere, as it is a power body not linked with the elemental pathway except through your nervous system, which runs everywhere throughout your physical body. I like to envision it near the chakra that houses the feeling that I'm working with.

3. Activate the superluminal body by simply commanding activation.

4. Allow the superluminal to receive incoming energies from your spirit. This body uses hypersonic waves much like condensed radio waves to shift energies from the divine into your physical self. You may perceive colors, sensations, or sounds; many people do. Allow these energies to saturate to the core of your superluminal body.

5. Now reconnect with the feeling that you've been working on. Center this feeling in the core of the superluminal body and allow the incoming energies to generate your feeling outward. You will probably feel physical sensations in your body. When these abate, you can ask these questions:

   a. What was the message of my body-based feeling?

   b. What belief has been connected to this feeling? Do I need to allow it to shift or change?

   c. What is this feeling transforming into?

   d. What need must I now meet?

   e. What must I do or know to meet this need?

Energy Fields

For a quick assessment of your relationship with other energies, consider these tips:

Ley-line involvement. All spiritual energetic forces can attach through a seal or chakra to a ley line in the ground. This can create elemental disturbances, including agoraphobia and other phobias, environmental toxicity, failure to thrive except in certain geographic regions, and culturally based diseases, such as Tay-Sachs disease among the Jewish population or sickle-cell anemia among persons of African descent.

Morphogenetic fields and lines. Spiritual energetic forces will almost always accentuate morphogenetic-generated strongholds and diseases. You can follow the images of the most potent forces to figure out which fields are impacting you.

The Vivaxis. Spiritual energetic forces can attach us to anything. For instance, I have a client who gets anxious every full moon, to the point of needing bed rest. His elemental-based water energy was latched to the spiritual energetic force of Chaos. When the moon moved the tides, it also affected his inner balance. We erased this connection and he's been fine ever since.

You can cancel out negative ley line, morphogenetic, and Vivaxis attachments through conscious directing of spiritual forces. Degenerative spiritual forces can erase your link to a harmful field. For instance, you can summon the force of Disharmony and break the connection between yourself and an elemental-based binding to an ancestral land. Bindings cause many illnesses; this type of work can eliminate their effects. You can also use generative spiritual forces to establish positive connections with fields. Want to prosper every time the planet Mercury goes retrograde or in reverse? Attach a spiritual force like Abundance to Mercury and trigger it every time this change occurs.

Patterns, Boundaries, and Habits

Most of the power pathway tips thus far have related to evaluating for negative patterns. Certainly you can attach a degenerative spiritual force and power to the lines of energy holding an elemental pattern in place. This is easiest to do through the power fields, which are organized in grid form. Look for the filaments or congestion on a power level continuum, attach the force, and—"Boom!" It works like dynamite.

But you can also create a brand-new pattern based on your spiritual genetics, and thus create a new power- and elemental-based neurological pathway for success. Sometimes the easiest way to break a bad pattern is to establish new boundaries and habits through the power pathway.

To do this, first evaluate the power energies present in regard to a certain pattern, behavior, or issue. Ask to intuitively see which forces would create healthy internal and external boundaries. Then ask to see which forces would automatically allow the subconscious to select habits that would reinforce health. Command this shift. In the end, you'll probably see an equal number of generative and degenerative spiritual forces. If these spiritual forces are not in balance, your chakric system will also lack balance. You'll be either too rigid, as often happens with an oversupply of generative spiritual forces, or too flexible, as occurs with too many degenerative spiritual forces.

Let's say you have pretty good boundaries and simply want some better habits. The conscious application of the spiritual energetic forces can make a hard job seem easy. Why not apply the virtue of Truth to replace the bad habit of lying? Or why not use the second ray of Love to heal a broken heart?

Times, Places, and Zones

The power pathway operates in dimensions one through six; therefore it will support the vast majority of elemental issues impacting you in these dimensions. Power forces can't tell time. Many organic issues involve spacetime distortions, and power spiritual energetic forces will merely reinforce causal issues across all times and spaces.

You can access a power force to help open the Akashic or Shadow Records and to peer into a Plane of Light for diagnostic or healing purposes. As noted in chapters 11 and 12 on the elemental pathway, each chakra relates to a corresponding Plane of Light, as do the corresponding seals. You can intensify the imaging of Plane of Light data by looking through a seal rather than merely a chakra center; you control the "dimmer switch" by adding forces like the ray of Intelligence or the virtue of Clarity to help your process.

Power diagnostics and healing can also apply in the Zones of life and death. If part of you is stuck in one of the Zones, this condition is probably supported by a misinformed power force—usually a spiritual force and sometimes a Power. Sometimes a misapplied virtue keeps us stuck. One may think it virtuous, for instance, to linger in the Gray Zone, trying to help a demonic entity out of its troubles, rather than to return to wholeness within oneself. The best way of working the various dimensions, Planes of Light, and Zones for healing is to use the elemental techniques suggested in the elemental pathway chapter and provide secondary support with power healing.

The Book of Life

The power pathway provides one of the best healing resources in existence: the Book of Life. Although the Akashic and the Shadow Records involve karma and must therefore be carefully interpreted, the Book of Life provides only truth. This truth is subjective in that it mediates among our spirit, the Greater Spirit, and our elemental self. The unfolding of Book of Life information provides the perspective that we often need to heal.

Means of Accessing

There are five different methods for accessing the Book of Life:

- Through the analog system and any of the seals. The analog is the ancient system and way of knowing, in which your intuitive faculties provide revelation and insight directly into your neurological system. Through this connection, information and light from the Book of Life can directly alter your current body, self, and perspectives through alignment with your spirit. Work through the seal that best reflects the issue you are considering or the question you have in mind.
- Through universal language. You can access Book of Life information for yourself or others through its encoded form in various materials. Such materials could include scriptures, ancient scrolls, mathematical formulas, sacred geometry and inspired music, poetry and writings.
- Through your highest spiritual gifts, which can be held in Divine principle for accessing your Personal Book of Life.
- Through any of the chakras. You can use intention to sense, touch, feel, or see the Book of Life "chapters" that apply to the life concerns regulated by specific chakras. The easiest way to read the Book of Life is by psychically holding it in front of your heart chakra.
- Through the spirit body. This aspect of your spirit works like an etheric covering for the eighth chakra through the eighth seal.

Applications

You can access the Book of Life for the following reasons:

- To read the spiritual truth, purpose, destiny, gifts, and original plan encoded within your Personal Book of Life.
- To enhance understanding of why you have chosen certain life circumstances. You can see which choices supported or support your destiny and which ones do not. Because of the intense compassion and understanding coding the information, you automatically forgive yourself and others for "mishaps" and subsequently heal on a deep level.
- To project into the possible future and gauge current life decisions.
- To gain information about superior or miraculous healing remedies, and to obtain clear input about whether to use them or not.
- To obtain information for others with spiritual permission; understand the Divine Plan; determine your own role in the plan;

summon spiritual forces and energies to bring the Divine Plan to earth; and become more instrumental in encouraging world change.

• To access your Personal Book of Life in order to actualize your spiritual genetics and align with your Divine History.

Deliberations

It can be easy to confuse the Akashic Records with the Book of Life, especially if accessing them by any digital means, which can include use of your spiritual gifts. The digital system is the linear nervous system. You can certainly gather information and make changes through this system, but it's slow. The digital system is one-way and electrical; the analog system is circular and energetic. Any and all strongholds can also affect interpretation and so you must be careful not to assume you are absolutely right in your readings.

Here are a few guidelines for distinguishing between the Akashic and your Personal Book of Life:

Akashic Records	Personal Book of Life
Contains negative and positive information	Includes only positive information
Counts mistakes and achievements	Emphasizes spiritual achievements
Records others' reactions to you	Records only information about yourself
Will establish blame	Empowers only grace
Emphasizes the human as frail	Sees human as divine
Implies need for self-correction	Establishes giving of grace and forgiveness
Outlines actions as good or bad	Does not differentiate between actions
Information can create self-hatred and a lack of goodwill	Information only increases goodwill and self-love

Energy Laws

Here are descriptions of the energy laws governing the power pathway.

Natural Laws

The power pathway must obey the laws of the land; for instance, supporting rather than changing the dictates of the elemental natural law. In diagnostics, the most helpful applications of natural law are those that help you speed up the process or access the knowledge that you need, as per techniques already described.

When healing, you have the right to direct a power force to quicken or slow. I once used this idea, for instance, to speed up a bad case of the flu, attaching degenerative spiritual forces and fire powers to the virus. I was dreadfully sick for twelve hours (instead of the two weeks for which everyone else was struck). I was then able to get on a plane to Disney World with my five-year-old and not spend my travel time in the bathroom. When applying power forces this way, you should proceed only after harmonizing with your spirit. In that instance, my spirit and subconscious were both keen on the plan. However, another time I wanted to speed up detoxification from a virus and got a resounding "no" from my spirit. I probably would have become too ill to function.

Conversion Laws

On the power pathway, you can read only the energy that is present, and you must ethically use power forces as they are. You can, of course, break the conversion law; for instance, you could pull a feeling thread out of a spiritual force and discard the rest of the force. But this will backfire, in that the remaining energy will form a new force with unpredictable results.

Spiritual Laws

The more you attune with your own harmonic, the greater the intensity of your intuition and the more likely you are to make an accurate and effective diagnosis. Healing on the power pathway is always optimum if you first harmonize with your spirit and command from there. If in doubt, go to the center of a set seal or the neutron base within a chakra.

Energy Shapes and Spin

If you want to diagnose or heal with shape, focus your intuitive faculties on the seal center. If you haven't yet set a particular seal, focus on the chakra. Imprinted there are the various geometric symbols, numbers, and shapes that are molding, deflecting, or attracting the various spiritual energetic forces, which are penetrating the elemental pathway from the power pathway. If you're tonally acute, you can see or hear the tones emanating from these centers. By harmonizing with your spirit, you can assess which symbols, tones, or shapes will assist you in meeting your goals. (Use the lists in chapter 12 to understand the symbology and tones.)

After you've set your seals, you can evaluate seal spin using your intuition or a pendulum. Seals spin in conjunction with the chakras, although at a much reduced rate. Other power energy bodies have spins of their own. All power spins are held in place by spiritual energetic forces, rather than the seals or the energy bodies themselves.

Each spiritual energetic force spins at an optimum rate, and therefore in a favorable shape. Within each power force is a band of frequencies, each of which spins at its own rate. This accounts for some of the intense power of a spiritual energetic force. You're not only accessing the overtone of the combined frequencies, which we could call a harmonic, but also the independent vibrations within the whole.

For diagnostic purposes, you can follow the general ideas for testing and evaluating chakra spin in chapter 11, applying this same information to work with the seals. An intuitive with aptitude for spin can also determine if all or only parts of their power forces are entering the elemental pathway, or if they are all operational once in the elemental pathway. To perform this procedure, compare a power force's intensity on the power side with its intensity in the elemental pathway.

Energy Contracts

It's not as easy to absorb others' energy through the power pathway as it is on the elemental pathway, but similar circumstances do occur.

Accessing powers that aren't our own can give us a false sense of authority. Sometimes we're modeling after family, gender, or cultural patterns. Some power energies decrease our natural abilities and therefore help us fit in a little better. Females might attach to a mother's virtue of Intuition to increase feminine wiles. Males might access a force like Strength from a group consciousness to mirror society's masculine mores. If we're naturally creative in an intellectual family, we might absorb a relative's Chaos to keep ourselves from demonstrating our gifts.

I encourage you to read the sections about absorbing other energies in chapter 12, as much of what occurs on the elemental pathway in this regard also happens on the power pathway. Following are considerations important on the power pathway. Here is what can happen:

- **Being corded or bound through power forces.** You can "share" a power force, particularly a spiritual force or a power, with someone or something else, which can be controlling either the energy flowing through the force to you or your choice of the force. Rays can also hold energy contracts from others, which can disempower, warp, or overemphasize this ray.

· **Cording or binding of others through power forces.** What if you're the one who wants more power or love? Sometimes we throw a power force at someone else as if playing with a lariat. For instance, you might not want to be abandoned, so you keep a lover close to you. Every time he or she tries to leave, a degenerative spiritual force steals energy. Maybe you don't want a parent to die—a generative spiritual force could be an attempt to keep him or her alive.

· **Cording or binding from a group consciousness.** This means that in case of viral infections ranging from the flu to HIV, you are dealing with a group consciousness. Spiritual energetic forces can bind directly to a physical organism or a group consciousness, reinforcing the power of these intruders.

· **Bindings that kill.** Certain familial bindings kill. Multiple sclerosis and several other diseases can run on family miasms that not only program the elemental body for certain diseases but also lock power forces into place. As I write this book, I'm working with a woman with breast cancer. Every woman in her family has died of cancer by age fifty. They have all inherited a strong degenerative spiritual force and the "virtue" of Suffering.

· **Feelings that hurt.** Feelings interlace within the various spiritual forces. Sometimes others can cord into us through these feelings and send other power forces into our system through the feelings.

Indicators of an intrusive energy, entity, or consciousness are the same on the power pathway as on the elemental pathway, as are many of the steps taken to release others' energies and interference. Reference the material in chapter 12 to evaluate for intrusion.

The steps for healing power energy contracts are similar to those used for dealing with others' energies on the elemental pathway, though there are some differences. You can use the following steps, adapted from those outlined in chapter 12 for the elemental pathway, for power pathway releases.

1. Center yourself in the issue, a chakra, or a seal and ask the Divine to separate your own from any others' power energies.

2. Intuitively examine the intruding spiritual energetic forces. Ask your own spirit to show you who or what these forces are and where they are connected.

3. As you envision the other entity, force, or consciousness, claim your right to understand the reason for the bond and its effect on you and the other bondholder.

4. Ask the Divine what will occur if you eliminate this connection and link with power energies appropriate to you.

5. Ask yourself (your spirit and your subconscious) if you are really willing to allow this shift. If you aren't, ask why and ask if there's additional work you need to do to prepare.

6. If you're ready, command the change and ask the Divine to send divinely appointed sources to help.

7. Ask what you need to do or know to allow integration of your new energies.

Here are some power-based processes that can speed the process and take care of cleansing from others' energies on a daily basis.

· Every morning, program a generative spiritual force with a water power into your morning shower. Know that as the physical water washes over you, you are being cleaned and invigorated for your day.

· Every evening, program a degenerative spiritual force with a calming power (such as earth or ether) to cleanse you of all energies that aren't your own. Program this force to automatically detach as soon as you are purified.

· If you're going to go into a difficult situation, such as a family function at which everyone dislikes you, prepare with virtues that keep you focused inside of yourself. You can also create a bubble of spiritual forces both generative and degenerative to wrap around you and strengthen your natural personality, while wiping away others' judgments and beliefs.

· Attach degenerative spiritual forces to feelings and beliefs that are not your own and allow them to be sent away.

· Attach generative spiritual forces to feelings and beliefs that you want to strengthen and so increase their intensity.

Sourcing

There are two factors to consider when sourcing on the power pathway. The first involves bindings. As I've already suggested, spiritual energetic forces can act like bindings when they join with entities or other energies instead of linking to the Primary Grid. To determine if this is an issue, use your intuition to track the two end points of a particular spiritual energetic force on either side of the seal. If on the power side it ends anywhere other than in a point or bubble of white light, you may be conjoined with a negative energy. You will need to perform a binding release, as described in the "Energy Contracts" section on pages 305–07.

The other factor is the fact that the power pathway is a catchall of sourcing possibilities. Through the power pathway, you can easily access all the entities and energies listed in chapter 6 and then some. You can do the same through the other three pathways as well, but the ability to command on the power pathway is ideal for consciously summoning help.

Power sources can help you diagnose, perceive issues, and strategize and perform healing. You can ask a specific guide to provide you information, or you can request that the Divine connect you with the necessary assistance.

It's also important to evaluate whether or not you're currently working with appropriate guidance. Interference is a major issue on all pathways, but can have serious ramifications on the power pathway. Following manipulative or naïve guidance can lead to catastrophe. Why do we assume intelligence from beings that we can't see, touch, or understand, simply because they're dead or "spiritual"? Many misinforming entities present themselves as wise or angelic. Some we connected to long ago, and we haven't questioned the link for centuries.

I worked with a client named Jean-Paul who was very psychic. He relayed that for his entire life he had received messages from an entity named Harold. I suspected foul play and instructed Jean-Paul to write down all of Harold's advice and the outcome of following it. A pattern emerged: every input had led to disaster for Jean-Paul. Now the relationship between Jean-Paul and Harold could qualify as an elemental-based association, although Harold could have been commanding power energies to trick Jean-Paul.

My client Marianne was clearly affected by interference on the power pathway. A medical doctor, she was able to look at her patients and, more often than not, will them into wellness. She was therefore called "Lucky Marianne." What she wished for herself, however, backfired. If she bid on a house, someone else would outbid her. If she wanted a certain man, another woman stole him out from under her. When working with Marianne, I heard the statement, "Find out who's receiving her messages." Intuitively, I perceived a host of entities listening in on her personal requests and then commanding oppositional forces. As soon as Marianne broke the bonds with these entities, her personal life reflected much more happiness and joy. She's now married and has a child, and she is dean of a medical school.

Discarnate sources are ideally available to provide encouraging advice, healing, and reassurance. I have a physician friend who is able to "weave color"—his phrase for the ability to shift power forces around someone's body. He perceives generative spiritual forces as gold and degenerative spiritual forces as black. He doesn't see one as good nor one as bad; both are effective healing tools. As a surgeon, he shifts these energies before, during, and after surgery to ensure the best outcome for his patients.

How does he know what to do? "When I'm in doubt," he says, "I pray. Immediately, an angel in gold appears in my mind's eyes and demonstrates what I'm to do next." This doctor, who will reveal his trade secret to only a chosen few, is known as the "surgeon with the golden hands."

All sources available on the elemental pathway are available for diagnosis and healing on the power pathway.

The important sources to understand on the power pathway are the Forces, the Powers, the Virtues, and the Masters.

The best way to open to beneficial assistance is to begin in your harmonic. Now ask for a gatekeeper—a helper appointed by the Divine. A gatekeeper screens all other incoming sources and acts as an intermediary, keeping out negative or delinquent forces. Having a gatekeeper is a good way to be safe when working with power energies or information. Over time, you can open to additional assistance.

If you haven't worked this way before, test your gatekeeper. Your right to command includes forcing an appearing entity or consciousness to show you its correct form. Many people ask if an approaching—or encroaching—being is "of the light," but an interfering entity or even an evil one can be made of light energy as easily as dark. Test a source against your harmonic and ask for signs to assure you of your gatekeeper's ethics.

Elements

Just as all elemental diseases involve nutritional strongholds, so too do they include elemental imbalances. From the elemental pathway, you can evaluate the nature of each of the eight elements in a disease, but doing a power diagnosis may ease and speed up healing.

For instance, I worked with a young woman named Serena who had experienced migraines during every menstrual cycle for over ten years. Traditional and alternative therapies hadn't touched the problem. We first made an elemental assessment through the elemental pathway. We found that from her time in the womb through the present she had operated on only 60 percent water throughout her system and only 40 percent fire in her uterus, but she had 60 percent too much fire in her heart. When I said "air," she said that her aura was full of holes; "stone" brought her an image of being encased in concrete. Her metal was 80 percent too high (migraines are often an expression of heavy-metal toxicity) and wood was nonexistent in her system. She felt smothered in earth, like she couldn't breathe, but she lacked earth underfoot. Her star or spiritual energy was interrupted by latent interference, a familial curse and miasm.

» Nutrients, Elements, and pH Balance: The Power Connection

TIME AND TIME AGAIN, clients look at me in despair, wondering why *no* medical treatment—traditional or alternative—is working. Problems this entrenched are held by elemental patterns locked into place by power forces.

Every elemental issue, energy, or particle is capable of attracting and holding power forces; these forces lock issues into place. Elemental healing will avail nothing if the power forces are stronger than your efforts. What good is a diet if the power pathway is imposing forces supporting an eating addiction? What benefit is a new job if the power pathway will only sabotage your work? What's the point of cancer treatments when your pH won't balance because the power pathway is holding you in acidity?

The purpose of this section is to help you picture the relationship between the power pathway and all elemental diseases and problems. I've highlighted the elemental pathway life components of nutrients, elements, and pH as these will be imbalanced in all disease processes. By attracting and activating the correct power energies—especially the spiritual forces and powers—you can exponentially bolster the nutritional, elemental, and pH shifts you are making on the elemental pathway. You are using spiritual energetic forces to assist in basic physical healing.

On the elemental pathway, nearly all conditions could be cleared if the body could assimilate nutrition effectively. From an elemental perspective, food allergies and sensitivities, and digestive and assimilation issues, create malnutrition, although the person might appear to eat well and may even be overweight.

The body has to break down food to use it for your well-being. Fats are converted into tiny particles, which attach to specks of bile that help continue to digest it even when passed into the intestine. Carbohydrates are fractured into simple sugars, which are used for instant or stored energy. Proteins are disassembled, first into peptide chains and then into single amino acids. But early-life issues—such as a mother's rejection, fear of the world, and loss of the spirit world—can cause the body to reject certain of these component food parts. Why assimilate fructose if you don't want enough energy to be alive? Why accept tryptophan, a calming amino acid, if the world is too dangerous for you to let down your guard?

I find that most of these responses start right in the womb, due to either current life conditions or prior life expectations. The interplay of issues between mother and child form the child's ability to absorb nutrients from the amniotic fluid. Often heavy-metal poisoning begins right there, as the child coats the pineal with metals as protection against a world that doesn't believe in the Divine. Good fats are rejected, because fat stimulates shame; simple carbohydrates are considered toxic, because they represent tainted love; and proteins are seen as undesirable if power and control issues are present. As we mature, we continue to develop reactions to the components of foods that mirror our life pains. By the time we're adults, we've assembled a mess of strongholds attached to the nutrients entering our bodies.

In unconsciously judging or repelling certain nutritional elements, we're really resisting the Divine available through the elemental pathway. We're also producing the external environment that we detest in our internal bodies. What we judge when incoming, we create internally.

Consider the physical digestive process. If we fear the uplifting effects of the amino acid tryptophan, this fear will "stick" to every tryptophan acid. When the body breaks a protein into its parts, all self-created peptide chains made with tryptophan will be encased in fear. Fear will permeate the physical systems receiving the influence of this "poison pill."

Infected proteins can disempower. They usually affect brain waves, hormones, stress levels, and all organ functions, especially those of the heart. Heart disease is often a reflection of contaminated proteins, as are other muscular

As complicated as this determination sounds, it painted a simple picture. She had felt unsafe in the womb as a female, mainly because of latent interference, and had established stone and heavy metals in her system in an attempt to protect herself. Every time her estrogen rose, she experienced the severe consequences of these in-womb decisions.

problems such as chronic fatigue. Dilapidated or unavailable sugars create blood-sugar problems, immune dysfunctions, diabetes, and often severe food cravings and disorders. Unnatural fats often underlie liver, gall bladder, intestinal, nervous system, and food-related disorders.

Physically, the marked nutrients are rejected by antibodies and body tissues that don't want the poison pill, yet they are accepted by tissues that mirror the strongholds. Only some of your body parts will adhere to the toxic messages and therefore accept the poison nutrients. These are the parts that hold the same strongholds, frequencies, and consciousness waves as the negative message. When you accept a certain negative belief or feeling, it relates to a certain chakra or chakras, and it will continue to impact that area more strongly than others. The internalization of a certain fear, for instance, will match the vibratory frequencies of a certain chakra and certain organs, glands, or tissues governed by that chakra. Hence, you'll develop the types of diseases, problems, and cravings that impact that chakra. The nutritional maladaptation will alter the biochemistry and, therefore, the pH of the fluids in that area of the body. This is why some parts of your body may be acidic and others alkaline. The energetics of the elemental pathway impose negative messages into the chakra, which can be psychically read through elemental means. The energetics, however, also affect the power pathway.

Remember that all spiritual forces are interlaced with feelings. Even a tiny, subatomic-sized particle of fat can latch onto a spiritual force. In other words, the "sticky feeling" attracts a spiritual force that contains that particular feeling. Advanced physical diseases are usually locked into place by thousands of spiritual forces, each linked with a tainted fat, sugar, or amino acid. The greater the buildup of these components in the body—such as in greatly overweight people—the more potent the spiritual forces supporting the problem. Think of someone with severe attention deficit disorder (ADD). Imagine the spiritual forces impacting that person's brain waves and the inability of nutrients to soothe the overexcited parts of the brain.

This is why diets for weight control or medicinal purposes so often don't work—they fail to penetrate the powers of the power holding patterns in place. Sometimes very extreme eating changes, such as a severe macrobiotic diet or a fast, break the hold of disease in the elemental pathway; however, unless you shift the power forces, these same forces will latch onto the same or a similar disease pattern and cause a different problem.

I worked with a woman named Jill who was thirty pounds overweight. I pointed out that she wasn't metabolizing her fats correctly, which was an elemental diagnosis. She already knew this information from her nutritionist, but endless amounts of supplements and rigorous eating discipline weren't working. I looked a little further into the elemental pathway and saw that the causative organ was her liver, the problematic feelings were fear and shame, and the mental issue was her belief that she was powerless in relationships. Guess what? Jill only gained weight while in relationships—and she had quickly put on those thirty pounds while dating her current boyfriend.

Jill had done a lot of work on her issues and was frustrated. She didn't want to work on her feelings or beliefs yet again. So I examined her power energies, and saw a Limitation spiritual force attached to her liver as well as generative spiritual forces connected to the fear and shame in the fats. Rather than simply eliminate the Limitation force, since Jill was now so skilled at accessing it, we connected it to the shame, thus "limiting" the power of shame in her system. She first added Health, a generative spiritual force, to her liver; later she added all lipid-processing places within her body and cells. We reduced the intensity of her fears by establishing, in her third chakra, virtues that emphasize self-reliance and self-esteem. Jill lost all thirty pounds (and her boyfriend) within three months. The weight loss was not the result of losing her boyfriend; since then she's been in another relationship for six months, and she hasn't gained an ounce.

Continuing with a power diagnosis, I guessed that she would have several spiritual forces connected to different elements and nutrients, locking in her patterns, strongholds, and food sensitivities. To determine which one might shift her most easily and quickly, I asked her to see if there was a power supporting all the unhelpful spiritual forces. There was. Serena spotted an Air power pushing spiritual forces into her system. We shifted this Air power to support a Health generative force. She hasn't had a migraine since.

The pH Balance

In general, the presence of too many strong degenerative spiritual forces indicates acidity, and an imbalance in favor of generative forces indicates an overly alkaline state.

If intuition or physical pH measurements indicate acidity, these degenerative forces are reinforcing negative, electrical-based issues, patterns, strongholds, and power levels and fields (such as fields one, three, five, seven, and nine). Your main issues will most likely lie within the chakras of the same numbers—often called the masculine chakras, because they impact how you interface with the external world. You are using strong spiritual energetic forces against yourself because at some point others used them against you.

If your intuition or a pH measurement indicates alkalinity, you are accessing generative forces to reinforce positive, magnetic-based issues and the like, with an emphasis on fields two, four, six, eight, and ten and the same numbered chakras. These are called the feminine chakras, because they regulate how you relate to the internal world. You are using seemingly positive spiritual energetic forces to reinforce spiritual beliefs and ideas that seem to support you, yet they actually injure your relationship with the Divine.

A note on pH: Most people test acidic on a general pH blood, urine, or saliva test. However, a more thorough test, whether physical or intuitive, will show that the body is often inconsistent in its pH. For instance, a woman's uterine or second chakra area can be alkaline while her digestive tract tests acidic. Therefore the balance of her vaginal excretions can test different from that of her urine. Intuitively, whitish, moldy, or lumpy looking areas tend toward alkalinity; dark, devoid, or bare spots tend toward acidity.

Moving through
the Mirror of the
Imagination Pathway

T he imagination pathway can seem confusing and leave us wondering which world we're doing what in! Yet for me, it's the easiest pathway to negotiate. There are two sides, and as long as you're willing to be truthful, shifting healing on the imagination pathway is nothing more or less than performing imaginative energy exchanges.

We've only to peer into the two sides of our own hearts and nature to understand this place of nothing and all. When Lewis Carroll wrote *Through the Looking-Glass*, he composed for us all a snapshot of the mirror-like quality of life. Alice fell through the looking glass and landed in a reality that seemed reverse of this one. It was just as real as that of her childhood life, but it operated by a set of rules that bent time and space. A cookie could make you bigger or smaller. Your head might be lopped off one day and returned the next. A baby could be turned into a pig, and, well, who was to say what was real or not?

The looking-glass land is the land of the imagination, and in it there are delusions and illusions. A delusion may be real or not in three-dimensional reality, but it is never true. An illusion may be real or not, but it is always true.

It is tempting to disregard this confusion altogether and regard the imagination pathway as a pass-through pathway. You can't. For all its seeming unreality, the imagination pathway is as important a pathway as the other three. You must sort real from not real and truth from fiction to gain illumination—or to be effective on the elemental or the power pathways. Each chakra invites you to a special acknowledgment of imagination truth and lie. As Shakespeare said, "All the world's a stage," and we are but players on it. What's your script? What stage are you on? Through the imagination pathway, you can rewrite the play, or

My hands trembled as I reached out toward Skellig's wings. I touched them with my fingertips. I rested my palms on them. I felt the feathers, and beneath them the bones and sinews and muscles that supported them. I felt the crackle of Skellig's breathing. I tiptoed to the shutters and stared out through the narrow chinks.

"What are you doing?" she whispered.

"Making sure the world's still really there," I said. [1]

—David Almond,
Skellig

get off the stage altogether. By playing on the imagination pathway, you learn the ultimate lesson of writing your own script.

The beauty of healing on the imagination pathway is that we have only to convince ourselves of being healed, and we can be. This is why the key to healing on the imagination pathway is imagination.

None of us really gets to where we want to be without imagination and pretending.

Healing on the Imagination Pathway

To understand the role the chakras play on the imagination pathway, it's important to understand the basic physics of the imagination pathway.

The imagination pathway represents both the everyday world and its opposite, the antiuniverse, the complement to what we consider as real. According to quantum physics, every concrete particle "here" is partnered with an equal but opposite particle "there." "Here" is the elemental; "there" is the antiuniverse. On the imagination pathway, you can shift energy between this world and the antiworld. Another way of saying this is that you can shift between the elemental and the opposite of the elemental. For every particle creating reality in the here and now, there is an antiparticle that could create a different reality.

Antiparticles explain tachyons, the energies that move information beyond the light-speed barrier. If a particle weighs, say, ten pounds here, it will move as a negative ten-pound particle in the imagination pathway. A negative ten-pound particle transferred into the elemental reality can pack a big wallop. And that's good, because, as I've been saying, might is right on the elemental pathway. If you can attract a "weighty" illusion into the elemental pathway, it will hold so much weight that it will become real.

Elemental-based electrons are called positrons in the antiworld. Electrons contain the lower-frequency charges, many of which we think of as negative. When most of us think of negativity, we think of dark and stuck emotions, destructive beliefs, fear-based ideas, and the like. These are the energies that materialize as life's problems. If our elemental-based self believes them to be true, we will hold onto these electrons. These potent charges will attract power forces that support the negativity, creating conditions that only reinforce your negative beliefs!

Working the imagination pathway provides another option. Let's say you could simply imagine a reality, a sensation, a relationship, a feeling, or a job as different from the situation causing distress. You now open the doorway between the elemental and the imagination pathways, the world and the antiworld. The actual doorways are multifold, but the easiest to open is the imagination mirror at the center of every chakra. By opening it, you create a vacuum. There's too much force in this world and no force on the imagination pathway. Anything you're ready to surrender will shift through the looking glass. In return, the opposite energy will enter. Once the worlds are balanced again, the doorway will slam shut.

Do you know what's going to exit through the door? Whatever was causing or holding that old reality in place. Know what will enter? The opposite of the negative energy—the tachyons exactly matching the new vision! *Your imagination can hold a new vision and, if powerful enough, supplant your old reality with a more desirable one.*

Let me give you an example. You have a tumor. You imagine yourself free of the tumor. The tumor is in your stomach, so you move into your third chakra, which is located in the stomach area. Holding onto the vision of wellness, you open the portal, the imagination mirror. Because you're holding onto an image of wellness, the energy holding the tumor is freed up. It's no longer staked into the elemental world, and so away it slides through the looking glass! What replaces it is the mirror image of the tumor existing in the antiworld. What's the mirror image of the tumor? The exact opposite of "tumor"—"antitumor." Antitumor tachyons flood your system and actually add weight to the imagined, but not-yet-real image of being clear of cancer. The tachyons (or positrons) convert to electrons; other entering particles transform into healthy protons and neutrons. The power forces must shift into alignment with these new marching orders—and if you've imagined with enough strength and force, the tumor might disappear. Then again, your feelings about the tumor might shift, leaving you in acceptance of what previously upset you. Your imagination, when used in the highest order, links you to your spirit and Higher Self, and you will manifest for the greatest ultimate gain.

The easiest way to work the imagination pathway is by imaging the center of the chakra corresponding to the problem. There is a sheen-like energy that reflects the symbols, shapes, spins, codes, and other determinants of disease and delusion. By reading and then changing these, you open the doorway between the worlds and can shape your reality. Shamans have been using this technique forever, and it is available to us all.

I've just explained one way to conduct imagination shift healing. It sounds easy, doesn't it? So, what's the catch? The human tendency to trick ourselves.

Delusion on the Imagination Pathway: Of Fallacies and Shams

Most of us are unwilling to release our negative problems. As I've suggested earlier, we hold onto "our stuff" because there's a payoff. Maybe I subconsciously or unconsciously want to stay sick because I like the attention. Maybe I realize that if I'm worthy of healing, I'm worthy of

» The Imagination Pathway in a Nutshell

THE IMAGINATION PATHWAY works like this:

Scene One: Illusion

1. Imagine wellness on the elemental pathway.

2. Be willing to surrender anything that is not creating wellness. For example, let's pretend your problems are caused by a bad belief held in your this-world electrons; you can also assess for issues locked into your this-world protons.

3. Open the imagination mirror between the elemental and the imagination pathways, located in the center of the causal chakra. This mirror works like a doorway, which you can use to assess for issues and causes.

4. The "freed" electrons flow into the antiworld, along with your harmful belief.

5. In the antiworld, the arriving bad belief is transformed from an electron state to a positron state. You now have more positrons than you need in the antiworld.

6. The imagination pathway naturally balances itself. The antiworld frees up energy that's already present so it can hold onto these new energies. It doesn't care whether the coded data is helpful or harmful. It just "is."

7. The opposing belief already exists in the antiworld. Floating in there is the antidote for your bad belief. This "good belief" exists in positive form and is now transferred over the imagination mirror to the 3-D realm. An exchange has been made and the door closes.

8. The "good belief" alters from a positron to an electron state. You have now successfully exchanged a "bad belief" for the opposing "good one."

Scene Two: Delusion

1. You think that you want to get well.

2. You really don't. You are unwilling to surrender the negative energies causing a problem. Let's say that your issues are caused by a bad spiritual belief held in a this-world proton. You have encircled this proton and locked it into the elemental pathway and aren't going to let go no matter what.

3. You envision wellness but continue holding the circle closed.

4. You open the imagination mirror between worlds.

5. The bad belief remains on the elemental pathway because you are unwilling to release it. It cannot shift to the imagination pathway.

6. The imagination mirror is open anyway, so free energy shifts from this world to the antiworld. Transferred over are electron-housed beliefs that are good.

7. In the antiworld, these beliefs lodge into place as positrons holding good beliefs. The antiworld now shifts in order to create balance. Bad beliefs exit the antiworld and enter the elemental pathway, shifting positrons to electrons once they hit the elemental pathway.

8. You now experience the strangulation of additional bad spiritual beliefs and probably continue the cycle.

love—and that means I'd have to leave my bad marriage. And on and on it goes, and where does it stop? In fantasyland.

We pretend that we want to be well, but maybe we subconsciously don't. We pretend that we want love or a lover, money or a nice house, but maybe we don't. Or maybe we're holding onto energies that don't want us to get what we want, such as bindings, family programs, genetic tendencies, interference, or the messages from our loved ones who are invested in having us remain the way we are. The usual recourse is to seem to try any number of elemental techniques, from diet and exercise to chanting and crystal therapies. But if we're still pretending, nothing's going to work.

If our own or others' energies are preventing change, our images, actions, intentions, and attempts are just so much fantasy. We're not actually willing to open the doorway between worlds and to release the negative energies. We're only willing to pretend. If there's no exchange between the elemental and the imagination pathways, between the this-world state and the antiworld, we're creating hallucinations, not real changes. This is why I always have people check two sources before doing healing work:

- **The subconscious.** By intuitively asking your own or another's subconscious, linked to the Lower Mind, Lower Self, and Lower Heart, you can see if there's a current willingness to heal or not. If there is, check the other source. If there's not, you must figure out which pathway to work on that might allow for willingness.
- **The spirit.** There are simply some life circumstances, events, and problems that are spirit-designed and necessary for growth, learning, and destiny. You absolutely should not attempt to avert a spirit plan; if you do try, bigger problems will arise.

Healing Disease through the Doorways

Healing traditionally involves release. The imagination pathway requires release and attraction or healing and manifesting. The inner wheel of the eighth chakra spins in reverse, as do the particles in the eighth auric field. Other energy bodies are also capable of reverse flow. This is how we clear our chakras and therefore our bodies, but it's also how we draw in new energy on the power pathway and especially on the imagination pathway.

Our energy system is designed to naturally clear and balance itself. The imagination pathway plays a key role in this process. Let's say you have psychic and physical toxins in your lymph system coagulating in breast tissue. In a few years, these toxins might cause cancer. If you're open to the imagination, at a certain point of toxicity your chakric system will be alerted. The inner wheel of your fourth chakra, sensing this critical increase in negative or dark-light energies in its region of control, will automatically spin backward. Where's this energy going? Into the imagination pathway or the antiworld. The "sick" electrons will be exchanged for "well" positrons. You complete the imagination cycle of release through surrender and healing through acceptance. If there are any precancerous cells, chances are they'll be erased immediately. You have just shift healed.

So why doesn't our energy system perform imagination healing automatically? Well, it would if it were allowed to. Unfortunately, most of us are afraid of the unknown. We either hold onto the negative charges building up, which will eventually make us sick, or we slam the door as soon as we've thrown the garbage into the antiworld, afraid to trust that goodness would replace it.

Know why disease seems to appear overnight in some people? Sometimes the strength of repressed emotions combines with power forces and discombobulates the system. The overall frequency or field created by these energies throws the two worlds out of balance. The door in the imagination mirror opens. You could decide to release the entire mess into the antiworld, in which case you'd get well. But most people are bonded to their problems and hold onto the negativity. Health-inducing energy that exists already in the elemental pathway releases through the imagination mirror. The imagination pathway balances by pouring tachyons into the real world. These tachyons hit gravity and turn into particles that reflect the opposite of the exiting positive energies. Now you get sick. If the feeling, belief, and forces you're accepting match the frequency of arthritis, you'll get arthritis. If they better mirror a certain type of cancer, you'll get cancer.

You might also attract sources or entities of like vibration. Fire beings, for instance, are supposed to stay in the center of the earth. If you're emitting a strong anger charge, along with a "the world is dangerous" philosophy, your body could start mirroring the exact conditions desirable to a center-of-the-earth fire being. They might very well take up residence in your body. After all, it seems like home! Some of these elemental beings actually transform into viruses in the body.

Diagnosing and Healing
on the Imagination Pathway

Diagnosing and healing through the imagination pathway is a profound experience. There are three steps to the process:

1. Using the mirror in the chakra center as a doorway to perceive what's true versus false. The power seal center also serves as a looking glass.
2. Exchanging energy as needed.
3. Locking new changes into place.

I'll cover ways to accomplish both diagnosis and healing throughout this section. Here are two specific exercises for working the imagination pathway no matter how you are approaching the issues.

Using the Imagination Pathway Mirror

1. Begin by grounding and centering. Imagine that the Divine has embraced you at all levels and that you fully accept attributes, issues, and energies no matter how they look or appear.

2. Key in on the presenting issue. Using elemental-based knowledge, energy mapping techniques, and your psychic senses, select the causal chakra.

3. Imagine yourself centered in this chakra and picture the mirror of the imagination. View this and the otherworld side of the mirror. Now ask to see, know, or hear a description of the issue in this world's mirror. You can work many different ways: electrons, protons, beliefs, feelings, patterns, strongholds, spacetimes, dimensions, symbols, tones, and so on.

4. Check for bindings, cords, and attachments as well as power energies.

5. Check for spin. Energy being drained from this side will be spinning out through a counterclockwise spiral, which duplicates the release spin of the inner or outer chakra wheel. Energy being shifted into this world from the antiworld will be incoming on a clockwise spiral, clearly channeling energy from the other side.

6. Ask for guidance to understand the full nature of the delusion or issue.

7. Now ask for guidance for healing the issue. What energies should you focus on? What bindings, cords, or attachments should you release? Which power energies need to be present or

released? Is any elemental processing necessary? What should you shift on this side alone? What spirals need to be released, inserted, or removed? Are these changes in spiral shiftings permanent, such as when you decide to continually allow in love or healing, or temporary, such as when you need to drain the elemental energy of a virus just until the infection is clear? And the chief question: What should you shift between this world and the antiworld in both directions to enable healing?

8. Use your imagination to conduct the shift through the imagination mirror.

9. Now ask what you need to do to support the shift on the elemental pathway.

10. Is it time to lock in this shift? If so, ask for guidance or an image in the mirror to do so. You can always lock with an equal-armed cross, and you should certainly do so if you found an "X" present in the mirror, signifying a cancellation of consciousness.

Working from the Middle of the Mirror

One of the most effective techniques for blending the divine and the imagination pathways is to stand in the center of the imagination mirror, between the light and dark—or this world and the antiworld—sides of the lens. This is the space of neutrality, where it is possible to petition for energetic qualities that meet the needs behind the presenting problem. Within this space, ask to know the baseline need and then the truth or quality that would meet this need. Now ask, picture, sense, know, or hear your life as it would be and *is* with this need fully met. Embrace this imagined reality and claim it as real. Sense its realness, taste it. Now radiate the energy of this reality in a full circle around you. This rippling energy will expand through both sides of the imagination lens and perform an exchange of imagination, power, or elemental energy necessary to complete your selected dreams in the here and now.

Manifesting through the Imagination Pathway

Manifesting, in relation to the imagination pathway, deserves a special note. Most people try to manifest their desires by working the chakric energy in front and in back of them. This doesn't work. Energy imagined through the front side is absorbed into the future, which you haven't stepped forward into yet. Reaching forward causes anxiety, which is really a clockwise chakric spin that goes so fast it keeps you from shifting energy from the antiworld to this world to solidify your wishes. Also, if you become too attached to a particular vision of the future, you may reject possibilities that come your way to assist in manifesting your dreams, because they won't precisely match the future you've projected.

All possibilities and resources exist in the here and now, in this spacetime, through the imagination.

Manifesting based on the past isn't any more lucrative than futuring. Many people either structure goals based on past achievements or evaluate opportunities based on similar past experiences. The past is done and can't be repeated, so your system cancels out these ideas. If you don't like what occurred in the past and your current possibility is comparable, you won't allow an imagination shift to take advantage of the opportunity. Your chakric spins in regard to your dreams will reverse in an attempt to discard the rejected goals. You won't allow transference of unneeded energies (of the past) from this world into the antiworld, and you become more stuck.

The best way to manifest through the imagination pathway is sideways.

These are a combination of energies in the antiworld and this world. What isn't represented in one place is alive in the other.

I once worked with a woman who really wanted a new job. She looked for another employer for over a year, to no avail. She energetically rejected any potential opportunity, because it didn't fit her long-term vision of enjoyable employment. Interviews never resulted in job offers because as soon as she walked into a company, she compared the current environment to former situations and sabotaged herself. After hearing that she had everything she needed in the present, she began to cry and asked how this could be. I showed her how she had energetically shaped her current job into a workable situation based on her aptitudes, strengths, and abilities. Why couldn't she shape a new job in similar ways? She could use her imagination to envision what she desired, then assume that it existed already in the antiworld. Physical action supports imagination pretending. My client began to act "as if" she had already landed a great job. Within two months, she received a job offer from an Internet application that exactly suited her envisioned desire. Not only does she love the new opportunity, but within six months she was promoted.

Specific Imagination Diagnostic and Healing Techniques

Here are several methods for performing diagnosing and healing on the imagination pathway.

Energy Particles and Charges

You can distinguish illusion from delusion and create a space for truthful diagnosis by simply recognizing the energy charges of an issue or in a chakra.

Protons create illusions and delusions that are spiritual in orientation. The information encoded in the protons states the view of love. Psychically, protons look like plus signs in the imagination mirror and the three-dimensional side of reality; in the antiworld, the charge will look like a negative or a minus sign.

Electrons carry illusions and delusions about the material universe; they look like a minus sign in this world and the imagination mirror, and a plus sign in the antiworld. By comparing these two worlds for proton-electron balance, you can determine where your energy is. You can also figure out if your problem stems from an unclaimed illusion or from a fantastical delusion. If in the antiworld there are more pluses around an issue than there are here, you have an unclaimed illusion. If there are more minus signs in this world than there are in the antiworld, you're working with a delusion. You can read the chakra-seal centers to determine the focus of the problem.

Neutrons are spaces of neutrality. There should be neutrons in the core of each chakra and in the center of the imagination mirror; these are the void areas for manifestation and exchange of antiworld and this-world energies. If you can't find any empty pockets in a chakra, summon forth the neutrons through power command and bring your consciousness to these spaces for diagnostics.

Life Energy and Kundalini

There is no energy on the imagination pathway; therefore there is no form of life energy. You can, however, call kundalini from either the elemental or the power pathway and direct it through the imagination pathway, usually with spin. For instance, you can eliminate incorrectly charged basic life energy from this world by reverse-spiraling it into the antiworld. Or you can access antiworld power energies, which are those that you've never owned, by spiraling them clockwise into this world.

Energetic Communication Method

The imagination pathway works through projection. The easiest way to retool this ability for diagnosis is to center yourself in a problem or a chakra and then ask questions. The answers might relay from the past, present, or future. Ask questions like these:

- If my problem originated in the past, what would have caused it?
- If my issue started in the here and now, what would have started it?
- If my problem could be understood in the future, what would that understanding be?
- If I could imagine the Divine explaining this problem to me, what would I imagine?
- If I could imagine healing for this issue, where would the healing come from, and when?

Energy Languages

The shadow language is slippery, like an eel in dark water. Reading a shadow involves shining light on an issue and then exploring the problem by looking at its reflection, rather than straight on—because problems and opportunities on the imagination pathway are caused by shadows or possibilities, not by anything substantial. When you read the reflection (or antireality) of an issue, you *are* summarizing the issue.

Here's an exercise that works for using the shadow language for imagination diagnosis:

Focus briefly on your problem by imagining that you are shining a light upon it. Now imagine that the light passes completely through the problem and onto the face of God. Instead of looking at the problem, you are staring upon God's visage. Even that is in shadows, for as it's said in the Bible, few of us can look upon the face of God and survive the great love present. Know that, whatever you see, you are looking into the presence of pure love and compassion.

The light of God's eyes and love enable you to peer into the shadows on one side of Him/Her. In the shadows is a reflection of what you consider to be the problem. You now understand everything that you need to know about this problem.

I once used this exercise with a famous speaker who was having problems with sex addiction. The phrase that came to him when peering through God's eyes into the shadows was this: "When the limelight increases, so does the blackness of the shadow behind you. Own the shadow as a light, and you will become the light."

He was finally able to break down and admit his problem and continue on to receive support for his humanness, which solved the problem over time.

Energy Bodies

There are no energy bodies on the imagination pathway, but the imagination pathway exists as a pinprick inside each elemental and power energy body. You can therefore access this pinprick and use imagination techniques in any energy body. Look for a small dark point in or near the center of the energy body. The eighth chakra is easiest to use—shamans have been exploring the imagination pathway through this chakra for eons. Through this point, you can access the antiworld for that energy body, a boon when performing healing. You can also bring through the opposite of any power force. Here is an overview of imagination healing, chakra by chakra.

Through the First Chakra The first chakra uses material energy, the basic stuff of life. On the elemental pathway, what you believe creates itself in form. If you think that a ball is hard, it will stay hard. If you think that a tumor—or an addiction, bad relationship, or money issue—is permanent, it will remain so. You can use the imagination pathway version of psychism, which is basically imagination, to manufacture energy into new forms in the antiworld and then transfer these into this world. As long as you're willing to surrender the lies you've established in the elemental pathway, the two worlds will be balanced and you can keep what you've just summoned.

Some individuals manipulate with this ability. Sorcerers often use misshapen symbols, such as a warped spiral, to send power or energies into the antiworld and then use a broken circle to keep the energy from returning. A really powerful sorcerer can enforce this process on others. An elemental curse, binding, or attachment is equivalent to an imagination lock that keeps the victim from reversing the sorcerer's demands. If you're stuck in a situation like this, know that the energy that you need to get free is available. It's probably just buried in the antiworld and needs to be summoned over. In exchange for it, you can release beliefs and energies that keep you fearful about your power in this world.

To work the first chakra, start with the power of one, which represents the ability to start over. This opens the door to energies sublimated in the antiworld and empties you of energies encasing you in entrenched patterns, recurring illnesses, addictions, shame cycles, sexuality and money issues, and all other first-chakra problems. The key is to be willing to accept goodness.

Through the Second Chakra The second chakra is like a chalice and feelings are the nectar that fills it. Own the fact that feelings can encourage a positive result. Through the imagination pathway, you release a so-called negative feeling or emotion by feeling the feeling and exchanging it for the energy available in the antiworld. Through this process, you are actually completing a feeling, not eliminating a feeling. When you feel your feelings, you're allowing the inner wheel of the second chakra to spin in reverse into the imagination pathway. The inner wheel will eventually go clockwise again, as long as you don't judge the feelings you just felt. This clockwise repositioning allows the return of a positive feeling.

We can use feelings to manipulate through the imagination pathway. As a child, did you ever pretend that you were sad so that your parents would buy you a toy? You were offering a delusion to the world. You weren't sad. You may have been greedy or needy or mad, but you were presenting a feeling that wasn't real. That locked the repressed feeling into this world. Over time, you will lose good feelings to the antiworld and receive more difficult feelings in return.

The second chakra is about twos. Two is about creating two out of one. When exchanged through the imagination pathway, all feelings increase in intensity and can be used for creative expression.

Through the Third Chakra Beliefs run the elemental pathway and consciousness directs power forces. On the imagination pathway, you can shift both thought particles and consciousness waves back and forth between this world and the antiworld.

Let's say you want to believe that you're lovable, but you think that you are unlovable. If you spin "I am unlovable" into the imagination pathway from this world and are ready to release it, you receive back the energy of "I am lovable." Now you're ready to rock and roll.

Basically, you need to be honest. The third center is the core of all self-esteem, and therefore of success and power issues. Want to know why you have liver problems? Stomach upset? Hypoglycemia? Unpin the negative belief and be honest about it. Then work the imagination pathway. By getting honest, you allow the imagination pathway to "convince" you of truth. Stay dishonest and you'll become further deluded.

One of the main self-confidence breakers comes from beliefs projected from someone else. Let's say that your dad looks at you and sends you the message, "You're stupid." Dad's probably projecting by sending you the belief that he holds about himself. He's not going to deal with the lie. He's not going to challenge and correct his belief. He's just going to pass the thought on to you! If you don't accept the lie, it will shimmer right into the imagination pathway and you'll actually end up feeling smarter! But maybe you want to make Dad feel smart, in which case you'll assume the lie as true and begin to live it. You'll keep it locked in your third chakra, and the inner symbol of your chakra will distort.

The third chakra is the place of threes and the pyramid. These are good symbols for holding desirable beliefs in place. Work with them when working in this place.

Through the Fourth Chakra The teacher in Elizabeth Haich's book *Initiation* suggests that the key to achieving unity consciousness is to "go down into the depths of your soul," where the subconscious forces dwell, and "awaken them to life in your consciousness" so as to experience them in real life.[2] The greatest impediment to actualization is fear, and the greatest fear is twofold: the fear of being alone and the fear of being intimate. Only relationships have the power to challenge you to be fully alone and intimate at the same time.

There are two forms of energy exchange on the fourth level of the imagination pathway: caregiving and caretaking. Imagination caregiving is accomplished by accepting love in both this world and the anti-world, and sharing it with others. If you establish a two-way spin of divine love back and forth, you achieve this objective. Love is the only energy that, when expressed into the imagination pathway, returns exactly as given—only tenfold! Caretaking is trickster energy. It involves taking love from others and giving it right back to them. Somewhere along the line, however, the caretaker twists the energy so the returned love bounces right back!

Tricksters often work with the four, the sign of balance, to imprison others. When caught by a trickster, you believe that you need him or her to be loved. You fail to perceive that the trickster is simply attracting all your love and using it for personal gain. A trickster can also manipulate a spiral by breaking, twisting, or reversing it, so you perceive a negative relationship as positive or just the reverse. The key to imagination pathway relationships is knowing that you can truly only give what you allow yourself to receive. Use fours, spirals, and the bond of a circle wisely, and you'll reap relationship rewards.

Through the Fifth Chakra In the New Testament, Jesus is compared to the Word, one with God and the basis of the created world. Words are symbols. They alter reality in the real world when serving as a channel for greater forces. This is the idea behind using symbols for healing, as is done in the Reiki energy healing system. Symbols are structures. You change the outcome of channeled energy by changing the structure.

Sorcerers often use words, the number five, or symbols like a twisted five-pointed star to create confusion and lies in the fifth chakric imagination pathway. We're all capable of performing sorcery unconsciously, such as when channeling our anger into the spoken word or an untruth onto the written page. You can also use symbols to clear reality of untruths and manifest truth. The best way to use symbols in the fifth chakra is to center them in the middle of the doorway between the here and there. Imagine what type of energy you want exchanged and it will be so. Practice with already noted symbols, shapes, colors, and tones, but also words themselves. For instance, say that you want to exchange a worry for faith. Imagine the word *worry* positioned in the middle of the doorway. Imagine it slipping through the doorway, and see the word *faith* sliding into its place.

Through the Sixth Chakra Which is most trustworthy: that which you perceive with your internal or with your external vision? An imagination master can use dreaming to create fresh choices. If you select goals only with your outer vision, however, you will fail to see the reality underneath reality. With inner vision, you can peer through the imagination mirror into the antiworld and see what lingers there, claim it as real, and birth it from the darker side of the moon into the sunlight of day. Placement of antiworld imaginings on imagination mirrors can bring a new reality into being.

Then again, you can also create hallucinations through imagination viewing. Hallucinations are fantasies that you begin to believe are valid and true. They have two causes. The first is denial. What you deny "here" is real "over there," and eventually transfers from the antiworld to this world. You can't run from anything! The second cause is confusing energies, interpretations, and sources. You might be imagining what you want, which is real in the antiworld, but it's not real in this world! See the "Sourcing" section at the end of this chapter for reflections on sources.

The sixth chakra is the place of the six, symbols such as the six-pointed star, and making your own choices.

Through the Seventh Chakra Spiritual growth depends upon submitting to the Spirit and your own spirit, which holds an encoded spiritual destiny. The imagination pathway poses a confounding truth: Your destiny changes all the time.

Each time you fluctuate, the imagination doorway opens and breathes in new energy. You change and, in some small way, so does your perception of purpose. The imagination pathway shatters the mindset of those who want a sure and solid future, a predetermined way to achieve spiritual destiny. Many people use spiritualizing to create walls and deny the constancy of change. This is the purpose of religiosity, most born-again Christian movements, fanaticism, legalism, excessive idealism, and even severe depression or apathy. Most often, a fundamental spiritualist decides to only accept his or her assumed version of religious truth as true. This magnetic energy is boxed into this world and secured tightly. The free electrical energy incorporates into the antiworld, which then spits back stored and denied electron-based issues, such as repressed feelings, sexual desires, hatreds, jealousies, and needs. These energies are either rejected or stored, thus attracting additional wrong spiritual beliefs.

The seventh chakra often calls forth the power of the seven—the number of the Divine manifesting in reality. It begs the question of willingness to surrender your truth for Truth.

Through the Eighth Chakra Here is the playground of the imagination maestro! The delusional love to force antiparticles into the particle world, but not return energy back—a process called *conjuring*. Most of us don't even question whether a toothpaste ad is true or not, so why would we question a shaman politicking his or her own truth? On the positive side, we can also *divine*, an ancient mystical term indicating the ability to predict and shape the future. We can divine what energy from the antiworld is needed in this world, bring it over, and exchange it for what needs to disappear from the here and now. I have a client who uses a bowl of water for divining; another uses a crystal ball. (Really!) These double as imagination mirrors for peering into the possibilities latent in the antiworld. Imagination can make these real when the diviner and the client join intention.

A solid use of the imagination pathway in the eighth chakra is to look at the other side of an issue. If the problem is an illness, seek for glimpses into wellness; if a relationship, search for aloneness. You don't have to select a choice until you finish questing.

The eighth chakra works with eights and the infinity sign. The true shaman understands that, essentially, you're creating something out of nothing—but if you give back again, you can keep the something that you've created.

Through the Ninth Chakra Have you ever just felt good about your own goodness? This isn't a bad thing—unless you're tricking yourself into thinking that good things make you good. That's the ultimate delusion of the ninth chakra.

Good acts run the gamut, from heading up a social activism program to serving as a multinational CEO. Imagination fantasies occur if you allow yourself to become an icon—a perfected representation of a standard—rather than a person who lives up to his or her standards. No one is an ideal. When it's impossible to live up to your own iconic self, what do you do? Usually, you deny, which creates the loops of problems that we've already considered, such as repression of needs, feelings, and desires, and, ultimately, the sacrifice of human happiness.

The true imagination master will see ideals as goals, not realities. After all, the opposite is always present in the mirror! If you really believe in a goal, it's possible to open the imagination doorway, release the goal, and receive the energies needed to activate the goal in the elemental pathway. The idea is "letting go" in order to manifest.

The ninth chakra works with the power of the nine, which can be used for completions.

Through the Tenth Chakra Let's say I hold an herb and tell you it's going to make you well. On the elemental pathway, the outcome all depends on the chemical reactions between you and the herb. On the power pathway, the result is affected by an infusion of force by either you or me. The imagination master will know that the herb is not really necessary for healing, but that its effects can be true. Therefore, imagination can bolster the herb's effectiveness by activating the herb's vibrations and harmonics, strengthening its potency.

To accomplish a goal like this, simply concentrate on your belief in the herb's vibrational healing powers. The belief is more important than the herb, as studies in placebo effects will affirm. You can also use imagination to perform an act called *endowing*. Endowing involves ascribing magical qualities to someone or to something that aren't real. Does a curse really have the power to kill? If the belief is carried in the antiworld of the victim, it sure does. The slightest encouragement in this world of a belief in curses creates an open door. Particles can transform into waves. You can ingest a consciousness wave of "belief in curses" from your own antiworld, after accepting the tiniest suggestion that curses are real in this world. Want to take the power out of an endowment? Release the belief in particle and wave form from here into there.

Endowment isn't necessarily a bad thing. I once told a child who was frightened of the dark that her teddy bear turned into an angel at night. When clutching this teddy bear, she was able to fall asleep at night. Is this manipulation? The teddy bear was only perceived as endowed with a magical quality; safety was a quality already latent in the child. Over time, she learned that she held this quality and didn't need the teddy bear.

The tenth chakra works with ten, the number of new life.

Through the Eleventh Chakra You must be careful to ensure that you are controlling forces through the eleventh chakra, not allowing them to control you! Want to know the key? Don't hold onto energy. Never, never, never seize energy eternally. What you own becomes you, and then you become it.

Here's an example: I worked with a man who had heart disease. He had already had four heart attacks. Glen was a very powerful executive, a top-notch CEO of a large computer company. When young, he had felt powerless and weak. As soon as he mastered the management of certain powers, he held onto the energy of them and refused to surrender them when they weren't needed. His wife saw him as heartless; his daughter, as a foreigner. The natural forces he was unconsciously commanding had rested in his physical heart and were creating a maelstrom. Through the imagination center, these forces were acting like magnets, attracting power-based issues from the antiworld. Glen rejected his own softness and need for love, the energies of which would slide into the antiworld and then return reasons and rationale for rejecting love. I showed him how to command a force and then release it when he was finished, and immediately his relationships and physical health improved.

Eleven is the sign of mastery and power; true masters know they aren't in charge. You don't cause effects—you allow them.

Through the Twelfth Chakra Jesus and other Ascended Masters— including Elijah of the Old Testament and the Chinese *hsien* who ascend in their bodies or immediately after death—remain in human form even after completing transmutation to the Divine. If human and divine are both equally unreal, then both are equally valid expressions of the other. If you only own your divinity, your humanity exits through the imagination pathway. If you only own your humanity, your divinity leaves through the imagination pathway. If you own both, you'll become both. You can remain in human form and be equally divine. You don't have to choose.

Twelve is a last number of the human dimension and a place to celebrate the human experience.

Energy Packages

On the imagination pathway, you can exchange information lodged in structures and thereby alter what appears in your life. You can obtain the "new data" from the antiworld and substitute it for the "old data" that doesn't serve anymore. You can also change structures and thus change the application of energy. Change a square into a circle and you have bonding instead of permanence. Alter a triangle into a square and you have solidity instead of growth. Imagination diagnosis and healing is truly a matter of shifting perspective rather than forcing change.

Beliefs You can hold beliefs on either side of the imagination pathway, but you'll never get anywhere trying to work beliefs just in this world. A positive belief here lingers in the negative over there, and vice versa. You must alter the story around a belief to effectively diagnose or heal on this pathway, rather than defining the actual belief creating your current life story. In the upcoming section on "Strongholds," I'll present ways to work storytelling to your advantage.

Feelings Feelings on the elemental pathway are frequencies; on the power pathway they are vibrational threads within spiritual energetic forces. On the imagination pathway, feelings are motivations that enable the mind to convince itself of illusions or delusions. If you really believe that an ancestral entity has cursed your family, the curse exists in this reality. You have transported the possibility from the antiworld to this world, usually through one or more chakras holding elemental-based beliefs that make you prone to this punishment. The belief allows the transfer between worlds, but the fear is the motivation for allowing the belief in the curse. If you were to stop thinking that you require this fear or that it has any power, you could shift the issue out of reality.

Strongholds Working with power field and level problems, as well as all emotional and mental strongholds, comes down to pinpointing singular thoughts and feelings and the combinations of these two on the imagination pathway. Remember that waves can emanate from particles. A vast power field can be constructed from a single point. If you can reduce the overwhelming size of an issue into a tiny pinprick of light or dark, you can flatten a building with an ice pick. You can use the imagination pathway to define the particular thoughts and feelings substantiating a problem, but only if you work with your imagination. Storytelling is one of the best ways to do this.

Storytelling is one of the most ancient and well-defined practices of healers across time. When you tell a story of how something came to be, you determine why it is. Knowing the "why" allows you to decide whether or not you want to hold onto your ideas (the originating beliefs or feelings motivating a problem). Imagination healing occurs when you release the "why" holding a problem in place and imagine a new storyline. Here's an exercise that will enable you to diagnose through storytelling on the imagination pathway.

Focus on the presenting problem. Now respond to the following statements, either by speaking to a friend or into a tape recorder, or in writing.

1. When I'm in this problematic state, my name is:
2. As _____ [say your name], I see the world in this way:
3. When I see the world in this way, this is how it responds to me:
4. And this is how I respond to myself:
5. Once upon a time, I was walking in the world as _____ [say your name], and this is what happened that made me create my problem:
6. When I inhabit the world of this problem, I am able to:
7. And I am not able to do this:
8. Therefore, I have created this problem so that I can do the following:
9. This is the story that I really want to create:
10. This is the single aspect of the current story that can change and therefore change my story:

Patterns, Boundaries, and Habits

Here are methods for addressing issues related to patterns, boundaries, and habits on the imagination pathway.

Patterns The imagination pathway will not cause patterns; rather, it responds to your desire for them. This can make it hard to diagnose patterns on the imagination pathway, except through means like storytelling. You can, however, psychically see patterns in the centers of the chakras by examining for shapes, tones, colors, and symbols.

Boundaries On the imagination pathway, boundaries are necessary to (1) deflect reverberating energy that could harm you and (2) support you in reverberating energy that you need. That said, there is only one boundary necessary to the imagination pathway: the division between here and there in the center of a chakra. Certain types of problems can indicate boundaries that are too flexible or too rigid in any of the chakras—or an absence of boundaries that should exist. You will perceive the chakric boundary holding the form that reflects the boundary problem. The following table provides examples.

Chakra	Boundaries Too Flexible	Boundaries Too Rigid	Boundaries Nonexistent
First	Overspending; sex addiction; promiscuity; workaholism; food, alcohol, or other addictions; diseases indicating lack of structure in body, such as anemia and varicose veins; adrenal dysfunction; cancers; skin problems; premature ejaculation in men	Lack of money and primary needs; lack of joy; controlling relationships; anorexia; diseases indicating tightness, such as lower back problems, constipation, and muscle tightness; skin problems; inability to be orgasmic	No ability to function in everyday life; severe mental illnesses and terminal illnesses
Second	Emotionalism; lack of separation between own feelings and others'; diseases such as endometriosis, fibroids, and Irritable Bowel Syndrome (IBS); some relation to ADD	Controlled or repressed feelings; difficulty relating to others; lack of creativity; diseases such as constipation, loose bowels, and fertility problems; some relation to autism	No management of feelings or relationship to them; inability to separate fantasy from reality or real from not real; severe second-chakra problems can result
Third	Lack of good judgment; inability to discern appropriate from inappropriate behavior; terrors and fears; lack of organization, logic, and reason; diseases including overproduction of chemicals in any digestive organ	Excessive criticalness; prejudice; self-righteousness; need to always be perfect; "good boy" or "good girl" issues; repressed anger and rage; overorganization, "anal" attitude, rigid logic; lack of a sense of fun; underproduction of chemicals in digestive organs	Irrationality; insanity; inability to deal with life's structure; severe digestive disturbances

Chakra	Boundaries Too Flexible	Boundaries Too Rigid	Boundaries Nonexistent
Fourth	Codependency and caretaking; love addiction; fear of being alone; heart and lung diseases involving overproduction of body chemicals	Loneliness and alienation; inability to relate to others; fear of intimacy; heart and lung diseases involving underproduction of body chemicals	Major relationship disorders; potentially terminal heart and lung disorders
Fifth	Inability to stop talking; obsessive learning; inability to tune out entities; some aspects of ADD; disc problems; auditory processing disorder; throat cancers and disorders; loose jaw; overeating; noise in ears; ear infections; hyperthyroidism	"Shut down" effect; inability to communicate; some aspects of autism; TMJ; disc problems; undereating; hypothyroidism; hearing difficulties; ear infections	Severe communication disorders; throat, hearing, and neck problems; some multiple-personality, ADD, and autism disorders
Sixth	Overstimulation by visuals; inability to separate own plans, visions, and dreams from others'; hyper-psychic visual sense; eye problems; over-stimulated pituitary	Lack of depth perception; inability to plan for self; lack of visions and dreams; narrow focus or goals; eye problems; understimulated pituitary	Totally controlled by the future—either fear of it, visions from it, or difficulties in perceiving it; severe eye or growth-related disorders; hallucinations; schizophrenic or borderline personality tendencies
Seventh	Religious fanaticism, susceptibility to brainwashing; awareness of God, perfection, spirituality, or spirits affecting ability to lead a normal life; pineal problems; anxiety	Inability to connect with spiritual entities or beliefs; no sense of the Divine; inability to forgive; pineal problems; depression	Severe depression, anxiety, or other mental health disorders; "Christ complex," thinking one is or must be perfect or a deity

Chakra	Boundaries Too Flexible	Boundaries Too Rigid	Boundaries Nonexistent
Eighth	Inability to separate other worlds from this one; constant visitations on or from other planes or dimensions; issues with time, karma, sorcery, power, and control	Inability to leave or forget the past; recycling of old issues; inability to connect with higher dimensions; issues with time; judgment against others	Overmysticism, leading to inability to regulate life or to insanity; can become societal outcast; any major illnesses can result, as these can penetrate from past lives
Ninth	Excessive idealism; unrealistic expectations; thoughts of grandeur and saving the world; judgment against others who are less than perfect	Lack of meaning or goals; depression from thinking oneself ineffective	Can cause any problem, as soul issues can penetrate from other souls or past lives
Tenth	Too attuned and affected by nature and natural energies; environmental sensitivities; allergies; bone and tooth problems from overproduction of chemicals	Out of touch with nature and natural energies and, therefore, own body and bodies' needs; allergies; bone and tooth problems from underproduction of chemicals	Total lack of boundaries between self and nature, leading to accidents; environmental toxicity; severe allergies; bone and tooth disorders; ancestral hauntings and influences; morphogenetically transferred issues; bindings and miasms
Eleventh	Severe negativity; controlling or violent behavior; power issues; calling of forces detrimental to self or others, such as storms or electromagnetic forces; physical boundary problems	Too nice; victimization; lack of power; ineffectiveness; physical boundary problems	Major power issues; inability to summon energies needed to lead life, manifest, or get well

Habits Habits can help you distinguish the difference between the sane and insane or illusion and delusion. Since time began, imagination shamans have performed ritual as a way of separating the two worlds and performing healing through imagination energy exchanges. I therefore emphasize the use of ritual and ceremony to perform imagination-based diagnosis and healing.

When used properly, ritual opens the doorways between the antiworld and this world. Shamans can consciously enter the antiworld from this plane and there gather diagnostic information and healing energies for themselves and their patients. This journey often involves entering a trance state, sometimes induced with the assistance of physical tools, such as spirit medicine, hallucinogens, aromas, dancing, or sex.

You don't have to go this far to gather data. I encourage you to instead develop a personalized ritual or ceremony that, when performed, allows you to access imagination-based information. This can include prayer, meditation, use of an altar, lighting candles, humming, singing hymns or chanting, journaling, listening to music, dancing, walking, using a mantra, or even thinking while you're brushing your teeth! The behavior matters less than the attitude you hold.

Some people use ritual so habitually that they turn the ritual into a pattern and thus gain only delusional rather than illusion-based information through the imagination pathway. It's easy to fool yourself. Prayer can open the door to holy sources and antiworld truths, but it can also access the Lower Mind or the subconscious, which are more than happy to continue fooling you. Do you know why so many people in mental institutions hear Jesus Christ, the Virgin Mary, or Buddha? They are often "channeling" an aspect of themselves that holds opinions or views about these figures.

To gain control over the uncontrollable, many people form fanatic or compulsive elemental habits, such as washing their hands fifty times a day to prevent disease, or praying over every food item to ensure God's blessings. Ritual must allow for a beneficial exchange of energy between the antiworld and this world. Any ritualistic behaviors that reinforce fear or act as an escape from living a productive, real-world life are not habits—they are delusional patterns.

Forms of Energy

On the imagination pathway, you can duplicate the appearance of any other energy. Therefore you must determine whether you're working with true or false energies, especially in a healing process. For instance, a cancer patient might wonder if the chemotherapy (or the acupuncture treatments, or the prayer, or the energy work) is effecting change. You can think something's working when it's not, and vice versa. An imagination evaluation includes psychically examining the center of the chakra originating or most affected by the cancer; say, the second chakra for uterine cancer. By examining the lens, you can intuitively sense if the energies used are working the way that you desire. Simply ask to see, hear, or know the effect of that energy on your well-being. If you want to select a cancer treatment, you can project each method onto the imagination lens and imagine the body's response. (However, you should not use this exercise as a replacement for professional medical input and treatment.)

Times and Places

Master imagination workers can access any and all times and places through the middle of the imagination pathway (the area actually inside of an imagination mirror). This neutral zone links to all spacetimes, Zones, Planes of Light, and other areas, including the various records and the Book of Life. You don't actually have to journey from or leave the imagination center to gain information or healing energy. Simply situate yourself in the mirror center and ask to perceive data or energies from the needed spacetimes.

You can also use imagination abilities to eliminate the veil between yourself and any of the thirteen-plus dimensions, but only if you've already set your seals on the power pathway. The imagination pathway naturally connects into dimensions one through eight, but it can extend into the higher planes if you desire. By linking the imagination self with the higher dimensions, you begin to open to the divine, and you will receive truth that is never delusion-based. Use the exercise "Working from the Middle of the Mirror," earlier in this chapter, to perform this task.

Energy Laws

There are no imagination laws, but you can peer through the imagination pathway and see what would happen if you broke a power, elemental, or divine law. You can also determine if a presenting problem results from rule-breaking by simply asking for the truth of that matter while in the center of any chakra. Imagine the law being or having been obeyed and see if you can correct a problem in this way.

Energy Shapes and Spin

By far the easiest imagination diagnosis can be made through perceiving symbols, shapes, numbers, tones, and spins through the imagination doorways in the centers of the chakras. The best way to gauge shape and spin is through psychic vision. Use the charts in the elemental pathway chapters to determine the meaning of what you see, sense, or hear.

Sourcing

Since time began, shamans have been contacting entities and helpers through the imagination pathway—sometimes fooling themselves and others into thinking that what they've perceived is what it appears to be. It's easy to think that an appearing being is an external entity, when it's merely a projection of your own mind.

Delusional sourcing can cause many problems, the least of which include hallucinations, bindings, hauntings, interference, schizophrenia, and just plain madness. Don't be ashamed if you think that you've been tricked. Most of us have; we just haven't known it. The "inner voice" that keeps sabotaging you? It might be an inner child or an internalization of your father's fears on the elemental pathway, but when empowered by power forces and perceived through the imagination pathway, it grows into a BIG GIANT that we think is Truth or even God—but it isn't.

The imagination pathway will reflect not only the worst but also the best of us. For diagnostic purposes, I recommend that anyone facing a chronic or difficult challenge check the chakras' centers to see if part of the problem involves sourcing external or internal "demons." You must check the eighth and tenth chakras; I would also check the first and the fourth. Return to chapter 11 and the information on bindings and contracts to know what to look for, in addition to performing a perusal for internal sources, such as those listed in chapter 6.

The Divine Pathway:
The Risen Heaven

Our divine self has been watching us all these many years. We dream of what we could be, not remembering that we are already that—and more. We decide to stop being a certain way and forget that we can't cease what is endless. The teaching of the imagination pathway is that everything and nothing might be real, but it must be true to be acceptable. On the divine pathway, we now continue to figure out what of the self is and should be made real, to be true.

Divination creates miraculous healings. Some of these healings appear as miracles in the three-dimensional reality. Some are merely events that touch us to the core. When we are divine, we know ourselves as centered with the Creator and can use any healing means at all to achieve a set end. The highest course is to petition—to ask for what we've already received. And the only real action needed for divine healing is willingness. Willingness to:

- Be imperfect
- Make mistakes
- Accept our divinity in the middle of our humanity
- Live with no regrets
- Release expectations of the "how"
- Accept that there are "whys"
- Return to the state of childlike wonder and accept the wonders as they unfold

As we allow divine learning, we stop trying to fix everything. We know it as already whole. We simply ask if *this* is the spacetime for the appearance of wholeness or not. But it's not at all simple to accept this revelation. We must "battle with the bowls"—the seven bowls of confusion, the illnesses from Pandora's box—to achieve hope and therefore wholeness. As we do this, our in-body chakras transform into the

Heaven watched through her lovely eyes that saw through all the trouble in the world to the heaven that lies beneath. She touched January with her webbed fingers as he passed.

She stood there in the hallway.

How did they know each other? Ancient dreams. Images from a stormy winter's night. Love. They watched each other. [1]

—David Almond,
Heaven Eyes

seven channels of light described in the book of Revelation and our twelve auric fields into the twelve spiritual gates that form us as a city of God. We change, and as we change, others change.

I've been open to this pathway for a while and I'm not an expert, only a student. But I've learned that when I think of a need, the need is met. I'm not surprised anymore when my washing machine breaks and a friend who does house repairs stops by unexpectedly. I assisted a woman with a brain tumor. The tumor disintegrated, not because of me, but because she finally understood who she really is. I worked on a woman with Cushing's syndrome. The disease disappeared, and she also believes she shed potential future illnesses such as breast cancer and heart trouble. I prayed with a good friend whose book was rejected at a publishing house. The publisher called my friend within hours, having changed her mind.

Writing this book has frankly been a divine process. I had already written three hundred pages of it as a sequel to *New Chakra Healing*, when Christ appeared and insisted that I work closer to the bone—that I write how he might present healing in a contemporary context. And so I scrapped all three hundred pages and started over. I received several revelations in the first few months, followed by dreams and then by learning through application. Near the end of writing this book, I received less spiritual insight and didn't think it was needed, until I was writing Part Five. I struggled over how to write that section, forgetting the "divine doctrine" of forgetting the how, setting the goal, and remembering that there was a reason for my struggling.

Finally I remembered to petition. That evening, I dreamed about an already-written book. I wasn't the author; the book was published by two medical doctors years in the future. There was page after page of information about various diseases. Placed in the middle section of each page was chakra-based information. I began reading the chakra information, and guess where it ended up? Yes, in this book! I heard a divine chuckle one night and had my own laugh. I don't believe that the future book can be written until this one is published. One begets the other, but which is the real chicken and which is the egg?

Most of the disease-based information I wrote quickly, as I had been working with it for several years. However, I couldn't figure out how to frame multiple sclerosis, because it's such a complicated disease. The morning I was to write the section, I petitioned for help, and immediately my car began acting up. Grumbling, I took it to a Midas station that had felt "intuitively right" that morning. I knew the fix would take forever and that I would miss my evening writing time. Well, the car had stopped banging and squeaking by the time I got there, and within two minutes the technician pronounced my car cured, in that it was never sick. But in those two minutes, I had paged through a magazine and found a research-based article on MS that gave me exactly what I needed for inspiration.

The divine pathway isn't just for great and grand issues. It's about real life. That's what healing is about—living a whole life and having wholeness within each moment of life.

Healing and Manifesting for the Self on the Divine Pathway

Expansion of the centered self allows change and growth. There are only two requirements for allowing an expansion of wholeness on the divine pathway:

1. The ability to accept divine love.
2. The surrender of your personal solution to the divine solution for a perceived need.

Problems on every pathway stem from a perceived need. Imagine a child unloved by her mother. She will grow up believing herself to be unlovable, yet she still needs love. To be loved, then, is her real need. Thinking that she doesn't deserve it, she will establish methods of getting love that keep her inner doubts covered up. Maybe she'll avoid relationships, as sex would bring up her inner hurt and pain. Maybe she'll become a sex addict, someone who leeches cold and uncaring energy from her partners in an attempt to meet her deeper need, while she remains distant. Underneath it all, this girl-woman feels separate from her mother and therefore separate from the Divine. She might even attend a church, synagogue, or temple and pray for healing, yet continue with behavior that only proves her unlovableness. Quite simply, she subconsciously wants to continue being in charge of her love life rather than allow divine healing. She doesn't want to take the chance that the Divine doesn't love her any more than her mother did. Healing will begin only when she surrenders her personal solutions to the need for love and accepts love from the Divine.

On the divine pathway, all healing begins and ends with your relationship with the Divine. If you can accept the unconditional reality and truth of divine love, seeing all else as illusion or delusion, then the only reality that will exist is one that is loving. You will always be linked with divine will. If you know that you are divinely loved, your personal will automatically desires only that which is loving, for yourself or others. At this point, you never need question if your will and God's will are the same. They are.

In the human state, we have needs. This is good! On the divine pathway, the Divine would chuckle at religious doctrines that negate human needs. Even the most rigorous spiritual standards require care and feeding of the body. It's pretty hard to pray all day without breakfast. A loving Supreme Being desires to meet our needs, because needs indicate where we are willing to grow and stretch! The Divine knows that it's not the object that we desire, it's the quality that object will provide. Money isn't the need—it's a vehicle for achieving a certain way of being.

From the divine perspective, lack, limitation, or illness simply indicates that we've attempted to come up with our own solution to a need, rather than one that is divinely willed. This is not to judge problems. What we think of as "bad" might be "good" from a higher perspective. When one of my closest girlfriends had cancer and entered the darkest time of her life, she wasn't a failure, nor was she refusing divine love. During her year of recovery, she found out that her husband didn't really love her and that her hormones had been off for years. These two understandings forced a change in her life and lifestyle that have left her extraordinarily happy just two years after diagnosis.

I had a client ask how he could heal from alcoholism through the divine pathway. I suggested in-patient treatment. He was astonished. "Can't prayer just fix me?" He didn't understand that from a divine perspective, going to chemical dependency treatment and Alcoholics Anonymous wasn't a punishment. Attendance wouldn't be an admittance of lack of faith. It would be the process of unfolding his deeper self to the conscious self, a welcoming into the world. Treatment was the divine healing! Sure, God could snap His/Her fingers and will away the compulsion to drink. The only issue is that the alcohol wasn't the issue, just the symptom. It was a personal solution for a genuine need. Until this man was willing to acknowledge the needs forcing him to drink and to deal with the pain covering up the inner needs, he wouldn't be "cured" of alcoholism.

Most of the time, the Divine isn't going to instantly and miraculously heal alcoholism or a cold or cancer or financial ruin, because the symptom isn't the need. The need lies under the problem. The need will always be about love. If you are willing to recognize and own divine love, you will be healed of your problems, because the underlying need will be met. But you'll have to surrender your personal solution to the problem, because whatever you're doing obviously isn't working, is it?

I have a client with chronic fatigue who prays all day for healing. For seven years, she has sat around and prayed while spending lots of money to work with some of the world's best healers. She hasn't gotten better. She lost her husband, who said he got tired of her whining. She lost her job because she wouldn't work more than five hours a week. The disease can involve an attempt to return to a womblike state to meet a childhood need for being tended. My client's behavior is an attempt to get others to take care of her, but it has backfired. She needs to take responsibility for the need and then petition for help, with the full willingness to follow the healing input provided her in life. Her husband's complaints about her impossible attitude could have brought her into the childhood pains that keep her in the straitjacket of chronic fatigue. However, she prefers to use the disease to meet a deeper need rather than go after the true need.

You might have to work hard to effect the healing that you desire. You can petition for a new job, but understand that the deeper pull is toward fulfilling your spiritual destiny. Your job will "pop in" once you accept the fullness of that responsibility and the joy of working toward it. You'll still probably have to write a résumé and make cold calls for interviews. If you have bad work patterns, such as never being on time, you'll have to change them and establish correct habits and protocol. You change behavior by changing behavior. Working the divine pathway can help you become willing to change the behaviors that need changing. Seen through the lens of the other pathways, the divine pathway adds the process for getting to the truest need, and the means for petitioning grace and help.

Keys to the Divine Pathway

The keys to working on the divine pathway are will, willingness, neutrality, timelessness and spacelessness, petitioning, and being at 100 percent. Here are notes about these divine pathway concepts:

• The divine pathway is a state rather than a place. You don't get there; you recognize that you are there. It is not heaven on earth; it is heaven in earth. The divine pathway is the state of Wakefulness. This consciousness implies that you are fully here and now.

• The divine pathway is in all here and nows. It is All Time.

• Because of All Time, the psychic gifts all combine. The numinous gift of one chakra accesses all the abilities of the other chakras. You know you're on the divine pathway and using numinous gifts when you feel, sense, hear, know, see, and become the revelation while receiving it.

- There are no polarities or dualities on the divine pathway. There is self and other, but they are completely linked. Hence it is a place of neutrality, where everything can come together and yet be separate.

- Because there is no separation, your issues are everyone's issues and someone else's problem is your problem. And God's powers are your powers, as is God's depth of love.

- You effect change by merging your will with divine will. If you know divine will, simply claim it. It now becomes your will. Use your will to petition change and it *absolutely will happen.* If you don't know what divine will is, wait. Let your personal will be revealed. If it matches divine will, your "wish" will be granted. If it doesn't, nothing will happen.

- Because the divine pathway is in All Time, your willed desire is granted before it occurs. You don't even have to finish a prayer, and the answer may already have arrived.

- In Wakefulness, you can petition anything for anything. If you need rain and you petition a cloud, the cloud consciousness will consider the request. If it can't meet the intent of your need, the petition is shared among unified consciousnesses until your need can be met.

- The key to effecting change, such as healing for the self or others, is willingness. You must be 100 percent willing to allow healing or manifesting. Someone else must be 100 percent willing to receive healing or manifested needs.

- No expenditure of energy is needed to make anything happen. To operate in this realm, you need be only 100 percent present and in the joy of living.

- Remember, rather than *acting intentionally,* as you must on the elemental pathway; or *commanding,* as on the power pathway; or *imagining,* as you do on the imagination pathway, you *petition* on the divine pathway.

Divine Tools

Here are several tools for working on the divine pathway. You can use these for diagnostics or healing.

Your Numinous Gifts

The numinous gifts are three-dimensional. If you ask and align with the Divine, your traditional psychic ability will transform into a numinous ability for gathering data and allowing healing.

Forgiveness Forgiveness is a gift to the self. On the divine pathway, it is the key to protection. It is also the key to dealing with others' energies. On the divine pathway, the word *forgiveness* means "for giving." Which energies are meant to be given to someone else and which are to be kept to yourself? Which energies were supposed to be kept by someone else and which are to be given to you?

Here is a forgiveness exercise that invites divine healing:

1. Invoke the Divine's energy of grace, which is power in love.

2. Center and ask the Divine to help you generate the actual substance of grace outward, from your center to all other aspects of yourself.

3. Petition the Divine to grant grace to anything and anyone who has harmed you or continues to negatively affect you, as well as to yourself for the same.

4. The conscious direction of grace offers three choices to all individuals, entities, and consciousnesses currently preying on you: to transform, to leave, or to receive consequences. Let's say you're dealing with an abusive husband whose energy is binding. Grace offers this person (or his energy) the chance to transform into the original spirit state. If your husband says "yes" psychically, the transformation completes. The victimizing energy moves out because your husband, executing free will, understands this choice as the most loving. If he doesn't want to change, but is willing to vacate your energy system, grace will help him exit and will heal you from the effects. If he won't go, grace reflects his own energy back to him. If he continues to try to hurt you, his own energy, such as horror and shame, returns to him tenfold. You aren't punishing or executing revenge; he's merely subjected to an ancient law regarding responsibility.

Prayer Prayer sends messages to the Divine. Although you can externalize prayer, know that every thought, word, deed, or feeling is a prayer to the Divine, as the Divine is within.

Meditation Meditation involves receiving inspiration from the Divine. There is no correct form to follow. Life is really a meditative act, as answers are provided to the self all the time.

Contemplation To contemplate is to recognize the presence of the Divine. By knowing the Divine in others or yourself, you are contemplating God.

Diagnosing and Healing on the Divine Pathway

It's almost misleading to discuss diagnosis on the divine pathway, because the divine pathway involves a state of total acceptance. Without duality, there is no good or bad. There isn't ease or disease or health, sickness, or wellness. Struggling to diagnose implies a judgment, and judgment doesn't exist on the divine pathway.

Discernment and truth, however, are valid ideas, as are such concepts and actions as choice, free will, and preference. You can discern the truth of the need under a presenting problem. You can then choose, through free will, a preferred way to meet that need. Therefore, discerning is less about working with individual energy particles, feelings, and laws, and more about conducting a few simple acts. Healing is less about changing something or yourself, and more about accepting a truth to meet your needs. As the Bible says, "The truth shall set you free." The truth not only acknowledges the need, but also opens to the energies required to meet your needs. These energies are metaphysically available through the chakras in their divine clothes as channels of light.

There are countless ways to allow divine healing. Here are but a few.

Standard Divine Diagnostic and Healing Technique

1. **Discern the truth of the need.** Through the divine state, you can figure out the need being met by your problem. Remember that there are no judgments on the divine pathway. Prosperity meets a need, as does cancer. When you're energy mapping, your evaluation will involve considering which bowl is a challenge. The first bowl of evil, for instance, can present as a fear of intimacy and the avoidance of a primary relationship. Are you trying to cancel out or ignore the need for love? It could also disguise itself in opposite terms, such as a love or sex addiction and the compulsion to keep finding new partners. The evil or anticonsciousness in this scene is equal to that in the first, except it appears different—as a resistance to being alone rather than the fear of being together. Work the bowls and your presenting issues, using the "Divine Healing through Feelings" exercise that follows, to summarize the original need.

2. **Select the chakra that houses the need.** Use elemental-based chakra processes to figure out which chakra (or combination of chakras) is holding the need hostage. Now look at the issue from a

divine perspective; evaluate the chakras as channels of light and the auric fields as gates of light. These descriptors are listed later in this chapter in "Energy Bodies." Each channel of light relates a certain truth needed to face your deeper need.

3. **Summarize the truth that will assist you in meeting your need.** For instance, if the presenting issue involves the first chakra, such as in a serious blood disorder, you can figure out which need or truth is being represented on the divine pathway. Light of the first chakra relates to the truth of being an I, or a self. The need presented by a blood disorder is therefore related to a need regarding selfhood and individuation. This interpretation will line up with the issues covered in the elemental-based first power level and field, and all issues ascribed to the first chakra, first auric field, and first seal.

4. **Determine your choices.** Divine healing involves forgiveness. Remember, forgiveness is a release of energy or information that is not yours to own and an acceptance of energies and information that are yours to own. You can only own that which aligns with your spiritual self. On the imagination pathway, you learned the difference between what is real and what is fantasy. On the divine pathway, disease and problems are a matter of perspective. Misunderstanding led you to accept energies (such as diseases) as a perceived way of meeting a true need. The need wasn't met, and so you contracted an imbalance in body, mind, and soul. You didn't have to take on these unfit energies, but it's okay that you did. However, to get to the point of acceptance and action, you must see that you had choices in the past and that you can now meet your need by accepting a different truth, energy, situation, event, job, or relationship.

5. **Make a new choice.** Ask for divine will if the choice is not clear.

6. **Forgive yourself and others for earlier choices and their consequences.** Decide that you are now whole, powerful, and fully loved by a compassionate God in the here and now.

7. **Own the Divine's free will.** Whatever you call God, the Divine Consciousness is fully human as well as divine, for "God" is All, and the All includes humanity. As humans have free will, so does the All. The diagnostic issue here is to own that God loves you so much that God has allowed you to be "sick" even though you are "whole." God's will, however, is to see you as whole. Now you must accept the diagnosis that you are as whole as God, as both of you are human. As God is whole, so are you.

8. **Illuminate from within.** See the exercise on radiating vital source energy in the "Life Energy and Kundalini" section later in this chapter.

Divine Healing through Feelings

Here is an easy exercise for performing divine diagnosis and healing when heavy emotions are involved. It involves working with your emotions and your feelings so you can better receive divine teachings over time. Practice and use it when shift healing.

1. Select an issue or a problem. Accept the discomfort it is causing in your life and in your body. On the divine pathway, everything that you resist becomes magnified. Don't resist.

2. Know that this discomfort does not exist in every aspect of yourself. As with the imagination pathway, there are different versions of the same reality. There is a place where you have illness, issues, a problem, or a need, and a space in which your needs are fulfilled in a way that makes the problems unnecessary. If there is discomfort inside of you, there is also a space of comfort.

3. Breathe deeply and associate with this state of comfort. Use the radiating exercise in the "Life Energy and Kundalini" section if you desire. Make sure you are still in your body. A visual psychic will picture the discomfort as a form and stand on the in-body side of the discomfort. I like to envision a big beach in my heart and the discomfort as an image in the sky in front of me. I see the problem as the moon over the water. A kinesthetic intuitive will have to feel the discomfort and move through it until finding a place of clearness in the body. Some kinesthetics prefer the hurricane concept, sensing the self centered in the eye of the storm. A verbal candidate will command him- or herself to a comfortable space. You can say that you want to be in your "place of purity" or the "state of comfort." If none of these means work, ask for divine help.

4. You may still actually feel the discomfort in your system, such as still wanting to vomit if you have the flu. Know that you can own discomfort and comfort at the same time. You simply want your consciousness placed in the state of comfort.

5. Now to the critical element: feel the feeling connecting you to the discomfort. And I mean feeling as in part of an emotion, not the emotion itself. A discomfort is always energetically composed of a variety of feelings, beliefs, energies, and even entities and forces. This congregate connects with you because at some moment

in time you had a feeling about what was going on. Get back to your original feeling.

6. Keep feeling. Usually, you can conduct this healing in one fell swoop. But sometimes I've found out that I didn't start in the original feeling, because I was so scared. If another feeling arises, stay with it or consider getting a friend or therapist to help you go to the core feeling.

7. Accept your awareness about the feeling and ask yourself why you had this feeling. This feeling arose historically because of a perceived need. What was it? What need is this feeling pointing out?

8. Petition to feel the Divine's acceptance of your need. All patterns, strongholds, illnesses, and issues stem from a need that you believe has not been met. The need has not been met because you judged it, not because the Divine judged it. When we judge a need, we freeze the feeling about the need, and then we go about creating backward and distorted ways to get our need met.

9. Petition for the Divine to meet the original need.

10. Know that you can now complete your relationship with the original feeling. This knowledge will open to an even deeper level of truth and eventually give way to a spiritual feeling. The spiritual feeling will generate through the superluminal body, activating the spiritual genetics and changing the conditions in your body.

11. Allow learning. If there's something you must learn, the knowing will be provided through the numinous gifts or maybe even by an elemental-based messenger.

12. Accept the learning. It will change you.

The Elemental Pathway and the Divine Pathway

The obvious spiritual nature of the divine pathway leads many to question the connection between it and the elemental pathway, between the profound and the mundane. Most spiritual and religious traditions discount the physical, especially the body and feelings. Consider the Catholic Church and its stand on celibacy for priests, a practice adopted despite the allowance of marriage by the early Christian Church. Read the Bible and see how little was written of the married life of the apostles, a clue to the overemphasis on sacrifice for the spirit. Look at the Zen Buddhist attitude of detachment, the "nonfeeling" of feelings, and the ascetic control over food. Watch the judgment against women's "emotionalism"; you see it in words such as *hysterectomy*, which was coined from a perceived "hysteria" or out-of-control feelings that required the elimination of the uterus. The American Puritan ethic of mastering and dominating nature, the body, and emotional impulses is still widespread.

The divine pathway embraces the elemental pathway, including the beautiful physical and emotional aspects of this here-and-now reality. I'll share a practical example to show you how and why.

I worked for some time with a very talented, intuitive woman named Ariana. She wanted to focus on expanding her gifts and beginning a healing and medical intuition practice. To do this, she wanted to eliminate the presence of entity intrusion and interference and her pattern of absorbing others' feelings and issues. We worked to no avail. One day her gifts would astonish me and her clients, and then the next they would implode into air.

Nothing changed until I asked her about her diet and her attitude toward her feelings. Ariana existed almost entirely on sugar and hated her own feelings. She was disgusted with the fact of being human and wanted to be like the angel she remembered being before birth.

Many spiritual people eat either almost nothing or a lot of sugar, white flour, nicotine, chocolate, and coffee. These substances provide a rush and take up no space in the body, leaving you feeling lightweight and like you can fly. Shamans I've met around the world use these substances medicinally. They also eat "real food."

In the body, sugar turns into carbon, a dense, black substance that causes congestion. White flour becomes pasty and thick. Chocolate clouds vision, nicotine covers grief, coffee blankets dislike of your work, and caffeine forces you to move forward when you don't want to. Essentially, the condensed material stops the electrical component of the electromagnetic system, which short-circuits the chakras. The chakras implode and, seeking energy, draw the auric fields toward the body so as to leech energy from them. Lacking their enhanced protective quality, the fields allow penetration of interference, including hovering bindings, ancestral and entity interference, morphogenetic programs, and others' feelings and issues. Over time, the collapsed auric field rigidifies and works like plastic wrap, holding fungus, mold, and germs inside the body, which stifles purification and the access to power forces.

The body is forced to repress feelings and turn to the imagination pathway. Now the buckled chakras become space stations for the shuttling of energies between the antiworld and this world. For some people, the entrapment makes them susceptible to fantasy. Sure, they perceive demonstrations of psychic information, but it is delusion rather than illusion. The body has no way to manifest a positive reality in its bowed state. The psychic perceptions will enhance the psychic interference or disengaged strongholds.

All of this from not eating right? Certainly. The same results can occur if you don't feel and deal with your feelings or care for all other aspects of the body. From a divine perspective, body is made of spirit and spirit is made of body. Electrons hold form, not just negative feelings. They establish the form for spiritual play.

When you eat correctly, the dense material, such as a heavy protein, is broken down into all the tiny particles of matter needed to support the cellular structure through which life energy flows. The abounding life energy enhances the electromagnetics and other natural forces of the elemental system that expand the chakras and the auric fields. Over time, you're full and free enough to set the seals and begin to command on the power pathway. The lesson of creativity available through the imagination pathway segues to the wisdom of the divine pathway. What you imagine can be. Think of something harmful, you can create it. Think of something helpful, it can be. The divine pathway links the need to take charge of your life with the full support of the universe for choices made. Elemental and divine are of one accord, just as you are a whole being.

For Ariana, the key was thinking that every time she was feeding her body or her feelings, she was feeding God. Since making that change, her spiritual gifts have truly blossomed. Her clients appreciate her wisdom, the interfering voices have stopped, and she now enjoys sharing her feelings through many newly developed friendships.

The Power Pathway and the Divine Pathway

Why should we command when we can petition? Why worry about forces—natural, supernatural, or otherwise—when we *are* a force?

The answer basically leads us to question the essence of God. On the divine pathway, we acknowledge our spiritual identity as *an extension* of the Great Spirit. But being *of* Spirit doesn't mean that we *are* the Great Spirit. My sons are my progeny, but neither is a duplicate of me. In fact, none of us is a copy or mirror of any other being. My identity is unique to me, as yours is to you.

We are each a note in a greater composition. The masterpiece is so much more than our singular sound, and yet our own song is an opus unto itself. If we are to conduct our own musical score, then we must know how to conduct.

Working the power pathway is like being your own conductor. The woodwinds double as generative spiritual forces, and the strings as rays. In this space called Creation the Divine wants companionship, not simple followers. What communion will there be unless we, too, act out of our spiritual strengths and powers?

I lead an intuitive development class that many call the "spoon-bending class." In this class, I present a hard-core process for moving intuitive gifts quantum leaps forward. At first, I provide data, information, charts, and graphs. Then comes the alchemy: the participants open their own innate gifts and basically become instructors to each other and themselves. Each and every class member grows in strength and emerges able to command at least certain energies in specific ways. One woman, a doctor, now mends her patients' illnesses by weaving colors. It's as if she braids wellness into the sore spots. Another doctor shifts energies from one space to another. A hospice care provider commands negative energies away from her dying clients. These and all other techniques involve standing in power and commanding change. You can't heal without knowing it's also your right to command.

The Imagination Pathway and the Divine Pathway

Many who hear of the imagination pathway see it as a place of trickery. Why not leapfrog over this place of potential sorcery, magic, and mayhem, they ask, and just be spiritual?

The imagination pathway isn't canceled out by the divine pathway. It's fulfilled by the divine truths. What good is free will if we're never presented with any choices? We can choose ease. We can choose disease. Either way, there is no judgment because it's all about experience.

Why don't our spirits just sit around in heaven and sing choruses to the Divine? Because that's boring! Because stillness without expansion becomes a black hole and implodes on itself. We are here to strive and try, to thrive and feel, to walk, talk, fall, and dance. The imagination pathway is the Divine answer to the call of love. Love doesn't destroy. Love is never wasted. It merely changes form. At a certain time in our lives, we might think it loving to live in an abusive marriage. Parts of us seem destroyed in this process. Because of divine love, however, these injured aspects of self are kept whole in the antiworld. When we're ready to claim them, they are ready and available.

How about the parts of the self that are in working order? What is in the antiworld of a successful businessperson who got all A's in college? The unsuccessful self, the one who wouldn't study, is alive in the antiworld, a testimony to the choice of successful expression. Love ensures choice. The choice for achievement would mean nothing if there hadn't been another road that could just as easily have been taken.

As I've trained people in the imagination and divine pathways, I've been thrilled to see how many combine the two. One healer learned to stand in the imagination mirror and see both sides of an issue. From this vantage point, she can most easily perceive the need presented by a problem. She then commands power energies to shift one image to the other side and benefit her client's health. Her success rate in healing is over 60 percent.

And think about this: Maybe the imagination pathway is only another way of looking at the divine pathway.

Healing for Others on the Divine Pathway

Jesus is my model of a divine healer. Did you know that he didn't heal everyone? Many weren't willing to ask. Others weren't willing to receive. And many didn't want to change.

The truth is, Jesus didn't really heal anyone. He never claimed to. In his own words, he knew that he and the Father were one. He understood himself as a vessel of divine will. If divine will matched the will of the sickly, poor, or needy, that person would be healed. Jesus was simply the bridge or the link. But he was a vital link in that he was willing to be healed personally every time he served as a healing conduit for another.

Let me show you how I believe he healed, and you'll see what I mean.

1. Jesus would be approached by someone who desired healing. This indicated a willingness in the petitioner.

2. Jesus linked with the Divine to find out if it was God's will to heal this person. A "no" simply meant that the person was actually not willing to accept divine love at that time.

3. If divinely willed, Jesus assumed the divined truth that another's problem is his own. He did not take on the energy of the other; he knew already that he and this other person, through God, were one with each other. Now he allowed any mutual place of need

within himself to receive divine love. By accepting healing for himself, Jesus shared this healing with another.

4. If the other could truly accept the healing, he or she would be healed. If not, Jesus received healing for himself anyway.

As Jesus himself said, love thy neighbor as thyself. What you desire for others becomes given unto you.

Specific Divine Pathway Diagnostic and Healing Techniques

Here are pointers for working with the divine pathway in our energy categories.

Energy Particles and Charges

The divine pathway presents choices, not judgments. When looking at an issue from a divine perspective, you will perceive information about love contained in protons and in magnetic energies and charges, information about power and your use of it in electrons and in electrical energies and charges, and a means of understanding grace in the neutrons.

Underneath the misunderstandings or incomplete data are truths. These are the truths of the channels of light. When tapped or divine, the "whole truth" under the "half-truth" alters the data in the particles and transforms the issue—and even the structure of the particles containing the issue.

Life Energy and Kundalini

On the elemental pathway, the red serpent winds upward, awakening full physical power. On the power pathway, the gold energy of truth descends, interweaving spiritual power. These two can be compared to electrical and magnetic energy, which, when joined, allow action and reflection, manifestation and healing. Both processes use a transformed aspect of vital source energy.

There actually is a form of kundalini on the divine pathway. I call it the *radiant process*. Unlike the other kundalini processes, it doesn't need to be activated, summoned, developed, or trained. It simply needs to be noticed. Within every single cell, organ, thought, and feeling is latent Wakefulness. This Wakefulness is fashioned from the living consciousness that I call vital source energy. This is the pulse of consciousness that, over time and through experience, motivates everyone toward goodness and love. Activating this radiant kundalini is simply a matter of recognizing it within your being or even in the center of a problem. This energy transmutes blocks and resistance on the elemental pathway, shifts power forces around, and transfers energies between the imagination worlds as needed.

I recently taught a class on the three types of kundalini and demonstrated a healing using all three. A woman named Cassandra had been suffering from illness for over a year. Though it wasn't diagnosed as such, she probably had some version of chronic fatigue. Doctors had removed her gall bladder a year before, but she continued to suffer from intense heartburn and digestive disorders, fatigue, and melancholy. She was a highly gifted intuitive and healer, and one of the happiest souls I've ever met, but she just couldn't get to the root of her problem.

I set my hand on the front and back of her third chakra, determining that this was the core chakra causing trouble. I then pointed out that her serpent kundalini was stuck near her liver. The kundalini wasn't doing anything wrong—it was actively trying to work on the emotional stronghold trapping the energy of this chakra. The heartburn was basically the reaction of the body to this intense fire energy. I shifted the kundalini through and beyond the block. She felt immediate relief and tingling throughout her body. Her face became red and lively. I quickly helped her set her seals and then gained permission to bring the golden kundalini down through her spiritual points and seals into the area of discomfort. Again, she felt relief.

And then I tapped her radiant kundalini, the truth latent yet bubbling inside of her. Using the numinous understanding, I asked her if she was willing to begin forgiving herself for knowing and sharing truth, even if it meant that someone might "get hurt" by her statements. In her family of origin, people never spoke clearly for fear of hurting others' feelings. She affirmed this issue as cutting to her soul and said, "yes." Within a matter of only a few minutes, she allowed a healing that could have taken years. She has felt immeasurably better since, after a short period of feeling sick while her body purged itself.

Energetic Communication Methods

The only way to thoroughly perceive your needs and choices in forgiveness is to involve all psychic gifts numinously. To do this, ask your questions and perform your querying in your chosen psychic center through divine love, which will blend your gifts into a unified whole. You can center yourself in the radiating kundalini energy inside an issue as well, to perceive the truth under the misunderstanding and the need that must be met.

Energy Languages

A client of mine described his divine knowings. Joshua had been allowing his numinous gifts to assist him in his work as a well-known therapist. As he put it, he was able to "help [his clients] see the difference between the choices they had made in the past and those they could make right now for their futures." When working in unity, he described a great light or presence that lingered in and near his heart. He doesn't know if he would call it Jehovah or the Light, for it seems "nearly human in its great compassion and understanding of human pain." When connected with this presence, Joshua says that he becomes one with the client, is reliant upon the light, and yet retains full responsibility for his own being, words, and insights. This is the best description of the language of unity that I can provide.

The language of unity blurs distinctions between "us" and "them," and yet leaves us within our own being in the here and now. It's an ideal state for diagnosing our own and others' issues, for it encompasses compassion and wisdom, both of the elements necessary to achieve truth.

Energy Bodies

You can enter the "state" of any incandescent energy body and discover truth for your entire system. The main energies on the divine pathway aren't really organized in energy bodies, only composites of truth. However, I will reference these truths as energy bodies so we can better understand them.

Body of the Eternal This is the ideal place to figure out if you're trapped in a spacetime, dimensional, interdimensional, Zone, or Planes of Light issue. You can check for bindings or any entity or untruth causing a warping of perspective that eventually leads to disruption on all other pathways.

You access this body by shifting into formlessness. It's easiest to meditate first and then imagine yourself stretching as vast as the ocean—and then even further. Feel the sense of waves inside your body and allow them to settle. The self now stretches into forever and into eternity. From here, evaluate for any disturbance by seeing if there is a weight or a sense of form in the stillness. Any heavy energy translates into a place of "stuckness" on another pathway. Now go to another of the pathways and see what the heaviness looks like there.

Body of the Infinite Through the body of the infinite, you evaluate for decisions that are shaping the present into something that is unattractive. When working with infinity, you're actually working outside of all spacetime, Planes, and Zones.

The easiest way to enter this incandescent body is to listen to your heartbeat. Now press your fingertips together. The fingers of each hand will maintain that hand's heartbeat for a few moments until you allow the energies of the two to connect through divine love. Once the rhythm of both hands matches, center your consciousness in the energy joining your fingers. Gradually evolve this field in and around your entire body. You are now sealed in the body of the infinite and will be able to neutrally concentrate on your problem or question. Diagnose with positive questions referencing the "here," such as:

- How is this person/problem/issue currently affecting my life?
- What decision led to this situation?
- What needs am I seeking to meet through my decision(s)?
- What choices are keeping me in this reality?

Questions such as these will lead to understandings about past choices that affect today. Healing will result from making new choices. You can use the Book of Life from the power pathway to attain forgiveness for decisions made and to ask about the next steps.

The Seven Bowls of Existence and the Seven Channels of Light The seven basic in-body chakras each link to one of the seven bowls of existence—evil, death, judgment, power, suffering, false miracles, and endings. In meeting the challenges of the seven bowls or plagues, our chakras transform into the seven channels of light, and all other aspects of the self unify until we truly Awaken.

It's relatively easy to diagnose which "plague" we're dealing with at any given time. You can trace the stuck chakra through elemental means, and then refer to the following list to pinpoint the bowl you're facing. The spiritual truth relating to the chakra is key to addressing the issues you're facing from the bowls.

Light (Chakra)	Spiritual Truth	Bowl
One	Truth of being an I, or a self	Evil
Two	Truth of the verb *to be*, a version of *am* that represents movement	Death
Three	Truth of decisions—the ability to determine one's thoughts	Judgment
Four	Truth of the other—the connection being love	Power

Light (Chakra)	Spiritual Truth	Bowl
Five	Truth of effect—the ability to shape others through communication	Suffering
Six	Truth of change—the key to becoming more of the I	False miracles
Seven	Truth of awareness—the ability to change reality through destiny	Endings

The higher chakras also illuminate and can be inspirational when working with the bowls, mainly because they aren't tied in to a certain bowl and so are more available when we're stuck. Here are the truths associated with these higher chakras.

Light (Chakra)	Spiritual Truth
Eight	Truth of undoing—the erasure of what never should have been
Nine	Truth of hope—the generating of change in ways that have never been
Ten	Truth of the Now—acceptance that everything ever needed is in the here and now
Eleven	Truth of grace—that love and power together create perfection out of imperfection
Twelve	Truth of grace—that love and power together make perfection and imperfection the same

From a divine perspective, you have only to enter the numinous state within any of your chakras to look for the focus bowl. Once you achieve the numinous state, simply ask and you'll know the answer. From there, you can ask questions like these:

· What strength am I summoning to meet this challenge?
· What beauty or other virtue am I developing to face this bowl?
· What truth am I realizing by surrendering to my fear of this bowl's contents?
· What aspect of the Divine is helping me in this quest?
· What gift is this bowl presenting to me?
· How am I being encouraged to present this gifting to others?

Here are questions that can lead to the spiritual truths inherent in the various channels of light:

Light One	What is the truth of myself in this situation?
Light Two	What is the truth that I long to creatively express?

Light Three	What is my truest thought about myself?
Light Four	What is the truth of my connection to others?
Light Five	What needs to be the truth of my communication?
Light Six	What is the truth of my future as I now need to see it?
Light Seven	What is the truth of my ability to change reality?
Light Eight	What is the truth of erasing what shouldn't have been?
Light Nine	What is the truth of creating what has never been?
Light Ten	What is the truth of the here and now?
Light Eleven	What is the truth of the seeming imperfection in this situation?
Light Twelve	What is the truth about the wholeness of this situation?

Twelve Spiritual Gates On the divine pathway, the twelve auric fields of the elemental pathway and the twelve doors of the power pathway update into the twelve spiritual gates, which serve as your buttress and filtering system. I recommend diagnosing and healing through these gates if you believe your issues involve problems with protection, boundaries, information filtering, maintaining a healthy ego state, and holding personal integrity. If your answer to the question "Do you give yourself away?" is "yes," you might benefit from work with the twelve spiritual gates.

How do you know if you give yourself away? Look at your relationships and behaviors. Do you sacrifice continually for loved ones? Do your daily systems run you, rather than the other way around? Do you worry about the perceptions of people that you don't care about? Do you get angry at political machinations or other issues that you can't do anything about? If these or other similar issues irk you, then you could use better boundaries.

You can work on the elemental or power pathway to pinpoint specific disturbances. Use the auric field chart at the end of this section for diagnosis.

For healing, you can work the elemental, power, or imagination pathway as discussed in those chapters. You can also work directly through the divine pathway, where diagnosis enables healing and repair.

The Divine Pathway Chakras

The chakras are key to the divine pathway, and they will transform during the maturation process. Over time, your chakras will actually change color psychically to reflect your spiritual qualities. Here are a few words about the capabilities of the divine chakras.

In completing this statement, you are both diagnosing the divine issue and Awakening the corresponding gate.

My client Pierre, for instance, used this gate-questioning process to evaluate his alcoholism. He drank only at social events but was clearly out of control, to the point that his wife threatened to leave him. I suspected a number of issues, but decided to work on Pierre's external rather than his internal system. After showing him a list of these gate statements, I asked which he had the most difficult time accepting. Pierre selected the fourth.

The fourth divine gate relates to the fourth channel of light, seal, and chakra, which is about relationship. Pierre didn't believe that people would love him for his true self, and so he disguised his fear by drinking. If he acted "strange" at a party, it wasn't him—it was the alcohol. Pierre began repeating the phrase of the fourth gate. Within a week, he had decided he was ready to quit drinking and had entered both marriage and personal therapy. While he was not "miraculously healed," the divine boundary of the fourth gate gave Pierre enough strength to look at his problems.

First Chakra Divine knowledge heals evil, the stuff of the first bowl that diffuses or deflects basic life or life spirit energy. The concept of evil causes all physical maladies, shame, and addiction. By believing in or following evil, we perceive disconnection from the Divine and refuse the vital source energy necessary for wellness. We remain below 100 percent on the first power level of Survival. Even after achieving power capacity or setting our seals, we might refuse to use these powers to help ourselves. We'll constantly trap our pain on this side of the imagination pathway or deflect our problems into the antiworld, pretending that they don't exist. In doing this, we're really pretending that *we* don't exist. The only way to heal from evil is to heal evil itself, essentially by forgiving yourself of anything and everything you've done to achieve perceived separateness from the Creator and your original self.

Forgiveness is the learning of the first spiritual gate. The face of God illuminated through this door is the face of a loving, kind parent. Here is the power of the number one, a new beginning. It is illustrated in the truth of a point or circle, the unbroken connection of love that begins with the Creator. By accepting this love, evil is healed and we can actually live in the Plane of Rest, bathed in eternal restoration. The psychic transcends into the numinous gift of *formation*.

Matter shapes according to the life that you are beginning. This is the chakra allowing a new life.

Second Chakra How do you heal death, the contents of the second bowl? The incandescent body of the eternal illuminates the secret: there is eternal continuance. If you stop fearing death, you can live in joy; if you live in joy, you stop fearing death.

Second-chakra illumination is reflected in the number two and the second dimension of the line. A line is a series of points of beginnings, ends, and middles. It continues forever; even when forming the stable square or rectangle, the walled lines continue without end and hold eternal creative space within. We create within the space, thus using the numinous gift of *creativity* through the spinning of feelings.

Feelings are frequency-based, the energy of the second power field of Functionality. You can use your feelings to petition for needs for self or others, allowing the spiritual gate of Manifestation to fully open. You end the endless cycle of forgiveness through reviewing your sins and actions—the task of the Plane of Evaluation—when you simply commit to creating with and for the Creator.

By knowing that feelings are basic to creation, you can manifest through this chakra.

Third Chakra Beliefs are judgments. Some seem to work for us and some do not. In illumination, we must confront our dogmatic need for beliefs, as posed by the bowl of judgment.

We release both judgments and beliefs in the third dimension, a cube with height for perspective. We now expand beyond the Ego power field on the Plane of Healing by using the numinous gift of *directing*. If we're not centered in the self, we're not controlled by dualistic beliefs and can create from higher consciousness. *This* is the basis of elemental-based super healing. Change the information holding a reality and you shift that reality. This is symbolized in the three-point triangle, which represents the consciousness of God. All cubes can be cut into triangles.

Here's the beauty of this illumination: everything you've ever needed for healing already lies in the third dimensional universe. The third spiritual gate of Illusion is now accessible and you can finally understand that the physical *is* divine.

You can obtain clear consciousness through this divine chakra.

Fourth Chakra It's interesting that the bowl of power relates to a divine fourth chakra, but that's exactly what the numinous gift of *loving* allows. Love is power. When power is wielded with love, it lifts us outside of the self through the bridging consciousness, so we can perform healing of great magnitude. Loving requires a perspective unattached to current time and accessible in the fourth dimension, a point outside of the cube. From this perspective, you can be here and there at the same time, in- and outside of your body at every moment. Through energy waves, you demonstrate the Relational power level, working with others and aspects of self to powerfully deliver love.

Illumination of this chakra will relate to the Plane of Knowledge. To really access Knowledge, you must assume divine love. How did Adam and Eve goof when eating of the Forbidden Tree of Knowledge? They didn't first assume the Creator's unconditional love, and in gaining knowledge without love they became shameful. Shame blocks the perception of connection with the Divine or others. The fourth-chakra illumination, then, ushers in the four of balance, symbolized by a cross with arms of equal length. This is the message Christ brought: You are not separate, on heaven or on earth, from Divine love. Through acceptance of divine love, you enter the gate of Completion. You don't have to be perfect, just yourself. The spiral symbolizes this eternal cycling of love.

Want fourth-chakra illumination? Accept the power of divine love to heal relationships and relationship-based wounds, especially shame.

Fifth Chakra Suffering begets more suffering—the plague of the fifth bowl—but as we access the numinous gift of *truth*, we begin to see through suffering to the pain underneath. Pain can be healed by Wisdom, the Plane of Light available at this level, which reveals everything as light. Light is the spiritual gate illuminating the fifth chakra.

Do you have pain? This chakra allows you to shift from being inside to outside of the third dimension. Sometimes, you need to escape the sensation of pain to heal the causes of it. When healed, you can then shift inside. This act employs the Merkabah, or five-pointed star, the vehicle for alchemy and movement. These understandings allow fulfillment of the fifth power level of Recognition, the use of harmonics to flow in the Divine, and it is key to transforming the elemental-based pain body into a passion body.

To shift pain and suffering, move like directed light.

Sixth Chakra In Peru, I was trained in psychic vision during a medicine ceremony. My teacher was the spirit of a plant, which worked with me night after night, beginning with how to see and expand a point. This is the basis of the numinous gift of *envisioning*, the ability to create a result through seeing what needs to be. All creation starts with a point, the basis of the sixth dimension in which cube lines dissolve and you're left with points.

A six represents choices, symbolized by the six-pointed star of resurrection. To resurrect means to bring up that which has been buried. Illumination on this level will exhume all darkness—or light—hidden underneath a presenting problem or opportunity.

There is light, dark, and everything in between. The sixth gate is Relationship. It isn't *about* relationships—it's about how one point, information particle, self, entity, or decision relates to another. You can certainly envision a desirable reality and force it to happen, but will it be a delusion or an illusion? Will you be hiding from reality or creating a new one?

The sixth bowl is about false miracles. Just curing someone doesn't produce a true healing, nor is there anything miraculous about the appearance of the impractical or impossible. To fulfill the power level requirement of Transformation, you must compose reality in cocreation with the Divine. This is the subject of the sixth Plane of Light about Truth, which provides instruction on creating as the Creator creates. Follow the ancient laws or you're simply a blind man causing your own blindness. This divine chakra is about healing perception, not necessarily about illness or issues.

For illumination, consider breaking your healing needs or perceptions down to the smallest points and then deliberately arranging them from there. Think about what really matters—not what you want to materially create.

Seventh Chakra We're completing our struggles with the seven known bowls afflicting humanity. The seventh is endings. How do we cope with endings? Through gate seven, we accept Infinite Faith. We believe in goodness even when it doesn't seem real. By doing this, we initiate the numinous gift of *inspiration*.

Inspiration isn't the typical psychic gift, which usually involves sensing or directing information-energy. Rather, it involves petitioning for the infusion of Spirit. This is an act of the seventh dimension, a space of no points or lines, upon which you exist in pure consciousness. Through free will, you can decide where and how to direct Spirit.

Seven is the key number of the third dimension. It signifies the Creator's great trust in us. Through the seventh power field of Applied Power, we can direct spiritual forces of our own accord. The energy is disharmonic, meaning that seventh-chakra action involves shifting the out-of-harmony or "illness" energies into a new state. A person skilled in healing on the divine pathway will simply infuse or call forth the Divine spirit, which will then order the illness or issue as needed. The delusional or ignorant will tell the Spirit what to do. If we trust the Divine, we assume grace and don't force an outcome. If we don't, we know that God loves us enough to allow us to do what we will. The universe will respond no matter our intentions, but what we create from our personal will ceases. Only that inspired by Spirit continues forever. Once we grasp this concept, we emerge from the Plane of Peace in full acceptance of our true self. We implement the spiritual principles of the universe, symbolized in a septangle or the rainbow.

By owning the faith to follow only Spirit, we achieve the peace of mind necessary to direct forces to heal the self and others.

Eighth Chakra You're beyond the bowls, but divine learning isn't over. It now shifts to pure free will. Now it's about behavior.

The eighth dimension is a place of nothing and everything. It is pure imagination. You must now understand the imagination pathway in order to illuminate the powers of the eight chakra and break free of karma. This involves using the same numinous *darkening* gift used by the Creator to emanate creation out of the dark waters of the void.

Here, the shaman is tested in his or her ability to truly Transmute—the task of the eighth power field—using the principles of conversion and inversion. The body of the infinite becomes important, as it insists that the truth of "no time" allows everything to be possible inside of time. The eighth gate, Creation, is opened and the divine pathway passes the testing of the Plane of Momentum, deciding to share the peace of the seventh-chakra illumination through acts of goodwill. The octagon represents the challenge of choosing only good in a dualistic world, through conversion of not good to good.

Illumination along the eighth chakra is ideal for breaking old patterns and establishing true and eternal new ones.

Ninth Chakra Here is advanced knowledge of love. I can describe the ninth dimension only as the pure expression of love, the numinous gift being the *allowing of life without intervention.* Love does not intervene. It accepts. This is highlighted for walkers of the Plane of Love. Choice is the gate of the ninth chakra. The choices that you make become reflected through what you do, and from there they create others' reality.

The nine is represented by three equilateral triangles, which can erase error and evil. The power level of Truth reveals that only universal truths are real. And the greatest of these truths is Love.

Ninth-chakra illumination is possible in holding one's own responsibility to be an expression of love. This can erase evil and the effects of injustice.

On the practical level, this energy merges well with the first chakra to complete healing from evils such as abuse, violence, addictions, incest, and other traumas.

Tenth Chakra Grace, the subject of the tenth dimension, is often described as what we receive from the Creator. Beyond the bowls, Grace is best echoed in the numinous gift of *tending*. It is what we give to others.

Severe wounds often accompany tenth-chakra violations. What if we were to grant grace to those who have caused the injuries? We would then graduate from the Plane of Power, because we've learned how to implement our powers for loving purposes. We maximize the tenth power field of One in All. The grace we provide others in turn empowers us. The gate reveals the oneness between the natural and the divine pathway.

While the tenth chakra has previously grounded us in earth, it now paradoxically releases us from the ground. We begin a new life, the meaning of the numerical ten—a one with a zero, the Divine emanating from the void. We become the void and the Divine manifests through us. Seen as a circle with a cross of eight arms, we know ourselves as the unbroken expression of the Divine, invested with the ability to change dark into light and bad into good, if we so choose. We become the cross in the seal. This illumination returns us to final healing of environmental, ancestral, chronic, genetic, and birth issues.

The key is the acceptance of the self as a giver of grace.

Eleventh Chakra We all want *the miraculous,* the numinous gift of eleventh-chakra illumination. The key is available on the eleventh dimension through purity with and for all. Through gate eleven, we now allow Renewal and an acceptance of innocence. We are healed from our own previous acts of cruelty and control.

Eleven is a master number. It looks like two parallel lines. We're back to the second dimension, with the addition of a line partnering all other lines. Through the eleven, we see ourselves in partnership with others, and sometimes with another human being as a mate. The path of the spiritual initiate isn't a lonely path; it's one of companionship. By grasping the call for charity on the Plane of Charity, the giving away of what you have, you release your personal mythology and become able to be fully joined in partnership.

This illumination can bring a final healing to issues about being and standing alone while in partnership. This allows merging of divine powers and the exponential command of forces.

Twelfth Chakra A twelve signifies the mastery of the human drama. In the Christian tradition, it looks like a corona or a rising sun with twelve lines. This is why you often see saints depicted with halos. Certain Hindu disciplines signify this concept with a twelve-petaled lotus. Through illumination of this chakra, you accept unity with the Creator through the gate of Freedom. You can choose what to do with your gifts, your time, and your self. This is the challenge of the Plane of Mastery. The decision inherent to this plane is best studied through an understanding of Jesus Christ. He became his own Enlightened Consciousness through his decision. The illumination of the twelfth chakra involves deciding your essential purpose. The numinous gift can only be called *knowing*.

What Next? Let's say that we do as did Christ or other masters and transcend through the twelve chakras. What next? I'm not there yet. I know only that there are other dimensions, such as the thirteenth, which reflect cocreation with the Creator. Here we become the Word, as Jesus was the Word with God. We move to the Transparency, the thirteenth Plane of Light. There is healing here for everything. And since there are no endings, there is continual growth.

Auras on the Pathways

Working the auric fields can be a strikingly powerful way to conduct pathway healing. The following table differentiates some of the qualities of each auric field, categorized by pathways.

AURIC FIELD BASICS, ALL PATHWAYS

Field Qualities	Location	Color	Pathway Qualities
First	In and around the skin	Red	*Elemental:* Protects against life-threatening illnesses and energies *Power:* Screens for primal spiritual forces *Imagination:* Creates illusions to ensure survival *Divine:* Channels vital source energy, the creative energy of existence
Second	Atop the tenth field	Orange	*Elemental:* Protects against others' feelings, sends messages about own feelings *Power:* Enhances or rejects feelings in spiritual forces *Imagination:* Allows feelings to be used to create illusions or delusions *Divine:* Translates feelings for creative expression

Field Qualities	Location	Color	Pathway Qualities
Third	Like a net around the second field, connected to spheres of knowledge	Yellow	*Elemental:* Screens for thoughts and ideas *Power:* Manages spiritual forces for learning and achievement *Imagination:* Allows ideas to be used for illusions or delusions *Divine:* Selects ideas that inspire
Fourth	Field around the third, connected to other planes	Green, pink, or gold	*Elemental:* Broadcasts and receives information about relationships *Power:* Accesses spiritual forces to heal or eliminate relationships *Imagination:* Projects ideals about relationships *Divine:* Uses love to create connections
Fifth	Field around the fourth, works like a convex lens	Blue	*Elemental:* Screens messages and input from all planes and dimensions *Power:* Directs energy for communication *Imagination:* Creates communication *Divine:* Conveys instant knowing of Truth
Sixth	Field around the fifth, made of light	Light, clear, or purple tones	*Elemental:* Selects options to materialize in reality *Power:* Delivers truth of options and spiritual forces to create them *Imagination:* Fashions the images of illusion or delusion *Divine:* Reveals truth
Seventh	Field around the sixth, also serves as part of the energy egg	Clear or a blue tone	*Elemental:* Screens for spiritual truths and beliefs; ideal exit point at death; pineal is ideal endocrine gland to run the body *Power:* Main access point for many spiritual forces *Imagination:* Projects beliefs about God and source of most religions *Divine:* Knowing of the Divine within and outside of self; place of exchange between spirit and the Divine Spirit

Field Qualities	Location	Color	Pathway Qualities
Eighth	Point above the head, opens like a pool	Black or silver	*Elemental:* Screens Akashic Records to access history for present *Power:* Screens Book of Life to create new perspectives *Imagination:* Attracts and projects energies that can make situations look like they come from the past, present, or future *Divine:* Allows the "Now" by bringing the future into the "here" so the present is all that exists
Ninth	One foot above the head	Gold	*Elemental:* Screens for energies and desires of the soul *Power:* Conducts spiritual forces according to soul desires *Imagination:* Creates illusions and delusions from the soul *Divine:* Enfolds the soul into spirit
Tenth	Around the first layer, doubles as etheric body	Clear or brown	*Elemental:* Templates the body and screens natural energies according to genealogy *Power:* Conducts spiritual forces according to genealogy *Imagination:* Absorbs illusions and delusions from family system *Divine:* Shares love and healing among all relatives, including those in nature
Eleventh	Around the entire body, strongest on the hands and feet	Pink or gold	*Elemental:* Screens for environmental energies according to desires and programming *Power:* Screens for spiritual forces to command or summon *Imagination:* Provides illusions or delusions of power for those who know how to manipulate energies *Divine:* Assumes powers
Twelfth	Around the eleventh layer and in the secondary chakra points	Clear	*Elemental:* Connects elemental and power realities and screens according to programs *Power:* Connection point to Primary or Star-Point Grid *Imagination:* Shifts according to "where" you think you are *Divine:* Becomes transfigured body when in full acceptance of love

Energy Packages

When working with beliefs, feelings, strongholds, and the like on the divine pathway, the most important point to remember is that there are no dualities; they exist on the other pathways, but not here. You must keep this in mind to do diagnostics and healing on the divine pathway.

Beliefs I have a friend who is a brilliant healer. He constantly says that all healing comes down to beliefs. You change a belief, you change reality. On the divine pathway, however, you never try to change a problem, so you don't even attempt to change beliefs.

On the elemental pathway, the belief that you are unworthy of goodness can attract victimization. On the power pathway, this belief can attract degenerative spiritual forces and entities. Through the imagination pathway, a disbelief in goodness will create evil in and around your life.

Logically, you could surmise that you can perform a similar diagnosis on the divine pathway. After all, here you're affected by the bowl of evil and the belief that you are unworthy of being free from evil. Yet the divine master refuses to argue whether or not evil should exist, or whether or not you are worthy of being victimized by evil. The diagnostic issue becomes what perceived need is being met through an association with the bowl of evil or through the belief that you are worthy or unworthy. You can work an issue by asking for Truth, in which case the diagnosis becomes a part of the healing. Ask what Truth must be represented to free you from needing a belief to tell you who you are.

Feelings When conducting divine healing, it's vital to consider the role of feelings. Feelings don't cause problems on the divine pathway. They connect you to the awareness that will solve them. All too often, a spiritual approach to healing eliminates the power of feeling, and so the healings fall short of the goal.

On the elemental pathway, feelings are frequencies that carry information, and on the power pathway they are components of the spiritual energetic forces. They are pure energetic structures or data on the imagination pathway, no more or less real than anything else. On the imagination pathway they serve as motivation to open the chakric doorways for exchanges.

On the divine pathway, feelings are emanations from spirit. They are about need, as on the elemental pathway. Elemental anger indicates violation and the need for a boundary or repair; fear indicates the need to shift direction. Sadness indicates a loss, disgust, a sense that something or someone is unhealthy for you; happiness reflects whole-ness. On the divine pathway, these feelings can be further understood as messages about how to better receive and give love, the only true need. Here is a divine perspective on feelings:

Anger. You can love yourself as you desire to love others. Bound-aries are necessary for self-definition and therefore self-love.

Fear. It is safe to depend upon the Divine. As a part of the Divine, you will know when to move forward or backward. All forces and energies are available to you at all times because you are a beloved of the Divine.

Sadness. At a certain moment in time, you are gifted with loving something or someone else even more than you love yourself. Since love is ever enduring and resurrecting, you can love the other and yourself.

Disgust. You are part of the Divine but don't need to be the whole of the Divine. Your wholeness allows separation between you and what is not of you, even while you are connected through the Divine. The Divine will attend to anything or anyone you currently need to perceive separation from.

Happiness. You can accept joy, the pleasure of experience.

Strongholds On the elemental pathway, you have to analyze emotional and mental strongholds for particular beliefs. On the divine pathway, you know that there is only one true misperception from which all incorrect beliefs stem. All strongholds reflect the belief that you are unloved by the Divine.

When you think that you're unloved by the Divine, you won't love yourself. You won't set and establish appropriate boundaries. Your anger won't do any good; you'll ignore it and so it will build. You won't recognize that others love you and so you'll be sad and sorrowful, easily despairing and pessimistic. You'll frighten quickly because you don't believe the Divine provides empowerment and protection. You'll be disgusted with yourself for failing and with others for failing you. And you'll do anything you can to be "happy" as a means of escape.

The escapism of happiness is actually the core motivation under-neath all addictions, diseases, problems, and issues. Essentially, you either believe you deserve to be happy—in which case your addictions of choice might be success, perfect relationships, sex, hard-core drugs, adrenaline rushes, and workaholism—or you'll believe that you don't deserve happiness, in which case your addictions might be failure, poverty, illness, bad relationships, food disorders, and sabotage. Here are indications that your feelings have become distorted.

Patterns, Boundaries, and Habits

Here's how you might perceive the differences between these three ways of conducting energy from a divine perspective.

Distorted Anger Feelings

Rage. You are angry and hurt. Your boundaries have been violated, and so you feel deeply sad. You don't want to accept the responsibility of feeling your sadness and moving to forgiveness.

Frustration. You keep setting boundaries or expectations for your desires and nothing seems to be working. You aren't fueling your boundaries with divine love.

Jealousy. You think the Divine has blessed someone else more than you've been blessed. You are failing to count your own gifts as worthy.

Envy. You think that the Divine has given someone else more power for attaining goals than you've been provided. You are failing to own your own abilities through the Divine to accomplish your spiritual mission.

Distorted Sadness Feelings

Sorrow. You have "frozen" a loved one, a positive situation, or a memory in time and space, and you refuse to move on. If you keep sorrowing, you don't have to get on with your life and accept new love.

Regret. You feel so guilty about missing love in the past, you believe that you have lost future opportunities to love. You are disbelieving in the grandness of divine love.

Despair. You think that you can move through sadness by giving up on love or by holding on to your pain forever. You are not allowing yourself the healing promise of love and the excitement of new adventures.

Distorted Happiness Feelings

Bitterness. Something or someone has judged you as bad when you were happy, and you have accepted this judgment as true. You are now afraid to let go of that shame-based person, being, or belief and just be yourself.

Cynicism. You are afraid of trusting current happiness; it might disappear. You don't understand the power of love to heal the past.

Distorted Fear Feelings

Terror. You do not trust the Greater Spirit or your own spirit. You don't think you have the energy, power, or right to be safe and happy. You must understand that divine love is powerful.

Fright. You are giving away your power to circumstances rather than to your inner knowing. By judging an event or a person on externals, you are disconnecting from yourself and therefore from your connection to the Divine.

Abandonment. You are failing to recognize the Divine's connection to you and, because of that, your connection to all that is spiritual. You are judging yourself and blaming someone else.

Distorted Disgust Feelings

Guilt. You have moved off of your spiritual path and need to move back onto it. Your actions, thoughts, or relationships need to better reflect the spiritual principles you are designed to follow.

Self-hatred. You are angry. Your boundaries have been violated. To spare someone you love, or to earn the love of another, you internalize your anger and hurt. While the other person—not you—should feel guilty, you feel their guilt for them, as a way either to keep them close or to avoid being rejected.

Shame. You believe that there is something wrong with who you are as a person and therefore you do not deserve the Divine's love. Because you are too scared to reject what or who is bad for you, or because you are unable to do so, you internalize your disgust and apply it to yourself.

Blame. You feel worthless and bad about yourself. You don't like this feeling, so you project it onto others or onto situations outside of yourself.

Patterns These include fixations or energy attachments to the bowls; lack of illumination or energy being expressed by the body; lack of energy emanating from any of the chakras; energetic snags or blocks in a formless state; energetic attachments to any time period—past, present, or future—and ragged, jagged, or heavy energy in response to the question "Do you accept Divine Love?" From a divine perspective, the problem with patterns is that they create division, dichotomy, and duality and limit the creative exchange of divine (and human) love.

Boundaries There are boundaries on the divine pathway. There is a Self; there is Other; there is "God" or "the Divine." In an Awakened person, these boundaries will remain true, and yet pass love just as cells perform osmosis and diffusion. If divine love doesn't exit or enter the Self or the Other, then the affected person doesn't truly understand divine love. If love only enters and doesn't exit, there is limited understanding of the purpose of loving others. If love only exits and doesn't enter, then there is no self-love. If there is no divine love, there won't be boundaries—there will be patterns.

Habits As any student of spirituality will tell you, it takes discipline to achieve a spiritual state while in human form. Good habits support the giving and receiving of love. A habit that doesn't result in increased love for self and others, in addition to respect of the Divine, isn't a habit. It's a pattern.

Forms of Energy

Understanding forms of energies is critical to living life in an Awakened state. They enable the establishment of boundaries for effectiveness. A boundary is the point at which something ends and something else begins. It is also the point at which something ends and beyond which it becomes something else.

These definitions provide two ways to establish boundaries. First, you can establish fixtures that allow permeation of certain energies while keeping other energies out. This takes a great deal of conscious control. On the positive side, you develop and hone skills and can use free choice. As you change, your boundary needs change. Updating the system creates conditions in which you are susceptible to harmful substances or people until you are transformed. Most people develop patterns—fixated responses—instead of the habits needed to maintain boundaries. This is the style for boundaries when working on the elemental, power, and imagination pathways. The second way to establish boundaries is to own your whole self and act from this place.

When working the elemental pathway, you use energy particles and charges to create physical and psychic boundaries around the physical self and then outward. Working the physical is slow and arduous because you have so many patterns holding you in place—often in bad places! Therefore, boundaries, set through intention, need constant monitoring and require disciplined habits. You can call these types of boundaries *parameters*.

When working the power pathway, you use electrical or magnetic waves and forces to establish boundaries. You must use the power of command to intuit needs and to alter power forces on demand. Habits involve developing processes for reviewing the location and use of these forces. Power boundaries are established through *resonance*—a matching of forces to your harmonics.

When working the imagination pathway, you use vibration to exchange energies through the imagination mirror. Therefore your boundary is the mirror itself, which can hold imprints; be altered, split into pieces, or used as a whole; refract energy; or serve as a centering point. You must constantly discern between illusion and delusion, imagination and fantasy, to maintain the proper boundaries between the antiworld and this world. The boundary-setting method on the imagination pathway could be called *reverberation*. Everything that you do here is reflected over there, and vice versa.

When working the divine pathway, boundaries are truths that reflect the need of a particular situation or "circle of yourself." All needs are evaluated for the good of the whole and the one. If you are hungry, a divine craving will suggest food healthy to your entire system, rather than just deferring to the desires of the moment. If you need a job, through the divine pathway you'll be led to a job that works for you and benefits the world. When setting boundaries through the divine pathway, you automatically shift or heal patterns by putting the harmonic sphere at the center of the self. You will now harmonize with your spirit, with the I Am that you are. Doing this aligns you with the good of all, not only the good of the self. Hence you are working the idea of *radiance*, the brilliance of expressing living vital source energy. By petitioning from this place, you create blessings for all.

Time and Places

The exercise for achieving stillness, provided in the preceding section "Forms of Energy," reduces all dimensions into the here and now, allowing you to instantaneously gain perspective on a problem from all points of view.

Energy Laws

The divine pathway doesn't tolerate the breaking of elemental, power, or imagination law.

I have a client who can gift people's wishes. She has only to pray for them, and the prayer comes true. Usually. As she says, there are times that the person is too blocked or cluttered to receive God's help. For instance, people in cluttered houses will seldom accept financial success or an improved relationship. The resistance actually lies within the person, who then reflects the resistance in his or her environment. Clutter = whatever is keeping you from good things. Clutter breaks the elemental law of intentionality. You must be 100-percent intentional on the elemental pathway for change to occur. Clear up the clutter, and you demonstrate that you are ready to address the resistance or at least to invite in a new understanding. Only after addressing the elemental behavior might the prayer work.

Jesus demonstrated that action on the elemental pathway can lead to miraculous and divine healing. In Mark 7:33, we see him touching a man's ears and then spitting before touching his tongue. The man's deafness and dumbness were then healed. In Mark 8:23, he spits on a man's eyes and the man is healed from blindness. In Matthew 23:23–26, he admonishes hypocrites to stop worrying about their external actions, but to first consider justice, mercy, and faithfulness—to "first clean the inside of the cup and dish, and then the outside also will be clean." What do these events and his words have in common? They reflect the sometimes-necessary presence of physical matter (as in the saliva) to prepare for healing and the usual need to clear internal negativities for enlightenment.

The divine pathway isn't a shortcut. It's not a way around the elemental law of action. It's not a way to avoid daily and personal responsibilities or the realities of the physical elemental universe. As Jesus says in Luke 11:36, "If your whole body is full of light, and no part of it dark, it will be completely lighted, as when the light of a lamp shines on you." The Divine shines on us all. However, we may emanate a darkness—such as a fear or resistance to love—that forces us to first clean the lamp of the self before we can fully appreciate and divine our own light.

The divine pathway doesn't allow the breaking of power laws, either. Certainly, you can achieve great life success by breaching power law. I once worked with a former Satanic Church leader who once would summon demons and air energy to force his victims to serve him before he cut their wrists and drank their blood. Certainly, this man was powerful. But was he enlightened? In working with me, he came to understand the importance of upholding power law, and not only for the sake of the victims. He hated himself. Deep inside, this man was void of compassion and love for himself. Self-loathing was his punishment.

The major imagination law is that of balance. All divine law stands on this single idea. There are no dualities, but there is balance. Love must come in and go out. Only then are the boundaries between people dissolved to allow merging into wholeness. And yet there must still be a balance between individuation and oneness. You must have a self to give up the self.

From a divine perspective, all elemental, power, and imagination laws do obey divine law, and therefore can be used to create miracles. Miracles don't break pathway laws. They don't even bend them. They achieve them.

Take the law of gravity on the elemental pathway. Is it so different from the divine spiritual Law of Clarity? The Law of Clarity attracts the correct truth to every situation. Gravity and truth both respond to attraction principles. You can conceivably attract a truth to an elemental situation and seemingly cancel out gravity. For instance, I have a client who insists that when she was a child in Ireland, two angels lifted her over a raging river. A dam near her town had broken, and without divine intervention she would have been drowned. Was the law of gravity really broken? Or did the truth of her needing help simply attract the forces needed to provide this help? If you pick a ball up from the floor, you aren't breaking the laws of gravity; you're just exerting a pressure needed to operate in spite of gravity.

When diagnosing, it can sometimes be helpful to just figure out if a problem exists because you've broken or ignored a pathway law. If you don't eat well, you'll get sick. The Law of Clarity will point out this truth, and a divine healing may assist you in becoming well, but you'll get sick again if you return to a diet of only doughnuts. Change your behavior to fit the law and a healing will follow.

Energy Shapes and Spin

On the divine pathway, the truth shapes according to need, the truth needed to meet that need, and the way that you need to apply that truth to make it true.

For instance, let's say that I'm in an abusive relationship. On the elemental pathway, the chakra might reveal the issues causing my stronghold as a broken circle in my first chakra. I was beaten by my father and so I attract similar, broken primary relationships. On the power pathway, I might perceive the numeric symbol two in the first seal, which illustrates that I think I must be paired with someone to be happy. I attract energies to support coupledom, rather than myself as an individual. On the imagination pathway, the imagination mirror might reflect a box. I keep my true self hidden and leak inauthentic energies from the antiworld, which all go to meet the other's needs, never my own.

On the divine pathway, you will not see an incorrect shape, number, or color, nor hear an incorrect tone. You will only perceive Truth, which is that which is most loving for you. For instance, in response to my question, "What's causing my problem in relationships?" I might see a white star on the divine pathway. The white star isn't a symbol of the problem—it's a symbol of the energy that I'm misapplying. It is a symbol of the energy that will meet my first chakra's need. It is, in fact, the answer. On the divine pathway, the diagnosis is also the healing solution. This white star in encoded with the truth that I must own to meet the real need, which is to love myself. Being abused isn't self-loving.

The white star also demonstrates the energies sent into the universe to establish correct boundaries and safe behaviors; thus it reflects the entire truth in symbol form. You can work with symbols on any of the pathways, including the divine pathway. You can also work with spin. If the white star had appeared spinning energy toward me, I could assume that I need to allow the truth reflected in this star into myself. If it had spun away from me, the energies might have needed to be shared.

Sourcing

On the divine pathway, you can source any consciousness anytime that you want. In fact, you are sourcing beings, entities, energies, waves, forms, and any other consciousnesses all the time, though you may not be Awakened to this knowledge. Recall that the contact tool of the divine pathway is to petition. If you ask a toad for help, the consciousness that can provide the help will provide it for you, even though you may not receive a response from the toad.

The Divine is pure consciousness. Pure consciousness is fully animate. It is so complete, it includes the profound and the mundane, the spiritual and the human. This means that the Divine is as human as you are. And that you, as a human, are completely acceptable to the Divine. Divinity blended with humanity becomes more than either could be on its own.

Energy Mapping

chapter sixteen

Mapping Your Way to Health

This final chapter is designed to help you create energy maps for shift healing. It covers a number of the major health concerns faced by individuals everywhere.

Many conditions interrelate. Allergies, for instance, are a component of several problems and can actually cause irritable bowel syndrome on the physical level. They are a symptom, however, of other problems, including PMS. Pain and inflammation underlie almost all major diseases, and viruses, bacteria, and fungi are often involved in life's medical challenges. The interrelationship between conditions begs the question: which is the cause and which the effect? That's the question that emerges as you energy map. In truth, when you're energy mapping the pathways you don't have to pinpoint a final answer! A shift in one area results in shifts everywhere. You can potentially produce drastic improvements in health and well-being by working on any component of a presenting problem.

This chapter has two sections. In the first, I present different types of energy maps, to get you comfortable energy mapping any life concern, past or present, as well as the strengths and assets that can help you in healing. The second section presents an overview of various diseases and life issues, each described along the four pathways. I begin with an outline of issues common to many problems. Depression and anxiety, for instance, underlie many life challenges. Next, I explore a number of common life issues presented in alphabetical order, with examples of healing experiences. This list is not comprehensive—it can't possibly be, as there are thousands of illnesses. The important point is to introduce you to the idea of the pathways and show you how to move around them.

Some illnesses strike in dozens of different ways. Heart disease, the leading cause of death in the United States, is such a culprit. So is cancer, the leading cause of death in the U.S. It's impossible to cover all the versions of these deadly diseases in this book. And so I have provided examples that show you how to work with only one form of a multiform illness.

I have provided just an overview of each of the four pathways for every life challenge for a reason. This is the breadth and depth of human existence! However, you can work on an issue on just one pathway or on all four. For a few conditions, such as AIDS, I have emphasized one pathway over another—this book is a presentation of energy work, and there are some diseases that energetically respond more quickly to certain pathways than to the others.

An Important Note

As stated in the introduction, in all cases, you should continue working with your medical and mental health professionals—if you don't already have one, I encourage you to seek one out. The Four Pathways approach isn't a substitute for medical, therapeutic, or alternative procedures. Always work with licensed professionals for medication, diet, exercise, and health-care treatments of any sort.

You won't see a listing of vitamins to take nor analgesics to use. This is not an integrative health-care book; rather, it presents breakthrough concepts on energy healing. Energy medicine should be used as an adjunct treatment to professional care. Energy is a supplement, not a substitute. It's an approach to asserting wholeness, not simply a way of repairing brokenness.

Core Concepts for Energy Mapping

I want to tell you to expect miracles. Don't make the mistake of assuming what these miracles will look like. A miracle can involve a shift in attitude rather than in health; in mind, not only in body; in spirit, not just in disease. To gain the most benefit, I encourage you to energy map from the divine perspective.

Pathway Core Concepts

As first introduced in chapter 1, there are several core concepts integral to pathway healing. This is a synopsis to those covered earlier.

- Know yourself as already whole.
- Accept that you are imperfect and perfect at the same time.
- Acknowledge that the Divine is imperfect and perfect at the same time.
- Consider that the imperfect and perfect become one in the "infinite now."
- Know that the only way to achieve the wholeness you'll desire in the future is to expand into the space of the "eternal here."
- Affirm that healing occurs when you open.
- Accept the current state of affairs.
- Accept yourself by assuming that you are already in the state of Wakefulness.
- And know that healing is more about Awakening the "health" than getting rid of a "lack of health."

Creating Energy Maps

In this section, you will learn how to create and use two main types of energy maps. The **Physical History Map** is designed to give you an overview of your physical health history, to help you spot patterns and overall needs that might be addressed through energy mapping and shift healing. It covers problematic issues as well as helpful attributes. The **Specific Energy Map** helps you energy map a particular issue and is the most useful tool to use on an everyday basis. From it you can build an action plan for healing and growth. Accompanying this map is a list of steps—a protocol to follow to diagnose or shift heal on each of the four pathways. You will learn how to fill out a specific energy map for problems and strengths.

Creating a Physical History Map

Before energy mapping a specific concern, it can be helpful to fill out a Physical History Map to acquaint yourself with your core patterns. Knowing these will help you more immediately pinpoint the issues to clear and the healing energies to access for specific concerns.

A Physical History Map can get complicated. I suggest that you get a large, art-size sheet of paper and a set of colored pencils. Draw a simple outline of a body, and record on your map what seems to matter or count to you. Trust your intuition.

Draw or write your core elemental symptoms on the Physical History Map. Here you are going to deal with the nuts and bolts of your everyday physical existence. I suggest you develop your own color code, so that you can indicate the following types of problems, noting next to them your age when each occurred or began.

Areas of pain	Sites of surgery
Areas of constriction	Sites of accidents
Areas of tension	Sites of severe injury
Areas that are too loose	Sites of missing body parts
Areas that are too rigid	Sites with chronic problems
Areas of diagnosed illness	Sites that have been abused
Areas that you have abused, for example, the stomach if you have been bulimic	Areas that you believe hold emotion or repressed feelings

For systemic physical issues, select the core organ or structure and write your description; for instance, osteoporosis mainly affects the bones; fibromyalgia, the muscles.

For systemic mental-emotional issues, either select a body part or chakra that houses the issue, or draw a circle around the entire body and label the basic feeling as well as you can; for instance, if you've been diagnosed as being bipolar, your moods will often change and this will affect your entire system. If you know what part of the brain is causing a mental or emotional issue, you can draw a line to a specific brain gland and then encircle the entire body to indicate that it affects every aspect of your life. You can skip selecting a body part if, for instance, you are commonly depressed or anxious—just draw a descriptive circle. If you have body dysmorphia, you can draw a circle around the entire body and write the word *image*.

For relationship problems, think of the places in the body that have been most affected. Does your marriage cause tightness in your breath? Does your mom make your stomach fall through the floor? Label the relationship and your idea of the problem, then connect the relationship to a location of tension or circle the entire body for systemic problems.

For systemic spiritual issues, draw a circle around the entire body and write about your core question or confusion.

For learning challenges or other educational issues, circle a body part if possible and then draw a descriptive circle around the part of the body most affected. For instance, if you are dyslexic, highlight your eyes. You can also draw a circle around the entire body if this condition affects every part of your life.

Once you have recorded your physical history, it's time to look for patterns.

1. Is there a strong indication of problems in a specific area? On one or the other side or half of the body? In the front or the back of the body? The front side indicates issues from this lifetime and those resulting from conscious decisions or your own or others' actions. The back-side issues stem from the unconscious, past lives, soul or interference. The left side of the body relates to issues of the feminine or spiritual nature or arising from female relationships; the right side of the body references problems with the masculine or active aspects of life or emanating from relationships with males.

2. Do your problems seem to result in certain issues more than others, such as pain, tension, mental anguish, fear, PMS, relationship challenges (the list is endless)?

3. Are there specific people, ages, or connections that have caused you the most challenges?

4. Do your issues leave you with an overwhelming impression about yourself? If so, what would you conclude about yourself from looking at this chart? Write that sentence down on your sheet.

5. Are there specific body parts, feelings, or assets that have always been healthy and beneficial? What got you through all of your life challenges? Write the answers on your map.

6. Are there specific goals that you would like to set, based on your conclusions? Write these goals by completing these statements:

- I would like to clear this resistance to health and happiness:
- I would like to accentuate these attributes for increased health and happiness:

This completes your Physical History Map.

Creating a Specific Energy Map

You can energy map any specific life concern. Usually, you'll prepare an energy map for a problem. Sometimes, however, it's helpful to map a strength so that you can better use it. That's the point of coming from wholeness! To map on each pathway for an issue or asset, follow these steps.

Tips on Energy Mapping for Specific Concerns You can select one or all pathways for energy mapping. The easiest way to energy map is to choose one pathway and create a single energy map. Select the pathway that seems easiest or most productive to work, and take action on this map. When complete with performing healing on this map, reflect on your progress. If you need further work, formulate another pathway map and shift heal according to this map, and so on.

Your other choice is to create maps for all four pathways around a single problem, then compare each map. Are there themes? Is there a similar situation on several or all four of the pathways? Is there a causal issue that "pops" on one of the maps, suggesting that you begin your shifting healing there?

To complete an energy map that will be helpful, you may have to refer back to previous chapters. For instance, step five in the "Elemental Issue: Creating a Specific Energy Map" section that follows will ask you to pinpoint the chakra that originally housed your issue. How can you know? First, remember that your psychic ability and your memory can work together to figure this out. Return to the appropriate chapter and review the energetic issues that can cause a problem. Perhaps you'll intuitively assess that your depression started in your heart, because that's where you are envisioning a box that holds an aspect of yourself. Use all the resources in this book and know that you can't "fail" at an energy map! Trust your intuitive faculties to provide you with the right answers. Any pathway change creates change on all levels. Now proceed with the following steps.

Elemental Issue: Creating a Specific Energy Map If mapping an elemental problem, remember that elemental concerns are those that can only be changed through *intention* and that actually make an *impression* on the world. This means that they follow the basic law of cause and effect and leave an imprint.

Remember your Physical Energy Map? Creating it was a good basis for learning how to create an elemental map, except that now you need to translate your knowledge into energy language. To do this, you will be connecting every major concern with a chakra or an auric field, a spiritual point or one of the secondary managing energy bodies. You can refer to the lists of all managing energy bodies in chapters 8 and 11. See this next list, "Elemental Mapping Considerations" for an outline of some types of issues that can cause problems and solutions or energies that can heal them.

Elemental Mapping Considerations

Energy Bodies:
Soul
Mind
Body
Spirit
Subaspects
Chakras
Auric fields
Causal body
Emotional body
Mental body
Pain body
Spiritual points
Tar body
Gray body
Silver body
Silver cord
Etheric bodies
Energy egg
Spiritual genetics
Seed of destiny
Star seed of destiny

Energies and Particles:
Electrical energies
Magnetic energies
Neutral energies
Charges
Congestion
Absence
Frequencies
Vibrations
Harmonics
Kundalini
Basic life energy
Elements
pH Balance

Energy Fields:
Morphogenetic
Ley line
Vivaxis

Times and Places:
Dimensions
Zones
Planes of Light
Past lives
In-between lives
Others' lives
Akashic Records
Hall of Records

Energy Packages:
Beliefs
Feelings
Consciousness issues
Mental strongholds
Emotional strongholds
Patterns
Boundaries
Habits

Grid Issues:
Power fields
Power levels
Star Point Grid
Secondary Grid

Energy Law:
Natural law
Conversion law
Spiritual law

Energy Symbology:
Shapes
Coloration
Tones
Numbers

Spin:
Depressed
Anxious
Counterclockwise
Clockwise
Inner wheel
Outer wheel

Sourcing Issues:
Interference, from others
Interference, from self
Group consciousness
Contracts
Bindings
Guidance, spiritual

**Energy Communication
and Languages:**
Psychic sense issues
Intuition issues

Pointers: If an issue lies in an organ, connect it to a chakra. For instance, the site of a removed kidney relates to the second chakra. A concussion is a head injury; if it resulted in headaches, it will relate to the seventh chakra; problems with your vision, the sixth chakra. If you needed cranial surgery as a result, you would also link the injury to the tenth chakra, which relates to bones. You can select more than one chakra for any particular problem.

A. Diagnostics for an Elemental Issue

To begin, take a piece of paper and draw an outline of a figure, such as the illustrations within the section "Energy Maps on the Pathways." You want to make energy mapping simple. A representative figure of a person is all you need.

You can reference the key used to energy map on the elemental pathway as a basis for your own elemental pathway mapping. Of course, you can always make up your own key, if you like. After creating a diagnostic energy map, read through B, "Shift Healing for an Elemental Issue" to perform healing. Following are steps for creating a diagnostic-based elemental energy map:

1. Think about your presenting problem. You might want to take notes as you reflect upon these questions.

2. What is the problem, exactly?

3. What is the nature of the problem?

4. How has it affected your entire being?

5. How is it affecting your entire being?

6. What parts of the body are affected by this problem?

7. Which chakras host these body parts and most likely, the problem?

8. Which auric fields are most likely affected by this problem?

9. Which chakra or chakras (or other energy bodies) originally hosted this problem?

Now illustrate the energetic information on your energy map, looking at the energy maps shown under the section, "Energy Maps on the Pathways" for ideas. You must depict the problem's originating chakra, charkas, or energy bodies.

Fill in your energy map to the degree of detail that you desire. Ask yourself these questions: What are the key energetic issues that would be beneficial to address in order to shift heal this issue? Who are the major players in the creation or healing of this drama? Refer to the list of "Elemental Mapping Considerations" in your pursuit. Be creative! Concentrate on the words intention and impress to depict energy particles, bindings, soul issues, feelings, strongholds, power levels, past life issues, and whatever else helps you better understand the core issues.

Complete the diagnostic aspect of this pathway by asking this question: What percentage of these various energetic issues, as well as the overall issue, involves your own energy versus energy from elsewhere? Make sure that you depict all cords, bindings, hauntings or absorbed feelings, as you will have to address others' energies differently than your own.

B. Shift Healing for an Elemental Issue

These questions can help you actually perform an elemental shift healing, based on your energy map. You can first create a special energy map as per the next section, "Elemental Asset: Creating a Specific Energy Map" to gain further understanding of your healing powers to use when shift healing.

1. What is the best way to release energies that are not your own?

2. What professionals do you need to include for working on your issue?

3. What support people or systems must you put in place to help yourself heal?

4. What is the most immediate energy technique to perform for providing yourself needed time and space for shift healing?

5. What energy technique is necessary to clear any interference that might not want you to heal?

6. What energy technique will help you pinpoint the necessary actions to take to heal?

7. What is the first step in shift healing on the elemental?

8. What is the second step in shift healing on the elemental?

9. What are subsequent steps in shift healing on the elemental?

10. What physical healing modalities will support your energy work?

11. What sources can support your energy work?

12. What energy laws, energy languages, and energy communications can be used to effect positive change?

13. Are there specific times or places to access to effect change?

14. Are there additional energy bodies, energy forms, energy packages, or energy shapes to access or use to effect healing?

15. Is there anything else to be done to allow the basic life energy to balance the entire system?

16. Are you willing to heal? If you do, what changes will occur in your life? Think about this.

17. Are you willing to begin living as if these changes have already occurred, as long as you are safe in doing so? Think about this.

Elemental Asset: Creating a Specific Energy Map

It can be helpful to fill out one of these maps in addition to an energy map examining your problem. Through an "asset energy map," you can clue into skills and powers you can use for shift healing.

Use the same energy map figure as you did when creating a diagnostic energy map. Now psychically examine your chakras and energy bodies for gifts, abilities, and powers, such as those described in chapters 9 and 10 on the psychic gifts. Mark the chakras that house your strongest gifts, and then next to the drawn chakras, write your responses to the following questions.

1. When using an asset, I am drawing on this part of myself:

2. When using an asset, I am relying on this chakra or chakras:

3. When using an asset, I am able to access these energy abilities within this chakra or chakras:

4. When using an asset, I am able to perform these energy actions through this chakra or chakras:

5. When using an asset, this auric field or fields can accomplish the following:

6. In order to fully use an asset, I have only to do or know the following:

7. I can use assets to shift heal my problem by doing this:

Power Issue: Creating a Specific Energy Map

Shift healing on the power pathway mainly involves dealing with powers that could possibly be commanded in or out of existence. Therefore you are chiefly looking for energetic issues involving *empowerment* versus *disempowerment*. To accomplish the goal of commanding power changes, you will be looking for spiritual energetic forces through your chakras, seals, auric fields, doors, and other energy bodies and considerations. Refer to the lists of power bodies in chapters 8 and 13, and use the following list, "Power Mapping Considerations" as a checklist for power issues.

Power Mapping Considerations

Energy Bodies:
Soul
Mind
Body
Spirit
Subaspects
Chakras
Auric fields
Spiritual points
Elemental bodies
Seals
Doors
Gold body
Life spirit body
Platinum body
Superluminal body
Energy egg

Spiritual Energetic Forces:
Generative spiritual forces
Degenerative spiritual forces
Virtues
Rays
Powers

Energies and Particles:
Electrical energies
Magnetic energies
Neutral energies
Charges
Congestion
Absence
Frequencies

Vibrations
Harmonics
Kundalini
Life spirit energy

Energy Fields:
Morphogenetic
Ley line
Vivaxis

Times and Places:
Dimensions
Zones
Planes of Light
Past lives
In-between lives
Others' lives
Book of Life

Energy Packages:
Beliefs
Feelings
Mental strongholds
Emotional strongholds
Patterns
Boundaries
Habits

Grid Issues:
Power fields
Power levels
Star Point Grid
Secondary Grid

Energy Law:
Natural law
Conversion law
Spiritual law

Energy Symbology:
Shapes
Coloration
Tones
Numbers

Spin:
Depressed
Anxious
Counterclockwise
Clockwise

Inner wheel
Outer wheel

Energy Communication and Languages:
Intuition issues
Spiritual gift issues

Sourcing Issues:
Interference, from others
Interference, from self
Group consciousness
Contracts
Bindings
Guidance, spiritual

Pointers: Concentrate first on the spiritual forces and whether the helpful or harmful ones were generative or degenerative. Most power healing is based on this simple difference. Then figure out if there are/were powers attached to these spiritual forces and if so, which elements were positive versus negative. Then check for virtues and finally for rays. You need to evaluate for spin, shape, particles, and more for outstanding issues or to check on patterns. For instance, if you've already spotted a strong, dramatic resistance spot on the elemental pathway and have determined whether the spin is depressed, check to see if the power energies are reinforcing this problem and if so, how.

A. Diagnostics for a Power Issue

To begin, take a piece of paper and draw an outline of a figure, such as the illustrations within the section "Energy Maps on the Pathways." You can reference the key used to energy map on the power pathway for your own power mapping, or make up your own. After preparing a diagnostic energy map, read through B, "Shift Healing for a Power Issue" to perform healing. Following are questions designed to help you prepare a power map.

1. Which spiritual forces are keeping the issue locked in on the elemental? Place these forces on your energy map, drawing lines from the force to the parts of the body or chakras that hold the issue. Label these forces as generative or degenerative. If you know the particular forces, label those, i.e. Creative, Chaotic, etc.

2. Are there feelings interlaced with these or other spiritual forces creating a link between the elemental and the power? Indicate the major feelings.

3. Which virtues are creating problems instead of benefits in regard to this issue? Indicate where these virtues are located.

4. Are there energies passing as virtues that are in essence nonvirtues causing problems? Indicate where and what these nonvirtues might be.

5. Are powers supporting the harmful spiritual energetic forces? Indicate which ones by looking at the elements involved.

6. Are other sources supporting the negative use of the various spiritual energetic forces? Indicate which ones, or highlight bindings or cords.

7. Are any rays causing problems? Are they damaged? Interfered with? Spinning wrong? Held by an inappropriate symbol? Energy map the problem with the ray.

8. Are there any spiritual energetic forces that are already working to solve the issue? Indicate these and their locations.

9. What other energies are preventing healing (as in shame, symbols, and so on) by blocking the connection points between the elemental and the power?

B. Shift Healing for a Power Issue

You can use your power energy map as a basis for power healing. Some people prefer to first access their power assets, as covered in the following section on creatng a power asset map, to empower the changes. These questions will help you enable potent power healing.

1. What spiritual forces need to be shifted, detached, or added to support a healing process?

2. Which feelings need to be processed through the superluminal body?

3. What virtues need to be shifted, detached or added to support a healing process?

4. What nonvirtues need to be transformed into virtues for a healing process to occur?

5. What powers need to be shifted, detached, or added to support healing? What elements do these need to be?

6. What sources and their bindings, cords or attachments need to be eliminated, transferred, or transformed for healing?

7. What sources need to be summoned or accessed for healing?

8. What rays need to be strengthened, enhanced, or altered for healing? How?

9. What other spiritual energetic forces need to be shifted, detached, or added to enhance healing?

10. Is there anything else that needs to be done in clearing the connection points between the elemental and the power pathways?

11. Are there any chakra seals that need to be set to facilitate healing?

12. Are there any doors that need to be specifically opened to facilitate healing?

13. What physical or elemental healing modalities will support your energy work?

14. What sources can support your energy work?

15. What energy laws, energy languages, and energy communications can be used to effect positive change?

16. Are there any specific times or places to access to effect change?

17. Are there any additional energy bodies, energy forms, energy packages, or energy shapes to access or use to effect healing?

18. Is there anything else to be done to allow the life spirit energy to balance the entire system?

19. Are you willing to heal? If you do, what changes will occur in your life? Think about this.

20. Are you willing to begin living as these changes have already occurred, as long as you are safe in doing so? Think about this.

Power Asset: Creating a Specific Energy Map Use the same energy map as when creating a diagnostic power map to find your hidden power attributes. Psychically examine your chakras, seals, and other power bodies for signs of your spiritual gifts, such as those highlighted in chapters 9 and 10. Depict your gifts in the chakras on your asset map, asking yourself which spiritual energetic forces you might best command. How you respond to these questions will help you better understand and empower your gifts.

1. When using an asset, I am able to command these spiritual energetic forces:

2. When using an asset, I am relying on this chakra seal or seals:

3. When using an asset, I am able to access these energy abilities within this chakra seal or seals:

4. When using an asset, I am able to perform these energy actions through this chakra seal or seals:

5. When using an asset, this field door or doors can accomplish the following:

6. In order to fully use an asset, I have only to do or know the following:

7. I can use my power assets to shift heal my problem by doing this:

Imagination Issue: Creating a Specific Energy Map   The easiest way to formulate an imagination energy map is to track issues through the imagination mirror in the center of each chakra. Your key words for recognizing an imagination block or asset are *imagining* and *exchanging*. Most of the time, you will be using your imagination to perceive problems caused by inappropriate placement of energies on this world versus the antiworld sides of the imagination mirror. To create your imagination map, refer to the descriptions of imagination bodies and ideas in chapters 8 and 14, and use the checklist, "Imagination Mapping Considerations."

Imagination Mapping Considerations

Energy Bodies:
Soul
Mind
Body
Spirit
Subaspects
Chakras
Auric fields
Spiritual points
Imagination mirror
Elemental bodies
Power bodies
Energy egg

Energies and Particles:
Electrical energies
Magnetic energies
Neutral energies
Charges
Congestion
Absence
Frequencies
Vibrations

Harmonics
Delusions
Illusions

Energy Fields:
Morphogenetic
Ley line
Vivaxis

Times and Places:
Dimensions
Zones
Planes of Light
Past lives
In-between lives
Others' lives
Akashic Records
Shadow Records
Book of Life

Energy Packages:
Beliefs
Feelings

Mental strongholds
Emotional strongholds
Patterns
Boundaries
Habits

Grid Issues:
Power fields
Power levels
Star Point Grid
Secondary Grid

Energy Law:
Natural law
Conversion law
Spiritual law

Energy Symbology:
Shapes
Coloration
Tones
Numbers

Energy Locations:
Antiworld
This world
In the mirror

Spin and Energy Flows:
Depressed
Anxious
Counterclockwise
Clockwise
Inner wheel
Outer wheel
From antiworld to this world
From this world to antiworld

**Energy Communication
and Languages:**
Phantasm gift issues

Sourcing Issues:
Interference, from others
Interference, from self
Group consciousness
Contracts
Bindings
Guidance, spiritual

Pointers: Concentrate on the basic energies, negative/electrons and positive/protons that are being exchanged or should be exchanged. Look for bindings, cords, and attachments and consider to whom or what they are attached. Ask yourself for key words to highlight the delusion or lie or the illusion or truth that you are showing. Symbols and colorations can be especially helpful to show on the imagination pathway, as they lend themselves to quick and easy healing.

A. Diagnostics for an Imagination Issue

To begin, take a piece of paper and draw an outline of a figure, such as the illustrations within the section "Energy Maps on the Pathways." Refer to the key used in this section as you create your own imagination energy map, or come up with your own symbols, and use the questions listed below when making your map. After forming an imagination diagnosis, you can apply the concepts in B, "Shift Healing for an Imagination Issue" for shift healing.

Remember that the left side of each imagination mirror represents the antiworld, and the right side, this world. A tip: In case you get stuck, look at the imagination pathway through your eighth chakra. This shamanic portal will activate the imagination storyteller within you.

1. Which chakras are holding the delusions that prevent the presenting issue from clearing to an illusion?
2. Which is the key chakra holding the affected in delusion?
3. What is the exact lie or delusion?
4. What is the fantasy you're hoping to achieve through believing in this delusion? Note your answer in writing.
5. What energies or sources, internal or external, are benefiting from this delusion?
6. What's the benefit? Note your answer in writing.
7. What symbols, shapes, colors, or numbers illustrate the delusion?
8. What energies are in the antiworld or this world that should be elsewhere?
9. What energies or constructs are lacking in these places?

B. Shift Healing for an Imagination Issue

Apply the information illustrated on your imagination map to perform your shift healing. If you desire, first energy map your imagination assets as per the next section so you have your full powers available for change, and then use the following questions as a springboard for healing.

1. What chakras need to be addressed to support an imagination exchange for healing?
2. What delusion needs to be shifted to allow this exchange?
3. What illusion needs to be created to allow this exchange?
4. What energies need to be exchanged, and how?
5. What energies or interfering sources must be detached or transformed to allow this exchange?
6. What symbols, shapes, colors or numbers will lock in the new illusion?
7. What's the story the imagination can use to make the full exchange permanently?
8. What elemental or power healing modalities will support your energy work?
9. What sources can support your energy work?

10. What energy laws, energy languages, and energy communications can be used to effect positive change?

11. Are there any specific times or places to access to effect change?

12. Are there any additional energy bodies, energy forms, energy packages, or energy shapes to access or use to effect healing?

13. What will be the new story in your life, after this exchange?

14. Are you willing to begin living as if these changes have already occurred, as long as you are safe in doing so? Think about this.

Imagination Asset: Creating a Specific Energy Map Create an asset energy map with the same map used for your diagnostic imagination map. Peering into the imagination mirror centered in each chakra, ask to perceive the various gifts and attributes available for healing. Reexamine chapters 9 and 10 for ideas. Depict the assets on your map, and then respond to the following questions.

1. When using an asset, I am able to make the following types of imagination exchanges:

2. When using an asset, I am relying on this chakra mirror:

3. When using an asset, I am able to access these energy abilities from this chakra's antiworld side:

4. When using an asset, I am able to access these energy abilities from this chakra's "this world" side:

5. When using an asset, I am able to perform these energy actions in the elemental pathway:

6. When using an asset, I am able to perform these energy actions through the power pathway:

7. When using an asset, I am able to accomplish the following:

8. In order to fully use all my assets to shift heal, I have only to do or know the following:

Divine Issue: Creating a Specific Energy Map Fashioning a divine energy map and using it for healing is mainly a matter of evaluating for unconditional love. It can be helpful to reflect upon times in your life in which you were able to accept unconditional love, power, and grace, as well as times in which this was difficult. This comparison will provide the basis for psychically sensing your divine issues. When psychically attuned, you will perceive the differences between being expanded or contracted in your spirit, mind or body, in reference to love. To formulate your divine map, refer to the descriptions of divine bodies and concepts in chapters 8 and 15, and use the following list, "Divine Mapping Considerations," as a checklist.

Divine Mapping Considerations

Energy Bodies:
Your own spirit
Others' spirits
The Divine Spirit
Chakras
Auric fields
Channels of light
Gateways
Body of the eternal
Body of the infinite
Seven bowls of existence
Energy egg

Energies and Particles:
Electrical energies
Magnetic energies
Neutral energies

Concerns:
Needs (the real need you hope to meet)
Lies (the way you tried to meet the need that caused the presenting problem)
Truths (the way you can allow your need to be met in health)

Energy Law:
Natural law
Conversion law
Spiritual law

Sourcing Issues:
Listened/followed own spirit
Listened/followed Divine spirit
Listened/believed something or someone else
Relationship with others' spirits

A. Diagnostics for a Divine Issue

You can create your divine energy map for diagnosis using the figure and symbols shown for divine energy mapping shown later in this chapter in the section, "Energy Maps on the Pathways." After forming a divine diagnosis, you can use the concepts in B, "Shift Healing for a Divine Issue" for healing. The following questions can help you construct your divine energy map.

1. What is the need that I'm attempting to meet through this issue?

2. What chakra/s did this original need lie within?

3. What is the lie I've been pretending as true in order to meet this need?

4. What decision did I make that allowed me to accept this lie as truth?

5. What chakra or chakras did I record this lie within, writing it over the original need?

6. What bowl or bowls of existence was I dealing with at that time?

7. What channels of light relate to the chakras involved in my problem?

8. What other divine energies or energy bodies are keeping me from accepting the Divine's unconditional love?

B. Shift Healing for a Divine Issue

Apply the revelations from your divine diagnostic map to allow shift healing. You can first prepare a divine asset map to assist you in allowing change, as shown in the next section. The following questions will help you accept wholeness through the divine pathway.

1. Am I willing to have my need met in a way that is loving for myself and all others?

2. Which channel of light holds a truth that can help me accept the truth that I need to become?

3. Which gateway can help me hold this truth as I become it?

4. What is the truth that I need to become?

5. What do I need to understand to forgive myself for becoming or reflecting a lie instead of the truth?

6. What do I need to understand to forgive others for seeing and treating me as this lie?

7. Is there a petition to enable an instant transformation of truth?

8. Is there a way that I can best allow the Divine to transform me into this truth?

9. Are there ways to use my vital source energy to support this transformation on the other pathways?

10. Am I willing to live in the here and now as this truth?

Divine Asset: Creating a Specific Energy Map Before you begin, know that divine assets tend to differ from those on other pathways in that they involve qualities rather than personal assets, such as "ability to give" instead of "manifestation." On the divine pathway, you don't actually "use" an asset, either; you become it. For instance, you don't "pray to Spirit;" you "pray Spirit." You don't apply healing, you *become* the healing. You don't channel wisdom, you *become* wisdom. The key is enhancing what you already are, not serving as a conduit for a quality outside of yourself. To apply this concept, you can either create a chakra-based asset map, using your divine energy map as a template, or simply reflect on these concepts.

1. When assuming Wakefulness, I become this quality:

2. When I petition this quality (e.g., praying "happiness,"), the following occurs:

3. In order to be this quality, I must understand the following:

4. To permanently be this quality on all pathways, I need only become this truth:

On every pathway, you work with the chakra primarily affected by, or primarily causing, your presenting illness. Your diagnostic energy map will center on occurrences within this chakra. You also conduct healing through the same chakra. In the case of the elemental pathway, you work directly in the chakra center; on the power pathway, you use the chakra-seal; on the imagination pathway, you employ the imagination mirror; and on the divine pathway, you apply the channels of light. All are versions of the fundamental chakra, the key to energy mapping.

Depending upon your starting pathway, you can access any other energy body for diagnosis or healing and still return to the primary chakra to check on progress and make corrections. You can jump to another pathway from your original chakra, conduct work, and return to the starting gate. Keep in mind that all pathway processes begin and end with the chakras, and you will easily sort through any challenges you meet.

In the following section, I will present sixteen different energy maps. These energy maps represent three universal issues and thirteen specific issues and life challenges. There are four maps for each pathway, each portraying one of the sixteen diseases.

Many of the case studies presented here may seem miraculous, and some might leave you questioning the healing process. I have seen miracles when working the pathway system, many more than those described in this section. Not all healings result in miracles, or even long-coming cures. In the final count, the place of divine within each of us makes the final decision regarding what needs to be healed and how. That which appears as a failure can be the ultimate success. Many believe that the person who finally dies from a long-standing illness hasn't been healed. Those final months, days, or minutes, however, might have been the most miraculous of his or her life. Perhaps a longing for love became fulfilled. Perhaps years of bitterness were finally eased. Perhaps a belief that caused hardening of the heart was challenged and changed. Perhaps the dying was the healing, a release from this body for freedom on the next plane.

Traditional medicine would consider it a failure if the symptoms don't disappear. Holistic therapies might have us doubtful if we don't challenge the traditional. On the Four Pathways, however, the end result can only be measured in the acceptance of love and peace, in the alteration of character that occurs when we substantiate what is truly important to our spirits. May all healing occur for you as you truly desire it to be.

Headaches

Marianne had been afflicted with severe migraines since she was twelve. Mainstream medicine didn't alleviate the pain. Headaches usually involve the first chakra and a secondary chakra, each of which represents a different point of view about a subject. To uncover the reason for the raging debate that eventually takes place in the head, regression is almost always a necessary tool. Once you figure out the issuing chakras and the subject matter, you can figure out the power-level dynamics, food and nutritional triggers, pH imbalance, and the nature of the mental or emotional stronghold. From there, you can determine a course of action on the elemental pathway.

Marianne pinpointed the two chakras through regression. One was her first chakra. Under trance, she recalled that her dad had screamed at her whenever she had cried as an infant. The resulting belief was subconsciously stored as a mental stronghold: "My needs are bad," a reflection of the first power level.

The sixth chakra engaged in the power struggle when Marianne developed sexually at age twelve. Again her father screamed, this time that she was a slut because she was kissing her boyfriend. The migraines began, the sixth chakra asserting Marianne's emerging desire to act like a woman and the first chakra inhibiting her primary drives.

With all migraines it's most important to address the originating chakra and the baseline conflict. Marianne's first chakra actually

Elemental Pathway Examples
Headaches
Irritable bowel
   syndrome
Allergies
Overeating

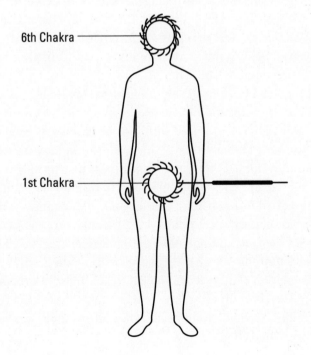

6th Chakra

1st Chakra

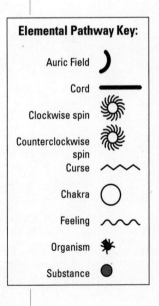

Elemental Pathway Key:

Auric Field	)
Cord	▬
Clockwise spin	✺
Counterclockwise spin	✺
Curse	∿
Chakra	○
Feeling	∿
Organism	✹
Substance	●

encompassed both points of view: "I have a need" versus "These needs are bad." Her primary emotions caused the chakra to cycle in a negative or "electrical" spin. Every time she felt torn regarding a need or desire, her first chakra spun in reverse, keeping her stuck in her old pain and emotions and causing an acidic condition in her body. She would then crave the very foods that increased the propensity of an adrenal rush and therefore a migraine: high-fat, milky, and sugary foods, which, of course, Marianne admitted to consuming a few days before a migraine attack. In Marianne, the sixth chakra attempted to balance this depressing energy by spinning fast, clockwise. The resulting state of anxiety set off another set of cravings, namely for chocolate and more sugar, which further exacerbated the first-chakra adrenal rush and eventually caused a blood-sugar low. After indulging in sugary substances, Marianne would overeat so-called "healthy foods," mainly of the alkaline producing variety. The first- and sixth-chakra foods combined to create a conflicting pH balance in Marianne's body: partly acidic and partly alkaline. All forces combined to close certain of her blood vessels and constrict nerves, hence the migraines.

Marianne and I continued to use regression to free her from the imprisoning messages from her father. She claimed her right to be in the world and to have needs. She established a connection with the Divine through the back side of her first chakra, thus correcting the reverse spin in the first chakra. She pulled out a first-chakra cord from her father and then owned her higher self's self-image, which she infused with gold light in her pituitary. This corrected the anxious spin in her sixth chakra. Next she envisioned a circle between her first and sixth chakras, holding this sense of internal oneness in place by putting an energetic cross within it.

At this point, Marianne was experiencing far fewer migraines, perhaps one every three months instead of every two weeks. Now we worked physically, as you must with first-chakra issues on the elemental pathway. Marianne chose spiritual exercise that emphasized her femininity; for her this was tai chi. She also took up weight lifting to help her "inner child" strengthen itself in regard to her father and her deep-seated fear of being shamed by men. Marianne worked the practical side of the sixth chakra by selecting clothes in colors related to her higher self and envisioning herself as desirable and safe. Finally, Marianne felt strong enough to restrict her diet and she greatly reduced her consumption of dairy foods and chocolate. Today, Marianne still gets migraines, but only every three to six months. She considers these reoccurrences as signs that she needs to face an emotional issue or take better care of herself physically.

Irritable Bowel Syndrome (IBS)

Sometimes the pain was so bad that Joe couldn't get out of bed in the morning. No, he didn't have PMS. Joe was diagnosed with a severe case of irritable bowel syndrome (IBS), a condition characterized by recurrent constipation, diarrhea, or both. Joe had both.

IBS is a second-chakra condition and therefore involves the neurotransmitters that process feelings. Scientific research supports the theory that IBS is caused in part by emotions, so I knew that Joe needed practical dietary advice, but also emotional processing.

Second-chakra food issues usually involve some sort of fungal growth. Yeast is often a culprit behind IBS, and heavy-metal toxicity is often a secondary factor. Stuck, sad feelings attract the element of water, and water appeals to yeast. The milky hue in Joe's eyes suggested Candida, a common intestinal yeast that feeds off sugars, including gluten and milk. And Joe did like his "comfort foods," especially pizza, muffins, and bread.

Foods high in sugar, yeast, milk, and gluten create a highly acidic environment in which healthy bacteria cannot grow, though pests like Candida can. Without certain flora, the intestines cannot break down food particles; this leads to constipation and diarrhea. Joe was addicted to second-chakra foods and was therefore feeding his own problem. I also guessed that Joe had some sort of heavy-metal toxicity because his skin was slightly yellow, indicating that his liver wasn't eliminating properly. Heavy metals often exist if someone feels threatened; the

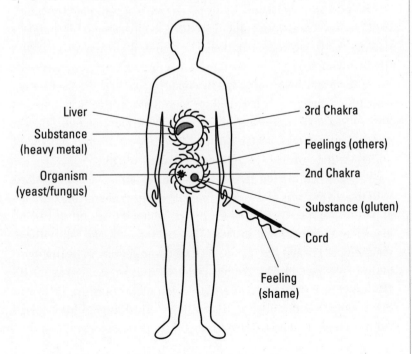

Liver
Substance (heavy metal)
Organism (yeast/fungus)
3rd Chakra
Feelings (others)
2nd Chakra
Substance (gluten)
Cord
Feeling (shame)

metals are perceived as being protective. Joe was a feeling sympathizer; I could tell by the amount of feelings stuck in his body. The body perceives the interference of others' feelings as a form of psychic invasion and so erects the armor of heavy metal as a defense. The fact that Joe's second chakra spun counterclockwise in the inner and outer rims supported my theories, as did the somewhat too-fast counterclockwise spin of the inner wheel of his third chakra and the too-fast clockwise spin of the outer wheel of this chakra. He was totally repressing feelings in his second and third chakras, holding on to heavy metals internally while trying to throw them (and extra feelings) off through the anxious outer wheel of his third chakra. Basically, his second chakra was storing everything, and the third chakra was trying for balance.

Joe wanted to first work physically. He changed his diet in consultation with a naturopathic doctor, who took him off all yeast-producing foods and started to detoxify the heavy metals in his system. Joe's diarrhea stopped, but his constipation did not. We then intentionally "triggered" feelings with special water I prepare with a business partner. Scott and I use blessing and prayer to create crystalline change in water, and these new-formed crystals support the body in making changes. After drinking the water, Joe began to feel extremely emotional. I spent several sessions helping him remember various childhood incidents involving anger or sadness, until we reached an emotional stronghold on the second power level that insisted that it was "bad to be angry."

Badness is about shame. Using psychic viewing, Joe could see small cords attached to all heavy gluten products from a cesspool of shame he had internalized from his mother. The shame also originated in a past life involving his mother. We eliminated the major cord between the two of them and used toning and fire imagery to dry up the shame pool, which Joe's higher self finished off by transforming the shame into love. When love replaces shame, there is no more shame. Joe was highly psychic and was able to lock this change into place with symbolism, using a white rectangle for personal strength.

We next had to stop Joe from absorbing others' feelings. Along with the shame, this blob of externalized energy was causing the constipation. We used the exercise "Freeing Yourself from Others' Energies: The Transpersonal Process" in chapter 11 to clear out others' feelings and I taught Joe various techniques to shift from feeling sympathy to feeling empathy, from psychic to intuitive. By this time, Joe's IBS was gone, except when he ate too much sugar or gluten. Every day, he is committed to "feeling his feelings," flushing others' feelings from his body, and restricting his use of triggering foods.

Allergies

My favorite story about a food allergy is one that I call "The Red Jell-O® Story."

Betty was curious. Every year around her birthday, she broke out in hives. I used my verbal intuition and her spiritual guidance informed me that she was allergic to red food dye. She was puzzled. Requesting more information, I was informed that the allergy first appeared at Betty's tenth birthday party and was related to a decision stored in her heart chakra.

Betty was astonished. "My mom served red Jell-O with strawberry whipped cream for every birthday!" We both laughed, but wondered what was so critical about red Jell-O. We used regression to return to her tenth birthday party.

Both Betty and I were raised in Midwestern Minnesota and so we chuckled as Betty recited the list of "Jell-O sins." "I observed that my mother had given up her life to make Jell-O, just because she was married," Betty relayed. "And so I decided I would never marry." Hence, Betty would be spared a life of Jell-O popular events, like church potlucks, funeral dinners, family get-togethers, and sewing club meetings. Betty had never married; now, at age fifty-five, she wanted a life partner.

If we had looked inside of Betty's chakra system, we would have seen her heart spinning counterclockwise, keeping her life energy from emanating through her auric field so as to attract a mate. We would

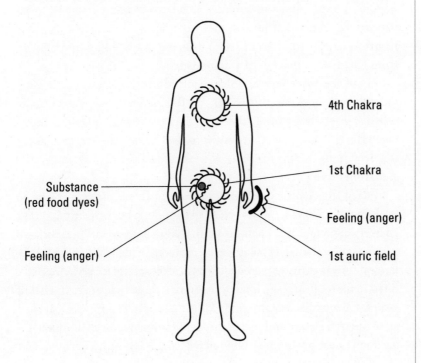

4th Chakra

1st Chakra

Substance
(red food dyes)

Feeling (anger)

Feeling (anger)

1st auric field

have found anger bonding to red dyes at every eating, forcing itself through to her first chakra and auric field—and therefore her skin, when intense enough—as happened on every birthday when Betty retriggered her strong frustration with her mother's life. We might have found memories of past lives in which Betty, forced into marriage, lost her independence and joy. We didn't need to work that hard. Instead, we worked homeopathically; we sought to stimulate Betty's deeper issues by exposing her to the energy that had established the original issue.

I had Betty prepare red Jell-O and stick it in her refrigerator for a week, where she had to look at it every time she opened the door. Betty wasn't happy. She reported feeling mad and frustrated for a week, often raging about her mother, her parents, and everything to do with marriage. Then, Betty reported, the anger simply stopped. She was fine.

At the end of her "treatment," Betty threw away the Jell-O and came to see me. Owning her anger had replaced the feeling from the attachments to the first auric layer, first chakra, and the food dyes. As her anger was now able to move freely through her system, her chakras balanced, and she could emanate her love needs through her fourth auric field. Betty decided it was time to meet a life partner. A year later, she celebrated her birthday without hives—and with a boyfriend.

Overeating

Stuart had been overweight his entire life. Diets, gastric bypass, weight-loss spas, and even traditional therapy had only created a yo-yo pattern so severe that he was now turning to what he saw as a last resort: energy work. He needed to drop at least one hundred pounds from his three-hundred-fifty-pound girth.

There are dozens of variables involved when working on the elemental level for overeating issues. On this pathway, you must usually select at least three initial actions, as the psyche will struggle to sabotage efforts. I have found it easiest to first isolate the major chakras involved in the binge-purge or overeating cycles and to select strategies from there.

I used the chakric development chart to figure out Stuart's basic problematic chakras. As he seemed to have been born overweight into an overweight family, I knew the tenth chakra was primary, as it houses genetic, ancestral, and soul issues. Stuart was "coded" for weight challenges. He was currently addicted to milk, cheese, and ice cream; as outlined in the section about food in chapter 11, these indicate first-chakra issues. Further discussion revealed that their father had sexually abused all of Stuart's sisters and that Stuart's mother had molested him. Serious food issues are often an attempt to gird oneself with an armor of fat as a protection following serious emotional or physical violation.

I had Stuart keep a food diary and record when and why he ate for a week, and he easily passed the "emotional eating" test. He ate when upset or scared, angry or shameful, guilty or even happy. This step indicated a second-chakra issue involved in overeating. We were now counting on chakras ten, one, and two, all of which spun counter-clockwise. There was one more. Every time Stuart talked with a woman, he would later escape to a fast-food restaurant and eat until he couldn't move. Bingo for the fourth (relationship) chakra. As illustrated by family-of-origin sexual issues, it was understandable that Stuart would be scared of women and would compulsively overeat to reinforce his lipid armor. Because of his anxiety, this chakra spun wildly clockwise. I constructed a simplistic view of Stuart's eating disorder. His family was energetically and genetically coded to use weight as a protection against the world. Given the history of family sexual abuse, the original reason might have been sexual. Stuart used food for emotional satiation, indicating an emotional stronghold as a personal pattern. His heart issues were secondary to those held in other chakras, in that he ate in reaction to relationship fears caused by early violation.

Stuart and I worked in several ways. First, I lined him up with a therapist specializing in sexual abuse, who used hypnotherapy to support his abuse recovery. I supported this work by helping Stuart psychically

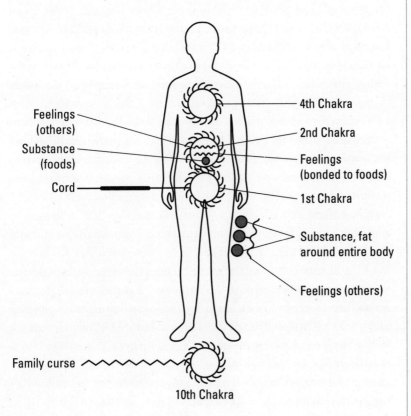

Feelings (others)

Substance (foods)

Cord

4th Chakra

2nd Chakra

Feelings (bonded to foods)

1st Chakra

Substance, fat around entire body

Feelings (others)

Family curse

10th Chakra

sense a life energy cord between himself and his mother through his first chakra. The day after we removed this cord, he lost five pounds. I then used regression through the Akashic Records to unpin the ancestral story that initiated the sexual abuse and eating patterns in his family. After freeing himself from a family curse coursing through his tenth chakra, Stuart lost twenty-five pounds within a month.

Because Stuart's issues so heavily involved the first chakra, I made him take action, first substituting healthier first-chakra foods for his addictive ones. Meat, berries, and tomatoes killed his appetite for the milk products, and supplements from a naturopath provided him energy and kept his blood sugar consistent, thus reducing cravings. After making these substitutions and additions, I used guided imagery to have Stuart break the bonds between the addictive food substances and his feelings, thus beginning to resolve the emotional disconnect that typifies emotional strongholds. Stuart reported a noteworthy reduction in his cravings after this work, although he continued to binge when under stress, or after talking to a woman.

We furthered Stuart's emotional work through second-chakra energy techniques. I determined that Stuart was highly psychic in his second chakra and constantly absorbing others' feelings. He used his fat partly as a shield from others' feelings and partly as a storage house for feelings not his own. I had him rid himself daily of others' feelings, as described in chapter 11; we used the process called "Freeing Yourself from Others' Energies: The Transpersonal Process." At this point, Stuart began to write his feelings down so he could track his own emotional reasons for eating. His second-chakra strengths were awesome, and I had him begin to use color work to fill in his chakras and auric fields every night when he was praying and meditating. By this time, he had lost seventy pounds.

Stuart regained ten pounds after meeting a woman whom he wanted to date. His therapist and I then had him check in with friends daily to share his fears, and we coached him in dating procedures. Stuart has now reached his goal of losing one hundred pounds; it took him eighteen months to do so. He "flushes" others' feelings daily, attempts to avoid his craving foods, and has maintained a 250-pound weight and his dating relationship for over a year.

As is common with addictive behaviors, however, managing one area of life often results in stress in another. Since losing weight, Stuart has been forced to confront other issues, including overspending and a fear of failure. Stuart repeatedly sabotaged efforts at gaining well-paying employment, while wracking up credit card debt. He is realizing that healing can be a continual process, one of constant change and ruthless honesty. I last recommended that he start working a different pathway, so he can make peace with this truth.

Pain and Chronic Inflammation

Jack was in constant pain from back problems stemming from a car accident eight years earlier. Some days he couldn't get out of bed, and at age thirty, he didn't want to continue living. Back surgery hadn't helped, nor had prednisone and steroids.

I worked on Jack with a fellow healer using power pathway techniques. Within twenty minutes we had completely eliminated Jack's current back pain, and months later the pain is still gone, despite his heavy schedule involving uncomfortable international travel.

I perceived a strong Fire power attached to a degenerative Chaotic spiritual force on Jack's first chakra. His pain body was full of red fire energy and forcing it into the first chakra. These three factors were causing severe inflammation in his coccygeal and cervical vertebrae and putting pressure on the lumbar area, where he actually felt the pain. My guess was that the Fire power became a factor during the accident, but the degenerative spiritual force had been an issue since early childhood. Jack confirmed that his father had physically abused and shamed him, which established some of the reasons that Jack was now working for a verbally abusive boss. I asked Jack if he also wanted energetic assistance to made a shift in his career, and he said yes. Basic career issues lie in the first chakra.

Power Pathway Examples
Pain and chronic inflammation
Fibromyalgia
Arthritis
Multiple sclerosis

Power Pathway Key:

Auric field	☽
Chakra	○
Cord	▬
Degenerative spiritual forces	∩
Energy Flow	↔
Energy body	☆
Energy marker	✕
Feeling	〜
Group consciousness	●
Generative spiritual forces	🌿
Negative-based energies	—
Organism	✳
Powers	≈
Positive-based energies	+
Ray	∠
Virtue	◇

Power (fire) 〜
Degenerative spiritual force
1st Chakra
Pain body

Together, healer Phil and I worked energetically to switch the degenerative spiritual force for the generative spiritual force of Love, and I asked the Divine and Jack's higher self to transform the pain body into a passion body. I then used my mind to envision a substitution of an Air power for a Fire power. Knowing that Jack needed new ideas to transform the old ones from his father, I thought Air would better provide input; as well, Air allows quickness of movement, and I knew he wanted a fresh vocation.

During the brief session, Jack reported feeling "expanded" in a way he had "never before felt." He felt "good about himself" and as "light as a bubble." The pain abated and left by the time Phil and I left Jack's home, and, again, it has stayed away.

Fibromyalgia

For years, Selma constantly ached, but had no name to attach to her pain. Finally a friend suggested that she consider the diagnosis of fibromyalgia. Reading a book, she decided that she was onto something and visited with several doctors before getting a definite "yes."

Selma was familiar with energy work and was a good candidate for the power pathway, as she was willing to use her psychic muscle to create change. With my assistance, she read her own chakras to figure out which might be at the core regarding the fibromyalgia. I suggested she

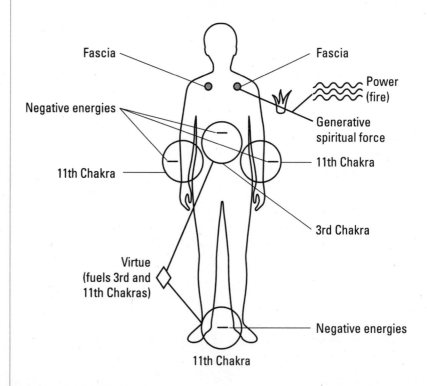

pay special attention to the eleventh chakra, which is usually involved in this condition. She highlighted the third and the eleventh, seeing both afflicted with dark and swirling energies reflecting off both chakras, and specifically the outer wheel of the third chakra. The inner wheel of the third chakra was almost dead with weight. These areas were fueled by virtues, such as Work. As well, she saw generative spiritual forces fueled by Fire powers connected into each of the many sore points in her muscles. The fire energy was generating fascia inflammation.

Selma wanted pain release. To accomplish this, she detached the generative spiritual forces—and therefore Fire powers—and inserted them where they might be needed, in her first, second, fourth, and seventh chakras. She selected spiritual forces that would support her life dream of becoming an artist instead of an accountant, her current line of work. Selma figured that the payoff for having fibromyalgia was related to her fear of pursuing her true goals. She revalued the virtue of Work and instead inserted a generative spiritual force of Healing with Water and Wood powers into the sore spots and experienced immediate pain relief, although at least half of the pain returned over the next few weeks. The up-and-down nature of healing is typical. Usually, there are layers to critical issues. As soon as you unpin one, you experience immediate but short-term relief, as the next layer soon surfaces. Within the next few weeks, we worked on Selma's third chakra. On the elemental pathway, the liver can be associated with fibromyalgia in that unprocessed toxins can end up stored in the fascia; as well, the liver can produce an overabundance of lactic acid, which causes muscle soreness. I suspected this was one of the physical factors underlying Selma's problem. The liver relates to power and anger issues, and Selma's restrictive beliefs coordinated the liver reactivity. To heal the liver, Selma stuck a degenerative spiritual force into the black areas in the liver short-term, setting a "time lock" so it would release as soon as the black energy cleared. She again experienced significant pain relief, which this time stabilized.

We then worked in the middle layer of the energy egg, the land of possibilities. Within this realm, Selma envisioned her new profession and then psychically transferred this image through the eleventh chakra and auric field throughout her body. At this point she felt finished with our work, but she decided to surround her entire auric field with a pyramid for the time being to assist her in building her self-confidence for her new direction. Selma's pain cleared up within a few weeks of our session. We assumed the fibromyalgia did as well. Given the difficulty in diagnosing the disease, it's also hard to know when it's gone.

Arthritis

Eric had been afflicted with osteoarthritis for several years. This common condition is usually based in the tenth chakra and reflects the belief that you haven't measured up to family expectations. It's often necessary to work the twelfth chakra as well, which is most easily accessed through the energy egg. Customarily I also check the seventh and ninth chakras. I worked all these chakras with Eric, plus his fourth. Eric's physical symptoms pointed to the fourth chakra, the home of inner children and the innocent child in particular. Chakras often store destructive charges in the joints to preserve the major organs. Eric's energetic issues therefore caused arthritis in his shoulders and elbows. Having been married to four alcoholic wives, it was obvious that Eric had incurred relationship damage. Most probably, his failure at relationships was triggering guilt and shame from the tenth-chakra ancestral bed and creating the arthritic conditions in his joints.

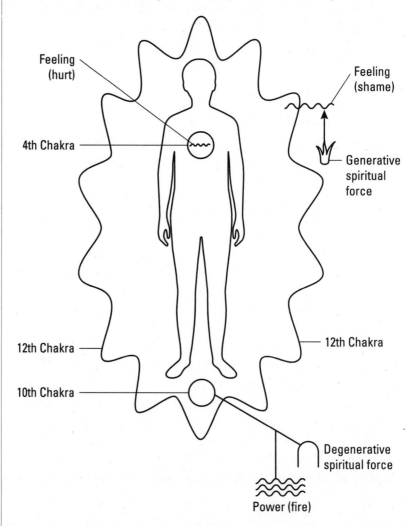

Usually, the tenth chakra will contain the keys to figuring out which degenerative spiritual forces are causing chaos in the body and which generative spiritual forces might be stimulating viruses, anger, or inflammation—all potential aspects of arthritis. In Eric, we found a strong degenerative spiritual force of Judgment fueled by a Fire power. There was a generative spiritual force of Judgment in the twelfth chakra feeding shame, which in turn was being stored in the body as bone growths and spurs. I psychically peeked into the source of these attachments and saw an inner picture of a Puritanical pastor, probably one of Eric's ancestors, whose religious fundamentalism had carried through to Eric's parents. Always treated as a failure unless he acted perfectly, Eric had unconsciously rejected his innocent child as impractical. The family believed that children are born evil. This "hellfire and brimstone" philosophy had caused Eric great anger, which he buried to adhere to dogma, though he acted out his rage by marrying women he didn't love or even approve of philosophically.

We switched the tenth-chakra degenerative spiritual force of Judgment for a generative spiritual force of Forgiveness connected to the power of Star, which adds ether or spiritual truth to fire. We still needed fire in Eric's system to burn out the shame. Forgiveness fit the situation; if in doubt, you can always use the generative spiritual force of Love. We then substituted a degenerative spiritual force of Release for the current generative spiritual force to clear the shame through the twelfth chakra. Next, we worked in Eric's heart and attached the Virtue of Love to his innocent child, so he could accept himself as pure and acceptable. Eric then expressed his feelings through the superluminal body, relieving himself of the anger, rage, and hurt caused by his judgmental family. Finally, we set his seals, taking special care to activate his seventh-chakra pineal gland and to connect him with the sense of his own personal principles through the ninth chakra. Eric's arthritic growths seemed to melt as soon as we worked on his innocent child, and they were gone by the time we finished our six months of meeting every other week.

Multiple Sclerosis (MS)

Elizabeth had been afflicted with multiple sclerosis for about six years, and was now confined to a wheelchair. She couldn't speak more than a few words without losing her breath, and her words were slurred. I hadn't worked often with the condition, but because Elizabeth was familiar to shamanism, we pursued the power pathway. This would give her the capability of moving energetic forces and of working with transgenerational issues.

People with MS are natural shamans. They believe that their job is to heal the family of shame and evil. Shame can bond with yeast or fungal-like conditions and other magnetically-stored energies, and create problems in the second chakra. This includes sensitivities and addictions to foods such as milk, sugar, yeast, and gluten. The chore of defeating shame engages the shamanic abilities housed in the eighth chakra and the life energy of the first chakra. Forces seeking to encourage evil often attack through one or both of the first or eighth chakras, linking with a virus to do the "dirty work." Put all this together and you find a cesspool of various energies and energy sources, especially if seen through the lens of the elemental pathway, to include curses and cords; virus, yeast, and fungus; and a range of feelings, including the energy of shame. This potpourri of physical and psychic conditions establish alkaline and acidic areas in the body, which is confusing to the immune system, and might partially account for the autoimmune aspect of this disease. In autoimmune dysfunction, the patient's body attacks itself. In the case of MS, the myelin sheaths of the nerves are the major losers, which eventually become scarred. Lesions also develop in the brain.

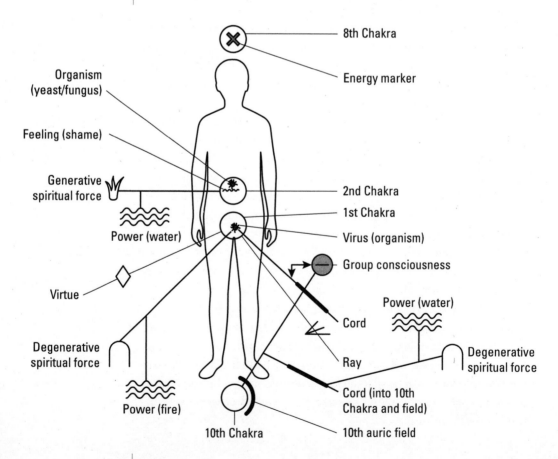

Clues are often spotted in the MS victim's morphogenetic field, which is associated with the tenth chakra and therefore the tenth auric field, the body's etheric coating. Here you will spot ancestral associations with evil. Children born under the spell of evil often absorb shame while in the fetal state, which initiates the first chakra involvement in later conditions. Not all of those affected will be susceptible to MS; only those with strong eighth-chakra predilection toward shamanism and ninth-chakra principles forcing the battle against evil to be vulnerable tend toward MS.

Thus, people with MS are seeking to battle evil. Seeing the shame within the body's fat particles (specifically, those laid within the nerves' sheaths), the inner shaman goes about attacking the shame, thus attracting the virus attached to group consciousness, the latter desiring to reinforce the evil. The shaman sublimates the virus, where it goes underground and eventually attracts the attention of the immune system, which attacks it—and various parts of the body. The immune system is now vitalized to attack the shame, which is bonded with the fats, as well as the virus. Seeking to destroy shame and evil, instead the shaman unfolds a process that wars against vital components of the body.

Meanwhile, the generative spiritual forces attached to the shame (as well as the fungus and incorrect spiritual beliefs) keep re-creating the shame, keeping the battle alive. (This process instills magnetic problems.) As well, the virus attached to group consciousness is usually associated with degenerative spiritual forces, which cause a loss of life energy. (This process is mainly electrical in nature.) Water powers often dampen the system, retain shame, and support the generative spiritual forces, while Fire powers animate the virus and degenerative spiritual forces. Over time, the body becomes fooled by the Fire powers, thinking that they are good substitutes for the life energy leaking out of the system.

A reading of Elizabeth's chakras through the power pathway showed all these key components of MS. She had a generative spiritual force with a Water power associated with her second chakra. This force was fueling shame and therefore, fungus and yeast overgrowth. A degenerative spiritual force with a Fire power affected her first chakra, supporting a virus that was corded to an ancestral group consciousness. This consciousness was feeding off the life energy in Elizabeth's first chakra. Life energy not desirable or needed by this group consciousness leaked out and was unavailable to Elizabeth.

This consciousness was actually corded through the morphogenetic field in the tenth auric field, and originated through the tenth chakra, which was associated with a degenerative spiritual force and a Water power. Besides this physical ancestral connection, Elizabeth held past life motives for battling evil. An energy marker connected into the eighth chakra, marked her as the family shaman. This chakra spun counterclockwise, making her shamanic powers unavailable.

We used the Book of Life to conduct regressions through first the tenth and then the eighth chakras, releasing the tenth chakra cord and the eighth chakra energy marker. These chakras were then ready to spin correctly. We were ready to work on the first and second chakras. At this point, Elizabeth was slightly more mobile than previously. She was able to speak with more clarity and feed herself. However, it turned out that she was unwilling to allow much more change in her life. When working with the virus and her first chakra, she balked. She didn't want to give up the virus and allow her life energy to return. Elizabeth was scared of the potential pain of life. She also didn't want to change her diet or feel her feelings, two necessary actions for working the second chakra. I worked as far as I could on the spiritual energetic forces, and then uncovered both a ray and a virtue that were part of the problem.

Elizabeth was holding tightly onto the virtue of Healing through her first chakra, but this virtue was being misused. She had linked it to the first ray of Will, and was determined to become the healer for her family. She didn't want to give up this role.

Unfortunately, Elizabeth remained steadfast. Rather than return energies to her family of origin, she sacrificed herself. After a few months of gain provided by the changes she did make, she began slipping quickly, and died a couple of years after we worked together. We had spent three sessions together in total.

Depression

On the elemental pathway, a box containing energetic aspects of the self often indicates depression. The corresponding chakra spins counterclockwise, as if to hold onto the negatively and emotionally charged energies of the past. It is seen similarly on the imagination pathway.

Since the death of his wife of forty years, Robert had been depressed. His children were worried because after five years of widowhood he still wouldn't leave the house or take care of his basic needs. He refused to see me, so his daughter Clara came instead.

The imagination pathway is relatively easy to work remotely. I intuitively read Robert's eighth chakra, peering specifically into the imagination mirror in the center. I looked on this world's side of the mirror to determine the cause of Robert's depression. I saw an image of a red heart held in a black box. A black cord pierced the heart and whirled counterclockwise, sending the red energy of the heart through the mirror to the other side. Robert had imprisoned his heart in the "box of death" and was sending his life energy to his wife on the other side of life.

You must have permission to heal another person. I spiritually requested Robert's subconscious and his spirit for permission to shift his depression, and I received a resounding "yes." The image of

Imagination Pathway Examples

Depression
Osteoporosis
Chronic fatigue syndrome
Cancer, general

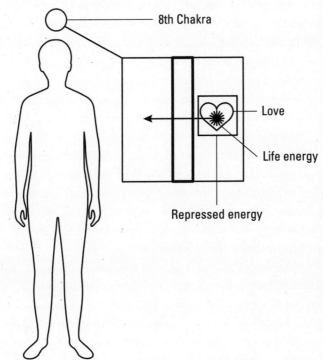

8th Chakra

Love

Life energy

Repressed energy

Imagination Pathway Key:

Energy lock	✕
Spiritual genetics	∨
Disease-producing	⟨
Repressed energy	▢
Love	♡
Energy flow direction	⇄
Life energy	✳
Energy cord	▬
Antiworld	▯▯
Imagination mirror	▯▯
This world	▯▯
Chakra	○
Positive-based energy	+
Negative based energy	−
Neutral-based energy	✳
Group consciousness	●

a book came into my mind, and I asked Clara if Robert was a writer. She was pleased that I perceived this, as it offered proof of the efficacy of the remote process. She said that he was a successful writer of children's books, but hadn't written since her mother died. Sensing that Robert had more to give the world, I used his spiritual guides to erase the black box around his heart and eliminate the cord into the afterlife. I "reached through" the mirror, asking the Divine to pull forth Robert's remaining life projects from the antiworld. Three books came forth, which I envisioned on the mirror on this side and locked into place with the sign of a cross with a circle around it. I then returned his heart to his fourth chakra. Understanding that Robert desired to remain connected to his wife, I surrounded his heart in this world with gold and pink within a symbol of three circles, representing the linkage of Robert and his wife through the Divine. Then I closed our session.

Clara reported that her father had left a message on her phone during our session, asking if she would help him clean his house. He had an idea for a book and wanted to start writing immediately. A few months later she called again; she said that her father was "like a new man," and that he often dreamed of his wife, who encouraged him to keep on with his life.

Osteoporosis

Suzanne was frightened. There had been a further 10% reduction in bone density since the year before, despite medication, calcium supplements, and weight-bearing exercise. Could I help?

Suzanne's foundational health was deteriorating quickly. I decided to use techniques from the imagination pathway, as they are fast. The imagination pathway is supportive of traditional and holistic therapies in that it can eliminate the blocks that are making these treatments ineffective. I believed that the drugs and supplements could work if we shifted Suzanne's reality—which we did in a single session.

We worked completely within the tenth chakra, where I envisioned the central mirror. I actually stood in the center of this mirror and asked to perceive the energies affecting Suzanne. I envisioned a string of women who shouted in my ear that Suzanne was too strong and independent. Women were supposed to be weak and dependent, they insisted, or they weren't feminine.

Suzanne was indeed a powerful woman—a national speaker and workshop leader. Her husband of thirty years seemed to like her that way, yet her ancestral leadership held different views—as Suzanne unconsciously must, too. I pictured the physical and then energetic genetics coding this belief system, which also showed me which chromosomes were compromising Suzanne's skeletal system. There were

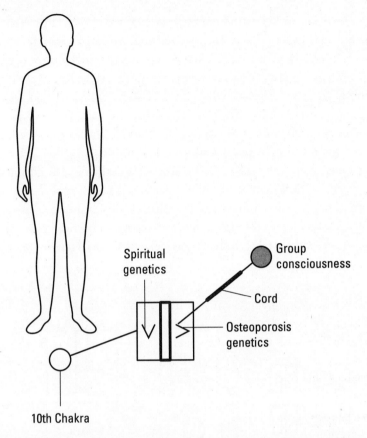

Spiritual genetics

Group consciousness

Cord

Osteoporosis genetics

10th Chakra

black circles connecting the osteoporosis genes with the ancestral representatives, serving as a form of a cord.

Serving as Suzanne's shamanic doctor, I summoned her spiritual genetics from the antiworld and pictured these replacing the genes in her body. At the same time, I took the circular lines and energies creating the cording and formed one great big circle, which I imaged as surrounding Suzanne. I turned this circle into the colors of her spiritual genetics and asked the Divine to pulse this circle so it would protect and assist her. Thus we used the material of the past, both energetic and genetic, to serve rather than imprison. I put a white square around the inner work so it would hold, and then ended our session.

Suzanne retested her bone density a few weeks later, just to see if our work was effective. There had been a 15% gain in bone density.

Chronic Fatigue Syndrome (CFS)

As is the case for most chronic fatigue victims, Talia was always tired, muddled, sore, and afflicted with insomnia. I worked the imagination pathway because she had already pursued many of the possibilities available through holistic medicine over the previous two years. Talia was also gifted psychically, which is an asset on the imagination pathway.

As we began, Talia used visioning to look into each chakric mirror. There was a black "X" in each. Also, red energy spun counterclockwise from her first and third chakras, from this world into the antiworld, as is common with CFS. This reverse spin indicates a bleeding of basic life energy from this world into the antiworld, which substantiates a loss of energy in everyday life. The black "X" in the chakras reflects a cancellation of life dreams in the chakras so marked. If you stop accepting your dreams from the antiworld, your life stops moving forward.

During our first session, Talia switched first and third chakra spins to regain her life energy. She then established a cross in these imagination mirrors, so as to lock in the shift. At this point, Talia experienced a sudden increase in fatigue, as if a wet blanket descended over her. I asked her to label the feeling associated with this fatigue, and she noted despair.

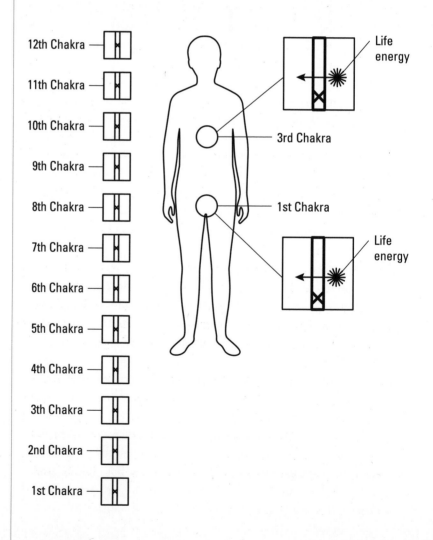

I encouraged Talia to explore this surfaced feeling, and any originating experiences associated with it. In essence, I was asking her to dip into the elemental pathway. In correcting her depressed and counterclockwise chakra spins, she had released feelings that had been held since childhood. Talia was disappointed in our work, as she felt physically worse, not better, and was now "stuck" dealing with her emotions.

The imagination pathway can be magical. It's also tricky. It can't be used for escapism, although it can open up an escape valve for long-held issues. In making a shift, you are often forced to confront the demons, feelings, beliefs, or issues that caused the illness in the first place. Knowing this, I encouraged Talia to face her feelings, as they had obviously been there for a long time anyway, and weren't about to disappear at this point.

I didn't hear from Talia for many months. She finally returned for a second session, telling me that she was now seeing her therapist again, whom she had stopped seeing several years ago. Apparently, the same feelings had arisen with this therapist, and Talia had fled therapy, as she had run from our work. Talia reported that in working with her therapist, her symptoms were gradually alleviating, and were now about 50 percent better. I double-checked her first and third imagination mirrors, and saw that the crosses were still intact, and that they looked healthy. With Talia's permission, I looked into these mirrors on the antiworld side, and saw various life choices available to her, ones that did not include CFS as a way to hide feelings. Talia selected a life choice that allowed for gradual healing of the CFS, and eventual acceptance of memories and experiences from childhood. At last report, Talia was still on the mend, and still in therapy.

Cancer, General

There are electrical and magnetic based cancers; electrical caused by connections to the past or carcinogens, and magnetic created by fears about the future. You can diagnose the specifics by looking at the spins of the chakras through the central imagination mirrors, or you can simply work neutrally, as I did with Joseph, a man with esophageal cancer.

I never actually met Joseph. He was the brother of a client who was very concerned about his recent diagnosis. Joseph was set to begin rotating bouts of chemotherapy and radiation within two weeks, and his sister wondered if there was any last-minute assistance I could provide energetically. I decided to work the imagination pathway as it provided the leap into quantum physics and instant change that we might need.

Technically, the esophagus is a third-chakra organ, although the issues imbued often come from the fourth chakra. Given our limited time, I decided to work the third chakra, and as structurally as possible.

I "stood" in the center of the third-chakra mirror, specifically asking that the Divine hold me in neutrality. In scientific terms, I wanted to check what was going on with the neutrons, which emit a gravitational pull to attract both electrons and protons. If we could get the neutrons sending out the right messages, then the electromagnetic aspects of Joseph's system could adapt and initiate health. From this place in space, I could "see into" the third chakra, where I saw a black mass. This was the cancer, so I knew that we were dealing with an electrically charged cancer—thus, it probably held emotional charges and physical toxins.

Indeed, the black mass was causing the third chakra to spin counterclockwise in both the inner and outer wheels. *Joseph must be very fatigued,* I thought. His sister confirmed that he was. All his life energy was draining into the antiworld through a reverse spin, leaving no energy to evict the cancerous cells. To shift this picture, I looked for the neutrons holding the malignancy in place. I always see neutrons as red or pink. There they were! Within them I spotted the genetic and energetic codes for cancer. Now I looked into the antiworld and imagined there a neutron that held a healthy code. I replaced the cancer neutron in this world with the healthy neutron from the antiworld and infused it with Divine love. I then exchanged the remaining cancer material in

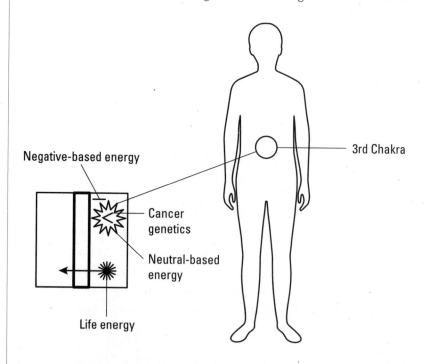

this world with healthy cells from the antiworld. Then I envisioned the future self of Joseph, healthy and free of cancer. I took the energy of this future self and put it into a circle around the cancer site.

At this point, we had a healthy neutron or base program placed within the cancer site, and we had surrounded the cancer area with another set of energies that are love based. I asked the Divine to establish the right motion and spin for the neutron, so it would correctly program the physical cells. I then asked the Divine to pulse the new and loving surrounding energy to strengthen Joseph's entire body and all physical and energetic structures. I locked the exchange in place with a cross within a circle in the center of the mirror, and I was done.

Guess what? A second MRI to establish parameters for the chemotherapy showed no mass or cancer.

Heart Disease

Fourth-chakra illnesses are always about love. This assumption was affirmed through my work with Casey, a former CEO of a large corporation who was willing to have one and only one session, as he didn't "believe in this kind of stuff."

Casey was hardly able to breathe and wheezed on his way downstairs to my office. I didn't know how he'd get upstairs again. He had survived a massive coronary attack six months previously, and though he was trying to obey doctor's orders regarding diet and exercise, he felt he was slipping. "I don't have much time left," he shared, as if embarrassed. "So let's just see if there's a God who has some time for me."

Casey's mention of God suggested that we should work the divine pathway. He didn't seem the type of man to struggle with herbs and potions and emotional healings, anyway. The heart through the divine pathway relates to the fourth bowl of power and challenges us to look at love as something more than an implement of power. Casey was used to being a powerful and strong person, not willing to sublimate his will to the Divine—much less a body that was betraying him. He had always used love to barter for his needs, giving his daughters money to earn their approval or paying for mistresses to gain nonthreatening touch. I asked Casey if he was willing to entertain a healing from God—the

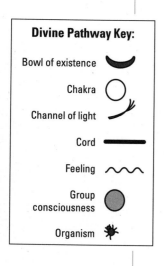

Divine Pathway Examples
Heart disease
HIV infection/AIDS
Premenstrual syndrome
Addictions

Divine Pathway Key:

Bowl of existence

Chakra

Channel of light

Cord

Feeling

Group consciousness

Organism

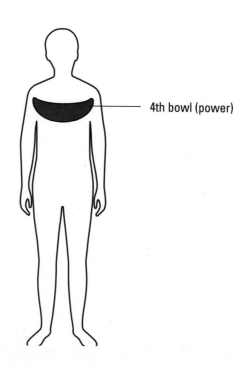

4th bowl (power)

word for the Divine that was comfortable to him—and he reluctantly said yes.

Casey asked if he needed to pray. I said no. I told him to imagine he was back in Catholic school and that God was holding His hands in a praying image around Casey's entire body. "Let God pray over you," I suggested, "rather than having you pray to God." Casey created this image and started to cry. I then asked Casey if he was willing to have God meet his real need, that of loving Casey no matter how big and strong and powerful he was or not. Casey said yes.

I gave Casey an assignment. I told him that his job from here on was to simply accept God's presence around him and to look at others through this bubble of Grace. Casey didn't know if his skills were passable, and I said this wasn't about perfection. He simply needed to know that he was encircled by God's light and would only be able to see through divine energy! This learning, empowered through the fourth channel of light, continued to work on Casey as he left, crying.

The divine isn't about "pretend magic" or "prayerful imagination." Casey actually allowed himself to be bordered with Divine energy. This bubble of grace is extremely high-vibration, and as it pulses it seeps healing energies through the auric field, which then transform the energies of the chakras and therefore the body. Casey had to let go of control—his major life issue—and let the power healing him be bigger than he was. This way he actually merged into his higher self and allowed the healing.

Was there a healing? Well, nine months later Casey called and left a message on my answering machine. He was grateful. He was exercising, eating well, and playing with his granddaughters, and his heartbeat had been strong since our session. He was allowing love and felt better than he had in years. The doctors said he was doing miraculously well. I received a call a few months later from one of Casey's daughters who told me that her father had died a week earlier. He had received a premonition in a dream prior to that week, in which an angel told him that it was time for him to prepare to "come home." God had provided him extra time, and was pleased that Casey had used it so well. Casey's daughter reported that her father had not seemed afraid to die.

HIV Infection/AIDS

Fred had been infected with HIV for ten years, and had just come down with full-blown AIDS. On the divine pathway, AIDS is a disease about group shaming. It involves a virus that is fueled by a group consciousness seeking to sublimate specific societal groups. Consider that AIDS affects people whose existence challenges the beliefs of traditional authority figures that hold onto fundamentalist attitudes. The challenge in getting free from the clutches of this virus is to avoid the temptation of destroying the group identity to save the self. The bottom line is that if you have AIDS, you must resist the desire to hate the societal groups that are attached to the virus. You must draw a circle big enough to allow all to thrive.

Like many people who contract HIV, Fred had been judged by people representing the establishment. We talked through his experiences until he could see that he held judgments against himself, as well as the people who appeared to be judging him. Ready to move into acceptance of self and others, Fred and I more directly began working with the eleventh channel of light, which relates to the spiritual truth of being one with all. This channel provides the lessons needed for anyone with AIDS. As I do with most people with AIDS, we also opened the third layer of Fred's energy egg, inviting spiritual energies into his system that would support his work in accepting loving attitudes.

Fred immediately reported the sensation of expansion. "It's as if my heart is now able to hold the world!" he exclaimed. He called me a few times over the next few months, and updated me as to his progress. Fred said that he felt physically stronger and healthier, although his blood tests didn't reveal any significant changes. He was channeling this increased energy into his job as a career counselor for people in abusive relationships, and was still able to meet with his friends at night. I asked Fred if he wanted another session, and he said that he didn't want

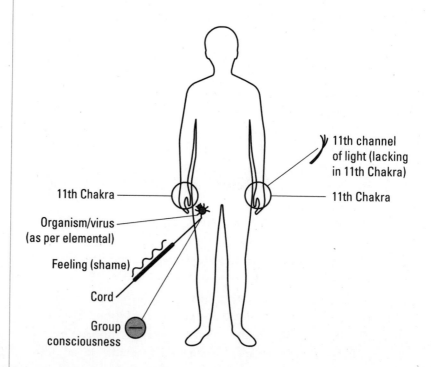

11th channel of light (lacking in 11th Chakra)

11th Chakra — 11th Chakra

Organism/virus (as per elemental)

Feeling (shame)

Cord

Group consciousness

to "push the envelope." He would take "feeling better" over "false hope," and I was happy that he carried some gain from our session.

Fred's partner, Gary, called me after Fred died, which was about eight months after our work together. Gary wanted me to know that Fred had reconciled with his parents a few days before his death. I hadn't known that Fred hadn't seen his parents in over twenty years. Fred's healing might not have earned him more time on earth, but it did seem to open his heart to a new way to walk in his body, while here.

Premenstrual Syndrome (PMS)

PMS involves a conflict between a woman's masculine self and its representative first chakra and her feminine self as embodied by her second chakra. Francine had long struggled with these seeming polarities in her personality. Her strength of character and ambition drove her into the corporate world, while her equally strong feminine nature had earlier in her life led to shopping sprees for pink satin sheets and shiny lipsticks. During the last decade, she had forgone the princess personality, as she figured it wouldn't help her become successful.

Francine came to me for severe PMS. I asked her when she had started to experience the severe cramping and bloating she so detested, and the timing correlated with her emphasis on career instead of self-care. From the Divine perspective, Francine was most affected by the second bowl of death that would have her die rather than surrender her independence to Cinderella fantasies. I encouraged her to open to the

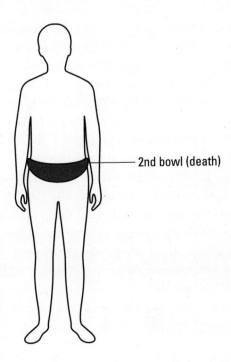

2nd bowl (death)

second channel of light, which surrounded her like a bubble of joy. Representing the creativity of movement, I asked Francine to allow the Divine to show her how best to stimulate her second chakra's personality and therefore relieve the tensions in her second chakra.

Francine felt prompted to take a free-style dance class. She couldn't imagine that this behavior would eliminate her monthly problems, but she said that she would take the class. Her PMS was a little better that month. We returned to the second channel of light and she next envisioned herself going social dancing. She was terrified; her last relationship had been five years before with a coworker. They had talked work all the time. Still game, Francine went dancing at a social club—and had fun. Her symptoms improved again. We worked together one more time. This time the Divine spoke, telling her to embrace her full feminine power, and it linked her with a religious figure related to her childhood faith. Francine believes that this being spoke to her throughout the next month, during which she experienced no PMS whatsoever. Once in a while some of her symptoms return, at which point she "checks in" with her spiritual guide and is informed of what to do.

Addictions

Jamie had taken her first drink at age ten, sipping it from a cup still clutched by her drunk, unconscious mother. By age thirteen, Jamie was a full-blown alcoholic, going to school "smashed" and bragging about it to her fellow "burnouts." She was now seventeen and wanted to stop, having met a "straight dude" who wouldn't date her unless she cleaned up her act. Jamie wouldn't see a real therapist, but was willing to see me.

Like all addictions, alcoholism deals with the first bowl of evil. Jamie was attempting to negate herself and her own needs for love. Never having received much attention from her single mother, much less love, she was scared to feel the pain of having been rejected. Maybe she wasn't a valuable person. Maybe she really was the "lost cause" her mother insisted that she was. Jamie's "evil" was to see herself as so worthless that she resisted the need for love.

Jamie needed to know that she was valuable simply because she was alive. This idea is represented in the first channel of light, which relates to the first chakra. It wasn't easy to convince her to try envisioning this energy coming from the Divine into her body, but she was finally able to do so when imagining herself as a fetus within her mother. Jamie saw angels surrounding her and her mother. They sang songs of love and welcome to her. They told her about her gifts and the reasons that the Divine wanted her to be alive. They showed her how her mother had been hurt in childhood, and Jamie was filled with

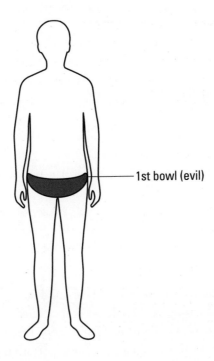

1st bowl (evil)

compassion for her mother. I then encouraged Jamie to let the Divine appear as a mother and a father figure. These beings helped her birth and she experienced what it would have been like to be raised by two unconditionally loving parents.

After the healing, Jamie was willing to see an alcoholism specialist, who worked with her for a few months. Jamie graduated from therapy with honors and now goes to Alcoholics Anonymous weekly. She has been in recovery and off alcohol for three years. As with many addicts, Jamie had multiple addictions. Addictions are a way to fill empty holes, and in the human state, it's hard to really believe that we are truly deserving of unconditional love. While Jamie has been sober from alcohol for three years, she continues to struggle with other addictions, such as sugar and cigarettes. I believe that when she is ready to meet her needs—that she now fills with substances—she will search for healthier solutions. Until then, she rests in the knowledge of having a mother-father in the Divine.

Afterword

Most of us won't really love our lives unless we break away from the thinking that leads us to believe that life is simply about existence, suffering, or even learning. As beneficial as the concepts behind traditional and alternative medicine and paradigms, I find that they focus on the search for problems instead of the expectation of delight. You are whole, not a conglomerate of parts and pieces. You might be a little rusty, like the Tin Man in the *Wizard of Oz*, or a bit dented around the edges, like a much-loved child's toy. You might be overly sad or living a particularly mundane existence at the moment. And underneath it all, you are your Greater Self, the self who exists on all Four Pathways and in every corner of the universe, right now.

If you could see yourself through the lens of wholeness, how might you evaluate yourself? If you could peer inside your heart wearing eyeglasses coated with compassion, how would you view your relationships? If you could look at another's behavior with the understanding of perfection within imperfection, how might you better relate to him or her? *Advanced Chakra Healing* isn't meant to answer these questions for you. Its purpose is rather to invite you to make your own, similar queries, so that you can shift out of questioning and get into living. There are Four Pathways, but only one true reality. There are many aspects of you, but only one genuine you. To find yourself on the journey of health and healing, you have only to own that you might already know yourself very well. God Bless, and be well.

Endnotes

Chapter One

1. Coehlo, Paulo, *The Fifth Mountain*. (New York: HarperPerennial, 1998), p. 204.

2. Daniels, A. M., and Sallie, R. "Headache, Lumbar Puncture and Expectation," *Lancet* 1 (1981), p. 1003.

3. Benson, Herbert, M.D., *Timeless Healing*. (New York: Scribner, 1996), p. 267.

4. Cherry, Reginald, M.D., *Healing Prayer*. (Nashville: Thomas Nelson Publishers, 1999), pp. 14–15.

5. Rose, Louis, *Faith Healing*. (Baltimore: Penguin Books, 1971).

6. Nolen, William, *Healing: A Doctor in Search of a Miracle*. (New York: Random House, 1974).

7. "They Haven't Got A Prayer," October 15, 2003, the Telegraph of London, an online publication owned by Telegraph Group Limited.

8. *JAMA*. 1998; 280(18):1569-1575; *and* Centers for Medicare & Medicaid Services. *1997 National Health Expenditures Survey*. www.cms.hhs.gov/statistics/nhe

9. Cleary, Thomas, *The Taoist I Ching*. (Boston: Shambhala, 1986), p. 277.

Chapter Two

1. Eco, Umberto, *Baudolino*. (London: Random House, Vintage, 2002), p. 31.

2. Dark, Tom, "African Avatars and the Third Secret of Fatima," from *Nexus* magazine, vol. 8, no. 5 (August-September, 2001).

3. Austin, James, M.D., *Zen and the Brain*. (Cambridge, Mass.: The MIT Press, 1999), pp. 427–428.

4. Ibid, p. 429.

5. Huai-Hai, Shih, and Cleary, T., *Sayings and Doings of Pai-Chang*. (Los Angeles: Center Publications, 1978), p. 81.

6. Austin, *Zen and the Brain*. p. 638.

Chapter Three

1. Haich, Elizabeth, *Initiation*. (Palo Alto, Calif.: Seed Center, 1974), p. 218.

2. "The Future of String Theory, A Conversation with Brian Greene," *Scientific American*. 289, no. 5 (November 2003): p. 71.

3. Russek, Linda G., and Schwartz, G., "Energy Cardiology: A Dynamical Energy Systems Approac h for Integrating Conventional and Alternative Medicine," *Advances*. 12 (1996): pp. 4–24.

4. Pearsall, Paul, Ph.D., *The Heart's Code: Tapping the Wisdom and Power of Our Heart Energy*. (New York: Broadway Books, 1988), p. 13.

5. Suplee, Curt, "The Speed of Light Is Exceeded in Lab: Scientists Accelerate a Pulse of Light," *The Washington Post*, July 20, 2000.

6. Hau, Lene Vestergaard, "Frozen Light," *Scientific American*. 13, no. 1, Special Edition 2003 (May 2003): pp. 44–51.

7. *Minneapolis Star-Tribune*. "Scientists Freeze Pulse of Light," December 11, 2003, 7A.

8. Gerber, Richard, M.D., *Vibrational Medicine* (Santa Fe: Bear & Company, 1988), p. 162.

Chapter Four

1. MacDonald, George, *Diary of an Old Soul*. (Minneapolis: Augsburg, 1994).

Chapter Five

1. Kerner, Elizabeth, *Song in the Silence*. (New York: Tom Doherty Associates, 1997), p. 171.

2. Hines, Brian, *God's Whisper, Creation's Thunder*. (Brattleboro, VT: Threshold Books, 1996), pp. 21–22.

3. Oschman, James, *Energy Medicine*. (New York: Churchill Livingston, 2000), p. 18.

4. Sheldrake, Rupert, *A New Science of Life*. (Rochester, Vermont: Park Street Press, 1995), p. 13

5. Ibid., p. 95

6. Ibid., p. 47

7. Hurtak, J. J., *The Keys of Enoch*. (Los Gatos, CA: The Academy for Future Science, 1977), p. 33.

8. Jacka, Judy, N. D., *The Vivaxis Connection*. (Charlottesville, VA: Hampton Roads Publishing, 2000), pp. 110–111.

9. Ibid.

10. Hawkins, David, *Power versus Force: The Hidden Determinants of Human Behavior*. (CA: Hay House, 2002).

11. Smolin, Lee, "Atoms of Space and Time," *Scientific American*. 290, no. 1 (January 2004): p. 73.

Chapter Six

1. Attanasio, A.A., *The Serpent and the Grail*. (New York: HarperPrism, 1999), pp. 90–91.

2. Oschman, *Energy Medicine*. p. 226.

3. Attanasio, A.A., *The Serpent and The Grail*. (New York: HarperPrism, 1999), p. 8.

Chapter Seven

1. Lackey, Mercedes, *Exile's Honor*. (New York: Daw Books, 2002), p. 154.

2. Benson, *Timeless Healing*, pp. 83–84.

3. Ibid., p. 87.

4. Hines, *God's Whisper, Creation's Thunder*. p. 200.

5. Ibid. p. 23.

Chapter Eight

1. Peck, Shannon, *Love Heals*. (Solana Beach, CA: Lifepath Publishing, 2003), p. 147.

2. Gerber, *Vibrational Medicine*.

3. Ibid.

4. Bruyere, Rosalyn, *Wheels of Light*. (Sierra Madre, CA: Bon Productions, 1989), pp. 247–259.

5. Knight, J. Z., *A Beginner's Guide to Creating Reality: An Introduction to Ramtha and His Teachings*, p. 177.

6. Ibid.

7. Gardner, Laurence, *Genesis of the Grail Kings*. (Boston: Element Publishing, 2000), p. 135.

8. Ibid., pp. 206–207.

9. Haich, Elizabeth, *Initiation*. (Palo Alto, Calif.: Seed Center, 1974), pp. 215–216.

Chapter Nine

1. Morrell, David, *The Fraternity of the Stone*. (New York: Ballantine Books), p. 350.

Chapter Ten

1. Maxwell, Cathy, *The Seduction of an English Lady*. (New York: Avon Books, 2004), p. 311.

Chapter Eleven

1. Cooper, Roger, *Impressions*. (Brainerd, Mich.: Evergreen Press, 2002), p. 27.

Chapter Twelve

1. Allende, Isabel, *Kingdom of the Golden Dragon*. (New York: Rayo Books, 2004).
2. Okada F, Tokumitsu Y, Hoshi Y, Tamura M, "Gender-Related and Handedness-Related Differences of Forebrain: Oxygenation and Hemodynamics." *Brain Research* 601 (1-2):337-342, 1993.
3. Harasty, J. et al, "Language Associated Corticol Regions Are Proportionally Larger in the Female Brain." *Neurology* 54, 2:171-176, 1997.
4. Sichel, Deborah M.D., Driscoll, Jeanne Watson, M.S., *Women's Moods*. (New York: Quill Publishing, 2000), p. 29–30.
5. Ibid.
6. Sherwin, B.B., "Estrogen Effects on Cognition in Menopausal Women." *Neurology*, 48, 1997.
7. Lab Report/Abstract, "A study into the relationships between cerebral lateralization, handedness, gender, and personality." *Biological Psychology*, BESC-1190, 2001.
8. Auger, A. P., Perrot-Sinal, T. S., & McCarthy, M. M., *Neurobiology*, 98 (14), 8059-8064. 2001.

Chapter Thirteen

1. Iles, Greg, *Footprints of God*. (New York: Simon & Schuster, 2003), p. 293.
2. Carter, Rita, *Mapping the Mind*. (Los Angeles: University of California Press, 1998), p. 13.
3. Austin, *Zen and the Brain*.
4. Morse, Melvin M.D. and Paul Perry, *Transformed by the Light*. (New York: Random House, 1992) p.11.

Chapter Fourteen

1. Almond, David, *Skellig*. (New York: Random House, 1998), p. 95.
2. Haich, *Initiation*, (Palo Alto, Calif.: Seed Center, 1974), p. 272.

Chapter Fifteen

1. Almond, David, *Heaven Eyes*. (New York: Random House, 2000), pp. 228–229.

Chapter Sixteen

1. Jensen, Jane, *Dante's Equation*. (New York: Ballantine Books, 2003), p. 203.

Index

Recommended Reading

Aczel, Amir, *Entanglement*, New York: The Penguin Group, 2003.

Austin, James, M.D., *Zen and the Brain*, Cambridge, MA: The MIT Press, 1999.

Benson, Herbert, M.D., *Timeless Healing*, New York: Scribner, 1997.

Brinkley, Dannion, *The Secrets of the Light*, Henderson, NV: HeartLight Productions, 2004.

Braden, Gregg, *The God Code*, Carlsbad, CA: Hay House, 2004.

Brennan, Barbara Ann, *Hands of Light*, New York: Bantam, 1988.

Bruyere, Rosalyn, *Wheels of Light*, New York: Fireside, 1994.

Childre, Doc, and Martin, Howard *The HeartMath Solution*, San Francisco: HarperSanFrancisco, 2000.

Chopra, Deepak, M.D., *Creating Health*, New York: Houghton Mifflin, 1995.

Choquette, Sonia, Ph.D., *Your Heart's Desires: Instructions for Creating the Life You Really Want*, New York: Three Rivers Press, 1997.

Dale, Cyndi, *New Chakra Healing*, St. Paul, MN: Llewellyn Publications, 1998.

Eliade, Mircea, *Shamanism: Archaic Techniques of Ecstasy*, Princeton, NJ: Bollingen Foundation, Princeton University Press, 1964.

Gardner, Laurence, *Genesis of the Grail Kings*, Gloucester, MA: Fair Winds Press, 2002.

Gerber, Richard, M.D., *Vibrational Medicine*, Rochester, VT: Bear & Company, 2001.

—-, *A Practical Guide to Vibrational Medicine*, New York: Perennial Currents, 2001.

Greene, Brian, *The Elegant Universe*, New York: Vintage, 2000.

Grof, Christina, Ph.D., *Spiritual Emergency*, New York: Jeremy P. Tarcher, 1989.

Grof, Stanislav, M.D., *The Cosmic Game*, Albany, NY: State University of New York Press, 1998.

Haich, Elisabeth, *Initiation*, Santa Fe, NM: Aurora Press, 2000.

Harner, Michael, Ph.D., *Hallucinogens and Shamanism*, New York: Oxford University Press, 1973.

Halpern, Paul, *The Great Beyond*, Hoboken, NJ: Wiley, 2004.

Hawking, Stephen, *A Brief History of Time*, New York: Bantam: 1988.

Hawkins, David, *Power versus Force: The Hidden Determinants of Human Behavior*, Carlsbad, CA: Hay House, 2002.

Herbert, Nick, *Quantum Reality: Beyond the New Physics*, New York: Doubleday, Anchor Books, 1985.

Hines, Brian, *God's Whisper, Creation's Thunder*, Brattleboro, VT: Threshold Books, 1995.

Houston, Jean, Ph.D., *Physicians of the Soul*, Ashland, OR: White Cloud Press, 2002.

Hubbard, Barbara Marx, *Conscious Evolution*, Novato, CA: New World Library, 1998.

Hunbatz, Men, *The Secrets of Mayan Science/Religion*, Santa Fe, NM: Bear & Company, 1990.

Hunt, Valerie, Ph.D., *Infinite Mind*, Malibu, CA: Malibu Publishing, 1996.

Hurtak, J. J., *The Keys of Enoch*, Ava, MO: Academy for Future Science, 1982.

Jacka, Judy, N.D., *The Vivaxix Connection*, Charlottesville, VA: Hampton Roads Publishing Company, 2000.

Johnson, Steven, *Mind Wide Open: Your Brain and the Neuroscience of Everyday Life*, New York: Scribner, 2004

Kaku Ph.D., Michio, *Hyperspace: A Scientific Odyssey Through Parallel Universes*, New York: Anchor, 1995.

Kelsey, Morton, *Healing & Christianity*, Minneapolis, MN: Augsburg Press, 1995.

Knight, J.Z., *A Beginner's Guide to Creating Reality: An Introduction to Ramtha and His Teachings*, Yelm, WA: JZK, Inc., 2000.

Livio, Mario, *The Golden Ratio*, New York: Broadway Books, 2002.

Long, Max Freedom, *The Secret Science Behind Miracles: Unveiling the Huna Tradition of the Ancient Polynesians* Marina del Rey, CA: DeVorss & Company, 1948.

Myss, Carolyn, Ph.D., *Invisible Acts of Power: Personal Choices that Create Miracles*, New York: Free Press, 2004.

Orloff, Judith, M.D., *Second Sight*, New York: Warner Books, 1997.

Oschman, James L., *Energy Medicine*, Philadelphia, PA: Churchill Livingstone, 2000.

Ouspensky, P.D., *In Search of the Miraculous*, New York: Harcourt Brace Jovanovoch, 1949.

Pearsall, Paul, M.D., *The Heart's Code*, New York: Broadway, 1999.

Pert, Candace, Ph.D., *Molecules of Emotion*, New York: Scribner, 1999.

Russell, Peter, *From Science to God*, Novato, CA: New World Library. 2003.

Shealy, C. Norman, M.D., *Sacred Healing: The Curing Power of Energy & Spirituality*, Lanham, MD: Element Books Ltd., 1999.

Sheldrake, Rupert, *A New Science of Life*, Rochester, VT: Park Street Press, 1995.

Skully, Nicki, *The Golden Cauldron: Shamanic Journeys on the Path of Wisdom & Power*, Rochester, VT: Bear & Company, 1991.

Steiner, Rudolf, *An Outline of Occult Science*, Hudson, NY: The Anthroposophic Press, 1972.

Strassman, Rick, M.D., *DMT: The Spirit Molecule*, Rochester, VT: Park Street Press, 2001.

Talbot, Michael, *The Holographic Universe*, New York: HarperCollins Publishers, 1991.

Targ, Russell, *The Heart of the Mind: How to Know God Without Belief*, Novato, CA: New World Library, 1999.

Templeton, John M., and Herrmann, Robert, *The God Who Would Be Known: Revelations of the Divine in Contemporary Science*, Radnor, PA: Templeton Foundation Press, 1999.

Virtue, Doreen, Ph.D., *Angel Medicine: How to Heal the Body and Mind With the Help of the Angels*, Carlsbad, CA: Hay House, 2004.

Villoldo, Alberto, Ph.D., *Shaman, Healer, Sage*, New York: Harmony, 2000.

Walsch, Neale Donald, *Tomorrow's God: Our Greatest Spiritual Challenge*, New York: Atria, 2004.

Walker, Evan Harris, *The Physics of Consciousness*, Cambridge, MA: Perseus Publishers, 2000.

Wolf, Fred Alan, Ph.D., *Taking the Quantum Leap*, New York: Harper & Row Publishers, 1981.

Zukav, Gary, *The Seat of the Soul*, New York: Simon & Schuster, 1989.